Risk Modeling for Appraising Named Peril Index Insurance Products

DIRECTIONS IN DEVELOPMENT
Agriculture and Rural Development

Risk Modeling for Appraising Named Peril Index Insurance Products

A Guide for Practitioners

Shadreck Mapfumo, Huybert Groenendaal, and Chloe Dugger

Contents

Boxes

Case Example Boxes

Risk Modeling for Appraising Named Peril Index Insurance Products
http://dx.doi.org/10.1596/978-1-4648-1048-0

Figures

Tables

Risk Modeling for Appraising Named Peril Index Insurance Products
http://dx.doi.org/10.1596/978-1-4648-1048-0

Foreword

This guide was written to introduce a wider audience of insurers to index insurance as a risk management tool for agriculture. Index insurance, which is a relatively recent innovation, has exciting potential for addressing the need for agricultural insurance in developing economies. Even more significant, index insurance is a tool for achieving broader financial inclusion and for increasing investment in smart agricultural technologies in the regions of the world that need it most. Index insurance thus has the potential to contribute to increased agricultural sustainability and improved food security.

Our experience working on index insurance in more than 20 developing countries has demonstrated its value as a tool for reaching a huge but largely unserved market segment: small, semi-commercial farmers and the array of service providers that they use. Small farmers can be an attractive customer base for more and more insurers—especially those in markets whose traditional life, property, and vehicle market shares are spoken for.

Developing business lines involving index insurance is not without challenges. For a successful index insurance market to develop, important prerequisites—such as the availability of historical data, product design capabilities, and distribution channels—must be in place. To safeguard the smooth development of index markets, insurers must rigorously evaluate the quality of the products they offer and must take extra care to ensure that distributors and policyholders fully understand the benefits and the limits of the purchased coverage. Without these extra steps to ensure responsible insurance practices, insurers can damage the implementation and potential of index insurance in the market.

In an increasingly competitive insurance market, creative product development and imaginative business strategies are becoming the norm. This guide will help emerging market insurers who seek to stay on the cutting edge to successfully penetrate new market segments.

Ceyla Pazarbasioglu
Senior Director
Finance and Markets Global Practice
The World Bank Group

Acknowledgments

The authors would like to thank numerous colleagues and peers who have provided invaluable contributions to this guide. The authors note that any errors, either of omission or commission, in this guide are entirely their own. The views presented herein represent those of the authors and are not an official position of the World Bank Group.

We thank Utako Saoshiro of the World Bank Group for her input, ideas, and assistance on the content, text, and diagrams throughout this guide, and Dr. Kurt Rinehart of EpiX Analytics for his valuable input to chapter 10.

We also thank Dr. Yong Bum Cho, Professor Gary Venter, and Dr. Fan Yang of the AIG Model Validation Group for their review of the models and text in this guide. We would like to acknowledge Dr. Erwann Michel Kerjan of the Wharton School of the University of Pennsylvania for his in-depth feedback on the drafts. We also acknowledge Dr. Francisco Zagmutt of EpiX Analytics for his critical review of chapter 10.

Over the past 12 years, the authors benefited from interactions with the following people: Carlos Arce, Mae Joy Armada, Erin Bryla, Martin Reto Buehler, Eric Chapola, Daniel Clarke, Julie Dana, Conrad De Jesus, Christopher Ereso, Gilles Galludec, Hanna Joy Germinal, Rose Goslinga, Ulrich Hess, Joseph Kakweza, Vijay Kalavakonda, Harini Kannan, Juliet Kyokunda, Geric Laude, Gift Livata, Peter Maina, William Martirez, Michael Mbaka, Agrotosh Mookerjee, Ronald Ngwira, Fredrick Odhiambo, Sharon Onyango, Gary Reusche, Rhoda Rubaiza, James Sharpe, Andrea Stoppa, Charles Stutley, Joanna Syroka, Daniele Torriani, Christina Ulardic, Anita Untario, Panos Varangis, Duncan Warren, Simon Young, and Andiry Zaripov.

Many thanks go to David Crush, Alejandro Alvarez de la Campa, and Samuel Munzele Maimbo of the World Bank Group for their support of this project and to Lucille Gavera, Bonny Jennings, and Anna Koblanck for making this guide a user-friendly resource.

We would also like to acknowledge our other colleagues, clients, and peers at the World Bank Group and EpiX Analytics for the many useful ideas and constructive conversations.

Finally, we greatly thank our families for their support, understanding, and encouragement during the process of writing and finalizing this guide.

About the Authors

Shadreck Mapfumo is senior financial sector specialist in the Finance and Markets Global Practice of the World Bank Group. He provides agricultural and index-based insurance advisory services to insurance companies and intermediaries in Africa, the Caribbean, and Asia. Shadreck has a master's degree in actuarial studies from the Australian National University, he is a member of the Institute of Actuaries of Australia, and he holds the Associate in Reinsurance and Associate of the Chartered Insurance Institute (U.K.) designations. He has worked in index insurance for more than 12 years.

Huybert Groenendaal is managing partner of EpiX Analytics LLC, a consulting firm specializing in probabilistic modeling and decision modeling. Huybert leads consulting engagements worldwide in a broad range of fields and industries, from pharmaceuticals and oil and gas to manufacturing, insurance, health, and epidemiology. Huybert holds a PhD from Wageningen University (the Netherlands) and an MBA in finance from the Wharton School of Business, University of Pennsylvania. Huybert is an affiliate faculty member at Colorado State University.

Chloe Dugger is a partner market executive at Vitality Group, the international expansion arm of the South African insurer Discovery Limited. Prior to this position, Chloe was an operations officer in the Finance and Markets Global Practice of the World Bank Group, where she managed advisory projects for companies looking to scale up agricultural and index-based insurance across Africa. Chloe has a master's degree in development studies from the University of Oxford.

Endorsements

"This guide, written by leaders in the field, is poised to become a go-to reference for anyone interested in index insurance. It is packed with useful information for both practitioners and regulators as well as individuals who simply want to learn more about this complex subject. As such, the Microinsurance Working Group of the International Actuarial Association recommends this guide as a very timely contribution to inclusive insurance literature."—**Nigel Bowman, Chairman, Microinsurance Working Group, International Actuarial Association**

"It is with great interest that I have read *Risk Modeling for Appraising Named Peril Index Insurance Products*. The authors provide a very useful guide for practitioners and academics alike. They show the great potential of index insurance and describe the critical success factors without ignoring trust-related and technological hurdles or market dynamics. This makes the guide an indispensable read for anybody interested in this domain, and I cannot applaud enough the World Bank Group for sponsoring this important initiative." —**Eckart Roth, Chief Risk Officer, Peak Reinsurance Company Limited, Hong Kong SAR, China**

"This book is an important step forward to harness the power of insurance to create value and bring hope to underinsured societies around the world, an important step toward creating more vibrant and sustainable economies in these critical and developing areas. This book provides a comprehensive and practical guide to microinsurance and its pricing implementation. It will be a business enabler within the insurance industry and development and governmental sectors, and a model for entrepreneurs in adjacent and unrelated areas to better understand economic opportunity outside the already industrialized and consumer-based economies." —**Sean C. Keenan, Senior Managing Director of Model Risk Management, AIG, United States**

"An instant classic! This guide will become the reference point against which the development and quality of index insurance will be measured, and the foundation for many further efforts and publications to come. An extremely useful go-to aid for general insurance staff, be they managers, sales force, outreach officers, or those with underwriting or claims handling functions, as well as the actuarial, product design, and development specialists. All will find the necessary information and tools to venture into the exciting new world of index insurance." —**Martin Buehler, Principal Insurance Officer, International Finance Corporation, United States**

"The importance of microinsurance for small entrepreneurs and their financial partners is gaining recognition. This guide gives a comprehensive introduction to the risk management and quantitative analysis an institution would want to undertake to offer this insurance in a sound, sustainable manner." —**Gary Venter, President of the Gary Venter Company and Actuary in Residence at Columbia University, United States**

"This guide will help insurance managers and actuaries navigate the challenging yet exciting journey of index insurance development. With the steps and considerations clearly laid out for interested stakeholders, this material should help accelerate the evolution of index insurance." —**Geric Laude, President and Chief Executive Officer, CARD Pioneer Microinsurance National Capital Region, the Philippines**

"This guide provides a necessary reference document on index insurance. It uniquely blends the qualitative and quantitative aspects of the subject, making it suitable for specialists and newcomers. It makes extensive use of case studies, ensuring engagement with the reader." —**Corneille Karekezi, Group Managing Director and Chief Executive Officer, African Reinsurance Company, Nigeria**

"This comprehensive guide promises to be an invaluable guide for actuaries, actuarial analysts, and insurance managers faced with the task of modeling index insurance products. Packed with useful tools, step-by-step guidance, and accessible explanations of applied statistics, this guide is a timely contribution to not only the world of impact insurance but also the financial inclusion agenda, supporting the goals of agricultural sustainability and food security." — **Lisa Morgan, Technical Officer, International Labour Organization's Impact Insurance Facility, Switzerland**

"This is an important book written by experts who know what they're talking about. The book is clear, educational, and consistent. The authors show how to implement index insurance step by step in a very transparent way. Without a doubt, it is the most prominent book I have come across in this area. From that perspective, the book fills a big vacuum." —**Auguste Mpacko Priso, Head of Microinsurance Working Group, Institute of Actuaries of France, France**

Abbreviations

ACRE   Agriculture and Climate Risk Enterprise
APPIU   average payout per insured unit
ARC2   African Rainfall Climatology, version 2 (NOAA)
AUS   average unit size
CIRAD   Centre de coopération internationale en recherche agronomique pour le développement (French agricultural research and international cooperation organization)
CVaR   conditional value at risk
EROC   expected return on capital
EVA   economic value added
FEWS NET   Famine Early Warning Systems Network (USAID)
GOF   goodness of fit
MFI   microfinance institution
MLE   maximum likelihood estimation
NGO   nongovernmental organization
NPL   nonperforming loan
NPR   nonproportional reinsurance
PERT   project evaluation and review techniques
PR   proportional reinsurance
RCPIU   required capital per insured unit
SAR   special administrative region
TVaR   tail value at risk
VaR   value at risk

A full glossary of terms follows at the end of the book. Terms included in the glossary appear in bold type upon first use in the book.

CHAPTER 1

Introduction

The main audience for this guide is the managers and **actuarial analysts** of insurance companies in developing countries interested in developing and evaluating **named peril index insurance** product lines. However, a number of other stakeholders could also find this guide useful, including

- Farmer organizations, financial institutions, and agriculture value chain actors and investors evaluating the potential benefits and risks of index insurance policies.
- Insurance regulators assessing insurance products for client value and consumer protection purposes.
- Students interested in quantitative risk analysis and **probabilistic modeling**.

Named peril index insurance is a financial instrument for transferring risk from individuals or groups to international risk carriers. Index insurance products trigger compensation to the **insured party** based on the deviations of a **proxy** such as rainfall, temperature, or humidity that is highly correlated with a named peril such as drought or excess rain. In turn, these named perils correlate with financial losses for the insured party, for example, decreased yield for a crop affected by drought, or the death of livestock.

As a relatively new instrument in developing countries, named peril index insurance products are often designed by specialized **product design teams** external to the **insurer** that **underwrites** the risk. Some examples of firms that provide these product design services include ACRE Africa, Columbia University's International Research Institute for Climate and Society, MicroEnsure, PlaNet Guarantee, EARS Earth Environment Monitoring BV, and CIRAD (Centre de coopération internationale en recherche agronomique). Index insurance product design is a very technical and labor-intensive, and thus expensive, process. Premium volumes generated from these products are often still too low to support a complete product design team at an insurer;

however, many external product design firms have accessed donor resources to partly fund their costs.

In many cases, insurers in developing countries are minimally involved in the setting of contract **triggers**, or the product review and refinement process. Concrete metrics and statistics that explain the product design team's reasons for recommending a specific product structure can help **insurance managers** make sound business decisions regarding what products to offer.

For example, insurers are sometimes asked to change a product's **premium rate** and coverage level to meet **policyholder** price expectations. Clear information on the implications of such a change on the insurer's profit objectives and risk tolerance will ensure that the manager makes an informed business decision. Without clear tools for evaluating these changes in product structure and price, insurance managers risk engaging in blind underwriting that goes against their business objectives.

However, with deeper involvement in product design and evaluation, insurers can develop the best contract wording for their market, wording that clearly explains issues like **basis risk** and **implied deductibles** to policyholders. They can also apply innovations and experiences from other classes of business in their market, contributing insights that product design specialists may lack.

The main objectives of this guide are to

- Promote informed business decision making among insurance companies by providing them with effective tools for evaluating named peril index insurance business opportunities and products;
- Support the improvement of named peril index insurance product offerings through structured and transparent collaboration and communication between insurers, product design teams, and policyholders;
- Encourage more insurance companies to write index-based insurance policies that protect against key risks and improve access to finance among the unbanked and underbanked market in developing countries;
- Improve the technical capacity of insurance companies in quantitative risk analysis of index insurance products and named peril index insurance pricing analytics; and
- Encourage practices in the index insurance industry that are in the best interests of various stakeholders (insured parties, policyholders, insurers, reinsurers, and regulators) and build confidence in the products offered (see box 1.1).

Index insurance is commonly perceived to be complicated and difficult to evaluate. This is one reason index insurance products have not yet achieved high penetration in developing countries, despite their clear potential to improve the risk management options for vulnerable populations. This guide attempts to close the knowledge gap to grow this important market and provide protection to more low-income customers.

Box 1.1 Promoting High Standards of Professional Behavior

The guide encourages practices in the index insurance industry that are in the best interests of various stakeholders (insured parties, policyholders, insurers, reinsurers, and regulators) and build confidence in the products offered. As such, it supports actuaries and other professionals involved in designing and pricing index-based insurance products in following the principles outlined in the Actuaries' Code of the Institute and Faculty of Actuaries, United Kingdom.

The main principles of the code that the guide promotes are as follow:

Principle 1: Integrity—Members will act honestly and with the highest standards of integrity.

Section 1.3 Members will be honest and truthful in promoting their business services.

The guide provides tools to support practitioners in being clear and honest about the workings, accuracy, and value of products developed, as well as about the implications of changing various parameters within the products offered to fit the needs of different stakeholders.

Principle 2: Competence and Care—Members will perform their professional duties competently and with care.

Section 2.2 Members will not act unless they have an appropriate level of relevant knowledge and skill.

Section 2.7 Members will keep their competence up to date.

The guide encourages practitioners to continue identifying and developing the best techniques to apply in the course of their work.

Principle 5: Communication—Members will communicate effectively and meet all applicable reporting standards.

Section 5.1 Members will ensure that their communication, whether written or oral, is clear and timely, and that their method of communication is appropriate.

Section 5.3 Members will take such steps as are sufficient and available to them to ensure that any communication with which they are associated is accurate and not misleading, and contains sufficient information to enable its subject matter to be put in proper context.

A central goal of the guide is to promote clear communication of the features of products developed to facilitate informed decision making by new and existing buyers of index-based insurance products, insurers, reinsurers, regulators charged with approving new products, and other affected stakeholders.

1.1 Guide Overview

Part 1 of this guide provides a summary of the insights and decisions required for the insurer to make an informed decision to launch and expand an index insurance business line. Part 1 explains each key decision the insurance manager makes at each step in the product design, evaluation, and pricing process, and the information the insurance manager and actuarial analyst need from the product design team and other sources to make these decisions. Insurance managers are the primary audience for part 1.

Part 2 of this guide provides a step-by-step guide to calculating the decision metrics used by the insurance manager in part 1. These metrics are calculated using probabilistic modeling that provides insights into risks related to the index insurance product. Probabilistic models generate thousands of possible future scenarios based on historical risk patterns, potential changes in those risk patterns over time, other relevant information, and uncertainty measures. The models use these thousands of scenarios to provide an understanding of specific elements of an index insurance product that are important for the insurance manager's decision making. Actuarial analysts are the primary audience for part 2.

This book complements the work on product reliability outlined in Morsink, Clarke, and Mapfumo (2016), which looks at the same issues of product quality but from a client value perspective. Mathematically, the approaches that they present, and the ones that we explain and promote in this book, end up being very similar.

It is also important to point out what this guide does not cover.

- First, the key objective of this guide is to provide a framework for approaching the assessment of index insurance. The book does not cover the comparison of index insurance with other potential risk mitigation products or the assessment of if and when index insurance is appropriate for a given situation. While some of the methods and analyses presented in this book can be useful in helping address these issues, the scope of this guide is limited to the appraisal of the index insurance product.
- Second, the book mainly focuses on the assessment of retail index insurance products and does not show examples of how to appraise sovereign index insurance products. The overall approaches and metrics discussed in this guide can, however, also be applied to sovereign index insurance.
- Third, the guide does not include assessment examples with indices that are based on area average loss or damage. Instead it focuses on indirect indices such as temperature and precipitation. Nevertheless, the main principles discussed in the guide do apply to other types of indices.

1.2 The Case Example

Throughout this guide, we will refer to a concrete example of a product design and evaluation process—our case example (case example box 1CB.1). This example uses hypothetical data that are based on our experience developing index insurance products in more than 20 developing countries. Wherever a reader sees a box labeled "Case Example," he or she will find new information on this hypothetical example.

Case Example Box 1CB.1 Excellence Insurance Background

Excellence Insurance was founded in 2008 in Mapfumoland. Mapfumoland is a lower-middle-income country with a population of 50 million people. Since its launch, Excellence has earned a reputation for innovation and a focus on bottom-of-the-pyramid, low-income consumers. The Mapfumoland market overall has low insurance penetration and a large unbanked and uninsured population. As part of its strategy to expand its customer base into the low-income population, Excellence is considering launching a named peril index insurance product line. Excellence has already been approached by Mass Bank, a commercial bank with a significant portfolio of loans to smallholder farmers, about developing an index product to protect its portfolio from defaults after drought.

Bibliography

Banks, E., ed. 2002. *Weather Risk Management: Markets, Products, and Applications.* Basingstoke: Palgrave.

Dick, W., A. Stoppa, J. Anderson, E. Coleman, and F. Rispoli. 2011. *Weather Index–Based Insurance in Agricultural Development: A Technical Guide.* Rome: IFAD.

Morsink, K., D. Clarke, and S. Mapfumo. 2016. "How to Measure Whether Index Insurance Provides Reliable Protection." Policy Research Working Paper 7744, World Bank, Washington, DC.

Risk Modeling for Appraising Named Peril Index Insurance Products
http://dx.doi.org/10.1596/978-1-4648-1048-0

CHAPTER 2

Critical Concepts in Named Peril Index Insurance

2.1 Why Is Insurance Useful for Smallholder Farmers?[1]

The purpose of insurance is to transfer a specific type of risk from an individual or a group to a third party capable of handling the financial impact of the loss. Most risks can be classified as either high frequency/low impact risks, or low frequency/high impact risks. High frequency/low impact risks have a short **return period** and are usually retained by the party concerned and managed through **risk mitigation** strategies, such as regular doctor's visits or the use of smoke detectors in the home.

However, low frequency/high impact events, such as death, a major medical emergency, or the destruction of valuable assets, can require the transfer of such risks to a well-capitalized third party that can absorb part or all of the financial impact. Insurance is one of the most common tools for transferring this type of risk.

Insurers are able to take on this risk because they pool a large number of different risks, thereby diversifying and reducing their overall exposure. This **risk pooling** is most effective when the insured risks are relatively **independent**, which means the risk events will not all occur at the same time. For example, when one health insurance policyholder undergoes an expensive procedure to address chronic heart disease, other policyholders will not all require the same procedure at the same time.

Another reason that insurers can take on risk is that they buy reinsurance for some of this risk. **Reinsurance** is a form of insurance for insurance companies that transfers a portion of the exposure to reinsurance providers.

It is important to note that insurance transfers only the monetary value of the **residual risk** that is not managed by the insured party's implementation of necessary risk mitigation measures. Farmers that use good farming practices undertake risk mitigation strategies such as the use of drought-resistant seeds

Case Example Box 2CB.1 Smallholder Agriculture and Household Finance in Mapfumoland

Rose Jituboh is a Mapfumoland farmer who lives in Bwanje, an area prone to short dry spells; she farms half a hectare of land. Agricultural production is her household's main source of income, but she and her family members also take on odd jobs at construction sites and other farms in her local area. The family also receives remittances from an older daughter in the nearest city.

Like her neighbors, in the past Rose has used saved seeds to plant her maize crop each year. In the past decade, though, she and her neighbors have lost large parts of their harvests when dry spells hit during the germination or flowering phases of the crop cycle. Rose remembers 2007 and 2010 as particularly bad years for dry spells.

This year, Rose applied for a loan from Mass Bank for $80 to buy drought-resistant seeds and fertilizer. With these improved inputs, she will be less likely to lose her harvest if a dry spell occurs this season.

and appropriate fertilizer against high frequency/low impact risk events like dry spells. These risk mitigation measures are part of why a high frequency event—like a dry spell in a specific location—can have a relatively low impact (case example box 2CB.1).

Insurance products transfer the residual risk of low frequency/high impact risk events to insurance companies. The insured party regularly pays a small amount for protection against the devastating effects of a rare but very severe event, such as a major drought or earthquake, against which it is very difficult to implement successful risk mitigation measures.

Although smallholder farmers can benefit from risk transfer through insurance products, the specific type of risks they face makes index insurance a promising tool for this population. Index insurance solves a major problem for insurers wishing to cover low frequency/high impact events that affect many insured parties at the same time, often in logistically challenging situations and typically with relatively low insured amounts per insured party.

Many risks, such as fire, accident, or death, affect insured parties independently. In these cases, insurance companies find it operationally and financially feasible to visit each affected party and assess his or her level of damage to determine the **claim** payment. This type of insurance is called **indemnity insurance**. For example, when a car covered by car insurance is in an accident, the insurance company sends an adjuster to evaluate the damage to the vehicle. Based on the adjuster's evaluation, the insurance company will make a claim payment for the estimated cost to repair or replace the car. This evaluation of actual losses is expensive and can often take significant time and resources to complete.

Table 2.1 summarizes the main differences between indemnity and index-based agriculture insurance from the perspective of the insurer.

Table 2.1 Key Differences between Indemnity Insurance and Index-Based Agricultural Insurance

	Indemnity insurance products (multi-peril crop insurance)	Named peril index insurance products
Coverage	• Most perils that affect agriculture production (for example, hail or drought) except for exclusions specified in the contract	• Only perils specified in the contract
Underwriting and product design requirements	• **Historical inventory damage data** for the individual farmer or for a population representative of the farmer's experience • Farmer location • Farmer acreage	• **Historical hazard data** (for example, time series for meteorological data) • Historical inventory damage data • Agronomic data • Location of the measurement point (for example, weather station or satellite pixel)
Underwriting and product design costs	• High because of requirement for farmer-level yield data	• High because of technical capacity needed
Target market	• Large and medium commercial farmers	• Governments • Smallholder farmers • Agribusinesses • Input suppliers • Financial institutions • Nongovernmental organizations
Contract monitoring activities	• Yield measured at the end of the season	• Real-time hazard data used to monitor the contract throughout the season
Loss assessment	• Completed for each farmer • Semi-objective process	• No field assessments • Transparent and objective evaluation using real-time hazard data
Risk of **adverse selection**	• High	• Low
Risk of **moral hazard**	• High	• Low
Basis risk	• Low	• Moderate to high

2.2 What Is Named Peril Index Insurance?

When risks affect a large population all at the same time—called **covariant risks**—and often in difficult on-the-ground circumstances, assessing the losses of each individual insured party that is affected is not feasible. For example, a major typhoon might affect tens of thousands of insured parties at the same time. The insurer will not have the resources to assess each claim individually in a short period even in the best conditions. Damage to infrastructure caused by the typhoon will make such assessments even less feasible.

In the case of small rural farmers in developing countries, a loss event such as a major drought will similarly affect large numbers of farmers. Smallholder land-holdings of fewer than two hectares would require an extremely high number of assessments, even over a relatively small area or region. Furthermore, each farmer will insure a relatively small value—for example $100—making the potential revenue per **insured unit** very small. These factors make indemnity insurance for smallholder farmers operationally and financially unattractive for the insurer. For covariant risks in logistically challenging environments, index insurance offers

Risk Modeling for Appraising Named Peril Index Insurance Products
http://dx.doi.org/10.1596/978-1-4648-1048-0

an efficient mechanism for providing coverage without relying on individual assessments for claim processing.

An important assumption of index insurance products is that insured units within a given geographical area have similar characteristics, and the effect of the deviation in the proxy is similar for all insured units. When a claim is triggered for a specific area, all insured units are compensated at the same payout rate, usually a percentage of the **sum insured**.

Individual payouts are calculated automatically based on deviations in a proxy, such as the cumulative amount of rainfall during a specific period, or the wind speed of a typhoon. Neither the number of individuals affected nor the on-the-ground conditions affect the claim process.

It is important to note that there will be situations in which an insured party experiences a loss attributable to a hazard event but does not receive a payout. The index product will only pay out for hazard events that are specifically covered by the policy—those for which the proxy(ies) meet the specified triggers.

An important element of index insurance product structuring is when the proxy triggers a payout. In some cases, proxies can trigger a payout for asset protection rather than for replacement. For example, in Kenya index-based livestock insurance products trigger a payout to pastoralists for the purchase of animal feed when pasture levels begin to decrease because of drought. An important feature is that the payout comes as the pasture is decreasing, not when it has disappeared. This way, the pastoralists can purchase feed to keep their animals alive rather than using a payout to replace animals that have died.

Named peril index insurance is a relatively new financial instrument for transferring risk from individuals or groups to international risk carriers. Although the instrument has been used for many years in developed countries such as Belgium, France, Germany, Italy, Switzerland, the United Kingdom, and the United States, its use in the developing world is fairly recent. See case example box 2CB.2.

Case Example Box 2CB.2 Insured Units and Proxies for Mass Bank Product

Mass Bank provides loans of between $75 and $160 to farmers like Rose Jituboh for the purchase of improved inputs. Most farmers use the loans to purchase drought-resistant seeds and fertilizer. Like Rose, Mass Bank's customers live within 20 kilometers of 10 ground-based weather stations—the geographical areas for the index insurance product.

Excellence Insurance is developing an index product for Mass Bank that covers maize crops against both dry spells like the ones experienced recently in Rose's area and more serious droughts. The loans from Mass Bank are the insured units. The product uses two proxies: cumulative rainfall in millimeters during the flowering period and the number of consecutive dry days during the entire cover period. Based on the deviations in these proxies, the product makes payouts of between 0 percent and 100 percent of the sum insured (the value of the loan). For Rose's $80 loan, the 100 percent payout will equal $80.

2.3 Who Are the Main Stakeholders in the Risk Transfer Process?

The key stakeholders in the risk transfer process are the regulator, the insured party, the policyholder, the insurer, the product design team, the **data provider**, and the **reinsurer**, each of whom are defined below.

Regulator—The regulator approves the issuing of the product in the market and also determines and implements consumer protection rules.

Insured party—The insured party is the individual or firm that transfers away the unwanted residual risk. The insured party can be an individual farmer or a small or medium enterprise, or it can be the same organization that is the policyholder.

Policyholder (the client)—As a market segment, smallholder farmers constitute a large number of insured units, each with small insured values, which makes issuing policies to each smallholder farmer operationally and financially unattractive for insurers. Working with a single policyholder organization, that is, an **aggregator**, such as an input supplier, a microfinance institution, a cooperative, or a commercial bank, provides insurers with a less expensive way of reaching smallholder farmers. A single policy is issued to the policyholder that covers all the insured units. In some cases, the aggregator will be both the policyholder and the insured party, such as when a commercial bank insures its own portfolio of loans. In other cases, the aggregator is the policyholder, but the policy specifies that the insured parties are the individual smallholder farmers. In the latter case, the aggregator is acting as an **agent** of the insurer and is therefore remunerated through an agreed-on commission structure.

Insurer—The insurer underwrites the risk. The insurer is the party legally responsible for the liabilities arising from the policy. The insurer issues the policy, collects premiums, reinsures part of the portfolio, and settles claims arising from the policy. If the product does not perform as expected by the end users, the financial and reputational risks fall on the insurer. For this reason it is critical that the insurer fully understand the features of each named peril product it underwrites.

See figures 2.1–2.3 for the potential configurations of policyholders and insured parties.

Product design team—The product design team possesses specialized skills in developing named peril index products. Often, this team is part of an **insurance intermediary**, but it can also be made up of members of the insurer's internal staff.

In the interest of the long-term sustainability of an index product line, we recommend that insurers and other key stakeholders work toward developing this product design capacity locally. If this capacity is not initially available locally, insurers can hire international resources to design index products and build local capacity. Remaining wholly dependent on international resources for product design services can be difficult and often financially imprudent. In the long run, local resources tend to produce better-designed products because of their understanding of the local environment. For agriculture index insurance products in particular, local agronomists play a crucial role in designing a Base Index that takes into account all the critical aspects of the local crop and soil characteristics.

Risk Modeling for Appraising Named Peril Index Insurance Products
http://dx.doi.org/10.1596/978-1-4648-1048-0

Figure 2.1 Individual as Policyholder and Insured Party

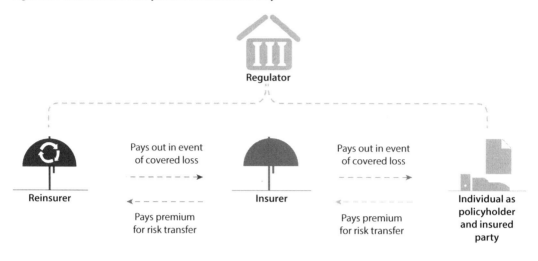

Figure 2.2 Aggregator as Policyholder and Insured Party

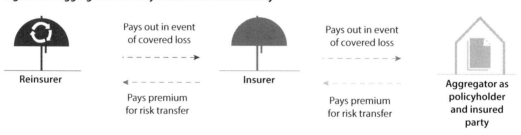

Figure 2.3 Aggregator as Policyholder (Agent) on Behalf of the Insured Party

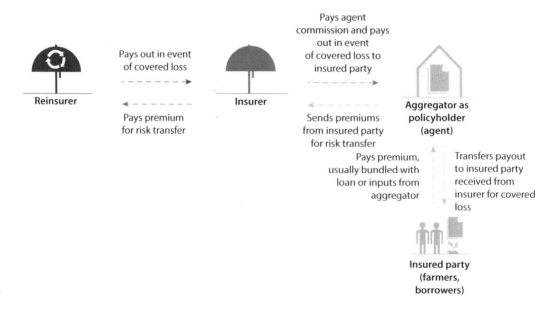

Risk Modeling for Appraising Named Peril Index Insurance Products
http://dx.doi.org/10.1596/978-1-4648-1048-0

Data processing team—Index insurance products require real-time hazard data for claim processing. These data can come from publicly or privately owned weather stations, remote sensing equipment, or satellites, and often must be processed and converted into a suitable format for analysis by the insurer. Many firms that provide product design services have also developed capabilities in processing data for insurance purposes.

Data provider—Depending on the country, data providers are public agencies, private firms, or a combination of the two. Data are collected through ground-based or satellite instruments. The data provider supplies the historical data needed for product design and pricing, and real-time data for claim settlement.

See figures 2.4–2.7 for various configurations of product design and data processing and provision.

Figure 2.4 Product Design and Data Processing Internal to Insurer

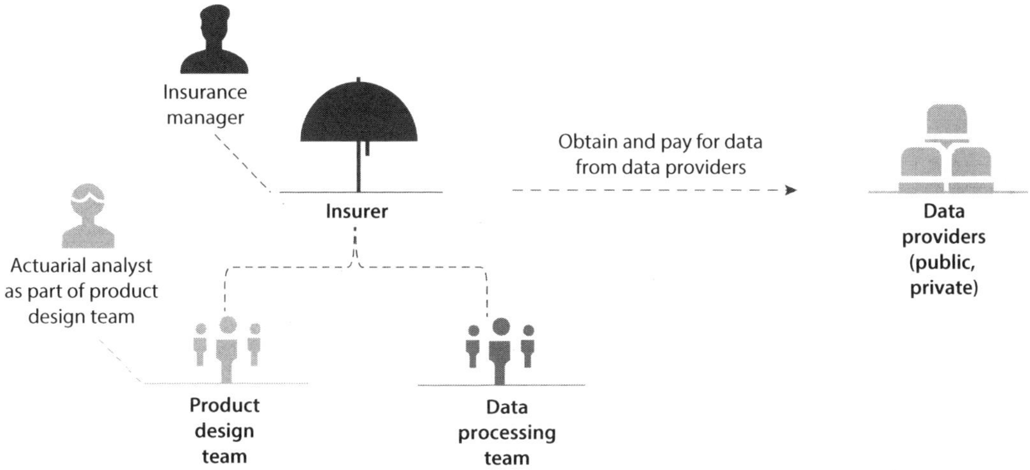

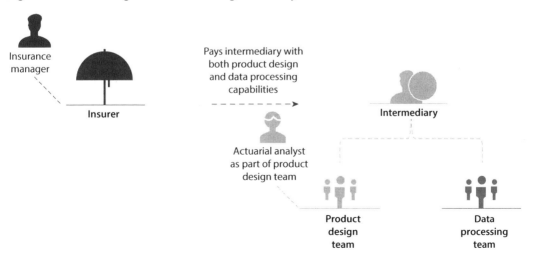

Figure 2.5 Product Design and Data Processing Provided by One External Firm

Risk Modeling for Appraising Named Peril Index Insurance Products
http://dx.doi.org/10.1596/978-1-4648-1048-0

Figure 2.6 Product Design and Data Processing Provided by Two Separate External Firms

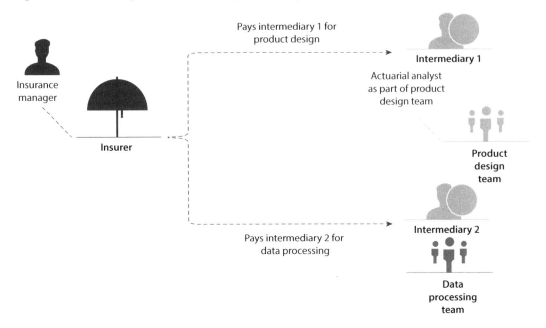

Figure 2.7 Product Design and Data Processing Provided by External Firm, with Actuarial Analyst Internal to Insurer

Reinsurer—The reinsurer, the insurer of insurers, accepts all or a portion of the risk underwritten by the insurer. Because of the covariant nature of the risks insured using index insurance, a significant portion of the risk should be reinsured on the international market. Reinsurance protects the **solvency** of the local insurance company and also provides a foreign exchange inflow when a major loss event occurs, which can benefit both the insurer and the national economy.

Risk Modeling for Appraising Named Peril Index Insurance Products
http://dx.doi.org/10.1596/978-1-4648-1048-0

Throughout this guide, most of the attention is placed on the interactions between two key roles: the insurance manager and the actuarial analyst. The insurance manager is the staff member of the insurer charged with decision making regarding the insurer's index insurance product line. The actuarial analyst uses analytics and **risk modeling** to provide the insurance manager with metrics for evaluating index insurance business opportunities and products. The actuarial analyst can be a part of an internal or external product design team, or a member of the insurer's staff who is charged with analyzing information provided by an external product design team. See case example box 2CB.3.

Case Example Box 2CB.3 Excellence Insurance Staffing and Resources

At Excellence Insurance, management has assigned a promising actuary on staff, Lindiwe Maneli, to serve as the actuarial analyst for the index insurance product line, and an experienced executive, Ghassimu Sow, to the role of insurance manager. Excellence is considering hiring the Mapfumoland specialist insurance intermediary firm Hazard Analytics to provide the product design and data processing services.

2.4 How Are Named Peril Index Insurance Products Developed?

Index insurance contracts are designed using historical hazard and inventory damage data to trigger payouts at specific frequency and severity levels. The index insurance product design process typically occurs in two phases. In the first phase, the product design team develops a product based mainly on input from local subject specialists (for example, agronomists), and evaluates (chapter 4) and prices (chapter 5) this initial product. This guide calls this product the **Base Index.** The Base Index is designed with the goal of providing maximum transfer of the risk of the named peril. It provides the highest level of coverage possible against damage to the farmer's inventory. The Base Index triggers a payment when the proxy's behavior indicates that any damage to inventory—no matter how small—is expected.

A major challenge for Base Index design is basis risk—the difference between the payout triggered by the index insurance product and the actual losses experienced by the insured party that are attributable to the named peril. **Insured party basis risk** describes the scenario in which the payout amount is less than the farmer's actual losses attributable to the named peril. In this case, the farmer experiences an economic loss from the named peril but is not adequately compensated by the claim payout. **Insurer basis risk** describes the scenario in which the payout is greater than the actual losses the insured party experiences from the named peril. In this case, the insurer suffers an economic loss because of unnecessary claim payments.

Risk Modeling for Appraising Named Peril Index Insurance Products
http://dx.doi.org/10.1596/978-1-4648-1048-0

Two types of basis risk cause these outcomes for the insured party and the insurer: product design basis risk and geographical basis risk. An example of **product design basis risk** is provided here. Imagine a very simple index insurance policy that stipulates that a payout will occur when less than 100 millimeters of rain falls during the entire growing season. Imagine that 105 millimeters of rain fell during the period, but all in the last week of the season. In this example, farmers will likely experience losses because of the very dry season overall, but the policy will not pay out. Product design basis risk is discussed, evaluated, and quantified in detail in chapter 4 of this guide.

An example of the other type of basis risk, **geographical basis risk**, occurs when a farmer's field is so far away from the location where the proxy is measured that the conditions in her field do not match the proxy measurement. This type of basis risk is not discussed or quantified in this guide. With the advent of satellite products, insurers can reduce geographical basis risk by using multiple, precise measurement locations.

Because it provides such a high level of coverage, the Base Index is also very expensive, and many policyholders will request a lower price—and lower coverage—product. However, it is extremely important that the insurer always produce a Base Index to explain to the policyholder the difference between complete coverage—that provided by the Base Index—and the coverage provided by other product options. Without this explicit comparison, policyholders often fall into the trap of expecting complete coverage even when they have purchased a lower coverage, less expensive product.

In some cases, the policyholder will purchase the Base Index. More often, however, the Base Index will cost more than the policyholder is initially willing or able to pay. This is when the second phase of the product design begins. The product design team must now use input from the policyholder on price to redesign and improve the product with new parameters so that the cost of the product decreases (case example box 2CB.4). This second product is called the Redesigned Index. The product design team also evaluates the Redesigned Index (chapter 6), just like the Base Index.

The trigger levels for the Redesigned Index proxies embody a specific implied deductible, which is the difference in coverage between the Base Index and the Redesigned Index. The deductible is the amount of residual risk that is carried by

---

Case Example Box 2CB.4 Base Index and Redesigned Index Triggers

Excellence Insurance's Base Index for Mass Bank is designed to pay out in seasons with less than 100 millimeters of cumulative rainfall (the trigger). The Redesigned Index for Mass Bank is designed to pay out in seasons that have less than 75 millimeters of cumulative rainfall. The Redesigned Index is cheaper than the Base Index, but in any season during which rainfall measures between 75 millimeters and 100 millimeters, the Redesigned Index will not pay out. If Mass Bank purchases the Redesigned Index, the bank retains more drought risk—the implied deductible.

the policyholder and not transferred to the insurance company by virtue of purchasing the Redesigned instead of the Base Index. The less residual risk that is transferred to the insurance company, the lower the cost of the index insurance product and the higher the deductible. Products with lower deductibles will be more expensive.

Policyholder understanding of the levels of triggers and the amount of the implied deductible is paramount to successful implementation of index insurance. If policyholders do not understand these factors, they will have incorrect expectations of when the product will pay out. For example, a policyholder with an incomplete understanding of a product designed to cover catastrophic drought may expect to receive a payout after a short dry spell.

One way in which the insurance provider can ensure policyholder understanding of the index product is by explaining the product's behavior with reference to previous experience in the insured area, as demonstrated in case example box 2CB.5.

Because named peril index insurance is relatively new, many people believe that an index that does not trigger when losses are experienced on the ground is always caused by product design basis risk. In many cases, however, the Base Index—which would have paid out for most losses—was too expensive and the policyholder selected the Redesigned Index and so is responsible for the implied deductible. It is critical to understand and distinguish between these two situations in which a low (or no) payout occurs despite significant loss of inventory.

The tools in this guide provide and explain quantitative and probabilistic tools and techniques that insurance managers can use to evaluate and communicate the characteristics, future behavior, and value of index insurance products. The processes suggested for the insurer's review of these products are critical strategies for practicing **responsible finance** and for the long-term sustainability

---

Case Example Box 2CB.5 Specific Years Comparison for Base Index and Redesigned Index

The Excellence Insurance manager, Ghassimu Sow, uses examples from 2010 and 2007 to explain the difference in coverage for the Base Index and the Redesigned Index to Mass Bank. Farmers in Rose Jituboh's and other areas remember these years as having very bad dry spells that affected their crops and harvests.

Ghassimu explains that in 2010, the Base Index would have paid out 61 percent of the sum insured for Area H. For a farmer with a loan of $80, the payout would have been $49. The Redesigned Index, however, would have paid out only 11 percent—$9 for a $80 loan. In 2007 in Area D, the Base Index would have paid out 40 percent of the sum insured ($24), while the Redesigned Index would not have paid out at all.

These concrete numbers help the Mass Bank managers understand that these are very different products. If they select the less expensive Redesigned Index, they will receive less coverage against drought and dry spells.

Risk Modeling for Appraising Named Peril Index Insurance Products
http://dx.doi.org/10.1596/978-1-4648-1048-0

of index insurance markets. Specifically, well-informed and educated providers, buyers, and users of index insurance will help further develop and sustain index insurance markets.

This guide provides methods for meeting consumer protection responsibilities such as providing transparent services and treating policyholders fairly. Failure to implement responsible insurance principles will lead to reputational challenges for the product, the insurer, and the market as whole, which in turn will lead to low product sales.

Although the framework and tools presented in this guide do allow for a much better understanding of index insurance, it is important to note that the concepts are very difficult. A thorough assessment of a product does allow for a clear explanation of the product's characteristics, but many insured parties will still find it difficult to fully understand the product. This guide does not cover how best to communicate index insurance concepts to insured parties or confirm their understanding. In many cases, the distribution channels and aggregators, who normally act as policyholders, will have a critical role in ensuring the insured party's understanding of the product characteristics.

Note

1. Named peril index insurance can also be useful for other stakeholders, such as micro, small, and medium enterprises engaged in nonfarming activities that are nonetheless exposed to weather risks. For example, microentrepreneurs in some coastal areas are vulnerable to typhoons or hurricanes that can damage or destroy their inventory. This guide focuses on index insurance for farming-related activities, but it is important to remember that the tools discussed here can also be applied to other types of insured parties.

Bibliography

Banks, E., ed. 2002. *Weather Risk Management: Markets, Products, and Applications.* Basingstoke: Palgrave.

Dick, W., A. Stoppa, J. Anderson, E. Coleman, and F. Rispoli. 2011. *Weather Index-Based Insurance in Agricultural Development: A Technical Guide.* Rome: IFAD.

Mahul, O., V. Niraj, and D. Clarke. 2012. "Improving Farmers' Access to Agricultural Insurance in India." Policy Research Working Paper 5987, World Bank, Washington, DC.

Morsink, K., D. Clarke, and S. Mapfumo. 2016. "How to Measure Whether Index Insurance Provides Reliable Protection." Policy Research Working Paper 7744, World Bank, Washington, DC.

PART 1

Decision Tools for Insurance Managers

The chapters of part 1 provide a summary of the insights and assessments required for the insurer to make an informed decision to launch and expand an index insurance business line.

Chapter 3 explains the process of completing a prefeasibility study, which establishes the presence—or lack thereof—of key prerequisites for launching an index insurance business line in a new market.

Chapters 4 through 6 cover the pilot phase of launching an index insurance business line, during which the insurer works with a small selection of policy-holders to design an initial product offering. These chapters detail the process of designing, evaluating, and pricing the Base Index, and evaluating the Redesigned Index.

Chapter 7 provides a description of a detailed market analysis to be completed following the pilot phase. The market analysis uses the insurer's experience during the pilot phase to provide an understanding of the market's potential for a commercial index insurance business line.

Finally, chapter 8 explains how to determine the value of index insurance to a **financier** that provides loans to small farmers. Given a particular financier's historical **default rates** and projected portfolio, the chapter illustrates to what degree index insurance can protect the financier against **nonperforming loans** caused by the named peril.

Part 2 of the guide (chapters 9 through 15) explains the quantitative models[*] that produce the metrics and results used in part 1.

---

[*] In part 2 of the guide, **Monte Carlo simulation** models are used (and explained in detail) to determine the expected outcomes of an index insurance product, as well as the risks inherent in such a product.

CHAPTER 3

Prefeasibility Study

3.1 Introduction

The purpose of the prefeasibility study is to determine whether the market possesses the basic prerequisites for the design and introduction of named peril index insurance products. The ability to develop, refine, and scale up named peril index insurance products opens opportunities for risk carriers (insurers and reinsurers) to reach large rural populations of potential customers. In the past few years, insurers have participated in pilot projects aimed at providing proof of concept for commercial index insurance products. With the focus on implementing pilots, relatively little energy was spent on analysis of the prerequisites for the successful expansion of coverage with these products.

Experience to date from various pilot project studies has shown that reaching commercially viable volumes for named peril index insurance in a given market requires the presence of several key resources. This chapter discusses how the insurance manager should assess the prerequisites for a specific market. The insurance manager must evaluate each prerequisite for every target area and for the market as a whole, and only proceed with the product if the prerequisites exist in enough target areas to provide sustainable business volumes.

The key questions that the prefeasibility study answers follow:

- Are potential policyholders interested in buying this product?
- Is a pool of subject specialists available to assist with product design?
- Are historical hazard data series available with which to design and price products?
- Are data providers able to provide real-time or near real-time hazard data for claim settlement during each **risk period**?
- Are qualitative and quantitative inventory damage data for product design and product evaluation available?
- Are local or international product design capabilities available?
- Are distribution channels available through which the product can be sold effectively?

- Are reinsurers willing to offer the necessary reinsurance **capacity**?
- Has regulatory approval been granted to underwrite this product?
- Are direct or indirect subsidies available?

These 10 key points are discussed in more detail in the following section, and concrete examples are provided in case example boxes 3CB.1–3CB.3.

Case Example Box 3CB.1   Excellence Insurance's Prefeasibility Study for Mapfumoland

For Excellence Insurance the market is a specific country—Mapfumoland. Agriculture is a major part of the Mapfumoland economy, and more than two-thirds of the population engage in agricultural production. Most of these households pursue subsistence farming, but a growing segment—about 25 percent—engage in semi-commercial farming, using improved inputs and selling a portion of their harvests.

Excellence hired a consulting firm, Research Plus, to complete a prefeasibility study for index insurance in Mapfumoland. The consultants submitted a detailed report on the availability of historical weather data, ground and satellite real-time data providers, historical inventory damage data, local and international product design capabilities, distribution channels, reinsurance capacity, and the local regulatory position on weather index insurance. Lindiwe Maneli, the actuarial analyst, is studying the report and will summarize the findings before discussing them with the insurance manager, Ghassimu Sow.

3.2 Outline of Emerging Managerial and Process Controls

STEP 1: Summarize the Status of Prerequisites for the Product Design and Risk Transfer Process

For each target area within the potential market, each of the following basic prerequisites should be in place and available to the insurer:

- *Potential policyholders:* A sustainable index insurance market is one with either a large number of potential insured parties or a small number of players with very large portfolios to be insured. The insurer must be convinced that the market has sufficient demand for the product.

- *Subject specialists:* Robust product structures are usually developed with assistance from subject specialists such as agronomists and hydrologists. It is therefore important to make sure that the product development team has access to this expertise as it designs the products.

- *Historical hazard data:* Most reinsurers require between 20 and 30 years of historical data—such as daily or **dekadal rainfall** data—to perform product pricing (box 3.1). This information is required for several stages within the product design, product evaluation, and product pricing processes. If such information is not available, designing a robust product will not be feasible.

Box 3.1   Changes in Risk Conditions over Time

The use of historical hazard and inventory damage data for product design, evaluation, and pricing makes an implicit assumption that past risk conditions (for example, weather patterns) will continue into the future. Sometimes, however, these conditions change over time. Section 16.1 briefly continues this discussion. For now, two main types of changes in risk conditions are considered:

• *Changes in the proxy due to changes in climate:* If weather events become more severe, we can expect more severe damage than is observed in the historical data.

• *Changes in the degree of damage to inventory:* In some cases, weather will not change, but the same events will cause significantly more or less damage. For example, environmental degradation or rapid urbanization may increase losses relative to previous, similar events. Conversely, new drainage systems or drought-resistant plant varieties may decrease losses relative to previous events of the same nature.

When insurers design, evaluate, and price index insurance products, changing risk conditions must be accounted for as accurately as possible using qualitative and quantitative methods.

• *Real-time claim settlement hazard data:* The intended use of an index insurance product is to offer prompt claim settlement during the risk period, at the end of the risk period, or both so that policyholders can have access to funds as soon as possible after the hazard occurs. If claims cannot be settled promptly because hazard data are not available, a major purpose of developing an index product is defeated. As a result, the data provider must be able to provide real-time or near real-time data throughout the entire risk period. In this way, all key stakeholders can monitor the index parameters throughout the season. In addition, the insurer and reinsurer must have the necessary information to ensure they are holding appropriate liquid resources to make the required payments within the agreed-on claim settlement period. Even with excellent historical hazard data, the insurer should not proceed with an index product if real-time hazard data are not readily available.[1]

• *Historical inventory damage data:* The product design team needs detailed qualitative data, quantitative data, or both on how the indexed peril has affected the insured parties in the past. Written records of historical yields are not available for most smallholder farmers. In these cases the product design team relies on farmers' recollections along with information from local experts, government, and international sources, such as FEWS NET (USAID's Famine Early Warning Systems Network), to rank the level of crop damage caused by the named peril in each year and geographical area. This process is termed **qualitative classification of past damages**, and is discussed in detail in section 4.3. Sometimes, the product design team has access to quantitative data, such as recorded yearly yields or loan write-offs. Using the available qualitative and quantitative data, the product design team will evaluate the Base Index against the information on inventory damage from previous years. The available data must be substantial and accurate enough to support the product design process.

- *Product design capabilities:* High-quality product design capabilities must be available to the insurer, either internally or externally. The product design team should be able to both design and statistically evaluate the performance of the products. As discussed in chapter 2, we recommend that insurers work toward developing this product design capacity locally in the long run.

- *Clear distribution channels:* Given the small sum insured per farmer, selling index-based insurance to individual farmers is usually uneconomic. Most successful index schemes use distributors such as agribusinesses, financial institutions, cooperatives, or other institutions that act as the aggregator and policyholder on behalf of groups of farmers or other low-income individuals. The use of aggregators leads to low administrative costs for underwriting and claim settlement. Before investing heavily in the development of named peril index insurance, the insurer should identify clear distribution channels.

In most cases, named peril index insurance is bundled with other services such as access to finance. Understanding the underlying service in which the farmer is interested is critically important to the success of index distribution. The insurer must evaluate the value chain for each crop to be insured. Farmers in a poorly organized value chain will likely be blocked from accessing financing to pay for farming inputs as well as insurance premiums. The insurer should also pay close attention to issues of market **liquidity** and the cost of finance when evaluating value chains because these will affect the potential market size for named peril index insurance.

- *Reinsurance capacity:* Named peril index insurance is normally used to transfer covariant risks that can affect a whole country or region at the same time. As a result, most of the risk is transferred to international financial markets instead of being kept locally. Therefore, before offering named peril index insurance, the insurer should make sure it has access to sufficient reinsurance capacity. As long as volumes are high and data are of good quality, reinsurance capacity is usually accessible. Reinsurance prices are, however, sensitive to market conditions and sometimes volatile. For example, a major disaster in Asia can increase reinsurance renewal prices worldwide. For this reason, insurers should consider the potential for reinsurance price increases when evaluating products.

- *Regulatory approval:* In many developing countries, index insurance is not specifically regulated but is included under the "miscellaneous" class. This classification is common during pilot index insurance projects that are supported by multilateral organizations that provide quality control and a degree of self-regulation. However, as the product line matures, comprehensive regulation is needed to ensure the functioning of the market and proper treatment of policyholders. Regulators' understanding and approval of index products are critical for scaling up index insurance product lines.

- *Premium subsidies:* The availability of direct or indirect subsidies is not a prerequisite, but can considerably support the development, scalability, and viability of index insurance products, especially during the early stages of the product life cycle. However, it is important to consider whether these subsidies will be in place for the short or long term. If for the short term, the insurer will have to determine whether the target market will be willing and able to pay higher premiums once the subsidies end.

Based on research into the prerequisites for index insurance in the market under consideration, the insurance manager and actuarial analyst evaluate the relative strength of each prerequisite for the target areas and the overall market. If all prerequisites are in place for the overall market, the insurance manager identifies the market as a priority for launching the pilot phase. If many prerequisites are missing from the market, the insurance manager should consider waiting to develop an index insurance product line until conditions improve and more prerequisites are met.

Although this list of prerequisites is not exhaustive, our experience working on index insurance in more than 20 developing countries suggests that these are the critical elements for scaling up index insurance business lines.

In addition to the prerequisites discussed above, the insurance company in its due diligence process should consider other important factors, including, for example, the following:

- In what ways does the firm have a comparative advantage in this market (is it already doing business there; is it able to leverage experience and expertise)?
- Is the cost-benefit analysis for this market superior to that for other investment or business development opportunities the firm may have?

Because the above points are not unique to the evaluation of an index insurance product, they are not discussed in further detail in this guide.

Case Example Box 3CB.2 Summary of Key Points from the Research Plus Prefeasibility Study on the Mapfumoland Market

Prerequisite	Key points from the Research Plus prefeasibility study
Potential policyholders	• More than 500,000 smallholder farmers work with the five distribution channels that have expressed interest in the index product. • The rural bank and the agribusiness Buyer Goods are also interested in purchasing an index product to protect their agrifinance and input advance portfolios.
Subject specialists	• In each area, a number of local extension officers, specialists from agribusinesses and suppliers, and employees of research institutions work closely with smallholder farmers. • The report provides a list of three to five recommended subject specialists for each area. These specialists helped the Research Plus consultant develop qualitative classifications of past damages.

box continues next page

Risk Modeling for Appraising Named Peril Index Insurance Products
http://dx.doi.org/10.1596/978-1-4648-1048-0

Case Example Box 3CB.2 Summary of Key Points from the Research Plus Prefeasibility Study on the Mapfumoland Market *(continued)*

Prerequisite	Key points from the Research Plus prefeasibility study
Historical hazard data	• The Mapfumoland meteorological department operates 100 weather stations, which have recorded 30 years of good quality daily historical rainfall data. Of these weather stations, 50 have also recorded 20 years of daily temperature, humidity, and wind speed data. The data can be accessed for a nominal fee. • ARC2 daily rainfall satellite data are available from 1983 at a pixel size of 10 kilometers by 10 kilometers.
Real-time claim settlement hazard data	• Of the 100 meteorological department weather stations, 80 are fully functional and can provide real-time data. • ARC2 daily rainfall satellite data are also available and can be accessed for free.
Historical inventory damage data	• Research Plus worked with selected subject specialists in each area to develop area-specific categorical classifications of past damages. • Substantial qualitative information is available from FEWS NET, local government agencies, farmers, and local agribusiness firms.
Product design capabilities	• Two Mapfumoland specialist insurance intermediaries offer product design services and charge a fair service fee. Hazard Analytics has the stronger reputation in the local and international market. • Several international product design firms can also be hired to build internal capacity at Excellence. • The report recommends outsourcing the product design function to Hazard Analytics.
Distribution channels	• Five distribution channels have expressed interest in bundling named peril index insurance with existing services provided to maize farmers: a rural bank, a microfinance institution, a seed company, the agribusiness Buyer Goods, and a nongovernmental organization. • The maize value chain is well organized. The government purchases 50 percent of yields for the national grain reserve, and several local and national input suppliers cooperate with financial institutions to provide inputs on credit.
Reinsurance capacity	• All five reinsurance companies currently working with Excellence have expressed interest in supporting this class of business.
Regulatory approval	• The regulator has agreed that the index product may be launched, but has requested sample policy documents.
Premium subsidies	• Premium subsidies are currently not available.

Note: ARC2 = African Rainfall Climatology, version 2; FEWS NET = Famine Early Warning Systems Network.

STEP 2: Evaluate, Document, and Communicate the Business Decision

At this stage, the insurance manager documents the presence or absence of each of the basic prerequisites in the market. Based on the status of the prerequisites, the manager decides whether it is worth the effort for the insurer to pursue a pilot phase. The more prerequisites that are in place, the more confident the manager can be in starting the product design process. Because this is a subjective decision, the manager may want to specify a minimum number of prerequisites that each market must have in place before recommending a pilot phase.

STEP 3: Plan For and Resource the Pilot Phase

If sufficient prerequisites are in place, we recommend that the insurer launch a pilot phase by working with a few potential policyholders to design, evaluate,

Case Example Box 3CB.3 Excellence Insurance Technical Evaluation of Prefeasibility Study

Insurance manager(s)	Ghassimu Sow		
Actuarial analyst(s)	Lindiwe Maneli		
Technical evaluation of the prefeasibility study			
		YES	NO
Are potential policyholders interested in buying this product?		X	
Is a sufficient pool of subject specialists available to assist with product design?		X	
Are sufficient historical hazard data series available to design and price products?		X	
Are data providers able to provide real-time or near real-time hazard data for claim settlement during each risk period?		X	
Are sufficient qualitative or quantitative inventory damage data for product design and product evaluation available?		X	
Are sufficient local or international product design capabilities available?		X	
Are distribution channels available through which the product can be sold effectively?		X	
Are reinsurers willing to offer the necessary reinsurance capacity?		X	
Has regulatory approval been granted to underwrite this product?		X	
Are premium subsidies available			X
Total		9	1
Final decision			
Should the company initiate a pilot project?		X	

launch, and monitor the performance of several products before moving to the commercial phase in which the insurer offers the products to the wider market. Pilot testing allows the insurer to evaluate whether named peril index insurance is the right product for the target market and risk in question. In some situations, other risk management products provide better solutions than index insurance. In other situations, index insurance is best combined with other agriculture insurance and risk management solutions to provide a **hybrid product**. These nuances are most effectively uncovered during the pilot phase. The insurer must dedicate sufficient resources to the pilot phase because it is a critical part of market research.

The activities undertaken during the pilot phase are similar to those implemented during the commercial phase; the only difference is the scale at which each activity is undertaken, that is, with one or two policyholders in the pilot phase rather than with many policyholders in the commercial phase. Chapters 4, 5, and 6 explain in detail how to undertake a pilot with one policyholder. Chapters 7 and 8 expand the discussion to rolling out the product line to the broader market.

Risk Modeling for Appraising Named Peril Index Insurance Products
http://dx.doi.org/10.1596/978-1-4648-1048-0

Note

1. In many developing countries, weather stations do not meet the international standards necessary for their data to be used for insurance claim settlement. Installing more and better quality weather stations can improve product quality by reducing geographical basis risk for products based on weather station data. Better weather station data can also help calibrate satellite-based data that are now widely used for product design.

Bibliography

Clarke, D. 2012. *Weather-Based Crop Insurance in India*. Washington, DC: World Bank.

Dick, W., A. Stoppa, J. Anderson, E. Coleman, and F. Rispoli. 2011. *Weather Index–Based Insurance in Agricultural Development: A Technical Guide*. Rome: IFAD.

Mahul, O. V. Niraj, and D. Clarke. 2012. "Improving Farmers' Access to Agricultural Insurance in India." Policy Research Working Paper 5987, World Bank, Washington, DC.

CHAPTER 4

Product Design and Evaluation— The Base Index

4.1 Introduction

Now that the insurer has verified the presence of the prerequisites for index product design in the chosen market (chapter 3), the pilot phase begins with the design and evaluation of the Base Index for one or two policyholders. The insurer will follow the same steps for product design and evaluation during the later commercial phase when it takes on a larger number of policyholders.

As discussed in chapter 3, product design is often outsourced to specialist firms. However, because the insurance company is ultimately responsible for the performance of the product, the insurer must fully understand product parameters and performance, including product design basis risk. Underwriting index insurance products without a solid understanding of the product can cause capital flight in the medium to long term because of unexpectedly high claims or basis risk events. Increasing the understanding of product performance and behavior by both the insurer and the policyholder is therefore critically important for the long-term sustainability of index insurance.

To help bridge the knowledge gap between product design teams and insurers, this chapter highlights key points for discussion that promote transparency in the product design and risk transfer process. The Base Index product design process, in particular the data required for the process, is discussed. In addition, the process for evaluating the level of product design basis risk for the Base Index, a critical process in making index insurance business decisions, is explained.

The key managerial questions answered during Base Index product design and evaluation are the following:

- How does the frequency of the Base Index's projected payouts compare to the frequency of actual inventory damage events?
- What is the Base Index's level of insured party basis risk? Specifically,
  - How frequently will damage to the insured party's inventory that is caused by the named peril exceed the payouts provided by the Base Index?
  - What will be the magnitude of uncompensated inventory damage?

- What is the Base Index's level of insurer basis risk? Specifically,
  - How frequently will payouts exceed the actual damage to the insured party's inventory that is caused by the named peril?
  - What will be the magnitude of claims that exceed the actual inventory damage?

This chapter discusses these key questions in detail and provides concrete examples in the case example boxes. See case example box 4CB.1 to start.

Case Example Box 4CB.1 Overview of the Base Index for Mass Bank

The Hazard Analytics product design team contracted by Excellence Insurance is developing a Base Index for Mass Bank. Mass Bank is new to lending to small farmers and is one of the few Mapfumoland financial institutions that does so. Although Mass Bank is excited to be a first mover in this market segment, it is still cautious about the many risks associated with agricultural lending. Mass Bank recently partnered with a local agricultural college to offer extension services to its customers to manage some production risks. Even so, because Mass Bank's customers practice rain-fed agriculture, it is very concerned about the risk of loan defaults following a severe drought.

4.2 Basis Risk and the Implied Deductible

Because named peril index insurance is relatively new, many people believe that basis risk is always the cause of an index not triggering when losses caused by the named peril are experienced on the ground. In reality, the term "basis risk" applies to a narrower set of scenarios related to the performance of the Base Index.

Basis risk is defined as the difference between the payout triggered by the Base Index and the actual losses attributable to the named peril. This difference can be positive or negative. Insurer basis risk describes when the payout is greater than actual losses—the insurer suffers economic losses caused by unnecessary payments. Insured party basis risk describes when the payout is smaller than the actual losses—the insured party suffers an economic loss from the named peril but the contract does not provide adequate compensation (figure 4.1).

Figure 4.1 Insurer and Insured Party Basis Risk

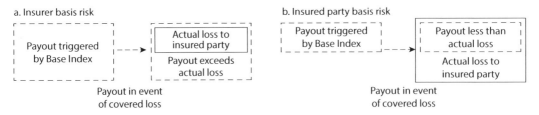

4.2.1 Product Design Basis Risk

Product design basis risk results from the inability of the Base Index to ever perfectly reflect the reality on the ground because its payouts reflect average losses, not the losses of the specific insured party. Product design basis risk is inherent in all named peril index insurance products; therefore, the insurer's focus should be on reducing instead of eliminating it.

Once a product has been marketed for a number of years and reliable quantitative inventory damage data have been collected, these data can be used to refine the index product. Over time, the product design team will have increasingly reliable information with which to analyze product design basis risk. This chapter provides a detailed process for using this type of information to evaluate the Base Index's product design basis risk, starting in the pilot phase.

It is important to note that changes in risk conditions over time must be addressed regularly as part of evaluating product design basis risk. Changes in the behavior of the proxy will lead to changes in the payouts triggered by the index insurance product, while changes in the degree of damage to inventory will cause changes in the actual losses attributable to the named peril. These elements are central to determining the magnitude of basis risk for the product.

4.2.2 The Redesigned Index's Implied Deductible

Index product design typically occurs in two phases. In the first phase, the product design team develops a Base Index using input from local subject specialists, and evaluates and prices it. The Base Index provides the highest level of coverage possible against damage to the farmer's inventory caused by the named peril. The Base Index triggers a payment when the proxy's behavior indicates that any damage to inventory—no matter how small—is expected. The Base Index is used as a point of reference for discussing product options with policyholders, and is extremely important for ensuring that the policyholder fully understands the product purchased. It is also extremely important that the insurer always produce a Base Index to explain to the policyholder the difference between complete coverage—that provided by the Base Index—and the coverage provided by other product options. Without this explicit comparison, policyholders often fall into the trap of expecting complete coverage even when they have purchased a lower coverage, less expensive product.

If the Base Index meets the policyholder's expectations, it is the final product purchased by the policyholder. In many cases, however, the Base Index will cost more than what the policyholder is initially willing or able to pay, so the second phase of product design begins. The product design team uses input from the policyholder on price to design the Redesigned Index with new parameters so that the premium decreases.

The implied deductible is the difference in coverage between the Base Index and the Redesigned Index. It is the amount of risk that the policyholder chooses to retain and not transfer to the insurance company. The Base Index is designed to transfer as close to all of the risk from the named peril as possible from the

Risk Modeling for Appraising Named Peril Index Insurance Products
http://dx.doi.org/10.1596/978-1-4648-1048-0

Figure 4.2 Redesigned Index Implied Deductible

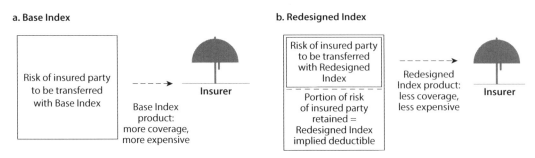

a. Base Index   b. Redesigned Index

Figure 4.3 Product Design Basis Risk versus the Redesigned Index Implied Deductible

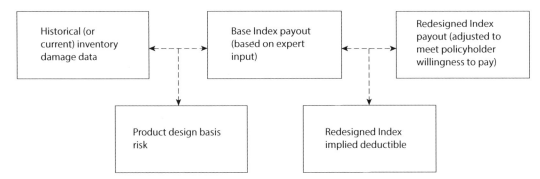

policyholder to the insurance company. The Redesigned Index, on the other hand, transfers less of the named peril risk from the policyholder to the insurance company (figures 4.2 and 4.3).

Of course, the insurer must make sure that the policyholder fully understands the implications of choosing the Redesigned Index. The best tools for explaining the differences between the Base Index and the Redesigned Index are discussed in chapter 6.

4.2.3 Identifying Examples of Product Design Basis Risk versus the Implied Deductible

Do not forget that the Redesigned Index is derived from the Base Index. If the Base Index suffers from product design basis risk, the Redesigned Index will too. So, when a policyholder experiences losses caused by a named peril but does not receive a payout from the index product that is equal to the damages, the insurer and other stakeholders should always try to determine whether the cause is product design basis risk or the implied deductible of the Redesigned Index.

In these cases, we suggest that the insurer calculate the payout values for the risk period for both the Base Index and the Redesigned Index. If the Base Index triggers but the Redesigned Index does not, the implied deductible is the reason for the difference. If neither the Base Index nor the Redesigned Index triggers, in spite of observed losses caused by the named peril on the ground, product design basis risk is the cause of the problem.

For example, imagine a very simple Base Index for drought and dry spell coverage that provides a payout of 100 percent of the sum insured when the cumulative rainfall for the period is less than 50 millimeters (**exit**) and no payout when the cumulative rainfall is more than 100 millimeters (trigger). It provides payouts equal to 2 percent of the sum insured per millimeter of rain below the trigger.

The Redesigned Index also provides a payout of 100 percent of the sum insured when the cumulative rainfall is less than 50 millimeters (exit), but it provides no payout when the cumulative rainfall is more than 75 millimeters (trigger). It provides payouts equal to 4 percent of the sum insured per millimeter of rain below the trigger.

As seen in figure 4.4, when cumulative rainfall is 50 millimeters or less, both the Base Index and the Redesigned Index will pay out 100 percent of the sum insured. When cumulative rainfall is 100 millimeters or higher, both pay out nothing. For cumulative rainfall between 50 millimeters and 100 millimeters, the Redesigned Index always pays less than the Base Index. This difference in payout is the implied deductible.

Take the case in which cumulative rainfall for the period is 80 millimeters. The Base Index payout will be 40 percent of the sum insured. This is the amount of damage to the insured farmers' inventory that we expect to see from drought and dry spells. However, the Redesigned Index will provide no payout. The difference in payouts here—40 percent of the sum insured—is the value of the implied deductible. The farmer experiences a loss of 40 percent but receives no payout, because this is the value of the risk retained when the insured party selected the less expensive, lower coverage product.

Now take the case of cumulative rainfall of 105 millimeters. The Base Index provides no payout for rainfall at this level, meaning that no damage to the farmers' inventory is expected from drought. But imagine that, although rainfall was at this relatively high level, temperatures were extremely high,

Figure 4.4 Identifying Product Design Basis Risk versus the Implied Deductible

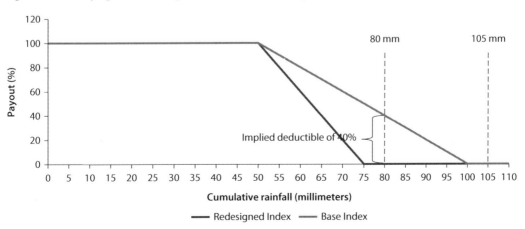

Risk Modeling for Appraising Named Peril Index Insurance Products
http://dx.doi.org/10.1596/978-1-4648-1048-0

resulting in drought conditions that caused damage to the insured farmers' crops. The damage to the farmers' inventory was caused by the named peril—drought—but the proxy used for the index was not sufficient to predict this damage. An additional proxy—temperature—is required to account for this scenario. This is an example of product design basis risk.

4.3 Steps in Product Design and Evaluation

This section discusses the steps in the Base Index design and evaluation process, including evaluating the Base Index for product design basis risk (see summary in figure 4.5). Chapter 11 provides a step-by-step guide to using the probabilistic models on which the decision metrics in this section are based. Product pricing is also an important part of evaluating the Base Index, and is discussed in chapter 5.

4.3.1 STEP 1: Collect Historical Hazard Data

To design the Base Index, the product design team collects historical hazard data. These data are used for designing and evaluating the Base Index in Step 7. Historical hazard data are available in many forms, for example, daily rainfall, daily temperature, and daily wind speed. The historical behavior of specific hazards helps determine the triggers for the Base Index. For example, to design a product that triggers based on average temperature and cumulative rainfall during a specific period of the crop cycle, the product design team will need historical daily temperature and rainfall data.

4.3.2 STEP 2: Collect and Summarize Historical Inventory Damage Data

Historical inventory damage data are often very scarce for the low-income market. Therefore, product design teams often produce a **categorical classification of past damages** for each year and geographical area. In this process, the product design team relies on farmers' recollections and information from local experts as well as government and international sources to categorize the level of crop damage caused by the named peril in each year and geographical area (case example box 4CB.2). Of course, these semi-quantitative data may be biased (for example, recall bias), so the analysis and results based on these data should be interpreted and used with care.

Once a product has been marketed for a number of years and reliable quantitative inventory damage data have been collected, these data can be used to refine the index product. Over time, the product design team will have more reliable information with which to analyze product design basis risk.

4.3.3 STEP 3: Collect Relevant Information from Subject Specialists and Policyholder

Successful index development relies heavily on inputs from subject specialists such as agronomists, hydrologists, and seismologists who provide information that helps the product design team set index triggers and payout rates (case example box 4CB.3). These specialists—and the prospective policyholder—can

Figure 4.5 Base Index Design and Evaluation Process

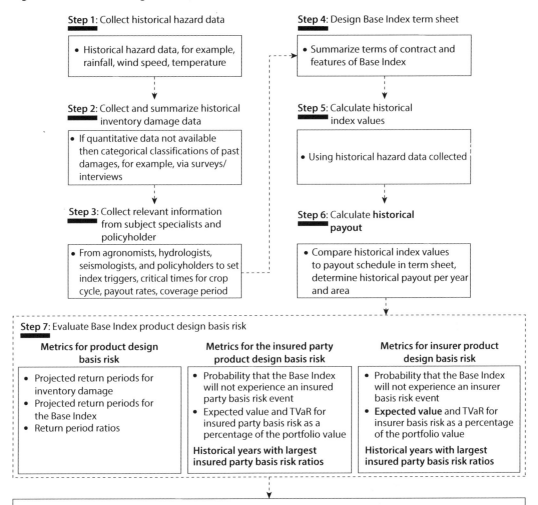

Note: TVaR = tail value at risk.

Case Example Box 4CB.2 Categorical Classification of Past Damages for Areas A to J, 1984–2013

The Hazard Analytics product design team uses historical rainfall data from the local meteorological service. The data show 30 years of daily rainfall for all 10 of the geographical areas needed.

Based on information from FEWS NET and interviews with local government agencies, the local agricultural college, farmers like Rose Jituboh, and agribusiness firms, the Hazard Analytics product

box continues next page

Case Example Box 4CB.2 Categorical Classification of Past Damages for Areas A to J, 1984–2013 *(continued)*

design team classified each year in each area as either good or bad according to inventory damage due to drought risk. Each good year was assigned a value of zero. The team rated each bad year on a scale of 1 to 5, where 5 corresponded to the highest damages from drought and 1 to mild damages from drought.

YEAR	AREA A	AREA B	AREA C	AREA D	AREA E	AREA F	AREA G	AREA H	AREA I	AREA J
1984					3				3	5
1985							1			
1986		2	2							
1987					2	3		2		1
1988				3						
1989		2							1	
1990			2	5	5		1			
1991						1				4
1992				3				1		5
1993										3
1994							1		1	5
1995										
1996	5									
1997				1	1	1		3	1	
1998							2		3	
1999							2	5		3
2000							3	2		
2001										
2002			2			1				
2003		1							2	3
2004				2			1			
2005										
2006				2	1					2
2007				2						
2008										
2009				1		1			3	4
2010								5		
2011	2									
2012										
2013								3	1	

Key	
0	Good year
1	1–20 percent loss
2	21–40 percent loss
3	41–60 percent loss
4	61–80 percent loss
5	81–100 percent loss

Note: FEWS NET = Famine Early Warning Systems Network.

Case Example Box 4CB.3 Subject Specialist Information for Base Index Product Design

The Hazard Analytics product design team hires a team of local agronomists identified in the prefeasibility report with experience working with maize farmers in the 10 geographical areas of interest. The agronomists design a product with two triggers. Having these two triggers is important because the dry days measure the spread of rainfall while the cumulative triggers measure the quantity. For a crop to do well, sufficient rainfall that is spread out across the season is required.

box continues next page

Case Example Box 4CB.3   Subject Specialist Information for Base Index Product Design *(continued)*

Trigger 1: Consecutive Dry Days

The agronomists report that local maize crops need a long duration of regular rainfall to grow, so they recommend looking at the number of consecutive dry days in a growing season and its effect on the crop's health. The number of consecutive dry days, defined as the number of days with less than 2.5 millimeters of rain during the crop cycle, will be the first proxy used in the Base Index design (Trigger 1).

The agronomists explain that there are two important thresholds for consecutive dry days. The first is the number of consecutive dry days after which the crop will suffer from water stress, which is 20 days. The second is the number of consecutive dry days after which the crop will die, which is 40 days, especially if the dry period occurs during the flowering stage in the crop cycle.

Based on the information from the agronomists, the product design team designs the Base Index so that it pays out 2.5 percent of the sum insured for each consecutive dry day above the first threshold (20 days). After 21 consecutive dry days, the payout will be 2.5 percent of the sum insured. By the 40th consecutive dry day—the day the crop will die—the total payout will reach 50 percent of the sum insured. The payout will also be 50 percent for any number of consecutive dry days greater than 40. Forty consecutive dry days is called the exit for Trigger 1, because this number (and above) receives the maximum payout of 50 percent.

Trigger 2: Cumulative Rainfall

Because maize is especially vulnerable to dry weather during the flowering stage of the crop cycle, cumulative rainfall (in millimeters) during the flowering period will be the second proxy used in the product design (Trigger 2).

The agronomists identify the threshold for cumulative rainfall during the flowering period as 100 millimeters of rain, which is the cumulative amount of rain that must fall during the flowering period for the maize to flower successfully. Any cumulative amount below this threshold will result in the loss of the crop.

Based on the information from the agronomists, the Hazard Analytics product design team designs the Base Index so that it will pay out 2 percent of the sum insured for every millimeter less than 100 millimeters of cumulative rain during the flowering period. So, if a cumulative total of 99 millimeters of rain falls during the flowering period, the payout will be 2 percent of the sum insured. If a cumulative total of 50 millimeters or less falls during the flowering period, the payout will be 100 percent of the sum insured (figure 4CB.3.1). The exit for Trigger 2 is 50 millimeters, because this amount (and lower) receives the maximum payout of 100 percent.

Final Payout

The product design team decides that the final payout will be the greater of the payout for Trigger 1 or Trigger 2.

box continues next page

Risk Modeling for Appraising Named Peril Index Insurance Products
http://dx.doi.org/10.1596/978-1-4648-1048-0

Case Example Box 4CB.3 Subject Specialist Information for Base Index Product Design *(continued)*

Figure 4CB.3.1 Base Index Trigger and Exit for Trigger 2

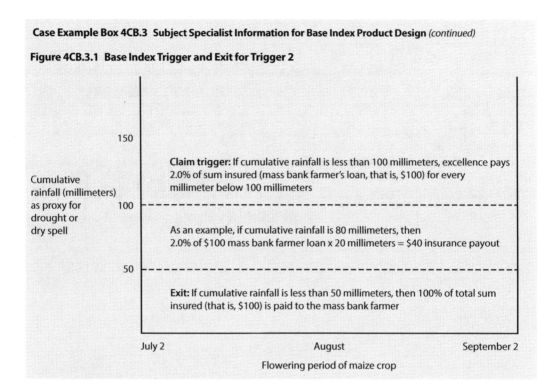

Flowering period of maize crop

Case Example Box 4CB.4 Term Sheet for Base Index

Insured areas	Areas A to I	Area J
Participating measurement stations	Stations A to I	Station J
Target crops	Maize	Maize
Type of insurance cover	Weather index insurance that pays out a defined percentage of the total sum insured when the following events occur at participating measurement stations during the total cover period: • A specified number of consecutive dry days **OR** • Total rainfall less than a specified level. These measures approximate weather conditions that may cause inventory damage for the policyholder that, as a result, cause losses for the insured.	Weather index insurance that pays out a defined percentage of the total sum insured when the following events occur at participating measurement stations during the total cover period: • A specified number of consecutive dry days **OR** • Total rainfall less than a specified level. These measures approximate weather conditions that may cause inventory damage for the policyholder that, as a result, cause losses for the insured.
Total contract period	June 20–September 17, inclusive	June 20–September 17, inclusive
Maximum payout	The greater of Trigger 1 payout or Trigger 2 payout (see below), up to 100 percent of the total sum insured	The greater of Trigger 1 payout or Trigger 2 payout (see below), up to 100 percent of the total sum insured
Maximum specified distance	20 kilometer radius	20 kilometer radius
Total sum insured	Total loan portfolio	Total loan portfolio

box continues next page

Case Example Box 4CB.4 Term Sheet for Base Index *(continued)*

Insured areas	Areas A to I		Area J	
Claim Trigger 1				
Payout trigger event definition	**Number of consecutive dry days**		**Number of consecutive dry days**	
	Days immediately following one another, where the total rainfall recorded on each day is 2.5 millimeters or less. Recorded rainfall is that taken from the participating measurement stations during the cover period for Trigger 1. The longest consecutive dry day period during the cover period is the index value, which is evaluated against the payout schedule.		Days immediately following one another, where the total rainfall recorded on each day is 2.5 millimeters or less. Recorded rainfall is that taken from the participating measurement stations during the cover period for Trigger 1. The longest consecutive dry day period during the cover period is the index value, which is evaluated against the payout schedule.	
Cover period	June 20–September 17, inclusive		June 20–September 17, inclusive	
Payout schedule	Trigger	20 consecutive dry days	Trigger	20 consecutive dry days
	Payout rate	2.5 percent per dry day above the trigger	Payout rate	2.5 percent per dry day above the trigger
	Exit	40 consecutive dry days	Exit	50 consecutive dry days
Number of payments allowed	Only one payment is allowed for this trigger.		Only one payment is allowed for this trigger.	
Timing of payment	Payments due according to the definitions above may be made at the end of the total cover period, that is, after September 17.		Payments due according to the definitions above may be made at the end of the total cover period, that is, after September 17.	
Claim Trigger 2				
Payout trigger event definition	**Total rainfall for flowering period**		**Total rainfall for flowering period**	
	Total millimeters of rainfall recorded during the flowering period. Recorded rainfall is that taken from the participating measurement stations. For the contract period, cumulative rainfall is obtained by summing daily amounts over the contract period. The resulting amount is the index value, which is evaluated against the payout schedule.		Total millimeters of rainfall recorded during the flowering period. Recorded rainfall is that taken from the participating measurement stations. For the contract period, cumulative rainfall is obtained by summing daily amounts over the contract period. The resulting amount is the index value, which is evaluated against the payout schedule.	
Cover period	July 25–September 2, inclusive		July 25–September 2, inclusive	
Payout schedule	Trigger	100 millimeters	Trigger	60 millimeters
	Payout rate	2 percent per millimeter below trigger	Payout rate	2 percent per millimeter below trigger
	Exit	50 millimeters	Exit	10 millimeters
Number of payments allowed	Only one payment is allowed for this trigger.		Only one payment is allowed for this trigger.	
Timing of payment	Payments due according to the definitions above may be made at the end of the total cover period, that is, after September 17.		Payments due according to the definitions above may be made at the end of the total cover period, that is, after September 17.	

Risk Modeling for Appraising Named Peril Index Insurance Products
http://dx.doi.org/10.1596/978-1-4648-1048-0

also provide detailed information for the coverage period, especially critical times during the crop cycle.

4.3.4 STEP 4: Design Base Index Term Sheet

Based on information from the subject specialists and the prospective policy-holder, the product design team writes the Base Index term sheet. The term sheet summarizes the terms of the contract and the features of the Base Index.

4.3.5 STEP 5: Calculate Historical Index Values

Now the product design team will begin evaluating the Base Index by calculating historical index values from the historical hazard data they have already collected (case example box 4CB.5). This process demonstrates how the product would have performed if it had been in the market during past growing seasons.

In this step, the product design team calculates the historical index value for each proxy, year, and geographical area.

4.3.6 STEP 6: Calculate Historical Payouts

Now the product design team compares each historical index value to the payout schedule in the term sheet to determine the **historical payouts** for each year and geographical area (case example box 4CB.6). The historical payouts are estimates

---

Case Example Box 4CB.5 Calculation of Historical Index Values for the Base Index

For each year and geographical area, the Hazard Analytics product design team follows the steps below.

Calculate the historical index values for Proxy 1 (number of consecutive dry days)

- Define cover period as June 20 to September 17 for each year.
- Define dry day as a day with 2.5 millimeters or less of rain.
- Define dry day trigger (level above which payment starts) as 20 days.
- Define dry day exit (level at or above which full payout is triggered) as 40 days.
- Classify each day as either dry (less than or equal to 2.5 millimeters of rain) or wet (more than 2.5 millimeters of rain).
- Find the longest stretch of consecutive dry days. The number of days in this period is the index value for Proxy 1.

Calculate the historical index values for Proxy 2 (cumulative rainfall during flowering period)

- Define the flowering period as July 25 to September 2 for each year.
- Define cumulative rainfall trigger (level below which payment starts) as 100 millimeters.
- Define cumulative rainfall exit (level at and below which full payout is triggered) as 50 millimeters.
- Add up the cumulative rainfall amount for each day during the flowering period. This value is the index value for Proxy 2.

Note: In many product design cases, a daily cap is included in the product design so that any amount above such a limit is not included in the cumulative total. In addition, the contract start date is often dynamic and not fixed, which means the contract starts once a certain condition has been met, such as having received a total rainfall amount of more than 50 millimeters within a three-day period.

Case Example Box 4CB.6 Calculation of Historical Payouts for the Base Index

For each year and geographical area, the Hazard Analytics product design team follows the steps below.

- Calculate the historical payout for Proxy 1: Compare the historical index value for Proxy 1 to the payout schedule in the term sheet (case example box 4CB.4) to find the historical payout for Proxy 1.
- Calculate the historical payout for Proxy 2: Compare the historical index value for Proxy 2 to the payout schedule in the term sheet (case example box 4CB.4) to find the historical payout for Proxy 2.
- Determine the final payout: Select the higher payout between that for Proxy 1 and that for Proxy 2. This value is the final payout for the specific year and geographical area.

See results in case example box 4CB.7.

Case Example Box 4CB.7 Historical Payouts for the Base Index

YEAR	AREA A	AREA B	AREA C	AREA D	AREA E	AREA F	AREA G	AREA H	AREA I	AREA J
1984	0.0%	0.0%	0.0%	0.0%	44.1%	0.0%	0.0%	0.0%	22.6%	90.4%
1985	0.0%	0.0%	0.0%	0.0%	0.0%	0.0%	0.0%	0.0%	0.0%	0.0%
1986	0.0%	0.0%	22.5%	0.0%	0.0%	0.0%	0.0%	0.0%	0.0%	7.5%
1987	0.0%	0.0%	0.0%	0.0%	22.5%	31.2%	0.0%	0.0%	0.0%	0.0%
1988	0.0%	0.0%	0.0%	47.5%	0.0%	0.0%	0.0%	0.0%	0.0%	0.0%
1989	0.0%	15.0%	0.0%	0.0%	7.5%	0.0%	0.0%	0.0%	0.0%	0.0%
1990	0.0%	0.0%	7.5%	100.0%	66.6%	0.0%	0.0%	0.0%	0.0%	2.5%
1991	0.0%	0.0%	0.0%	0.0%	0.0%	0.0%	0.0%	0.0%	0.0%	42.5%
1992	0.0%	0.0%	0.0%	50.0%	0.0%	0.0%	0.0%	0.0%	0.0%	86.0%
1993	0.0%	0.0%	0.0%	0.0%	0.0%	0.0%	0.0%	0.0%	0.0%	44.4%
1994	0.0%	0.0%	0.0%	0.0%	0.0%	0.0%	0.0%	0.0%	5.0%	96.0%
1995	0.0%	0.0%	0.0%	0.0%	0.0%	0.0%	0.0%	0.0%	0.0%	0.0%
1996	79.2%	0.0%	0.0%	0.0%	0.0%	5.8%	0.0%	0.0%	0.0%	27.5%
1997	0.0%	20.0%	0.0%	0.0%	0.0%	15.0%	0.0%	65.4%	0.0%	0.0%
1998	0.0%	0.0%	0.0%	0.0%	0.0%	0.0%	30.0%	0.0%	63.2%	0.0%
1999	0.0%	0.0%	0.0%	0.0%	2.5%	17.5%	2.5%	86.2%	0.0%	39.0%
2000	0.0%	0.0%	0.0%	0.0%	0.0%	0.0%	53.4%	0.0%	0.0%	0.0%
2001	0.0%	0.0%	0.0%	0.0%	0.0%	0.0%	0.0%	0.0%	0.0%	0.0%
2002	0.0%	0.0%	5.0%	0.0%	0.0%	0.0%	0.0%	0.0%	0.0%	0.0%
2003	0.0%	0.0%	0.0%	0.0%	0.0%	0.0%	0.0%	0.0%	29.0%	60.0%
2004	0.0%	0.0%	0.0%	19.2%	0.0%	0.0%	0.0%	0.0%	0.0%	0.0%
2005	0.0%	0.0%	0.0%	0.0%	0.0%	0.0%	0.0%	0.0%	0.0%	0.0%
2006	0.0%	0.0%	0.0%	2.5%	0.0%	0.0%	0.0%	0.0%	0.0%	39.4%
2007	0.0%	0.0%	0.0%	40.4%	0.0%	0.0%	0.0%	0.0%	0.0%	0.0%
2008	0.0%	0.0%	0.0%	0.0%	0.0%	0.0%	0.0%	0.0%	0.0%	17.5%
2009	0.0%	2.5%	0.0%	0.0%	0.0%	0.0%	0.0%	0.0%	32.8%	64.0%
2010	0.0%	0.0%	0.0%	0.0%	0.0%	0.0%	25.0%	61.2%	0.0%	0.0%
2011	2.5%	7.5%	0.0%	16.6%	0.0%	0.0%	0.0%	0.0%	0.0%	0.0%
2012	0.0%	5.0%	0.0%	0.0%	0.0%	2.5%	0.0%	0.0%	0.0%	0.0%
2013	0.0%	0.0%	0.0%	0.0%	9.0%	0.0%	0.0%	45.2%	0.0%	0.0%

of what the Base Index would have paid out to the policyholder if the contract had been in place during previous seasons. These are used in Step 7 to evaluate product design basis risk and in chapter 5 for Base Index product pricing.

4.3.7 STEP 7: Evaluate Base Index Product Design Basis Risk

The actuarial analyst now uses the historical payouts and the historical inventory damage data provided by the product design team to evaluate the Base Index's product design basis risk. Using the probabilistic model detailed in chapter 12, the actuarial analyst calculates the following metrics to provide a quantitative description of the index's basis risk.

Risk Modeling for Appraising Named Peril Index Insurance Products
http://dx.doi.org/10.1596/978-1-4648-1048-0

4.3.7.1 Metrics for Product Design Basis Risk

- The *projected return period for inventory damage* is the frequency at which inventory damage caused by the named peril occurs at specific **damage levels** (for example, damage to 10 percent of the inventory, 30 percent of the inventory, 50 percent of the inventory, and 70 percent of the inventory). For example, if two droughts that damage 10 percent of crops are observed in a 20-year period, the return period for drought at this damage level is 1 in 10 years.

- The *projected return period for the Base Index* is the frequency at which the Base Index makes a payout at specific **payout levels** (for example, payouts of 75 percent of the sum insured, 50 percent of the sum insured, 25 percent of the sum insured, and 5 percent of the sum insured).

- The *return period ratio* is calculated as the ratio of the projected return period for inventory damage to the projected return period for the Base Index at specific damage and payout levels. When the return period ratio is equal to 1, the Base Index triggers a payout at the same frequency as the occurrence of actual inventory damage caused by the named peril. When the ratio is greater than 1, the Base Index triggers a payout more frequently than the occurrence of inventory damage caused by the named peril (insurer basis risk). The greater the value of the ratio, the greater the amount of insurer basis risk. When the ratio is between 0 and 1, the Base Index triggers payouts less frequently than the occurrence of actual inventory damage caused by the named peril—farmers experience damage from the named peril but the contract does not trigger a payout (insured party basis risk). The greater the value of the ratio, the smaller the amount of insured party basis risk.

4.3.7.2 Metrics for Insured Party Product Design Basis Risk

- The *probability that the Base Index will not experience an insured party basis risk event* is the likelihood that the product will either trigger a payout when there is inventory damage caused by the named peril, or trigger no payout when there is no inventory damage due to the named peril.

- The *expected value and **tail value at risk** (TVaR) for insured party basis risk as a percentage of the portfolio value* are the magnitude of underpayments to the policyholder due to product design basis risk expressed as a percentage of the total portfolio value for all areas covered by the product.

- *Historical years with largest insured party **basis risk ratios*** lists historical years when the Base Index would have triggered insufficient compensation to the insured party because of product design basis risk.

4.3.7.3 Metrics for Insurer Product Design Basis Risk

- The *probability that the Base Index will not experience an insurer basis risk event* is the likelihood that the product will not trigger a payout when there is no inventory damage due to the named peril.

- The *projected value and TVaR for insurer basis risk as a percentage of the portfolio* are the magnitude of overpayments to the policyholder due to product design basis risk expressed as a percentage of the total portfolio value for all areas covered by the product.

- *Historical years with largest insurer basis risk ratios* lists historical years when the Base Index would have triggered excessive compensation to the insured party because of product design basis risk.

The insurance manager, the actuarial analyst, and the product design team review the values of these metrics and evaluate them against a set of guidelines developed by the insurer's **risk management committee**, with input from international reinsurance brokers or international reinsurers where necessary (case example boxes 4CB.8 and 4CB.9). The risk management committee guidelines should indicate the acceptable range of values for each metric. These agreed-on guidelines are critical for managing the insurer's reputational risk, which is linked to the product's quality. When a product's metrics fall outside of this range, the insurance manager should request that the product design team review and improve the Base Index structure.

In cases in which the Base Index meets all the requirements outlined in the evaluation guidelines, the insurer moves on to the next step: policyholder engagement. However, if the Base Index does not meet the requirements, the product design team must review the product to identify changes to the structure that will improve the Base Index's basis risk evaluation. These changes should still align with the recommendations provided by the subject specialists.

Case Example Box 4CB.8 Excellence Insurance Product Evaluation Guidelines for the Base Index

Decision metric	Risk committee guidelines for index products	
	Insured party basis risk	*Insurer basis risk*
Projected return period for inventory damage and the Base Index	Must be as close as possible to each other for each area, especially for damage or payout levels of 50 percent and 70 percent	
Return period ratio	Must be between 0.7 and 1.2 for each area and damage or payout level	
Probability that the Base Index will not experience a basis risk event	Must be greater than 75 percent for each area	Same as insured party basis risk
Expected value for basis risk as a percentage of the portfolio value	Must be less than 5 percent	Same as insured party basis risk
TVaR at 95 percent for basis risk as a percentage of the portfolio value	Must be less than 20 percent	Same as insured party basis risk
Final decision	**Present Base Index to policyholder**	
	Restructure index for specific areas	
	Consider alternative solutions (non-index)	

Note: TVaR = tail value at risk.

Risk Modeling for Appraising Named Peril Index Insurance Products
http://dx.doi.org/10.1596/978-1-4648-1048-0

Case Example Box 4CB.9 Product Evaluation Decision Metrics for the Base Index

INVENTORY DAMAGE RETURN PERIODS

				AREA A	AREA B	AREA C	AREA D	AREA E	AREA F	AREA G	AREA H	AREA I	AREA J
RETURN PERIOD	@	10%	DAMAGE LEVEL	13	9	9	4	6	6	5	4	4	3
RETURN PERIOD	@	30%	DAMAGE LEVEL	18	13	12	6	9	9	6	6	6	5
RETURN PERIOD	@	50%	DAMAGE LEVEL	30	20	19	9	14	14	10	10	9	8
RETURN PERIOD	@	70%	DAMAGE LEVEL	62	40	42	19	29	27	22	20	19	17

BASE INDEX RETURN PERIODS

				AREA A	AREA B	AREA C	AREA D	AREA E	AREA F	AREA G	AREA H	AREA I	AREA J
RETURN PERIOD	@	10%	PAYOUT LEVEL	14	7	11	5	6	7	9	8	7	3
RETURN PERIOD	@	30%	PAYOUT LEVEL	20	11	16	8	9	11	12	12	10	4
RETURN PERIOD	@	50%	PAYOUT LEVEL	30	17	24	12	14	16	18	18	16	7
RETURN PERIOD	@	70%	PAYOUT LEVEL	52	30	43	22	26	27	33	34	29	12

RETURN PERIOD RATIOS

				AREA A	AREA B	AREA C	AREA D	AREA E	AREA F	AREA G	AREA H	AREA I	AREA J
RETURN PERIOD RATIO	@	10%	DAMAGE/PAYOUT LEVEL	0.93	1.25	0.83	0.76	0.99	0.86	0.53	0.55	0.6	1.14
RETURN PERIOD RATIO	@	30%	DAMAGE/PAYOUT LEVEL	0.93	1.15	0.78	0.73	0.98	0.82	0.52	0.54	0.59	1.13
RETURN PERIOD RATIO	@	50%	DAMAGE/PAYOUT LEVEL	0.99	1.21	0.81	0.77	1.02	0.87	0.57	0.55	0.61	1.18
RETURN PERIOD RATIO	@	70%	DAMAGE/PAYOUT LEVEL	1.18	1.33	0.99	0.88	1.08	0.98	0.66	0.57	0.67	1.41

PROBABILITY THAT THE BASE INDEX WILL NOT EXPERIENCE AN INSURED PARTY BASIS RISK EVENT

90%	88%	88%	81%	81%	84%	82%	79%	74%	78%

PROJECTED INSURED PARTY BASIS RISK AMOUNT

	AMOUNT	% OF TOTAL SUM INSURED
LOWER	0	0%
EXPECTED	276,655	3%
UPPER	978,750	12%
TVaR	1,310,579	16%

HISTORICAL YEARS WITH LARGEST INSURED PARTY BASIS RISK RATIOS

	AREA A	AREA B	AREA C	AREA D	AREA E	AREA F	AREA G	AREA H	AREA I	AREA J
HISTORICAL YEAR WITH LARGEST INSURED PARTY BASIS RISK RATIO	2011	1986	2002	2006	1990	1987	1999	2000	1984	1991
BASIS RISK RATIO	28%	30%	25%	28%	23%	19%	28%	30%	27%	28%
HISTORICAL PAYOUT RATIO	3%	0%	5%	3%	67%	31%	3%	0%	23%	43%
HISTORICAL INVENTORY DAMAGE RATIO	30%	30%	30%	30%	90%	50%	30%	30%	50%	70%

PROBABILITY THE BASE INDEX WILL NOT EXPERIENCE AN INSURER BASIS RISK EVENT

97%	84%	97%	87%	88%	84%	88%	94%	94%	72%

PROJECTED INSURER BASIS RISK AMOUNT

	AMOUNT	% OF TOTAL SUM INSURED
LOWER	-	0%
EXPECTED	159,939	2%
UPPER	709,878	9%
TVaR	1,009,740	13%

HISTORICAL YEARS WITH LARGEST INSURER BASIS RISK RATIOS

	AREA A	AREA B	AREA C	AREA D	AREA E	AREA F	AREA G	AREA H	AREA I	AREA J
HISTORICAL YEAR WITH LARGEST INSURER BASIS RISK RATIO	1984	1997	1984	2011	2013	1999	2010	1997	1998	1996
BASIS RISK RATIO	0%	20%	0%	17%	9%	18%	25%	15%	13%	28%
HISTORICAL PAYOUT RATIO	0%	20%	0%	17%	9%	18%	25%	65%	63%	28%
HISTORICAL INVENTORY DAMAGE RATIO	0%	0%	0%	0%	0%	0%	0%	50%	50%	0%

The product evaluation model outputs above give the Excellence Insurance team important insights into different characteristics of the Base Index. With regard to insured party basis risk, Lindiwe, the actuarial analyst, observes the following:

- *The projected return period for inventory damage and the Base Index*: At the 70 percent damage level, Bwanje (Area B) has an inventory damage return period of 1 in 40 years, but a Base Index return period of 1 in 30 years.
- *The return period ratio*: Insured party basis risk is likely to occur in Areas C, D, F, G, H, and I at the 70 percent damage-to-payout rate (catastrophic level). The ratios for Areas C and F, however, are close enough to 1 that we can disregard them. Areas G, H, and I, however, have return period ratios that are too low to meet the risk committee's criteria (below 70 percent). If the other metrics for these areas also do not meet the criteria, the insurance manager will ask the product design team to improve the Base Index structure for these areas. If the return period ratios and other metrics do not improve with the changes in structure, then index insurance may not be a good risk management tool for the risk in these areas.
- *The probability that the Base Index will not experience an insured party basis risk event*: Except for Area I (74 percent), the probabilities for each area are greater than 75 percent. In other words, for each of the nine other areas, there is at least a 75 percent probability that no insured party basis risk event will occur in the next risk period. Since Area I failed to meet the risk committee criteria for both the return period ratio and this metric, the product design team should revisit the structure for this area.

box continues next page

Case Example Box 4CB.9 Product Evaluation Decision Metrics for the Base Index *(continued)*

- *The expected value and TVaR for insured party basis risk as a percentage of the portfolio value*: On average, we expect this portfolio to suffer a 3 percent insured party basis risk loss, but the insured party basis risk for a 1-in-20-year event could be as high as 16 percent of the portfolio (TVaR).
- *Historical years with largest insured party basis risk ratios*: The most recent year in which the Base Index would have provided an insufficient payout because of product design basis risk was 2011 (Area A). In this year, the Base Index would have triggered only a 3 percent payout, but the underlying data for this year (not shown in the table) show that the actual loss to the policyholder would have been 30 percent.

With regard to the insurer basis risk, Lindiwe observes the following:

- *The return period ratio*: Insurer basis risk is projected in Areas A, B, E, and J at the 70 percent damage-to-payout level. However, since Area E's ratio of 1.08 is very close to 1, we can disregard it. Only Areas B and J have ratios greater than the risk committee's guideline of 1.2.
- *The probability that the Base Index will not experience an insurer basis risk event*: The probability for Area J (72 percent) is less than 75 percent—the risk committee's cut-off.
- *The expected value and TVaR for insurer basis risk as a percentage of the portfolio value*: The projected value and TVaR of insurer product design basis risk are 2 percent and 13 percent of portfolio value, respectively, both of which are within the committee guidelines.
- *Historical years with largest insurer basis risk ratios*: In 1997, the policyholder would have lost about 50 percent in Area H, but the Base Index would have paid 65 percent.

Based on this analysis, Lindiwe completes the product evaluation for the Base Index as in case example box table 4CB.9.1. Lindiwe and her manager, Ghassimu, determine that the index needs restructuring for Areas B, I, and J.

Case Example Box Table 4CB.9.1 Base Index Product Evaluation Summary

	Basis risk evaluation for the Base Index	
Decision metric	*Insured party basis risk*	*Insurer basis risk*
Projected return period for the inventory damage and the Base Index	Requirement is not fulfilled for Bwanje (Area B; 1 in 40 years versus 1 in 30 years at 70 percent damage and payout levels)	
Return period ratio	Requirement is not fulfilled for Areas B, G, H, I, and J at the 70 percent damage-to-payout level	
Probability that the Base Index will not experience a basis risk event	Requirement fulfilled except for Area I	Requirement fulfilled except for Area J
Projected value for basis risk as a percentage of the portfolio value	Requirement fulfilled	Requirement fulfilled
TVaR at 95 percent for risk as a percentage of the portfolio value	Requirement fulfilled	Requirement fulfilled
Decision	**Present Base Index to policyholder**	
	Restructure index for specific areas	✓ **Areas B, I, and J**
	Consider alternative solutions (non-index)	

Ghassimu notes that, before launching a product based on this Base Index, Excellence Insurance will need to decide how it will manage insured party basis risk events. Excellence will also inform the regulator

box continues next page

Case Example Box 4CB.9 Product Evaluation Decision Metrics for the Base Index *(continued)*

of its strategy for managing basis risk events so that it can be evaluated against consumer protection guidelines.

As discussed in part 2 of this guide, an important consideration when interpreting the results for product design basis risk is what data and assumptions were used. For example, in this case example 30 years of historical data are used to estimate the return period ratio. Only some of those years experienced weather that would have triggered payout amounts. Therefore, the return-period ratios are based on relatively few observations (fewer than 30). As a result, it is not certain that the very low return period ratio for Bwanje (Area B) is definitely an indication of product value. Instead, the data may include outliers that are causing this result, and in fact the product may work very well for Bwanje. All of the product evaluation results need to be interpreted taking into account the data and assumptions used.

Note: TVaR = tail value at risk.

4.3.8 STEP 8: Document and Communicate Business Decision

Once the insurer has a Base Index that meets its internal guidelines for evaluating basis risk, the insurance manager and actuarial analyst present the Base Index to the policyholder and explain the basis risk evaluation. They should explain each metric so that the policyholder clearly understands the Base Index's strengths and weaknesses.

Even though the Base Index meets the insurer's internal guidelines for basis risk, the policyholder may not be satisfied with the product. In this case, the product design team must review the product to identify changes to the structure (for example, the addition of new proxies) that will improve the Base Index's basis risk evaluation.

The sample of historical insured party basis risk events can be especially helpful for this conversation. For each area, the insurance manager can refer to the year in which an insured party basis risk event occurred and compare the historical damage level with the payout triggered by the Base Index. The insurance manager must explain that, had the product been in place in that year, the payout would have been less than the value of the damage caused by the named peril because of product design basis risk.

Only once the insurer presents a Base Index that meets the policyholder's expectations for basis risk can the product design team move on to pricing the Base Index (chapter 5).

As highlighted earlier, basis risk can never be eliminated, only minimized. It is important for the insurer to clearly explain to the policyholder how the basis risk will be managed. Because of limited data points per geographical area, area-specific metrics will be subject to higher uncertainty and may be biased; therefore, we advise using them with extra care. Critical decisions should be based on portfolio-level metrics and statistics that will have less uncertainty. This caveat applies to all metrics covered in this and all subsequent chapters.

Bibliography

Crouhy, M., D. Galai, and R. Mark. 2006. *The Essentials of Risk Management*. New York: McGraw-Hill.

Dick, W., A. Stoppa, J. Anderson, E. Coleman, and F. Rispoli. 2011. *Weather Index–Based Insurance in Agricultural Development: A Technical Guide*. Rome: IFAD.

Lam, J. 2003. *Enterprise Risk Management: From Incentives to Controls*. Hoboken, NJ: Wiley.

Morsink, K., D. Clarke, and S. Mapfumo. 2016. "How to Measure Whether Index Insurance Provides Reliable Protection." Policy Research Working Paper 7744, World Bank, Washington, DC.

CHAPTER 5

Product Pricing—The Base Index

5.1 Introduction

At this stage in the pilot phase, the insurer has designed and evaluated the Base Index (chapter 4). Now the insurance manager needs to determine the price for the Base Index. Many policyholders who have risk exposure in multiple geographical areas will want to purchase an insurance product with a single premium rate across the different areas (case example box 5CB.1). These products, called **portfolio-priced products**, must account for the risk profiles in each area, the **correlations** in risk between all the areas, and the value insured in each area.

This chapter explains the process for determining the price for a portfolio-priced Base Index under three scenarios: (1) the policy is not reinsured, (2) the policy is reinsured through **proportional reinsurance** only, and (3) the policy is reinsured through a combination of **nonproportional reinsurance** and proportional reinsurance.

Each geographical area covered by a portfolio-priced product in reality has a different risk profile corresponding to a different premium rate. Therefore, the policyholder may want to know the specific premium rates for each geographical area in the portfolio, called the **equitable premium rates**. The policyholder may find these risk ratings useful in making future decisions about lending in specific geographical areas. This chapter also explains the process for providing the equitable premium rate for each geographical area.

The key managerial questions answered during Base Index product pricing are the following:

- What portfolio-priced premium rate for the Base Index meets the profit objectives and risk tolerance of the insurer when
  - The policy has no reinsurance?
  - The policy is reinsured through proportional reinsurance?
  - The policy is reinsured through nonproportional reinsurance, or a combination of nonproportional and proportional reinsurance?

Case Example Box 5CB.1 Mass Bank Loan Portfolio

Mass Bank has made loans to maize farmers for the purchase of inputs in 10 geographical areas, including Bwanje (Area B). The farmers will repay the loans with their earnings from crop sales at the end of the season. The total loan amount for each area is the sum of the loans to each farmer in that area. These total loan amounts vary from $140,160 in Area A to $2,252,250 in Area E. Mass Bank has requested a product to cover the farmers' crops against drought, because drought damage is a main reason that farmers fail to repay the loans. Mass Bank would like the product to have one premium rate for all 10 geographical areas.

- What profit margins, **combined ratios**, and **economic value added** could the insurance firm expect under different premium rates?
- What is the equitable premium rate (that is, the risk-based premium rate) for each geographical area that makes up the policyholder's portfolio?

5.2 Outline of Emerging Managerial and Process Controls

To address the key questions related to product pricing, we recommend the decision-making processes described below and summarized in figure 5.1. Chapter 12 provides a step-by-step guide to using the probabilistic models that produce the values for the decision metrics discussed.

5.2.1 Portfolio Product Pricing—No Reinsurance

5.2.1.1 STEP 1: Determine Key Model Inputs and Assumptions

Before the modeling and pricing analysis process begins, the insurance manager and the analyst agree on the inputs into the model for the specific product. These inputs are assumptions based on data from the prospective policyholder, data from the insurer, and data from the product design team (case example box 5CB.2).

The insurance manager and the analyst determine the following inputs:

Internal data from the policyholder

- Number of insured units per area
- Average sum insured per unit per area ($)

Internal data from the insurer

- **Starting fund value** ($)
- **Expense loading** (as a percentage of premiums)
- Target profit margin (percent)
- **Required return on capital** (percent)

Figure 5.1 Portfolio Product Pricing Managerial Decision Process—No Reinsurance

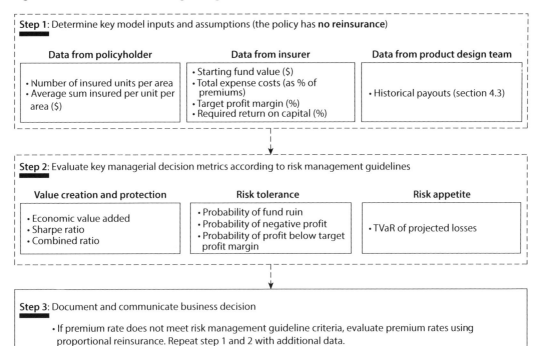

Note: TVaR = tail value at risk.

Case Example Box 5CB.2 Pricing Model Inputs for the Base Index—No Reinsurance

Internal data from Mass Bank

Mass Bank provides information on the number of loans in each geographical area (number of insured units) and the average loan size (average sum insured per unit) as shown in the table in this box. The total loan portfolio—the total loan book that has been approved and for which individual contracts have been signed between Mass Bank and the individual farmers—is $8 million.

Internal data from Excellence Insurance

The starting fund value refers to the policyholder funds for this class that are available at the start of the season and can be used to pay claims. The value of this fund is equal to the total premiums received during all previous periods less claims paid from this fund during all previous periods. Excellence's accounting department reports that the starting fund value is $50,000. Because this is the first time the product will be offered and no premiums have yet been collected, the starting fund is the amount that Excellence has decided to invest in the new product.

The Excellence accounting department estimates that the acquisition, general, and administrative costs related to all activities for this product (**expense costs**) are equal to 15 percent of the gross premium. Excellence management has indicated that a profit margin of 10 percent is required to meet

box continues next page

Risk Modeling for Appraising Named Peril Index Insurance Products
http://dx.doi.org/10.1596/978-1-4648-1048-0

Case Example Box 5CB.2 Pricing Model Inputs for the Base Index—No Reinsurance *(continued)*

profit objectives. Management also reports that the required return on capital—the return that share-holders require to keep their capital in this business line—is 5 percent. The required return on capital is equal to the difference between the expected return to shareholders from the business line and the return currently realized from the liquid assets in which the capital funds are invested.

Data from the product design team

The historical payouts are provided in case example box 4CB.7.

Ghassimu, the insurance manager, decides to evaluate portfolio premium rates between 3 percent and 12 percent.

Lindiwe, the actuarial analyst, uses these inputs to calculate the values of the different pricing-related metrics for the Base Index for the Mass Bank portfolio.

EXPOSED UNITS

	AREA A	AREA B	AREA C	AREA D	AREA E	AREA F	AREA G	AREA H	AREA I	AREA J
# OF INSURED UNITS	1,168	3,773	7,500	4,250	21,450	3,000	8,267	12,635	3,865	7,620
UNIT SIZE ($)	120	75	160	100	105	94	120	95	110	105
EXPOSED UNITS ($)	140,160	282,975	1,200,000	425,000	2,252,250	282,000	992,040	1,200,325	425,150	800,100

INSURER ASSUMPTIONS

TOTAL SUM INSURED ($)	8,000,000
STARTING FUND VALUE ($)	50,000
EXPENSE LOADING (%)	15%
TARGET PROFIT MARGIN (%)	10%
REQUIRED RETURN ON CAPITAL (%)	5%
RISK FREE RATE (%)	2%
PREDICTION INTERVAL (%)	
LOWER	5%
UPPER	95%

PORTFOLIO GROSS PREMIUM RATES TO BE EVALUATED (%)

ITERATION #	GROSS PREMIUM RATE (%)
1	3%
2	4%
3	5%
4	6%
5	7%
6	8%
7	9%
8	10%
9	11%
10	12%

Data from the product design team

- Historical payouts (section 4.3)

The insurance manager also selects the portfolio premium rates to evaluate.

After the analysis and modeling process, the insurance manager must ensure that the inputs used in the modeling were indeed the agreed-on values. In cases in which the analyst has deviated from these values—for example, by reducing the expense cost or profit margin to produce a lower price—he or she must provide full explanations for the changes and provide sources for the values used.

Risk Modeling for Appraising Named Peril Index Insurance Products
http://dx.doi.org/10.1596/978-1-4648-1048-0

5.2.1.2 STEP 2: Evaluate Key Managerial Decision Metrics

Based on the agreed-on inputs, the actuarial analyst produces several metrics to be used by the insurance manager to better understand the product's performance under a variety of premium rates. The values of these metrics will help the insurance manager identify the premium rates for the product that will meet the insurer's profit objectives and risk tolerance.

For each portfolio premium rate, the actuarial analyst calculates the following metrics:

- **Projected losses**
- Projected combined ratio (percent)
- **Projected loss ratio** (percent)
- **Projected profit margin** (percent)
- **Probability of fund ruin** (percent)
- **Probability of negative profit** (percent)
- **Probability of profit below target profit margin** (percent)
- Economic value added (percent; shareholder value)
- **Sharpe ratio.**

The insurance manager evaluates these metrics against guidelines set by the insurer's risk committee (see template in table 5.1 and sample guidelines in case example box 5CB.3), which should indicate the acceptable range of values for each metric. When a product's metrics fall outside of this range, the insurance manager and analyst should consider either a higher premium rate or the effect of reinsurance options.

When evaluating each portfolio premium rate, the insurance manager follows a hierarchical evaluation structure in which the manager first evaluates a rate by looking at the value creation and protection measures. If these are satisfied,

Table 5.1 Template for Risk Management Committee Guidelines on Index Product Pricing

Decision metrics	Risk management committee guidelines
1. Value creation and protection	
Economic value added	
Sharpe ratio	
Combined ratio (projected loss ratio + total expense costs)	
Indicative decision	
2. Risk tolerance	
Probability of fund ruin	
Probability of negative profit	
Probability of profit below target profit margin	
Indicative decision	
3. Risk appetite	
TVaR of projected losses	

Note: TVaR = tail value at risk.

Risk Modeling for Appraising Named Peril Index Insurance Products
http://dx.doi.org/10.1596/978-1-4648-1048-0

Case Example Box 5CB.3 Excellence Insurance Risk Management Committee Guidelines for Index Product Pricing

Decision metrics	Risk management committee guidelines
1. Value creation and protection	
Economic value added	Must be greater than 0 percent unless supporting business and reputational benefits can offset the loss
Sharpe ratio	Must be greater than 0 unless supporting business and reputational benefits can offset the loss
Combined ratio (projected loss ratio + total expense costs)	Must be less than 100 percent
Indicative decision	
2. Risk tolerance	
Probability of fund ruin	Must be less than 2 percent
Probability of negative profit	Must be less than 25 percent
Probability of profit below target profit margin	Must be less than 25 percent
Indicative decision	
3. Risk appetite	
TVaR of projected losses	TVaR net reinsurance must be less than $200,000

Note: TVaR = tail value at risk.

the manager can then look at the risk tolerance measures before finally evaluating the risk appetite measures (see case example boxes 5CB.4 and 5CB.5). When a premium rate fails the higher criteria, it should be eliminated from consideration unless it can be shown that the policyholder is also bringing in supporting business that has positive value creation and protection and has an overall portfolio that is profitable to the insurer.

In general, a good portfolio premium rate will have a low probability of fund ruin, a low probability of negative profit, and a low probability of profit below the target profit margin. In addition, it will have a positive economic value added. It is important to note that this model does not take into account that with higher premium rates, the demand for the product may be lower. The level of demand will not affect the projected loss ratio or projected profit ratio, which are relative values, but it will affect the projected payouts, which is an absolute value. Client price sensitivity is taken up in chapter 14.

5.2.1.3 STEP 3: Document and Communicate the Business Decision

The insurance manager uses the risk committee guidelines for index product pricing to document the hierarchical evaluation of the premium rates. If a premium rate or rates meet all the criteria, the insurance manager lists the premium rates and explains the projected impact on the insurer's profit margins

Case Example Box 5CB.4 Product Model Outputs for Base Index—No Reinsurance

ITERATION	GROSS PREMIUM RATE (%)	PROBABILITY OF NEGATIVE PROFIT (%)	PROBABILITY OF FUND RUIN (%)	PROBABILITY OF PROFIT MARGIN BELOW TARGET (%)	PROJECTED LOSSES ($)				PROJECTED COMBINED RATIO (%)				PROJECTED PROFIT MARGIN (%)				PROJECTED EVA (%)				SHARPE RATIO
					5% Lower	Expected	95% Upper	TVaR	5% Lower	Expected	95% Upper	TVaR	5% Lower	Expected	95% Upper	TVaR	5% Lower	Expected	95% Upper	TVaR	
1	3%	66%	62%	64%	619,287	2,038,858	2,524,657	15%	273%	869%	1087%	768%	173%	85%	109%	-77%	6%		-0.68
2	4%	60%	54%	63%	619,287	2,038,858	2,524,657	15%	209%	652%	804%	-554%	129%	85%	-105%	-24%	57%		-0.58
3	5%	55%	51%	58%	619,287	2,038,858	2,524,657	15%	170%	525%	646%	-426%	70%	85%	84%	30%	13%		0.47
4	6%	50%	47%	56%	619,287	2,038,858	2,524,657	15%	144%	440%	543%	341%	44%	85%	92%	56%	17%		-0.37
5	7%	46%	42%	49%	619,287	2,038,858	2,524,657	15%	126%	375%	466%	-280%	29%	85%	-69%	-13%	39%		-0.27
6	8%	41%	39%	45%	619,287	2,038,858	2,524,657	15%	112%	334%	409%	-254%	12%	85%	45%	9%	24%		-0.17
7	9%	38%	35%	42%	619,287	2,038,858	2,524,657	15%	101%	298%	366%	-199%	1%	85%	82%	-5%	28%		-0.07
8	10%	34%	32%	38%	619,287	2,038,858	2,524,657	15%	92%	270%	333%	-170%	-8%	85%	-78%	-2%	31%		0.01
9	11%	31%	29%	35%	619,287	2,038,858	2,524,657	15%	85%	247%	302%	-147%	15%	85%	-74%	2%	35%		0.14
10	12%	28%	26%	32%	619,287	2,038,858	2,524,657	15%	80%	227%	278%	-128%	20%	85%	-71%	6%	39%		0.24

Note: EVA = economic value added; TVaR = tail value at risk.

Case Example Box 5CB.5 Pricing Decisions for Base Index—No Reinsurance

On the basis of the company guidelines, Ghassimu and Lindiwe agree on the following:

Decision metrics	Managerial and actuarial decisions (indicate minimum acceptable premium rate)
1. *Value creation and protection*	
Economic value added	11 percent
Sharpe ratio	10 percent
Combined ratio (projected loss ratio + total expense costs)	10 percent
Indicative decision	10 percent
2. *Risk tolerance*	
Probability of fund ruin	Not met by any rate considered
Probability of negative profit	Not met by any rate considered
Probability of profit below target profit margin	Not met by any rate considered
Indicative decision	Consider reinsurance options
3. *Risk appetite*	
TVaR of projected losses	Consider reinsurance options
Final decision	**Write**
	Do not write
	Consider next reinsurance scenario ✓ **or other risk management tools**

Note: TVaR = tail value at risk.

and risk exposure. If the premium rates do not meet the criteria, the insurance manager and the actuarial analyst move on to evaluate the same premium rates under the second scenario—the policy is reinsured through proportional reinsurance only.

5.2.2 Portfolio Product Pricing—Proportional Reinsurance Only

To address the key questions related to product pricing with only proportional reinsurance, we recommend the decision-making process summarized in figure 5.2.

Risk Modeling for Appraising Named Peril Index Insurance Products
http://dx.doi.org/10.1596/978-1-4648-1048-0

Figure 5.2 Portfolio Product Pricing Managerial Decision Process—Proportional Reinsurance Only

Step 1: Determine key model inputs and assumptions (policy with proportional reinsurance)

Data from policyholder	Data from insurer	Data from product design team
• Same as in figure 5.1	Same as in figure 5.1 plus • Percentage ceded to reinsurer	• Same as in figure 5.1

Step 2: Evalute key managerial decision metrics according to risk mangement guidelines set

Value creation and protection	Risk tolerance	Risk appetite
• Same as in figure 5.1	• Same as in figure 5.1	• Same as in figure 5.1

Step 3: Document and communicate business decision
- If premium rate does not meet risk management guideline criteria, evaluate premium rates using proportional and nonproportional reinsurance.

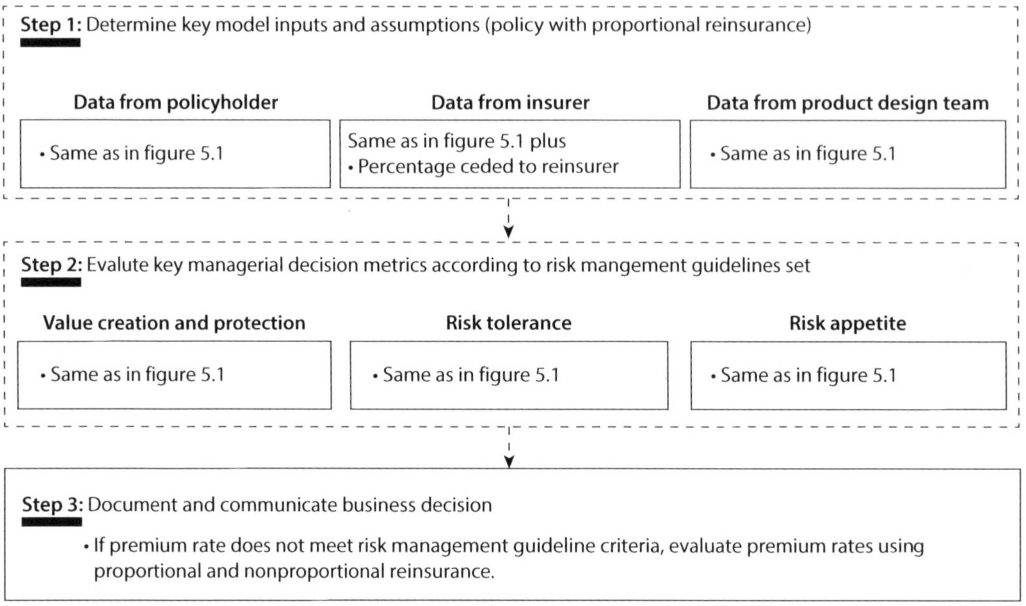

5.2.2.1 STEP 1: Determine Key Model Inputs and Assumptions

The insurance manager and the analyst use the same inputs into the model as for the analysis with no reinsurance (section 5.2.1), but add percentage ceded to the reinsurer as an input parameter (case example box 5CB.6).

This guide does not provide a discussion of the mechanism for determining the parameters for reinsurance arrangements, whether for proportional or nonproportional reinsurance. For further information on this topic, see Cass et al. (1997).

5.2.2.2 STEP 2: Evaluate Key Managerial Decision Metrics

Based on the agreed-on inputs, the actuarial analyst again produces the product pricing metrics (case example box 5CB.7). The insurance manager evaluates these outputs against the insurer's profit objectives and risk appetite as in section 5.2.1 (case example box 5CB.8).

Case Example Box 5CB.6 Pricing Model Inputs for Base Index—Proportional Reinsurance Only

Ghassimu and Lindiwe decide to evaluate a proportional reinsurance policy with 80 percent of the insured portfolio ceded to the reinsurer.

Internal data from the insurer
- Percentage ceded to the reinsurer: 80 percent

All other inputs are the same as in case example box 5CB.2.

Case Example Box 5CB.7 Pricing Model Outputs for Base Index—Proportional Reinsurance Only

ITERATION #	GROSS PREMIUM RATE (%)	PROBABILITY OF NEGATIVE PROFIT (%)	PROBABILITY OF FUND RUIN (%)	PROBABILITY OF PROFIT BELOW TARGET (%)	PROJECTED LOSSES ($)				PROJECTED COMBINED RATIO (%)				PROJECTED PROFIT MARGIN (%)				PROJECTED EVA (%)			SHARPE RATIO
					Lower	Expected	Upper Higher	TVaR	Lower	Expected	Upper Higher	TVaR	Lower	Expected	Upper Higher		Lower	Expected	Upper Higher	
1	3%	86%	47%	68%	123,857	407,772	504,931		18%	273%	686%	1057%	-766%	-173%	86%	100%	-27%	6%		0.00
2	4%	60%	43%	63%	123,857	407,772	504,931		18%	208%	652%	804%	-553%	-100%	85%	-100%	-24%	10%		-0.58
3	5%	55%	39%	58%	123,857	407,772	504,931		18%	175%	525%	645%	-426%	-70%	85%	-68%	-20%	12%		-0.47
4	8%	50%	35%	53%	123,857	407,772	504,931		18%	144%	440%	541%	-3x1%	-44%	85%	-52%	-16%	17%		-0.37
5	7%	46%	32%	49%	123,857	407,772	504,931		18%	126%	375%	465%	-280%	-26%	85%	-40%	-13%	20%		-0.27
6	8%	41%	29%	45%	123,857	407,772	504,931		18%	112%	334%	436%	-234%	-12%	85%	-31%	-9%	24%		-0.17
7	9%	38%	26%	42%	123,857	407,772	504,931		18%	101%	298%	380%	-199%	-1%	85%	-52%	-5%	28%		-0.07
8	10%	34%	24%	38%	123,857	407,772	504,931		18%	93%	270%	331%	-170%	8%	85%	-78%	-2%	31%		0.03
9	11%	31%	22%	35%	123,857	407,772	504,931		18%	85%	247%	302%	-147%	15%	85%	-74%	2%	35%		0.14
10	12%	28%	20%	32%	123,857	407,772	504,931		18%	80%	227%	278%	-128%	20%	86%	-71%	6%	39%		0.24

Note: EVA = economic value added; TVaR = tail value at risk.

Case Example Box 5CB.8 Pricing Decisions for Base Index—Proportional Reinsurance Only

Decision metrics	Managerial and actuarial decisions (indicate minimum acceptable premium rate)
1. Value creation and protection	
Economic value added	11 percent
Sharpe ratio	10 percent
Combined ratio (projected loss ratio + total expense costs)	10 percent
Indicative decision	10 percent
2. Risk tolerance	
Probability of fund ruin	Not met by any rate considered
Probability of negative profit	Not met by any rate considered
Probability of profit below target profit margin	Not met by any rate considered
Indicative decision	Consider more reinsurance options
3. Risk appetite	
TVaR of projected losses	Consider combined proportional and nonproportional reinsurance options
Final decision	**Write**
	Do not write
	Consider next reinsurance scenario or other risk management tools ✓

Note: TVaR = tail value at risk.

Because the insurer receives a commission that only covers its costs (that is, expense loading) for this product, adding proportional reinsurance does not change the metrics for value creation and risk tolerance. The reinsurer's fortunes follow those of the insurer. However, the absolute value of the TVaR is proportionately reduced.

5.2.2.3 STEP 3: Document and Communicate the Business Decision

The insurance manager uses the risk committee guidelines for index product pricing to document the hierarchical evaluation of the premium rates. If a premium rate or rates meet all the criteria, the insurance manager lists the premium rates and explains the projected impact on the insurer's profit margins and risk exposure. If the premium rates do not meet the criteria, the insurance manager and the actuarial analyst move on to evaluate premium rates using nonproportional reinsurance, or a combination of nonproportional and proportional reinsurance.

5.2.3 Portfolio Product Pricing—Proportional and Nonproportional Reinsurance

To address the key questions related to product pricing with proportional and nonproportional reinsurance, we recommend the decision-making process summarized in figure 5.3.

5.2.3.1 STEP 1: Determine Key Model Inputs and Assumptions

The insurance manager and the analyst use the same inputs for the pricing model as for the analysis with proportional reinsurance only (section 5.2.2), with the addition of the following input parameters (case example box 5CB.9):

Internal data from the insurer

- Amount retained under nonproportional treaty ($)
- Aggregate loss limit under nonproportional treaty ($)
- Percentage carried by the reinsurer under nonproportional treaty (percent)
- Estimated nonproportional reinsurance premium rate (percent)

Figure 5.3 Portfolio Product Pricing Managerial Decision Process—Proportional and Nonproportional Reinsurance

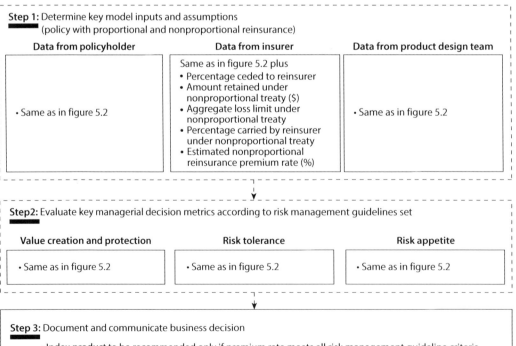

For a discussion of how to determine reinsurance agreement parameters, we again refer the reader to Cass et al. (1997).

5.2.3.2 STEP 2: Evaluate Key Managerial Decision Metrics

Based on the agreed-on inputs, the actuarial analyst again produces the product pricing metrics. The insurance manager evaluates these outputs against

Case Example Box 5CB.9 Pricing Model Inputs for Base Index—Proportional and Nonproportional Reinsurance

Ghassimu and Lindiwe decide to evaluate the Base Index with pricing that combines the proportional reinsurance policy discussed in section 5.2.2 with a nonproportional reinsurance policy with the terms discussed below.

Internal data from the insurer

- *Amount retained under nonproportional treaty ($):* Excellence Insurance will retain the first $85,000 of claim amounts per season.
- *Aggregate loss limit under nonproportional treaty ($):* Any loss that exceeds $709,000 will be covered by Excellence.
- *Percentage carried by the reinsurer under nonproportional treaty:* The reinsurer will pay 90 percent of the losses for any loss greater than $85,000 but less than $709,000.
- *Estimated nonproportional reinsurance premium rate (percent):* The reinsurance will cost 5 percent of all premiums.

See figure 5CB.9.1 and table 5CB.9.1.

Figure 5CB.9.1 Base Index Proportional and Nonproportional Reinsurance

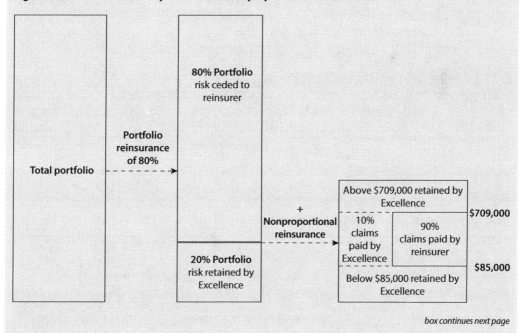

box continues next page

Risk Modeling for Appraising Named Peril Index Insurance Products
http://dx.doi.org/10.1596/978-1-4648-1048-0

Case Example Box 5CB.9 Pricing Model Inputs for Base Index—Proportional and Nonproportional
Reinsurance *(continued)*

Table 5CB.9.1   Reinsurance Terms

PROPORTIONAL REINSURANCE TERMS, IF ANY

% CEDED TO REINSURER	80%

NONPROPORTIONAL REINSURANCE TERMS, IF ANY

TREATY RETENTION ($)	85,000	
AGGREGATE LOSS LIMIT ($)	709,000	
% CARRIED BY THE REINSURER UNDER NONPROPORTIONAL TREATY	90%	OF TOTAL RISK PERIOD LOSSES
ESTIMATED REINSURANCE PREMIUM RATE (%)	5%	OF TOTAL RETAINED PREMIUMS

All the other inputs are the same as for case example box 5CB.2 and case example box 5CB.6.

the insurer's profit objectives and risk appetite as in sections 5.2.1 and 5.2.2 (case example boxes 5CB.10 and 5CB.11).

5.2.3.3 STEP 3: Document and Communicate the Business Decision

The insurance manager uses the risk management committee guidelines for index product pricing to document the hierarchical evaluation of the premium rates. If a premium rate or rates meet all the criteria, the insurance manager lists the premium rates and explains the projected impact on the insurer's profit margins and risk exposure. If the premium rates do not meet the criteria, the insurance manager and the actuarial analyst should not recommend proceeding with the index product, or alternatively recommend that the product design team redesign the Base Index.

5.2.4 Equitable Premium Pricing

As discussed in section 5.1, each geographic area covered by the portfolio-priced index product has a different risk profile (for example, less rain or more extreme maximum temperatures), which corresponds with a different premium rate. The premium rates that are specific to each area in the portfolio are called equitable premium rates (figure 5.4).

Case Example Box 5CB.10 Pricing Model Outputs for Base Index—Proportional and Nonproportional Reinsurance

Note: EVA = economic value added; TVaR = tail value at risk.

Risk Modeling for Appraising Named Peril Index Insurance Products
http://dx.doi.org/10.1596/978-1-4648-1048-0

Case Example Box 5CB.11 Pricing Decisions for Mass Bank Base Index—Proportional and Nonproportional Reinsurance

Decision metrics	Actuarial and managerial decisions (indicate minimum acceptable premium rate)	
1. Value creation and protection		
Economic value added	6 percent	
Sharpe ratio	6 percent	
Combined ratio (projected loss ratio + total expense costs)	6 percent	
Indicative decision	6 percent	
2. Risk tolerance		
Probability of fund ruin	7 percent	
Probability of negative profit	9 percent	
Probability of profit below target profit margin	10 percent	
Indicative decision	10 percent	
3. Risk appetite		
TVaR of projected losses	Requirement fulfilled	
Final decision	**Write**	✓ 10 percent and above
	Do not write	
	Consider other risk management tools	

Note: TVaR = tail value at risk.

Figure 5.4 Equitable Premium Pricing

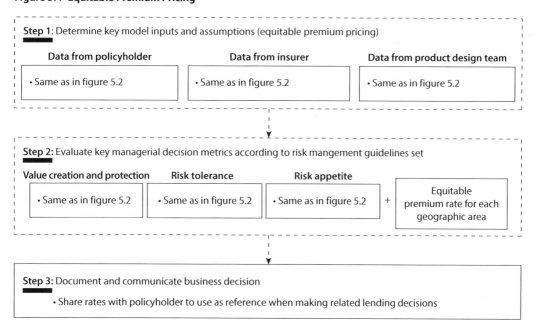

Step 1: Determine key model inputs and assumptions (equitable premium pricing)

Data from policyholder	Data from insurer	Data from product design team
• Same as in figure 5.2	• Same as in figure 5.2	• Same as in figure 5.2

Step 2: Evaluate key managerial decision metrics according to risk mangement guidelines set

Value creation and protection	Risk tolerance	Risk appetite	
• Same as in figure 5.2	• Same as in figure 5.2	• Same as in figure 5.2	+ Equitable premium rate for each geographic area

Step 3: Document and communicate business decision
• Share rates with policyholder to use as reference when making related lending decisions

Risk Modeling for Appraising Named Peril Index Insurance Products
http://dx.doi.org/10.1596/978-1-4648-1048-0

5.2.4.1 STEP 1: Determine Key Model Inputs and Assumptions

The insurance manager and the analyst use the same inputs into the equitable premium model as for the analysis with proportional reinsurance only (section 5.2.2). No additional inputs are needed because the insurance manager and actuarial analyst will just be identifying the premium rates specific to each geographical area. The client may find these risk ratings useful in making future decisions about lending in these areas.

It is important to note that the final commercial price for each geographic area will not be equal to the pure equitable premium rates because the insurer adds expense and profit loading. Often clients expect to be charged a product's pure risk premium rate. However, this approach is not possible because the insurer has to meet the costs of running the insurance fund (such as staff salaries and rentals). The attractiveness of the insurance product to prospective clients is affected by the size of these extra loadings. For example, a potential policyholder would need to be very risk averse to accept loadings as high as 50 percent.

5.2.4.2 STEP 2: Evaluate Key Managerial Decision Metrics

Based on the agreed-on inputs, the actuarial analyst produces equitable premiums for each geographical area (case example box 5CB.12). In this case, the goal of the analysis is not to find one overall premium rate that can be applied to the total portfolio of geographical areas, but to find the equitable premium for each area that takes into account each area's specific characteristics and risks.

It is important to note that the equitable premium is for the area, not for individual insured units. No attempt is made to calculate equitable premiums for the insured unit because index insurance is based on area averages. All policyholders in a geographical area pay a single premium rate. Individual insured units within the geographical area may in fact have different risk profiles, but are all considered to be one homogeneous class.

Also, the equitable premium rates are based on historical hazard or inventory damage data, so the results can be influenced by, for example, several recent years of high losses in a particular area, even though this area has the same actual risk profile as an adjacent one. Testing the significance of the differences in equitable premium rates for areas in this scenario is important, but beyond the scope of this guide.

Case Example Box 5CB.12 Equitable Premiums for the Base Index

ITERATION #	GROSS PREMIUM RATE	AREA A	AREA B	AREA C	AREA D	AREA E	AREA F	AREA G	AREA H	AREA I	AREA J
1	3%	-1%	2%	0%	4%	3%	2%	1%	1%	2%	13%
2	4%	0%	3%	1%	5%	4%	3%	2%	2%	3%	14%
3	5%	1%	4%	2%	6%	5%	5%	3%	3%	4%	15%
4	6%	2%	5%	3%	7%	6%	6%	4%	4%	5%	16%
5	7%	3%	6%	4%	8%	7%	7%	5%	5%	6%	17%
6	8%	3%	7%	5%	9%	8%	8%	6%	6%	7%	18%
7	9%	4%	8%	6%	10%	9%	9%	7%	7%	8%	19%
8	10%	5%	9%	7%	12%	10%	10%	8%	8%	10%	20%
9	11%	6%	10%	7%	13%	11%	11%	8%	9%	11%	21%
10	12%	7%	11%	8%	14%	12%	12%	9%	10%	12%	23%

5.2.4.3 STEP 3: Document and Communicate the Business Decision

At this stage, the insurance manager documents the equitable premium rates for each area covered by the product. The manager shares these rates with the policyholder so that the policyholder can review them and keep them as a point of reference when making related lending decisions.

Bibliography

Cass, M. R., P. R. Kensicki, G. S. Patrik, and R. C. Reinarz. 1997. *Reinsurance Practices*. 2nd ed. Malvern, PA: Insurance Institute of America.

Clarke, D., O. Mahul, and N. Verma. 2012. "Index Based Crop Insurance Product Design and Ratemaking: The Case of Modified NAIS in India." Policy Research Working Paper 5985, World Bank, Washington, DC.

Crouhy, M., D. Galai, and R. Mark. 2006. *The Essentials of Risk Management*. New York: McGraw-Hill.

Harrison, C. M. 2004. *Reinsurance Principles and Practices*. Malvern, PA: American Institute for Chartered Property Casualty Underwriters/Insurance Institute of America.

Lam, J. 2003. *Enterprise Risk Management: From Incentives to Controls*. Hoboken, NJ: Wiley.

CHAPTER 6

Product Evaluation—The Redesigned Index

6.1 Introduction

At this stage in the pilot phase, the insurer has designed and evaluated the Base Index (chapter 4) and determined its price under different reinsurance arrangements (chapter 5). The Base Index provides the highest possible level of coverage against damage to the farmer's inventory and is used as a point of reference for discussing product options with policyholders. Based on feedback from the policyholder on price, the insurer now designs the Redesigned Index (case example box 6CB.1) and calculates its historical payouts using the same process as in section 4.3 on the Base Index (case example box 6CB.2).

Case Example Box 6CB.1 Term Sheet for Redesigned Index

Based on the product pricing analysis, the Base Index has a minimum acceptable premium of 10 percent with proportional and nonproportional reinsurance. However, Mass Bank is only willing to pay for a product with a premium of 4 percent or less. Ghassimu and Lindiwe instruct the Hazard Analytics product design team to formulate a Redesigned Index with triggers, exits, and payout rates that provide less coverage than those for the Base Index.

Insured	Areas A to I	Area J
Participating measurement stations	Stations A to I	Station J
Target crops	Maize	Maize
Type of insurance cover	Weather index insurance that pays out a defined percentage of the **total sum insured** when the following events occur at participating measurement stations during the total cover period: • A specified number of consecutive dry days **OR** • Total rainfall less than a specified level.	Weather index insurance that pays out a defined percentage of the **total sum insured** when the following events occur at participating measurement stations during the total cover period: • A specified number of consecutive dry days **OR** • Total rainfall less than a specified level.

box continues next page

Case Example Box 6CB.1 Term Sheet for Redesigned Index *(continued)*

Insured	*Areas A to I*	*Area J*
	These measures approximate weather conditions that may cause inventory damage for the policyholder that, as a result, cause losses for the insured.	These measures approximate weather conditions that may cause inventory damage for the policyholder that, as a result, cause losses for the insured.
Total contract period	June 20–September 17, inclusive	June 20–September 17, inclusive
Maximum payout	The greater of Trigger 1 payout or Trigger 2 payout (see below), up to 100 percent of the total sum insured	The greater of Trigger 1 payout or Trigger 2 payout (see below), up to 100 percent of the total sum insured
Maximum specified distance	20 kilometer radius	20 kilometer radius
Total sum insured	Total loan portfolio	Total loan portfolio

Claim Trigger 1

Payout event definition	**Number of consecutive dry days** Days immediately following one another in which the total rainfall recorded on each day is 2.5 millimeters or less. Recorded rainfall is taken from the participating measurement stations during the cover period for Trigger 1. The longest consecutive dry day period during the cover period is the index value, which is evaluated against the payout schedule.	**Number of consecutive dry days** Days immediately following one another in which the total rainfall recorded on each day is 2.5 millimeters or less. Recorded rainfall is taken from the participating measurement station during the cover period for Trigger 1. The longest consecutive dry day period during the cover period is the index value, which is evaluated against the payout schedule.
Cover period	June 20–September 17, inclusive	June 20–September 17, inclusive

Payout schedule	Trigger 25 consecutive days
	Payout rate 2.5 percent per dry day
	                         above the trigger
	Exit 45 consecutive dry days
		Trigger 25 consecutive days
		Payout rate 2.5 percent per dry day
		                         above the trigger
		Exit 45 consecutive dry days

Number of payments allowed	Only one payment is allowed for this trigger.	Only one payment is allowed for this trigger.
Timing of payment	Payments due according to the definitions above may be made at the end of the total contract period, that is, after September 17.	Payments due according to the definitions above may be made at the end of the total contract period, that is, after September 17.

Claim Trigger 2

Payout event definition	**Total rainfall for flowering period** Total millimeters of rainfall recorded during the flowering period. Recorded rainfall is that from the participating measurement stations. For the contract period, cumulative rainfall is obtained by summing daily amounts over the contract period. The resulting amount is the index value, which is evaluated against the payout schedule.	**Total rainfall for flowering period** Total millimeters of rainfall recorded during the flowering period. Recorded rainfall is taken from the participating measurement station. For the contract period, cumulative rainfall is obtained by summing daily amounts over the contract period. The resulting amount is the index value, which is evaluated against the payout schedule.
Cover period	July 25–September 2, inclusive	July 25–September 2, inclusive

box continues next page

Case Example Box 6CB.1 Term Sheet for Redesigned Index *(continued)*

Insured	Areas A to I		Area J	
Payout schedule	Trigger	75 millimeters	Trigger	55 millimeters
	Payout rate	2 percent per millimeter below trigger	Payout rate	2 percent per millimeter below trigger
	Exit	25 millimeters	Exit	5 millimeters
Number of payments allowed	Only one payment is allowed for this trigger.		Only one payment is allowed for this trigger.	
Timing of payment	Payments due according to the definitions above may be made at the end of the total contract period, that is, after September 17.		Payments due according to the definitions above may be made at the end of the total contract period, that is, after September 17.	

Case Example Box 6CB.2 Historical Payouts for Redesigned Index

Lindiwe points out to Ghassimu that 1986 in Area C provides a good example of the Redesigned Index's lower level of coverage compared with the Base Index. The historical payout value for 1986 in Area C is 10 percent for the Redesigned Index, or $8 for a sum insured of $80. For the Base Index, the historical payout value is 22.5 percent, or $18.

YEAR	AREA A	AREA B	AREA C	AREA D	AREA E	AREA F	AREA G	AREA H	AREA I	AREA J
1984	-	-	-	-	-	-	-	-	-	80%
1985	-	-	-	-	-	-	-	-	-	-
1986	-	-	10%	-	-	-	-	-	-	-
1987	-	-	-	-	-	-	-	-	-	-
1988	-	-	-	35%	-	-	-	-	-	-
1989	-	3%	-	-	-	-	-	-	-	-
1990	-	-	-	72%	17%	-	-	-	-	-
1991	-	-	-	-	-	-	-	-	-	30%
1992	-	-	-	50%	-	-	-	-	-	76%
1993	-	-	-	-	-	-	-	-	-	34%
1994	-	-	-	-	-	-	-	-	-	86%
1995	-	-	-	-	-	-	-	-	-	-
1996	29%	-	-	-	-	-	-	-	-	15%
1997	-	8%	-	-	-	3%	-	15%	-	-
1998	-	-	-	-	-	-	18%	-	13%	-
1999	-	-	-	-	-	5%	-	36%	15%	29%
2000	-	-	-	-	-	-	3%	-	-	-
2001	-	-	-	-	-	-	-	-	-	-
2002	-	-	-	-	-	-	-	-	-	-
2003	-	-	-	-	-	-	-	-	-	50%
2004	-	-	-	-	-	-	-	-	-	-
2005	-	-	-	-	-	-	-	-	-	-
2006	-	-	-	-	-	-	-	-	-	29%
2007	-	-	-	-	-	-	-	-	-	-
2008	-	-	-	-	-	-	-	-	-	5%
2009	-	-	-	-	-	-	-	-	-	54%
2010	-	-	-	-	-	-	13%	11%	-	-
2011	-	-	-	-	-	-	-	-	-	-
2012	-	-	-	-	-	-	-	-	-	-
2013	-	-	-	-	-	-	-	-	-	-

The actuarial analyst and the insurance manager price the Redesigned Index using the same process used for the Base Index, described in chapter 5. Because the Redesigned Index provides less coverage, its premium will be lower than that for the Base Index.

Now the insurance manager has two products to discuss with the client: the Base Index and the Redesigned Index. This chapter explains how to determine

Risk Modeling for Appraising Named Peril Index Insurance Products
http://dx.doi.org/10.1596/978-1-4648-1048-0

and explain to the client the most important differences in level of coverage between the Base Index and the Redesigned Index.

It is important to note that the three main elements of the Redesigned Index—the product design, the price, and the level of coverage—are, of course, all highly interrelated. A product design team could devise many different Redesigned Indexes based on the same Base Index. Each of these Redesigned Indexes would provide a different level of coverage and have a different price. Changing any one of these three elements—product design, product price, or product coverage—affects the other two.

The key managerial questions answered during Redesigned Index product performance evaluation are the following:

- What level of coverage is provided by the Redesigned Index compared with the Base Index?
  - How often does the Resigned Index pay out compared with the Base Index (that is, what is the Redesigned Index's return period compared with that of the Base Index)?
  - How much less does the Redesigned Index pay compared with the Base Index (that is, what is the size of the implied deductible for the Redesigned Index)?
  - In what percentage of years is there no implied deductible for the Redesigned Index?
  - What are the largest differences in historical payouts between the Redesigned Index and the Base Index?
- In years with especially high losses, will the Redesigned Index provide payouts?

Recall that the Base Index and the Redesigned Index that is developed from it have the same level of product design basis risk. If the policyholder has questions about product design basis risk for the Redesigned Index, the insurance manager should repeat the explanations covered in section 4.3 on the Base Index.

6.2 Outline of Emerging Managerial and Process Controls

To address the key questions related to Redesigned Index evaluation, we recommend the decision-making processes described below and summarized in figure 6.1. Chapter 13 provides a step-by-step guide to using the probabilistic models that produce the Redesigned Index product evaluation metrics discussed in this section.

6.3 Step 1: Determine Key Model Inputs and Assumptions

Before the modeling process begins, the insurance manager and the actuarial analyst agree on the inputs into the model. These inputs are assumptions based on data from the prospective policyholder, data from the insurer, and data from the product design team (case example box 6CB.3).

Figure 6.1 Redesigned Index Evaluation Managerial Decision Process

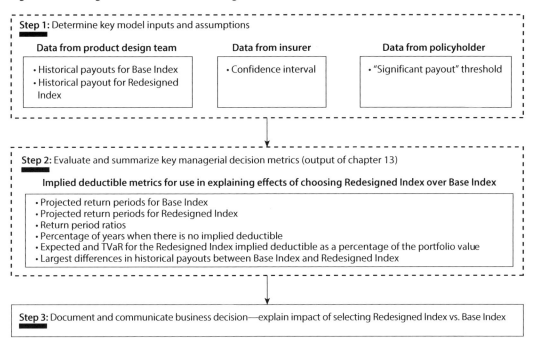

Step 1: Determine key model inputs and assumptions

Data from product design team
- Historical payouts for Base Index
- Historical payout for Redesigned Index

Data from insurer
- Confidence interval

Data from policyholder
- "Significant payout" threshold

Step 2: Evaluate and summarize key managerial decision metrics (output of chapter 13)

Implied deductible metrics for use in explaining effects of choosing Redesigned Index over Base Index
- Projected return periods for Base Index
- Projected return periods for Redesigned Index
- Return period ratios
- Percentage of years when there is no implied deductible
- Expected and TVaR for the Redesigned Index implied deductible as a percentage of the portfolio value
- Largest differences in historical payouts between Base Index and Redesigned Index

Step 3: Document and communicate business decision—explain impact of selecting Redesigned Index vs. Base Index

Note: TVaR = tail value at risk.

Case Example Box 6CB.3 Product Performance Model Inputs for the Redesigned Index

Internal data from Mass Bank
Mass Bank tells Ghassimu that their threshold for a significant payout is 10 percent of the sum insured.

Internal data from Excellence Insurance
Ghassimu and Lindiwe select a 90 percent prediction interval by setting the low at the 5th percentile and the high at the 95th percentile. This allows Excellence Insurance to understand the range of a number of key outcomes (for example, profit margin) that are likely to be observed over the next risk period with a 90 percent confidence level.

SIGNIFICANT PAYOUT/DAMAGE LEVELS (%)

MILD IMPACT	10%
MILD-MEDIUM IMPACT	30%
MEDIUM IMPACT	50%
SEVERE IMPACT	70%

PREDICTION INTERVAL (%)

LOWER	5%
UPPER	95%

TOTAL SUM INSURED PER AREA

AREA A	AREA B	AREA C	AREA D	AREA E	AREA F	AREA G	AREA H	AREA I	AREA J
140,160	282,975	1,200,000	425,000	2,252,250	282,000	992,040	1,200,325	425,150	800,100

Data from the product design team
The product design team provides the historical payouts for the Base Index and the Redesigned Index.

Internal data from the policyholder

- Threshold for a significant payout. Based on our experience from pilot studies, policyholders generally consider a payout that is 1.5–2 times the gross premium rate significant, that is, if the premium rate is 10 percent of the insured amount, any payout above 15–20 percent of the sum insured is "significant."

Internal data from the insurer

- **Prediction interval**

Data from the product design team

- Historical payouts for the Base Index (section 4.3)
- Historical payouts for the Redesigned Index (calculated as in section 4.3)

6.4 Step 2: Evaluate Key Managerial Decision Metrics

Based on the agreed-on inputs, the actuarial analyst produces the values of the metrics to be used by the insurance manager to better understand the Redesigned Index's performance compared with the Base Index. The metrics will help the insurance manager explain these differences to the policyholder so that the policyholder can make an informed decision about what product to purchase.

The actuarial analyst calculates the values of the following metrics for each geographical area (case example box 6CB.4):

Implied deductible metrics

- Projected return periods for the Base Index
- Projected return periods for the Redesigned Index
- Return period ratios
- Percentage of years when there is no implied deductible
- Projected value and tail value at risk (TVaR) for the Redesigned Index implied deductible as a percentage of the portfolio
- Largest differences in historical payouts between Base Index and Redesigned Index

Because the Redesigned Index is in response to the policyholder's request for a lower premium, the policyholder is the best party to evaluate the above metrics. As long as the Redesigned Index provides meaningful coverage to the policyholder in catastrophic years and the policyholder is clear on the limits of the coverage, the risk management committee does not need to set internal guidelines for acceptable return periods.

Case Example Box 6CB.4 Product Performance Model Outputs for the Redesigned Index

BASE INDEX RETURN PERIODS

				AREA A	AREA B	AREA C	AREA D	AREA E	AREA F	AREA G	AREA H	AREA I	AREA J
RETURN PERIOD	@	10%	PAYOUT LEVEL	14	7	10	5	6	7	8	8	7	3
RETURN PERIOD	@	30%	PAYOUT LEVEL	21	10	15	8	9	10	12	12	10	4
RETURN PERIOD	@	50%	PAYOUT LEVEL	32	15	23	12	13	15	18	18	15	7
RETURN PERIOD	@	70%	PAYOUT LEVEL	61	27	47	21	24	29	32	32	27	12

REDESIGNED INDEX RETURN PERIODS

				AREA A	AREA B	AREA C	AREA D	AREA E	AREA F	AREA G	AREA H	AREA I	AREA J
IMPLIED RETURN PERIOD	@	10%	PAYOUT LEVEL	22	13	21	10	20	14	11	11	14	3
IMPLIED RETURN PERIOD	@	30%	PAYOUT LEVEL	39	24	37	17	37	25	19	19	25	6
IMPLIED RETURN PERIOD	@	50%	PAYOUT LEVEL	85	50	73	34	87	52	39	39	55	12
IMPLIED RETURN PERIOD	@	70%	PAYOUT LEVEL	294	145	263	106	217	159	110	103	159	38

RETURN PERIOD RATIOS

				AREA A	AREA B	AREA C	AREA D	AREA E	AREA F	AREA G	AREA H	AREA I	AREA J
RETURN PERIOD RATIO	@	10%	PAYOUT LEVEL	0.64	0.50	0.49	0.53	0.30	0.49	0.79	0.77	0.48	0.87
RETURN PERIOD RATIO	@	30%	PAYOUT LEVEL	0.54	0.41	0.41	0.44	0.23	0.39	0.63	0.82	0.41	0.73
RETURN PERIOD RATIO	@	50%	PAYOUT LEVEL	0.38	0.30	0.31	0.34	0.15	0.29	0.45	0.45	0.27	0.53
RETURN PERIOD RATIO	@	70%	PAYOUT LEVEL	0.21	0.19	0.18	0.20	0.11	0.18	0.29	0.31	0.17	0.31

PERCENTAGE OF YEARS WITH NO IMPLIED DEDUCTIBLE

AREA A	AREA B	AREA C	AREA D	AREA E	AREA F	AREA G	AREA H	AREA I	AREA J
91%	80%	87%	75%	78%	81%	84%	84%	81%	55%

PROJECTED IMPLIED DEDUCTIBLE AMOUNT

	AMOUNT	% OF SUM INSURED
LOWER	0	0%
EXPECTED	309,342	4%
UPPER	990,402	12%
TVaR	1,283,575	16%

HISTORICAL YEARS WITH LARGEST IMPLIED DEDUCTIBLE RATIOS

	AREA A	AREA B	AREA C	AREA D	AREA E	AREA F	AREA G	AREA H	AREA I	AREA J
HISTORICAL YEAR WITH LARGEST IMPLIED DEDUCTIBLE RATIO	1998	1989	1986	2007	1990	1987	2000	2010	1998	2008
IMPLIED DEDUCTIBLE RATIO	50%	12.50%	13%	40%	50%	31%	50%	50%	50%	13%
BASE INDEX PAYOUT RATIO	79%	15%	23%	40%	67%	31%	53%	61%	63%	18%
REDESIGNED INDEX PAYOUT RATIO	29%	2.5%	10%	0%	17%	0%	3%	11%	13%	5%

Note: TvaR = tail value at risk.

- *Comparison of projected return periods—Base Index versus Redesigned Index:* For Bwanje (Area B), the Base Index pays a claim that is greater than 10 percent once in seven years, whereas the Redesigned Index pays such a claim once in 13 years. This means that Mass Bank will retain more risk with the Redesigned Index than with the Base Index.

- *Percentage of years with no implied deductible:* Looking at Bwanje, 80 percent of the time the payouts for both the Base and Redesigned Indexes are equivalent. The Base Index provides higher payouts than the Redesigned Index 20 percent of the time. In other words, once in every five years, the Base Index is expected to trigger a higher payout than the Redesigned Index. The higher the percentage of years with no implied deductible, the closer the coverage of the Redesigned Index to the Base Index.

- *Projected implied deductible amount:* If it chooses the Redesigned Index, Mass Bank will retain additional risk valued at 4 percent of the portfolio value that would be transferred to Excellence Insurance if it instead chose the Base Index. Once in every 20 years, the Redesigned Index's implied deductible could be as high as 16 percent (tail value at risk, or TVaR). In other words, in these extreme years, losses equal to 16 percent of the portfolio value will be absorbed by Mass Bank (Redesigned Index) instead of transferred to Excellence (Base Index).

box continues next page

Case Example Box 6CB.4 Product Performance Model Outputs for the Redesigned Index *(continued)*

• *Largest differences in historical payouts between Base Index and Redesigned Index:* If both products had been in place in the past, the Redesigned Index's largest implied deductible would have occurred in 1996 when the Base Index would have triggered a 79 percent payout, but the Redesigned Index would have triggered only a 29 percent payout. By choosing the Redesigned Index, Mass Bank would have retained an additional 50 percent in risk costs that would have been transferred away by the Base Index.

6.5 Step 3: Document and Communicate the Product Options and Business Decision

The insurance manager and the actuarial analyst summarize the key managerial decision metrics for the Redesigned Index (case example box 6CB.5). The insurance manager must then clearly explain to the prospective policyholder and other key stakeholders the impact of selecting the Redesigned Index over the Base Index. The message to the policyholder must be unambiguous: by selecting the Redesigned Index with the lower premium, the policyholder is choosing a product with a lower level of coverage.

The insurance manager should demonstrate the Redesigned Index's lower level of coverage by explaining the metrics for the historical payouts, the return periods, and the implied deductible, and by providing specific examples of years in which the Redesigned Index produces different historical payouts than the Base Index.

After a thorough discussion of the options, the policyholder decides whether to purchase the Redesigned Index. The policyholder may instead decide to purchase the Base Index at the higher premium level. Either way, the insurance manager documents the main discussion points and the product selected, and includes these as an appendix to the policy document.

In many cases, however, the policyholder will purchase neither the Redesigned Index nor the Base Index. Instead, the policyholder will ask the insurance manager to provide a new product with a different premium rate—one that is more expensive than the Redesigned Index but still less expensive than the Base Index. Once this new Redesigned Index is designed and priced, the insurance manager and the actuarial analyst will repeat the managerial decision process from this section with the new product.

Case Example Box 6CB.5 Outcome of Mass Bank Negotiations

After in-depth discussions with Excellence Insurance, Mass Bank decides to purchase the Redesigned Index for the coming season. The team at Excellence Insurance celebrates the breakthrough.

Bibliography

Brehm, P. J. 2007. *Enterprise Risk Analysis for Property & Liability Insurance Companies: A Practical Guide to Standard Models and Emerging Solutions.* New York: Guy Carpenter.

Crouhy, M., D. Galai, and R. Mark. 2006. *The Essentials of Risk Management.* New York: McGraw-Hill.

Lam, J. 2003. *Enterprise Risk Management: From Incentives to Controls.* Hoboken, NJ: Wiley.

Risk Modeling for Appraising Named Peril Index Insurance Products
http://dx.doi.org/10.1596/978-1-4648-1048-0

Detailed Market Analysis

7.1 Introduction

After completing the pilot phase (chapters 4, 5, and 6), the insurer now has the necessary information with which to complete a detailed analysis of the broader market for index insurance. Even with the necessary prerequisites in place (chapter 3) and a successfully implemented pilot, a market may still lack important characteristics for a named peril index insurance business line to be profitable and sustainable.

The key managerial questions that are addressed during the detailed market analysis are the following:

- Which market segments (rural banks, microfinance institutions [MFIs], seed companies, agribusinesses, and nongovernmental organizations [NGOs]) provide the highest projected volumes and profit for the investment of the insurer's resources and should therefore be prioritized?
- For which market segments should the insurer pursue a full business case?
- Which premium rates for each prioritized market segment meet the target policyholders' price requirements and the insurer's profit and risk profile?

For the market analysis, the insurer designs and prices a Base Index and a set of Redesigned Indexes to test the coverage and price combinations preferred by specific market segments. The insurer can use information gleaned from the pilot phase—such as characteristics of agricultural lending portfolios and typical yields for specific areas—as well as additional research to design these **prototype** products.

The design, evaluation, and pricing process for these products is the same as for the pilot phase, but these indexes are now referred to as prototype products. The Base and Redesigned Prototypes must meet the risk management committee's guidelines for product quality (basis risk metrics for the Base Prototype and product performance metrics for the Redesigned Prototypes) and product pricing.

The insurer shares the products with a number of key players in each market segment, clearly indicating the return periods, premium rates, basis risk evaluation (Base Prototype), and implied deductibles (Redesigned Prototypes). Based on feedback from these discussions, the insurer identifies the preferred products, if any, for each market segment.

Next, the insurer uses information about each market segment to determine whether they represent sufficient potential business volumes to meet the insurer's profit objectives and risk tolerance.

One issue that the insurer should keep in mind is the effect of liquidity on aggregators' ability to pay for insurance (case example box 7CB.1). Most named peril index product sales occur through bundling with financial products such as input finance. To estimate future sales in this case, the insurer needs to fully understand and evaluate the availability of liquid resources for both input financing and premium payments. A lack of liquidity in a market can prevent the expansion of products like named peril index insurance.

7.2 Outline of Emerging Managerial and Process Controls

To address the key questions related to the detailed market analysis, we recommend the decision-making processes described below and summarized in figure 7.1. Chapter 14 provides a step-by-step guide to using the probabilistic models that produce the decision metrics discussed.

Case Example Box 7CB.1 The Effect of Client Liquidity on Excellence Insurance's Premium Volumes

Progressive Agriculture has been operating a contract-farming business in Bwanje for 10 years. Progressive supplies inputs to smallholder farmers, provides them with extension services, and buys their maize produce at the end of the season. Most farmers in this program are very happy with Progressive Agriculture because it pays prices that are above market rates. In the past, Progressive Agriculture has used its own resources to provide input loans to the farmers, but with its expanding reach it no longer has the financial capacity to provide the necessary loans. Progressive approaches ABC Bank, a competitor to Mass Bank, to provide financing for its input program.

ABC Bank agrees to provide $10 million in financing to Progressive Agriculture. The loan amounts per farmer differ by area. If repayment rates are high in the first year, ABC Bank will increase the total financing by 20 percent every year, in line with Progressive Agriculture's expansion plans.

In the past, farmers' repayment rates to Progressive Agriculture have always been higher than 90 percent, except in those years when farmers were affected by drought. ABC Bank insists on making drought insurance part of the financing package.

Progressive Agriculture purchases an index product from Excellence Insurance to cover the $10 million in financing, greatly increasing Excellence's index insurance premium volumes.

It is important to note that Excellence Insurance's business volume from Progressive Agriculture is dependent on ABC Bank or another bank continuing to finance this program.

Figure 7.1 Detailed Market Analysis Managerial Decision Process

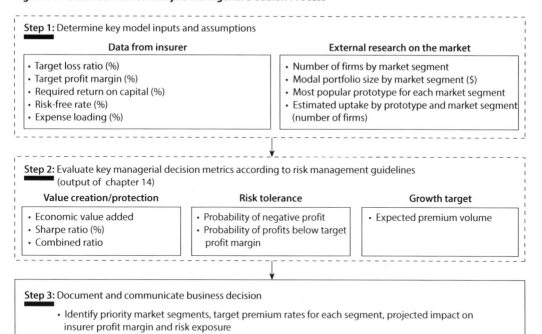

7.2.1 STEP 1: Determine Key Model Inputs and Assumptions

Before the modeling and pricing analysis process begins, the insurance manager and the analyst agree on the inputs into the model for the specific product. These inputs are assumptions based on data from the insurer and external research on the specific market.

To perform this detailed market analysis, the insurance manager and the analyst determine the following inputs (case example box 7CB.2):

Internal data from the insurer

- Target loss ratio (percent): This is based on the loss ratio of a successful product from the pilot phase. The specific values will be the 25th percentile (minimum), projected value (expected), and the 75th percentile (maximum) of the loss ratio for this product.
- Target profit margin (percent)

Case Example Box 7CB.2 Market Analysis Model Inputs for Prototypes

Excellence Insurance was pleased with the results of the pilot phase and got the go-ahead from its board to do a detailed market analysis for a commercial launch. Based on the experience during the pilot phase, Ghassimu and Lindiwe work with the Hazard Analytics product design team to design three prototype products—the Base Prototype, which has a premium rate of 10 percent; the Redesigned Prototype 1, which has a premium rate of 6 percent; and the Redesigned Prototype 2, which has a premium rate of 4 percent.

box continues next page

Risk Modeling for Appraising Named Peril Index Insurance Products
http://dx.doi.org/10.1596/978-1-4648-1048-0

Case Example Box 7CB.2 Market Analysis Model Inputs for Prototypes (continued)

Ghassimu and Lindiwe determine the inputs in the "insurer assumptions" table for the detailed market analysis for the Mapfumoland market segments. They use the loss ratio for the Redesigned Index launched during the pilot phase as the target loss ratio for this analysis. The information under "external research on the market" comes from a detailed value chain analysis that Excellence commissioned from an international consulting firm.

Internal data from Excellence Insurance

INSURER ASSUMPTIONS

TARGET LOSS RATIO (%)	
MINIMUM	13%
EXPECTED	79%
MAXIMUM	114%

TARGET PROFIT MARGIN (%)	10%

REQUIRED RETURN ON CAPITAL (%)	5%

RISK-FREE RATE (%)	2%

PREDICTION INTERVAL (%)	
LOWER	5%
UPPER	95%

EXPENSE LOADING (%)

MARKET SEGMENT	FIRM SIZE		
	Small	Medium	Large
Rural Banks	20%	15%	10%
MFIs	20%	15%	10%
Seed Companies	20%	15%	10%
Agribusinesses	20%	15%	10%
NGOs	20%	15%	10%

Note: MFI = microfinance institution; NGO = nongovernmental organization.

External research on the market

MARKET RESEARCH DATA

A) SUMMARY OF MARKET INFORMATION

	NUMBER OF FIRMS				
	Rural Banks	MFIs	Seed Companies	Agribusinesses	NGOs
Small	10	5	12	15	8
Medium	5	3	6	6	5
Large	2	0	3	2	3

	MODAL PORTFOLIO SIZE				
	Rural Banks	MFIs	Seed Companies	Agribusinesses	NGOs
Small	$ 1,000,000	$ 1,000,000	$ 1,000,000	$ 2,500,000	$ 500,000
Medium	$ 2,500,000	$ 2,500,000	$ 7,500,000	$ 7,500,000	$ 1,000,000
Large	$ 5,000,000	$ 5,000,000	$ 10,000,000	$ 15,000,000	$ 2,500,000

B) PRODUCT DEMAND INFORMATION

Premium Rates

	SMALL FIRMS				
	Rural Banks	MFIs	Seed Companies	Agribusinesses	NGOs
Base Prototype	10%	10%	10%	10%	10%
Redesigned Prototype 1	6%	6%	6%	6%	6%
Redesigned Prototype 2	4%	4%	4%	4%	4%

Most Popular Prototype (per market segment)

	Redesigned Prototype 1	Redesigned Prototype 1	Redesigned Prototype 2	Redesigned Prototype 1	Base Prototype
Minimum Uptake	2	3	5	3	2
Most Likely Uptake	6	4	5	4	3
Maximum Uptake	8	4	6	5	5
Total Firms	10	5	12	15	8

Premium Rates

	MEDIUM FIRMS				
	Rural Banks	MFIs	Seed Companies	Agribusinesses	NGOs
Base Prototype	10%	10%	10%	10%	10%
Redesigned Prototype 1	6%	6%	6%	6%	6%
Redesigned Prototype 2	4%	4%	4%	4%	4%

Most Popular Prototype (per market segment)

	Redesigned Prototype 1	Redesigned Prototype 1	Redesigned Prototype 2	Redesigned Prototype 1	Base Prototype
Minimum Uptake	2	2	2	2	2
Most Likely Uptake	3	2	4	4	2
Maximum Uptake	4	2	5	6	4
Total Firms	5	3	6	6	5

Premium Rates

	LARGE FIRMS				
	Rural Banks	MFIs	Seed Companies	Agribusinesses	NGOs
Base Prototype	10%	10%	10%	10%	10%
Redesigned Prototype 1	6%	6%	6%	6%	6%
Redesigned Prototype 2	4%	4%	4%	4%	4%

Most Popular Prototype (per market segment)

	Redesigned Prototype 1	Redesigned Prototype 1	Redesigned Prototype 2	Redesigned Prototype 1	Base Prototype
Minimum Uptake	1	0	1	1	1
Most Likely Uptake	1	0	2	2	2
Maximum Uptake	2	0	3	3	3
Total Firms	2	0	3	2	3

Note: MFI = microfinance institution; NGO = nongovernmental organization.

- Required return on capital (percent) per risk period
- **Risk-free rate** (percent) per risk period
- Expense loading by market segment and portfolio size (percent)

External research on the market

- Number of firms in market by size and market segment
- **Modal portfolio** size by firm and market segment
- Premium rates for each product type for each market segment and size
- Most popular prototype for each market segment and size
- Minimum, most likely, and maximum uptake for the most popular prototype for each market segment and size

7.2.2 STEP 2: Evaluate Key Managerial Decision Metrics

Instead of spreading its resources too thinly, it is important for the insurance company to focus its resources on market segments that have the highest expected premium income and satisfactory profit potential, particularly because availability of reinsurance capacity for named peril index insurance is critical. Reinsurers are interested in supporting classes of business for which there is sufficient volume and profit potential. Prioritizing segments to focus on is crucial to the insurer's success in launching an index insurance business line.

We suggest that the insurer prioritize the market segments into different tiers to first focus resources on the most attractive market opportunities (table 7.1; case example boxes 7CB.3–7CB.5). For each market segment, the insurance manager evaluates the preferred prototype for that segment against guidelines set by the insurer's risk committee,[1] which should indicate the acceptable range of values for each tier and metric.

Based on this analysis, the insurance manager categorizes each market segment into a respective tier, with Tier 1 segments receiving first priority for product launch. Some market segments will fail to meet the insurer's minimum profit

Table 7.1 Template for Risk Management Committee Guidelines on Market Segments

Decision metrics	Risk management committee guidelines
1. Growth target	
Expected premium income	
Tier 1	
Tier 2	
Tier 3	
Do not qualify	
2. Value creation and protection	
Economic value added	
Sharpe ratio	
Combined ratio	

table continues next page

Risk Modeling for Appraising Named Peril Index Insurance Products
http://dx.doi.org/10.1596/978-1-4648-1048-0

Table 7.1 **Template for Risk Management Committee Guidelines on Market Segments** *(continued)*

Decision metrics	Risk management committee guidelines
3. Risk tolerance	
Probability of negative profit	
Probability of profits below target profit margin	
4. Overall performance	
Total expected premium income across all qualifying segments	

Case Example Box 7CB.3 Excellence Insurance Risk Management Committee Guidelines for Market Segments

Decision metrics	Risk management committee guidelines
1. Growth target	
Expected premium income	
Tier 1	≥$1million
Tier 2	≥$500,000 and <$1million
Tier 3	≥$250,000 and <$500,000
Do not qualify	<$250,000
2. Value creation and protection	
Economic value added	>0 percent
Sharpe ratio	>0 percent
Combined ratio	<100 percent
3. Risk tolerance	
Probability of negative profit	<50 percent
Probability of profits below target profit margin	<50 percent
4. Overall performance	
Total expected premium income across all qualifying segments	>$3 million

Case Example Box 7CB.4 Market Analysis Outputs for Mapfumoland Market Segments

Note: EVA = economic value added; MFI = microfinance institution; NGO = nongovernmental organization.

Case Example Box 7CB.5 Managerial and Actuarial Market Analysis Decisions for the Mapfumoland Market Segments—Redesigned Prototypes

Tier	Firm size	Market segment	Projected premium income	Value creation and protection			Risk tolerance		Qualifying premium income
				Is EVA criterion satisfied? (YES/NO)	Is Sharpe ratio criterion satisfied? (YES/NO)	Is combined ratio criterion satisfied? (YES/NO)	Is the probability of negative profit criterion satisfied? (YES/NO)	Is the probability of profits below target profit margin satisfied? (YES/NO)	Projected premium income for each segment meeting all value creation and risk tolerance criteria
Tier 1	Large	Agribusinesses	$1,772,010	YES	YES	YES	YES	YES	$1,772,010
	Medium	Agribusinesses	$1,800,990	YES	YES	YES	YES	YES	$1,800,990
	Medium	Seed companies	$1,150,680	YES	YES	YES	YES	YES	$1,150,680
Tier 2	Large	NGOs	$499,500	YES	YES	YES	YES	YES	$499,500
	Large	Seed companies	$798,680	YES	YES	YES	YES	YES	$798,680
	Small	Agribusinesses	$600,840	YES	YES	YES	YES	NO	0
Tier 3	Large	Rural banks	$310,020	YES	YES	YES	YES	YES	$310,020
	Medium	MFIs	$300,000	YES	YES	YES	YES	YES	$300,000
	Medium	Rural banks	$450,150	YES	YES	YES	YES	NO	0
	Small	Rural banks	$339,984	YES	YES	YES	YES	YES	$339,984
Total projected premium									$6,971,864

Final decision

Pursue business opportunity ✓

Defer investment in the product until market conditions improve

Name of actuarial analyst

Signature of actuarial analyst

Name of insurance manager

Signature of insurance manager

Note: EVA = economic value added; MFI = microfinance institution; NGO = nongovernmental organization.

and risk appetite guidelines, and should not be selected for investment. In some cases, no market segments will meet the guidelines, meaning that the overall market does not warrant further investment of firm resources.

7.2.3 STEP 3: Document and Communicate Business Decision

At this stage, the insurance manager documents the market segments identified for prioritization (Tiers 1–3).

Note

1. The model automatically calculates the decision metrics for the favorite prototype product for each segment. In the book's case example, this will be the Base Prototype for small NGOs, medium NGOs, and large NGOs; the Redesigned Prototype 1 for small rural banks, small MFIs, small agribusinesses, medium rural banks, medium MFIs, medium agribusinesses, large rural banks, large MFIs, and large agribusiness; and the Redesigned Prototype 2 for small seed companies, medium seed companies, and large seed companies.

Bibliography

Brehm, P. J. 2007. *Enterprise Risk Analysis for Property & Liability Insurance Companies: A Practical Guide to Standard Models and Emerging Solutions.* New York: Guy Carpenter.

Crouhy, M., D. Galai, and R. Mark. 2006. *The Essentials of Risk Management.* New York: McGraw-Hill.

Lam, J. 2003. *Enterprise Risk Management: From Incentives to Controls.* Hoboken, NJ: Wiley.

CHAPTER 8

Value of Index Insurance to a Financier

8.1 Introduction

Based on the results of the detailed market analysis (chapter 7), the insurer has identified the market segments it will target with specific prototype products. The next step is to attract the major players in these segments as policyholders through sales and marketing activities. This chapter looks at offering index products to a specific market segment: financiers such as commercial banks, microfinance institutions, and agribusinesses that provide financing to smallholder farmers. This market segment is important for providers of index insurance because financiers' loan books are often large, and when insured as a whole portfolio, can provide significant premium volumes. Using the tools in this chapter, the insurer can identify the market players for which the index products are most valuable.

The key managerial questions addressed in this chapter are as follow:

- Does the named peril affect the nonperforming loan or default rates of the prospective policyholder—a financier lending to small farmers?
- What is the maximum amount a rational financier will be willing to pay to protect its capital by purchasing named peril index insurance?
- Is the index product commercially attractive to the financier (that is, are the costs lower than the forecast expected benefits)?

Our discussions with financiers in developing countries indicate that they have limited access to capital resources and have particular difficulty raising capital after a disaster has affected their portfolio. These financiers note that in the past, donor organizations helped some financiers that lent to the low-income market recapitalize, but donor funds are now less available. As a result, these financiers require new ways to protect their capital while also growing their lending portfolios.

The standard risk mitigation strategy used by financiers to protect their portfolios is general provisioning—setting aside capital to cover the income that will be lost from restructuring (extending the term of) or writing off (forgiving) loans. These restructured or written-off loans are called nonperforming loans (NPLs). This risk mitigation strategy involves a cost to the financier in the form of the capital set aside (opportunity cost) and the expenses incurred in attempting to recover the debt.

Lending to smallholder farmers, however, is a relatively risky enterprise and can require strategies beyond general provisioning because of covariant risks. Perils such as droughts, floods, and tropical cyclones can result in the total loss of a smallholder farmer's crop or livestock. If the farmer's income comes mainly from farming activities, these loss events can lead directly to loan defaults. If a financier has lent to a large number of such farmers, the impact of the risk event on its loan portfolio—increased NPLs—can be significant. In this case, an affordable risk transfer solution that protects the financier's loan portfolio from adverse weather events may be an attractive product for the financier.

However, if the farmer's income comes mainly from nonfarming activities that are not affected by the same weather perils, the farmer may still be able to pay back the loans received. Such farmers generally pay back their loans weekly or biweekly rather than at the end of the season. As a result, a poor agricultural yield caused by weather events will not necessarily affect the overall default rate for the portfolio of a financier that has lent to a large number of this type of farmer. These farmers—and the financier's portfolio—will not be very sensitive to weather perils. In this case, a financier may not be interested in a risk transfer solution for adverse weather events.

To effectively sell an index product to a financier, the insurer must first determine whether there is a clear link between the specific named peril and the financier's default rates. A necessary first step in making this determination is gaining access to the financier's historical records on defaults—both restructured and written-off loans (case example box 8CB.1). The actuarial analyst will use these data to determine the extent to which named peril index insurance can reduce the financier's losses during years with bad weather. Finally, the actuarial

---

Case Example Box 8CB.1 Approaching Buyer Goods

Ghassimu and Lindiwe present the results of the detailed market analysis to the Excellence board and receive approval to prioritize the large agribusiness market segment with its Redesigned Prototype 1 product, which has a premium rate of 6 percent. Excellence Insurance is now targeting Buyer Goods, a leading cotton buyer and processor, as a new client for index products. Buyer Goods provides its contract farmers with $24 million worth of inputs at the start of each growing season, and recoups the cost from each farmer at the end of the season when purchasing the cotton harvest.

After an initial meeting with Ghassimu and Lindiwe, Buyer Goods has agreed to provide Excellence with detailed information about its provision of in-kind advances of farming inputs to farmers in 10 geographical areas over the past 10 years, including repayment rates.

analyst will identify the maximum price the financier will be willing to pay for this reduction in losses—the value of the index insurance.

8.2 Outline of Emerging Managerial and Process Controls

To address the key questions related to the value of index insurance for a financier, we recommend the decision-making processes described below, summarized in figure 8.1. Chapter 15 provides a step-by-step guide to using the probabilistic models that produce the decision metrics discussed.

8.2.1 STEP 1: Determine Key Model Inputs and Assumptions

Before the analysis and modeling process begins, the insurance manager and the analyst agree on the inputs into the model for the prospective policyholder, the financier. These inputs are assumptions based on the internal data of the financier and data from the product design team.

The insurance manager and the analyst determine the following inputs (case example box 8CB.2):

Internal data from the policyholder (financier)

- Target maximum annual default rate (percent; this provides an indication of the financier's risk tolerance)
- Financier's **cost of capital** (percent)

Figure 8.1 Value of Index Insurance Managerial Decision Process

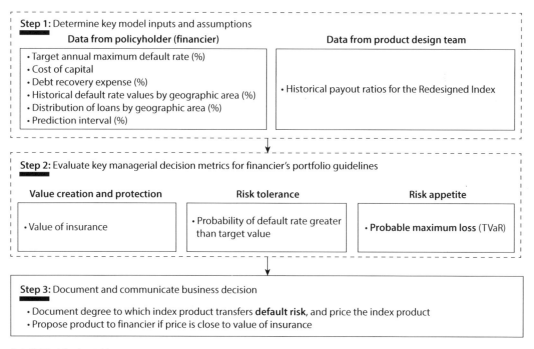

Note: TVaR = tail value at risk.

Case Example Box 8CB.2 Value of Index Insurance Model Inputs for Buyer Goods

Ghassimu and Lindiwe decide on the inputs below for the value of index insurance analysis for Buyer Goods.

TARGET MAXIMUM DEFAULT RATE

TARGET MAXIMUM DEFAULT RATE	4%

FINANCING COST PARAMETERS

COST OF CAPITAL (%)	5%
EXPENSE (%)	20%

PREDICTION INTERVAL (%)

LOWER	5%
UPPER	95%

GROSS DEFAULT RATES (%)

YEAR	AREA A	AREA B	AREA C	AREA D	AREA E	AREA F	AREA G	AREA H	AREA I	AREA J
2004	2%	3%	1%	3%	2%	15%	3%	3%	4%	1%
2005	2%	2%	1%	1%	8%	2%	3%	2%	4%	1%
2006	2%	3%	2%	1%	2%	3%	3%	2%	4%	1%
2007	5%	4%	1%	2%	2%	2%	25%	3%	27%	34%
2008	0%	2%	1%	16%	2%	20%	3%	34%	4%	27%
2009	9%	3%	4%	2%	2%	4%	4%	5%	4%	5%
2010	1%	15%	1%	2%	1%	3%	3%	2%	10%	3%
2011	1%	3%	1%	4%	3%	2%	5%	1%	4%	5%
2012	1%	3%	1%	2%	10%	1%	3%	2%	3%	4%
2013	1%	3%	2%	5%	2%	3%	3%	2%	3%	4%

LOAN DISBURSEMENT DISTRIBUTION (%)

AREA A	AREA B	AREA C	AREA D	AREA E	AREA F	AREA G	AREA H	AREA I	AREA J
10%	10%	10%	10%	10%	10%	10%	10%	10%	10%

HISTORICAL PAYOUT RATIOS (%)

YEAR	AREA A	AREA B	AREA C	AREA D	AREA E	AREA F	AREA G	AREA H	AREA I	AREA J
2004	0.0%	0.0%	0.0%	0.0%	0.0%	15.0%	0.0%	0.0%	0.0%	0.0%
2005	0.0%	0.0%	0.0%	0.0%	4.0%	0.0%	0.0%	0.0%	0.0%	0.0%
2006	0.0%	0.0%	0.0%	0.0%	0.0%	0.0%	0.0%	0.0%	0.0%	0.0%
2007	0.0%	0.0%	0.0%	0.0%	0.0%	0.0%	23.0%	0.0%	22.0%	23.0%
2008	0.0%	0.0%	0.0%	13.0%	0.0%	19.0%	0.0%	31.0%	0.0%	24.0%
2009	5.0%	0.0%	2.0%	0.0%	0.0%	0.0%	0.0%	0.0%	0.0%	0.0%
2010	0.0%	11.0%	0.0%	0.0%	0.0%	0.0%	0.0%	0.0%	7.0%	0.0%
2011	0.0%	0.0%	0.0%	0.0%	0.0%	0.0%	0.0%	0.0%	0.0%	0.0%
2012	0.0%	0.0%	0.0%	0.0%	7.0%	0.0%	0.0%	0.0%	0.0%	0.0%
2013	0.0%	0.0%	0.0%	1.0%	0.0%	0.0%	0.0%	0.0%	0.0%	0.0%

- **Debt recovery expense** (percent of loan amount; costs incurred by financier to try to recover debt)
- Historic default rates by geographic area (percent; restructures and write-offs)
- Distribution of loans by geographic area (percent)
- Prediction interval (percent)

Data from the product design team

- Historical payout ratios for the prototype product.

8.2.2 STEP 2: Evaluate Key Managerial Decision Metrics

To understand and explain the benefits of the index insurance product for the financier, the actuarial analyst evaluates the financier's portfolio under two scenarios:

- The financier's portfolio has no insurance coverage (gross default rate)
- The financier's portfolio is covered with the insurer's named peril index insurance prototype (net default rate)

By comparing the two situations, the insurance manager can determine the value of the index insurance coverage to the financier.

The actuarial analyst calculates the following metrics for the financier's portfolio:

Gross default rate (without index insurance coverage)

- Probability of default rate greater than target value
- Expected default rate and probable maximum loss (tail value at risk [TVaR])
- Projected cost of gross default risk

Net default rate (with index insurance coverage)

- Probability of default rate greater than target value
- Expected default rate and probable maximum loss (TVaR)
- Projected cost of net default risk

Value of insurance

- Value of index insurance to financier (the difference between the cost of the gross default risk and the net default risk)

We recommend that the insurance manager work with the client to produce guidelines for evaluating the value of index insurance and the net default rate decision metrics before the insurer begins the analysis of the value of insurance (table 8.1). The financier should base the guidelines on its own risk management policies.

Using the metric "probability of net default rate greater than target value," the insurance manager determines the degree to which the named peril affects the financier's defaults. Here, lower output values mean that the named peril has a higher impact on the defaults.

Using the metric "net default rate probable maximum loss," the insurance manager determines whether insurance lowers defaults in the years with the worst named peril events to a level that is acceptable to the financier's management. If the net TVaR is higher than the financier's target default rate, the NPLs or defaults may be caused by factors other than those captured by the index. Alternatively, the index structure may need to be improved to better capture losses for the financier.

Risk Modeling for Appraising Named Peril Index Insurance Products
http://dx.doi.org/10.1596/978-1-4648-1048-0

Table 8.1 Template for Client Guidelines for Value of Index Insurance and Net NPL Decision Metrics

Decision metrics	Client's guidelines
1. Value creation and protection	
Value of insurance	
2. Risk tolerance	
Probability of net default rate greater than target value	
3. Risk appetite	
Net default rate probable maximum loss (TVaR)	
Decision	Index insurance is a good solution for default risk
	Index insurance is not a good solution for default risk

Note: NPL = nonperforming loans; TVaR = tail value at risk.

Using the metric "value of insurance," the insurance manager determines the approximate amount that the financier will be willing to pay for the named peril index insurance product. In most situations, the financier will not be willing to pay a premium rate that is much higher than the value of the insurance calculated by the model.[1] However, to arrive at the final premium for the product, the insurer will need to include expense and profit loading in the value of insurance. See case example boxes 8CB.3–8CB.5.

8.2.3 STEP 3: Document and Communicate the Business Decision

At this point, the insurance manager documents the degree to which the named peril index product transfers the financier's default risk and the premium rate for the product that will make it commercially attractive to the financier.

Now the insurance manager returns to the pricing process completed in chapter 5. If the pricing for the prototype product is less than or equal to the

---

Case Example Box 8CB.3   Buyer Goods Guidelines for Value of Index Insurance

Decision metrics	Client's guidelines
1. Value creation and protection	
Value of insurance	Greater than 2 percent
2. Risk tolerance	
Probability of net default rate greater than target value	Less than 5 percent
3. Risk appetite	
Net default rate probable maximum loss (TVaR)	Less than 5 percent
Decision	Index insurance is a good solution for default risk
	Index insurance is not a good solution for default risk

Note: TVaR = tail value at risk.

Case Example Box 8CB.4 Value of Index Insurance Model Outputs for Buyer Goods

GROSS DEFAULT RATE

PROBABILITY OF GROSS DEFAULT RATE GREATER THAN TARGET	59%
EXPECTED GROSS DEFAULT RATE	4.42%
PROJECTED GROSS DEFAULT RATE FOR 1 IN 20 YEAR EVENT	7.81%
PROJECTED COST OF GROSS DEFAULT RISK	5.73%

NET DEFAULT RATE

PROBABILITY OF NET DEFAULT RATE GREATER THAN TARGET	0%
EXPECTED NET DEFAULT RATE	2.41%
PROJECTED NET DEFAULT RATE FOR 1 IN 20 YEAR EVENT	3.44%
PROJECTED COST OF NET DEFAULT RISK	3.08%

VALUE OF INDEX INSURANCE

VALUE OF INDEX INSURANCE	2.65%

Lindiwe notes that with no insurance coverage (gross default rate), Buyer Goods' probability of a default rate greater than the target is 59 percent, the projected default rate for a 1-in-20-year event (tail value at risk) is 7.81 percent, and the projected cost of retaining the gross default risk is 5.73 percent.

With coverage using Redesigned Prototype 1 (net default rate), the probability of a default rate greater than the target value declines to 0 percent, the projected default rate for a 1-in-20-year event declines to 3.44 percent, and the projected cost of the retained default risk is 3.08 percent.

The value of index insurance in this case is the difference between the cost of the gross default risk and the net default risk—2.65 percent. A premium rate of about 3 percent should be acceptable to Buyer Goods.

However, the Redesigned Prototype 1 has a premium rate of 6 percent. It is not likely that Buyer Goods will be willing to purchase the product at this premium rate. Excellence Insurance may need to restructure the product and go through the evaluation process again until a good balance between coverage and a cost that is acceptable to the client is achieved.

value of the insurance, the insurance manager can use the value-of-insurance metrics to present the product to the financier.[2] Alternatively, the insurance manager may determine that it is not feasible to offer the product at the necessary rate and inform the financier of this finding. Another option is to seek collaboration with a donor organization to provide funding to cover a portion of

Risk Modeling for Appraising Named Peril Index Insurance Products
http://dx.doi.org/10.1596/978-1-4648-1048-0

Case Example Box 8CB.5 Managerial and Actuarial Value of Index Insurance Decisions for Buyer Goods—Redesigned Prototype 1

Decision metrics	Actuarial and managerial analysis	
1. Value creation and protection		
Value of insurance	2.65 percent	
2. Risk tolerance		
Probability of NPL value greater than target value	0 percent	
3. Risk appetite		
Net default rate probable maximum loss (TVaR)	3.44 percent	
Decision	Index insurance is a good solution for default risk	(but premium is too high)
	Index insurance is not a good solution for default risk	

Note: NPL = nonperforming loan; TVaR = tail value at risk.

the cost of the index product so that it is more attractive to the financier. Through this intervention, the donor organization would help provide coverage against extreme weather events to low-income producers, but would not have to pay for all future damages. This intervention would also help develop the index insurance industry by making the products accessible to smallholder farmers.

Part 1 Conclusion

Part 1 of this guide provides insurance managers with a guide to index insurance business line development and decision making. Launching an index insurance business line is an innovative approach to reaching new market segments in the agriculture sector. Small and semi-commercial farmers and the many service providers with whom they engage—financial institutions, input suppliers, and agribusinesses—are a large and mostly untapped market. Using the tools provided in this guide, insurers will be able to prudently navigate this new market.

Notes

1. In some situations, financiers may be willing to pay more, for example, if they expect the impact of perils to increase over time, have a very high cost of capital, are otherwise very risk adverse, or will use the product as part of a customer loyalty program.

2. In some cases, the financier may still be interested in purchasing the index product even though the price for the insurance is greater than the value of insurance, for example, because of very high cost of capital for the financier, or because the financier wants to use the product in a customer loyalty program.

Bibliography

Brehm, P. J. 2007. *Enterprise Risk Analysis for Property & Liability Insurance Companies: A Practical Guide to Standard Models and Emerging Solutions.* New York: Guy Carpenter.

Crouhy, M., D. Galai, and R. Mark. 2006. *The Essentials of Risk Management.* New York: McGraw-Hill.

Lam, J. 2003. *Enterprise Risk Management: From Incentives to Controls.* Hoboken, NJ: Wiley.

PART 2

Probabilistic Modeling for Insurance Analysts

Part 1 of this guide (chapters 3 through 8) provides a description of the insights and decisions required for the insurer to make an informed decision to launch and expand an index insurance business line. Chapters 11 through 15 in part 2 of this guide provide a step-by-step guide to using the probabilistic models that can be used to calculate the decision metrics discussed in part 1.

Chapter 9 gives an overview of how to use part 2 of the guide, including an overview of its models and helpful Monte Carlo software tools.

Chapter 10 provides the reader with an overview of the main terms and techniques that are used to perform probabilistic analysis. The goal of this chapter is to help the reader understand the remaining chapters in part 2. Chapter 10 starts with an explanation of probabilistic analysis, the use of Monte Carlo simulation for probabilistic analysis, and the main building blocks of Monte Carlo simulation models. The chapter also discusses a variety of probability distributions, the correlation of different variables, and how to incorporate expert opinion into probabilistic models. Anyone who already has significant expertise in probabilistic modeling and Monte Carlo simulation can skip chapter 10.

Chapters 11 through 13 explain the probabilistic modeling for the pilot phase of launching an index insurance business line, which includes evaluating the Base Index for product design basis risk, pricing the Base Index, and evaluating the Redesigned Index. The probabilistic calculations for each chapter include guidance on implementing the analysis in the Excel files provided on the guide website (https://www.indexinsuranceforum.org/).

Chapter 14 details the modeling for identifying and prioritizing the market segments that have the highest projected volumes and profit compared with the investment of the insurer's resources.

Chapter 15 explains how to determine the extent to which index insurance can reduce a financier's losses during years with high default rates caused by the named peril as well as the maximum price the financier may be willing to pay for this reduction in losses (that is, the value of the index insurance). The insurer can use this analysis in marketing the product to specific clients.

Finally, all probabilistic models have inherent assumptions, and those presented in this guide are no exception. Therefore, chapter 16 explains the models' key assumptions and discusses alternative modeling approaches that analysts can also use with index insurance products.

In general, we recommend that the reader approach chapters 11–15 sequentially, but each chapter can also be read independently. Each chapter mentions any overlap or interdependencies between models in the relevant chapters.

How to Use Part 2

9.1 Introduction

When reading this guide, as well as when developing or using any probabilistic model, always be critical of what assumptions are made in the use of the data, the analysis, and the development of the model. The main, simplifying assumption in a model should be well articulated to all stakeholders so that they are aware of the assumptions and can decide whether the model framework needs refining. Typically, such refinements involve making changes to the existing model rather than building a new model.

The probabilistic approach used for the modeling throughout this guide is not the only one available. Especially when it comes to simulating payout ratios and **inventory damage ratios**, alternative, retrospective approaches to modeling index insurance products can help analysts understand pricing, basis risk, and other characteristics.

No single modeling approach is always the best for index insurance because of important differences across cases, including the following:

- *Different situations*, with different dynamics and types of uncertainties. For example, in certain regions the weather patterns may change rapidly over time, while in others they may be more stable. As a result, the model may or may not need to include dynamics and parameters to reflect such changing weather.
- *Differences in data availability:* In some regions very little or no historical loss data may be available, while in other regions reliable data may be available because the insurer has already provided coverage there for many years. Depending on the availability of reliable data, a probabilistic model could be built differently and be more or less complex.
- *Different modeling capabilities:* Different insurers will have different capabilities in developing and using probabilistic models. Depending on the capabilities, more or less complex probabilistic models will be appropriate.
- *Different decisions:* Depending on the specific decision to be made, different probabilistic models are needed. For example, within the approach in this

guide a number of different models are used that relate to product pricing, evaluating basis risk, and changes in coverage levels with price. Each of these questions requires different models, although in some situations it may be possible to develop one comprehensive probabilistic model to support all decision points at once.

The form, scope, and complexity of probabilistic models depend on many factors. However, we believe that a simple model with clearly understood assumptions and limitations is often better than an extremely complex model that is more difficult to handle. Still, keep in mind that a model that does not fully capture the key building blocks or important dynamics can be misleading if used for decision making under the belief that it is comprehensive when in fact it is not.

Chapter 16 discusses in detail the main assumptions underlying the models presented in this guide and explains a few alternative probabilistic modeling approaches. Example models of these alternative probabilistic approaches are available online at http://www.indexinsuranceforum.org.

9.2 Website

The website http://www.indexinsuranceforum.org provides links to important supplementary materials for this guide, including the following:

- Excel files for the models discussed in chapters 11–15
- References to relevant papers and books
- Links to index insurance–related websites.

We recommend that all readers visit the guide website and download the various Excel files before reading chapters 11–15.

9.3 Overview of Key Assumptions and Limitations of This Guide's Models

The probabilistic models used in this guide rely on specific assumptions that have important limitations.

First, the models assume that the index insurance product that is evaluated is the only product that the insurer offers. For example, when calculating the Sharpe ratio (an important risk metric explained in chapter 10), only the risks and returns of the specific index insurance product are included. In reality, an insurer should not consider the Sharpe ratio of the product in isolation, but should also consider how the index insurance product will affect its overall Sharpe ratio, which includes the products it already offers. Analyzing only the index insurance product in the absence of the insurer's entire portfolio also affects the calculation of other metrics discussed in the guide, such as the probability of ruin and the probability that the profit margin will be less than a certain target set by the insurer.

Second, the models consider only a one-year (or one-season) time frame. In other words, when estimating metrics such as the capital required or the probability of ruin, the models only consider these risks over a one-year horizon. Insurers, however, should also look at these metrics over multiple years (for example, a three- or five-year horizon) to obtain a clearer picture of the longer-term performance, risks, and profitability of the product.

Third, the models assume that the historical patterns related to the index are not changing significantly over time. Such changes might include an increase in the frequency of drought in a specific area or a decrease in the severity of drought in the same area. Such changes can be incorporated in a probabilistic analysis (see chapter 16), but to prevent the analysis from becoming too complex this dynamic is not incorporated.

As an example of an alternative model, for sovereign programs, the World Bank Group would commission a catastrophe risk model that combines historical data with physical science to get a more accurate estimate than just a historical-based approach. The approach of combining historical data with physical science is also taken in many mature agriculture insurance markets (for example, the AIR WORLDWIDE model in China). However, to ensure that the reader will understand the modeling approach, appreciate its limitations, and develop a good foundation for building or refining models that are appropriate (and potentially more complex) for any given situation, the models are kept relatively simple in this guide.

Chapter 16 provides a more in-depth look at the various assumptions, limitations, and alternative approaches to the probabilistic models that are presented in this guide.

9.4 Monte Carlo Software Tools

The models discussed in this guide and on the website use Monte Carlo[1] simulation models and were developed using both Microsoft Excel and a commercial Excel add-in called ModelRisk. However, many different commercial and open-source software tools can be used to build and run Monte Carlo simulation models.

9.4.1 @RISK™
@RISK is a commercial Excel add-in for conducting Monte Carlo simulations. Using a graphical interface (point and click), users can assign distributions to variables, perform simulations, and display and inspect results. More information is available at http://www.palisade.com.

9.4.2 Crystal Ball
Crystal Ball is a commercial Excel add-in for performing Monte Carlo simulations. The Crystal Ball interface is similar in appearance and functionality to @RISK. More information is available at http://www.oracle.com/us/products/applications/crystalball/overview/index.html.

Risk Modeling for Appraising Named Peril Index Insurance Products
http://dx.doi.org/10.1596/978-1-4648-1048-0

9.4.3 ModelRisk™

ModelRisk is a commercial Excel add-in for performing Monte Carlo simulations. Using a graphical interface (point and click), users can assign distributions to variables, perform simulations, and display and inspect results. More information is available at http://www.vosesoftware.com.

9.4.4 RiskSolver

RiskSolver is a commercial risk analysis add-in for Excel that is built around a set of optimization functions. The RiskSolver interface is similar in appearance and functionality to @RISK and Crystal Ball but in addition draws on a wide range of optimization capabilities. The RiskSolver tools also work in online spreadsheets and with application program interfaces. More information is available at http://www.solver.com.

9.4.5 R

R is a free, open-source statistical analysis software system that is easily downloaded and installed, and is operated using the R programming language to perform mathematical and statistical functions. It is well suited to a wide range of statistical analysis and simulation. The language is very flexible and users can design custom functions to perform analyses, as well as download and install function packages designed by others for specific problems. A host of functions have been developed for risk analysis in R. The biggest hurdle for most new users is that because R is a general tool and does not have built-in automated outputs and sensitivity analysis features in a simple point-and-click interface, modeling must be performed by entering and running a series of commands. More information is available at http://www.r-project.org/.

Note

1. Chapter 10 discusses Monte Carlo simulations in detail. For the moment, the reader can interpret it as a technique for performing a probabilistic analysis.

Bibliography

Bolker, B. M. 2008. *Ecological Models and Data in R*. Princeton, NJ: Princeton University Press. http://ms.mcmaster.ca/~bolker/emdbook/.

ModelAssist. "A Free and Comprehensive Quantitative Risk Analysis Training and Reference Software." http://www.epixanalytics.com/ModelAssist.html.

CHAPTER 10

Fundamentals of Probabilistic Modeling

The objective of this chapter is to provide a brief and accessible introduction to probabilistic modeling, in particular Monte Carlo simulation. Readers who are already familiar with these concepts should skip to chapter 11.

Probabilistic modeling is a wide and evolving field; many excellent books and other resources are available for learning about different aspects of probabilistic modeling. A few good books and resources include the following:

- Bolker, B. M. 2008. *Ecological Models and Data in R.* Princeton, NJ: Princeton University Press. http://ms.mcmaster.ca/~bolker/emdbook/.
- Cherubini, U., E. Luciano, and W. Vecchiato. 2004. *Copula Methods in Finance.* Hoboken, NJ: John Wiley & Sons.
- Embrechts, P., F. Lindskog, and A. McNeil. 2003. "Modeling Dependence with Copulas and Applications to Risk Management." In *Handbook of Heavy Tailed Distributions in Finance,* edited by S. T. Rachev, 329–84. Amsterdam: Elsevier.
- Forbes, C., and M. Evans. 2010. *Statistical Distributions.* 4th ed. Hoboken, NJ: Wiley. http://www.wiley.com/WileyCDA/WileyTitle/productCd-0470390638 .html.
- Gelman, A. 2013. *Bayesian Data Analysis.* 3rd ed. Boca Raton, FL: Chapman & Hall/CRC. http://www.stat.columbia.edu/~gelman/book/.
- Jewson, S., and A. Brix. 2005. *Weather Derivative Valuation: The Meteorological, Statistical, Financial, and Mathematical Foundations.* Cambridge: Cambridge University Press.
- Law, A. M., and W. D. Kelton. 2006. *Simulation Modeling and Analysis.* 4th ed. New York: McGraw-Hill.
- ModelAssist. "A Free and Comprehensive Quantitative Risk Analysis Training and Reference Software." http://www.epixanalytics.com/ModelAssist.html.

This chapter was written with key contributions from Dr. Kurt Rinehart, Risk and Statistical Consultant, EpiX Analytics LLC.

- Yan, J. 2006. "Multivariate Modeling with Copulas and Engineering Applications." In *Springer Handbook of Engineering Statistics*, edited by H. Pham, 973–90. London: Springer-Verlag.

When discussing specific topics or techniques, we will occasionally refer the reader to these titles for more in-depth study.

10.1 The Case for Probabilistic Modeling in Index Insurance

Will there be a drought next year? How many typhoons might occur? How likely is it that an index insurance product will pay out if there is a large drought or typhoon? How much capital should the insurer have on hand to cover a season of potentially high claims?

When assessing an index insurance product, there are typically a number of different uncertainties about the future and the index product's characteristics. How can we make sense of all of these uncertainties and understand the likely performance of a new index insurance product in a region of the world where weather may vary from year to year?

Probabilistic modeling (or quantitative risk analysis[1]) can help us take into account a large variety of risks and uncertainties to develop an understanding of what to expect on average,[2] as well as for the best case and worst case scenarios. As a result, probabilistic modeling is very helpful for the evaluation of index insurance products. The objective of this chapter is to describe the fundamentals of probabilistic modeling, with special emphasis on its application in the field of index insurance.

In the early years of index insurance development, instead of probabilistic analysis, practitioners working in developing countries favored using the **burn analysis contract valuation method**. This method uses historical payout ratios as the inputs for calculating the statistics for product evaluation and pricing. The advantages of using this method are its simplicity and the client's ability to easily relate the premium charged to previous experience.

However, the burn analysis method has two main drawbacks. First, it assumes that future experience will be similar to past experience, which is not always the case in reality. If an extreme event has not occurred in the past, the burn analysis method will not produce pricing that accounts for extreme events. This limitation in the analysis results in challenges for most perils that are covered with index insurance because extreme events can and often do occur. The insurer needs to have set aside sufficient capital to manage this risk of extreme events. Second, the historical sample used for the burn analysis contract valuation method is usually very small, likely biasing the results. More information on burn analysis and other alternative methods of valuing contracts can be found in Jewson and Brix (2005).

What is probabilistic modeling? A quick definition is that probabilistic modeling is a quantitative modeling approach based on the theory of probability that provides a prediction of a range of possible outcomes with their accompanying probabilities.

We consider probabilistic modeling the most appropriate and flexible method for evaluating, pricing, and understanding index insurance products because, when applied correctly, it can provide significant quantitative insights into the product and take into account the different types of risks for index insurance products. A critically important characteristic of a good probabilistic analysis is that it predicts the full range of possible future scenarios and does not underestimate the risks. Probabilistic analysis typically forecasts a large set of possible outcomes that go beyond what has occurred in the recent past. In other words, probabilistic analysis considers scenarios that have not yet occurred.

In addition, probabilistic analysis can take into account new circumstances that have not been observed in the past. For example, if a country is about to invest in flood mitigation measures such as flood walls, the probabilistic analysis can incorporate the impact of these measures on the probability and severity of flood claims.

One disadvantage of the probabilistic modeling approach is that a probabilistic model needs to be carefully developed, a process that relies on numerous assumptions and significant input data. Obtaining valuable insights from probabilistic modeling therefore requires an understanding and appreciation of the mathematical techniques, main assumptions, and different data sources upon which the results rely.

10.1.1 What Is a Model?

Before we discuss the probabilistic part of probabilistic modeling, let us first discuss the idea behind a model. A model is a simplified representation of reality that can help us better understand how a system works and can support more informed decision making about that system. In our daily lives, we typically focus on the most relevant factors of a complex reality or system to gain insight and make sound decisions.

For example, the geographical maps that we use to find our way in the real world are "models" of the earth's surface. There is no way to represent every rock and tree and the exact curvature of the earth at every point, but we do not really need those details to find our way. What we need is a way to represent distances and directions accurately so that we can find our way from place to place reliably.

The world is full of models. A map is a model of a location. A musical score is a model of the sound of a symphony. An architectural drawing is a model of a house or other building. A company's financial statement is a model of the financial health of the company.

Models come in many forms, fields, and applications. Models can also be mathematical representations of certain situations or systems. For example, in economics, models are used to provide an understanding of how changes in supply or demand influence a country's economic output. In operations research, models are used to help us understand how much inventory a retailer or manufacturer should carry. In atmospheric science, climate models are used to simulate the interactions of the atmosphere, oceans, land, and ice to determine the potential influence of carbon on future climates.

Risk Modeling for Appraising Named Peril Index Insurance Products
http://dx.doi.org/10.1596/978-1-4648-1048-0

What unites these models is that, by definition, they all include simplifications, selections of what is and is not included, and assumptions. The best models strike just the right balance between simplicity and realistic behavior. Including too much detail in a model results in longer development and run times and may obscure the insight we hope to gain.

The best models make realistic assumptions and document them clearly for the users of the model. Some assumptions are implicit in the mathematical tools themselves, while others are necessary to simplify the problem so that an efficient, useful model can be built. In the end, whatever type of model is developed of whatever complexity, it is critically important that the assumptions and limitations of the model are clear so that decisions based on model outputs take them into account. We emphasize this point because all too often decision makers that use models to inform and support their decisions come to "believe" in the model outputs without much critical review.

Models also often contain submodels. Probabilistic models typically comprise a mathematical description of a system in which multiple components of the system are uncertain or affected by chance. For example, an insurance product may cover multiple regions where the future weather of each of these regions will be uncertain and will vary. A model for this index insurance product brings together many submodels for all of the constituent variables to account for the future weather in each area. Another way to think about it is to start at the high level and work to the lower levels. At the high level, we intend to model insurance payout amounts for all covered units in all regions. To create such a model, we have to create submodels for drought **frequency** and drought **severity** for each of the regions. Each of these submodels, in turn, includes models for their parameters, such as the probability of a drought in any given year. A probabilistic model can include a large number of submodels.

10.1.2 *Deterministic versus Probabilistic Models*
Before we get into how probabilistic models work and how to interpret their results, let us look at what they are not: they are not deterministic.

In elementary school, we all learned that 2 + 2 = 4. This is an example of a deterministic calculation that provides a simple, invariable answer. Adding 2 and 2 always gives 4, and multiplying any number by 2 always gives twice that number. There is no gray area here. We know this outcome exactly and precisely. With **deterministic models**, the assumption is that the inputs and output are perfectly known. These models can be very helpful for examining some situations, but they do not provide insight into how likely some outcomes are to occur, that is, how much **uncertainty** is associated with a particular outcome.[3]

An example of a deterministic analysis for index insurance would be to calculate how often (and how much) an index product would have paid out over the past 30 years, and use these data to evaluate the product's performance. If this product's highest payment in the past 30 years was 40 percent of the insured amount, will the maximum possible payout for next year also be 40 percent?

Even when we have data from 30 years, it is possible for future payouts to be higher than any that have occurred in the past. But how *likely* is it that future payouts will be higher? And what if the insurance company has policies in multiple regions with different weather profiles?

In contrast to deterministic models, probabilistic models take into account **variability** and **uncertainty**, both in the inputs and in the outputs. When we have a coin and ask ourselves how many times it will show tails in the next 10 tosses, there is no single answer because the results are affected by chance. Any answer between 0 and 10 is possible, and each of these outcomes has its own probability.

Determining the outcomes of coin tossing and the accompanying probabilities is a problem a probabilistic model can help us with. The outcome in this case is conceptually very different from the outcome of a deterministic model. The output of the deterministic model is fully determined by the parameter values, which are assumed to be known, and the initial conditions. In contrast, probabilistic models incorporate the fact that we are typically uncertain about what the future may hold. Therefore, the output of a probabilistic model shows the range of possible outcomes and includes the probabilities for each of the different outcomes.

Two specific types of uncertainty are important when quantifying risk using a probabilistic model:

1. *Variability* (also called **aleatory uncertainty, secondary uncertainty, stochastic** variability, or interindividual variability): This uncertainty results from chance (that is, randomness) and is a function of the system being modeled. Two examples are the variability in the cumulative rainfall or the number of hours of sunshine per year.
2. *Parameter uncertainty* (also called **epistemic uncertainty**, primary uncertainty, or fundamental uncertainty) is a characteristic of measurement inaccuracy or the analyst's incomplete understanding of the phenomena (that is, level of ignorance). For example, we may be uncertain about the true average rainfall level in a particular area or the true annual probability of a claim. Unlike variability, parameter uncertainty decreases as we collect more data or expand our knowledge. We discuss this type of uncertainty more in section 10.2.2.2.

Both types of uncertainty need to be included in probabilistic models for index insurance because both affect the model's forecast of the product's performance, profitability, and so on. For example, the year-to-year variability in the payout ratios, driven by variability in annual weather, must be taken into account to understand risk metrics such as the potential magnitude of annual payouts in certain years. In addition, our epistemic uncertainty (that is, ignorance or lack of knowledge) about the true average annual rainfall in a certain area may be considerable, especially if we have limited historical weather data or weather patterns are changing, and needs to be taken into account.

Risk Modeling for Appraising Named Peril Index Insurance Products
http://dx.doi.org/10.1596/978-1-4648-1048-0

10.1.3 What Is a Probability Distribution?

Evaluating and pricing of index insurance products require an analysis and appraisal of what the future may hold. None of us knows exactly what will happen in the future, but we can assume that some results are more probable than others. In a classic demonstration of probability, if a **fair coin** (a coin with an equal probability of landing heads or tails for each throw) is flipped 100 times, it is extremely unlikely that the result will be 100 heads and 0 tails. It is much more likely that the result will be closer to equal amounts of heads and tails. This outcome can be demonstrated by actually flipping a coin 100 times and summarizing the results.

A **probability distribution** is a mathematical expression of the chances of observing various outcomes from a specific situation or experiment. One type of probability distribution, a **binomial distribution**, allows us to build a simple, quantitative risk model of the coin flip problem. Binomial distributions show the results of multiple events or trials that each have an outcome that can take one of two values (for example, success or failure).[4] Suppose you are asked to predict the number of times a coin will land head side up out of 10 flips. The result could be any number from 0 to 10, but not all of these outcomes are equally likely. With this model, we can identify the most likely outcome (5 heads) and the least likely outcomes (0 heads and 10 heads). We can also determine the probability of seeing at least 5 heads, more than 8 heads, either 5 or 6 heads, and so forth.

In an insurance context, a probability distribution can compute figures such as the average annual claims for a specific product or the probability that claims will exceed a specific amount. Because probability distributions provide an understanding of the probability of various outcomes, they are central to index insurance product evaluation and pricing. They provide a way to gain an understanding of what might happen, how large the risk might be, and how much required capital the insurer needs.

There are hundreds of different probability distributions[5] and most probabilistic models combine many different types to represent various uncertainties. The choice of probability distribution depends on the type of uncertainty. In fact, one of the fundamental tasks of probability modeling is to bring together the appropriate probability distributions to stand in for the most important elements of the problem.

10.1.4 What Is Monte Carlo Simulation?

Real-life problems that we wish to model often cannot be summarized as one simple mathematical equation or one probability distribution. For example, suppose that for an index insurance product, we need to forecast the probability that a given area will experience drought during the next season or year. One way of looking at this is that we have two possible outcomes: drought or no drought. Because a **Bernoulli distribution**[6] can represent the result of a single event that has two possible outcomes, we can easily use it to solve this problem. However, the Bernoulli distribution only tells us whether drought will or will not occur. It tells us nothing about the severity of the drought. To model drought severity, which will determine the payout amount for our index insurance product, we need another distribution (see section 10.2.1.2). Not surprisingly, the more complexity in the model (for example, more probability distributions), the more difficult the calculations become.

What if we also want to estimate total payouts for the following year for 10 areas, each with weather patterns that are different but also somewhat related because the areas are close together? The model for estimating the total payouts will need to include even more distributions now. At some point, calculating the probabilities for complex, real-life problems becomes mathematically too difficult using probability calculations. This is where Monte Carlo simulation provides a solution.

Monte Carlo simulation (or probabilistic simulation, or sometimes just simulation; box 10.1) is a way of running many "experiments" and then looking at a summary of the observed outcomes. It is a computerized mathematical technique for generating a range of possible outcomes that also provides the associated probabilities. In Monte Carlo simulation, we use a computer to "roll the dice" according to the probability distributions in our model and then report back on the outcome. It is a formal way of looking at many possible scenarios arising from a system with various risks and uncertainties and summarizing the results (box 10.2).

We often use the term "draw" to mean a random value resulting from a given probability distribution. This evokes the image of drawing a card from a randomized deck. So a **random draw** is a realized value that results from a random process. Each **scenario** or **iteration** of the Monte Carlo simulation depends on random draws from all the distributions from which the probability model is built. Some of the scenarios will be very unlikely, but they must all be possible. The model results will not properly reflect the spectrum of possible outcomes if they include outcomes that could never actually occur. If the model outputs include impossible results, the model is not built properly.

Box 10.1 A Brief History of Monte Carlo Simulation

Monte Carlo simulation was developed in the 1940s at Los Alamos National Laboratory by Stanislaw Ulam and John von Neumann. The technique was instrumental in solving some of the difficult analytics required for the Manhattan Project, the research program that developed the first nuclear weapons. Because the Manhattan Project was secret at the time, the method was given the code name "Monte Carlo," after the Monte Carlo Casino in Monaco.

In the 1950s, Monte Carlo simulations started to also be used in physics, chemistry, and operations research, and in 1964 David B. Hertz introduced Monte Carlo methods to finance with his *Harvard Business Review* article "Risk Analysis in Capital Investment."

Nowadays, with the availability of relatively inexpensive computing power, Monte Carlo simulation is used in a great number of fields, ranging from engineering, biology, and medicine, to business and finance.

Box 10.2 When to Use Monte Carlo Simulation

Imagine that you live in a country where 30 percent of the population is allergic to a certain food item. What is the probability that four randomly selected individuals will have the allergy? Most people will answer that this is $0.3 \times 0.3 \times 0.3 \times 0.3 = 0.0081$ or slightly less than 1 percent. This is a probability calculation.

The probability could also be determined by Monte Carlo simulation. To do so, we would put together a probability model with four distributions, each representing one of the four people. If we then simulate this Monte Carlo model 10,000 times, in about 81 of the iterations all four individuals would have the allergy. In other words, based on the results of the 10,000 Monte Carlo iterations, we could state that the probability of randomly selecting four allergic people would be approximately $81/10{,}000 = 0.0081$.

So, why would we ever want to perform a Monte Carlo simulation, which gives approximate answers, rather than a probability calculation that gives an exact answer? The reason is that when probability models get more complex (for example, more distributions, or intricate relationships between distributions), using probability calculations to calculate the answer becomes too difficult. In Monte Carlo simulation, we use the computer to simulate thousands of scenarios instead of doing the calculations ourselves. For example, what if we do not exactly know the proportion of patients with the food allergy? Or what if we use a diagnostic test that is not 100 percent accurate? These additional uncertainties can make the probability calculations too difficult, but including them in a Monte Carlo simulation is relatively easy.

Monte Carlo simulation relies on the **law of large numbers**. The principle is that if we simulate the Monte Carlo model many times, the result will be close to an exact answer. In the food allergy example, if we simulate the model many times the answer will be extremely close to the 0.0081 probability.

In summary, if possible, manual probability calculations in a probabilistic model are preferred to Monte Carlo simulation because the answer is exact. However, in most index insurance models the probability models will be too difficult to solve with probability calculation, and Monte Carlo simulation is the best approach. In this guide, Monte Carlo simulation is used for all probabilistic models.

How many scenarios should be run for a Monte Carlo simulation? There is no universally correct answer, but we recommend running at least 10,000 scenarios. With fewer scenarios, the resulting statistics, especially the statistics in the **tails** of the distributions, such as the 90th, 95th, or 99th percentile, become less reliable. Running more scenarios is never incorrect because it simply gets closer to the true answer. However, more scenarios will take more time while the computer runs the model. The marginal benefit of doing more scenarios after 30,000 or 100,000 becomes lower and lower. Depending on the complexity of the model and the software platform used for the simulation, 10,000 scenarios may take a few seconds (for a simple model) or several hours (for more complex models).

Let's take our index insurance example from above. With a Monte Carlo model, the computer simulates the drought/no drought frequency variable by taking a random draw from a binomial distribution. At the same time, the computer takes a random draw from a distribution for the payout amount associated with the drought (severity). For each Monte Carlo scenario, the value for the payout amount will be the random draw from the distribution when drought occurs or when no drought occurs. Each scenario represents one possible outcome for the system we are modeling. If we now run many scenarios, say 10,000 or more, and summarize the results, we end up with a distribution for the total drought-related payout for the index product for the following year. Monte Carlo simulates the **aggregate distribution** of the frequency (drought/no drought) and severity distributions (payout amount).

From this aggregate distribution we can quantify many risk-related aspects of the index product. For example, if 95 percent of the scenarios from the Monte Carlo simulation produce values of less than $75,000, we can say there is a 95 percent chance that the total payout amount for the following year will be $75,000 or less. Put differently, there is only a 5 percent chance of the total payout amount exceeding $75,000.

As you can see, a great advantage of Monte Carlo simulation is that the computer runs thousands of possible scenarios very quickly, typically in a matter of seconds or minutes. Doing this manually would take days or longer, and would not show us how likely it is that different scenarios will occur.

But, before running a Monte Carlo simulation model, it first must be built. The next section addresses three critical building blocks of Monte Carlo models.

10.2 Key Building Blocks for Probabilistic Modeling

Building sound Monte Carlo simulation models requires careful consideration of the three main building blocks of probabilistic models:

- Use of appropriate probability distributions
- Correct use of the input data for these distributions
- Proper accounting for the associations and relationships between variables

Some probabilistic models also include a fourth element, time series, which combine probability distributions and relationships between sequential time steps. For the index insurance models covered within this book, however, the three building blocks above are the most important.

10.2.1 Probability Distributions

Many different distributions can be used in a probabilistic risk model. Selecting the best distribution to apply in a specific situation is partly dictated by science and partly by art. The first thing to consider when picking a distribution is the nature of the variable that will be modeled.

Risk Modeling for Appraising Named Peril Index Insurance Products
http://dx.doi.org/10.1596/978-1-4648-1048-0

First, all distributions represent either **discrete variables**, which can only take integer values, or **continuous variables**, which can take any value. Counts of events are discrete (for example, number of typhoons per year), while rainfall and temperature are continuous because they can be measured to any numerical precision.

Second, many distributions are either right- (also called **positive**) or left- (also called **negative**) **skewed** (see figure 10.1), which means that the distribution is asymmetric, with one of the tails extending further than the other (see section 10.2.1.1.4 for more on tails). Skewed distributions are suitable for some variables and not others. The distribution of individual incomes is a classic example of a skewed distribution because the distribution peaks at relatively low values and then the right tail extends far to the right to account for the relatively few, extremely high incomes.[7]

Third, many distributions are bounded at specific values, meaning that all the values must be above, below, or both above and below a certain value. An income distribution, for example, is bounded on the left by zero because income is a positive value. However, a distribution for a probability or proportion will be bounded on the left at zero and on the right at 1.

Fourth, some distributions are designed for stochastic, or random, processes. Recall the binomial distribution discussed earlier in this chapter. This distribution should automatically come to mind whenever you consider a series of events, each of which has two possible outcomes. The **Poisson distribution** is ideally suited to some either/or processes. Poisson distributions represent random, discrete events

Figure 10.1 Skewing and Bounding in Distributions

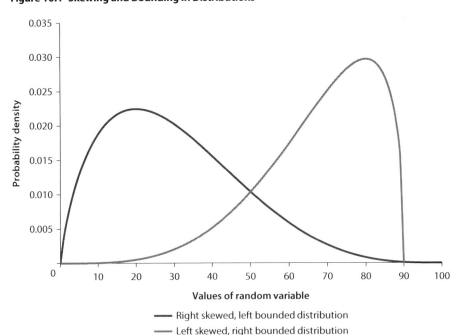

Right skewed, left bounded distribution
Left skewed, right bounded distribution

Risk Modeling for Appraising Named Peril Index Insurance Products
http://dx.doi.org/10.1596/978-1-4648-1048-0

that occur at some underlying rate, for example, counts of customer visits, auto-mobile accidents, typhoons, and many other "count" variables (see sections 10.2.1.2 and 10.2.1.2.3). Special distributions such as the **PERT distribution**[8] have been specifically created for cases lacking hard data on the parameter to model, for which expert opinion therefore could be used (see section 10.2.1.2).

This section first takes a detailed look at how to interpret a probability distribution and then introduces common distributions that will be used in this guide. For a more complete and comprehensive discussion of probability distributions, we encourage the reader to consult the references listed at the start of this chapter.

10.2.1.1 How to Interpret Probability Distributions

Probability density charts are represented on an x-y axis. The horizontal axis, conventionally called the x-axis, shows the random variable, the thing that we want to know or predict. This variable can be anything: net profits, crop yield, number of home runs by a certain baseball player, number of typhoons in the coming year, total insurance claim value in a calendar year, and so on. The vertical axis (y-axis) shows the probability for the x-axis variable. Probabilities can only take values from 0 to 1, so the y-axis is scaled from 0 to 1 and the total probabilities across all x-axis values also add up to 1.[9] Three concepts will be important for interpreting probability distributions: cumulative probabilities, percentiles, and distribution tails.

10.2.1.1.1 Discrete and Continuous Probabilities. As discussed in paragraph 10.2.1, a key characteristic of a probability distribution is whether it rep-resents a discrete or continuous variable.[10] Figure 10.2 shows a discrete

Figure 10.2 Probability Density Chart of a Discrete Probability Distribution

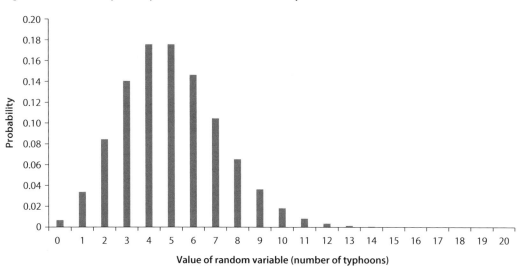

Figure 10.3 Probability Density Chart of a Continuous Probability Distribution

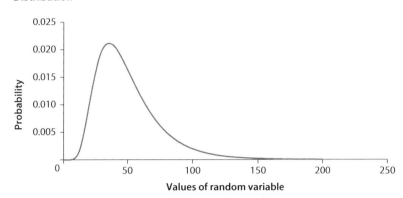

probability distribution for number of typhoons. The typhoon distribution is a **discrete probability distribution**, formally called a **probability mass function**, because the count of typhoons per year can only be an integer. There is no such thing as 1.5 typhoons.

Figure 10.3 shows that the probability of the number of typhoons being equal to 2 is about 0.08, or an 8 percent probability. According to the model that generated this distribution, there is an 8 percent chance of two typhoons occurring in the next year.

Continuous probability distributions are formally called **probability density functions,** and one is shown in figure 10.3. Note that there are no bars as in figure 10.2, just a smooth line. This smooth line indicates that a probability for any value on the x-axis can be found, for example, at x = 50, x = 50.01, x = 50.1, and so on. Of course, the continuous variable has limitless precision, so really when we say x = 50, we mean x = 50.00000000…. There are an infinite number of possible values of X, so there is essentially an infinitely small (that is, 0) probability that x is *exactly* 50. The probability density function, on the other hand, returns the density for a continuous distribution. Because continuous variables can take any number of decimal points, it does not make sense to talk about an exact probability of observing a value. Instead we use the more abstract concept of the density, which is proportional to, but not the same as, the probability of observing a certain value.

The formulas for the probability mass function (discrete probability distribution) and the probability density function (continuous probability distribution) are both expressed as

$$f(x),$$

with f being the probability function, and x being the value evaluated.

Risk Modeling for Appraising Named Peril Index Insurance Products
http://dx.doi.org/10.1596/978-1-4648-1048-0

The Bernoulli distribution, for example, is a probability mass function expressed as

$$f(x) = p^x (1-p)^{1-x},$$

where p is the probability of success for a Bernoulli trial.

For the less mathematically inclined readers, probability functions can be confusing, so this guide provides explanations of the concepts behind each distribution. More detailed mathematics for the distributions used and discussed in this guide are covered in the additional texts recommended at the start of this chapter.

10.2.1.1.2 Cumulative Probabilities. Both continuous and discrete probability distributions can represent the probability of X being within a certain range. To find the probability of the number of typhoons in the discrete probability distribution in figure 10.2 being equal to any value up to and including 2, we add the probabilities for the x-axis values 0 (0.01), 1 (0.03), and 2 (0.08). Adding these up gives a value close to 0.12, or 12 percent. In other words, there is a 12 percent chance of two or fewer typhoons occurring in the next year.

The conventional way of expressing this problem is as follows:

$$\text{Probability}(X \leq 2) = 0.12.$$

In this notation, X represents the random variable. A lower case x is used to indicate a specific instance of that variable, so the more general form of the relationship above is as follows:

$$\text{Probability}(X \leq x) = \ldots.$$

Probability($X \leq x$) is a very common method of interpreting probability distributions, as is probability($X > x$). Another term for both of these probabilities is **cumulative probability** because they are the accumulation (that is, the sum) of all probabilities of X up to the threshold of x ($X \leq x$) or beyond the threshold of x ($X > x$).

We can show cumulative probabilities in cumulative distributions. Whereas the distributions seen so far show the probabilities associated with individual values of the random variable, the cumulative distribution for Probability($X \leq x$) shows the probability of all values up to and including a certain value. The cumulative distribution is built by adding the probability for each value of the variable to all the preceding values. Once this is done for every variable value, we end up with a cumulative probability distribution (or **cumulative distribution function**).

Notice that the cumulative probability distribution in figure 10.4 is discrete. The variable value moves in discrete steps of 1. The variable cannot take a value of 1.5 so there is no unique probability associated with 1.5. The cumulative probability of the variable being less than or equal to 1.5 is exactly the same as

Risk Modeling for Appraising Named Peril Index Insurance Products
http://dx.doi.org/10.1596/978-1-4648-1048-0

Figure 10.4 Cumulative Probability Chart of a Discrete Probability Distribution

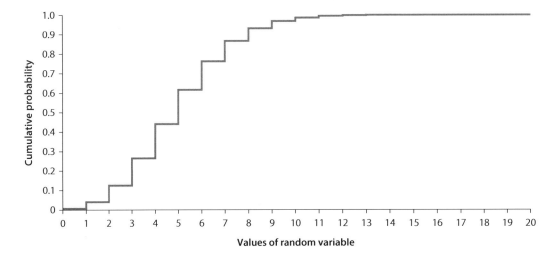

the cumulative probability of the variable being less than or equal to 1, hence the flat lines at each step in the cumulative probability distribution.

The cumulative probability up to a given x value is computed for continuous distributions in a comparable way. The only difference is that where we could *add up* the probabilities in the discrete distribution, with a continuous distribution, we *integrate* the area under the curve to determine the cumulative probability. Once we do this for every variable value, we get a continuous cumulative probability distribution (cumulative distribution function).

The cumulative probability distribution makes it much easier to find the kinds of probability measures that are of interest in risk and insurance modeling. For example, in figure 10.5 we can readily see that there is about a 65 percent chance of values less than or equal to 50, and about a 90 percent chance of values less than or equal to 100.

10.2.1.1.3 Percentiles. One type of probability measure that we often use with continuous distributions is the **percentile.** When we use a cumulative probability distribution, the percentiles are the points along the x-axis that correspond to certain cumulative probabilities. For example, the 10th percentile (P10) is the value of x such that the Probability(X ≤ x) = 0.10.

In figure 10.6 the vertical line represents the P10. The line touches the distribution at the y-axis value of 0.1. The corresponding x-axis value is 138. From this we know that the P10 is approximately 138. There is a 10 percent probability that a random x will be less than or equal to 138 and there is a 90 percent chance that a random x will be greater than 138.

We can also find percentiles for a continuous distribution using a probability density chart (as opposed to a cumulative probability chart). With a continuous probability density chart, the probability is proportional to the area under the

Figure 10.5 Cumulative Probability Chart of a Continuous Probability Distribution

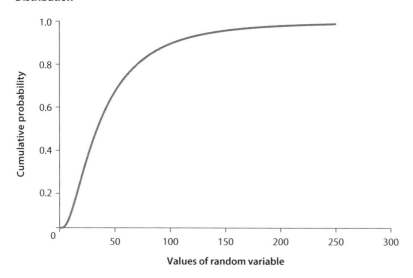

Figure 10.6 Cumulative Probability Chart of a Continuous Distribution with the P10 Displayed

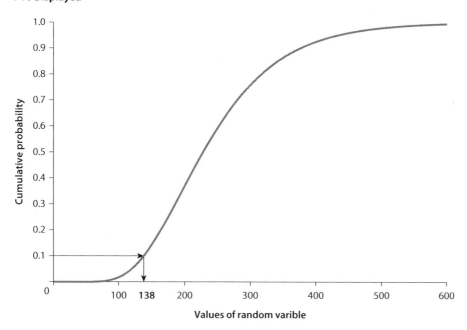

Note: P10 = 10th percentile.

Risk Modeling for Appraising Named Peril Index Insurance Products
http://dx.doi.org/10.1596/978-1-4648-1048-0

Figure 10.7 Probability Density Chart of Continuous Distribution with the P10 Displayed

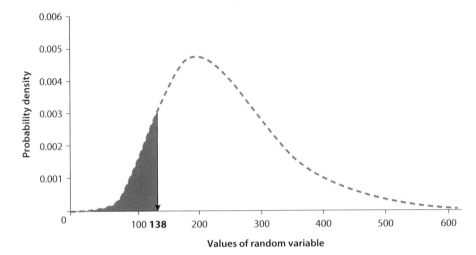

Note: P10 = 10th percentile.

curve. As illustrated by the vertical line in figure 10.7, the P10 divides the area under the curve such that 10 percent of the area under the curve is to the left and 90 percent of the area under the curve is to the right of 138.

In general, probability distributions rather than cumulative probability distributions are used throughout this guide because most people find them easier to interpret and they are the default in most modeling software. When it comes to finding specific percentile values we rely on the modeling software to provide the correct figure. When we show probability distributions we generally leave out any numbering along the x-axis but label the percentiles and other key metrics to orient the viewer to the scale of the distribution.

10.2.1.1.4 Distribution Tails. Figure 10.7 also illustrates a term that is common in probabilistic modeling: tail. When we look at this distribution, we see a peak on the left side and a long, extending tail on the right, in the positive direction. This distribution is positively skewed. We can readily tell that low values of x are more likely than high values. As a result, the P50 is far to the left. Although the curve extends far to the right, there is very little area under the curve on the right. For the distribution shown in figure 10.7, 50 percent of the area falls to the left of x = 228. The long right tail tells us that there is still some chance of getting values of x higher than 500, even if it is very unlikely. This is the nature of long-tailed, positively skewed distributions. They can show us low-likelihood, extreme-value situations. These are very important for risk assesments of index insurance products.

Although less relevant for index insurance, we want to briefly mention the importance of **fat-tailed distributions**. These distributions have one or both tails that are both long (x-values very far from the median) and fat (x-values on the tail have a higher probability of occurring than for thinner tailed distributions). These distributions can be helpful for modeling inventory damage and can model very large (or very small) damages. The Pareto distribution has the fattest tail of all probability distributions.

The models used and discussed in this guide do not use the **Pareto distribution** to simulate inventory damage levels (for example, a dollar amount of losses). Instead, the models in this guide simulate the payouts of the index insurance product as a percentage of the sum insured, which does not correspond exactly to the damage experienced on the ground. Since the payout ratio is a percentage, and percentage payouts can only range from 0 percent to 100 percent, this guide uses, as a default, the **beta distribution** to represent the payout ratio (which ranges from 0 to 1; see section 10.2.1.2.4).

10.2.1.2 *Selecting Probability Distributions*
This section explains a select group of probability distributions that are most helpful when modeling index insurance products. These specific distributions were selected using the same four considerations discussed at the start of section 10.2.1:

- *Type of variable (discrete or continuous):* One of the uncertainties in our models, for example, is whether the product will pay out or not pay out in the next season. Because there are only two potential outcomes for this variable (payout/ no payout) we selected a Bernoulli distribution that represents such discrete situations.
- *Right or left skew of the distribution:* For example, a left-skewed distribution may be appropriate for representing the annual rainfall in a particular area if there are many years with similar amounts of rainfall but some years with extremely low rainfall.
- *Bounding of the distribution:* One of the uncertainties is what the size of the payouts should be, which is a percentage of the amount insured. Because such percentages can only range from 0 percent to 100 percent, a beta distribution (which is bounded at 0 and 1) was selected to represent this variable.
- *Specific design of the distribution for stochastic processes:* Poisson distributions, for example, represent random, discrete events that occur at some underlying rate. Poisson distributions are often used to model events such as accidents.

Not all distributions are discussed in this section and for those that are discussed, the descriptions are fairly brief. We again encourage the reader to refer to the additional texts recommended at the start of this chapter to become more familiar with the different probability distributions that are available to represent uncertainties in Monte Carlo simulation models.

10.2.1.2.1 Bernoulli Distribution. The Bernoulli distribution models whether a single trial results in success or failure, for example, winning a coin toss (or not), winning the lottery next week (or not), or defaulting on a loan in the next year (or not).[11] It models a single event that has an outcome that can take one of two values, which are usually denoted as 1 for a success and 0 for a failure. The outcome of the single event is governed by the probability of success, which is conventionally represented by the letter p, which is the only parameter for this simple distribution.

$$f(x) = p^x (1-p)^{1-x}$$

For a fair coin, the probability of success (p) is 0.5, or 50 percent, but for winning the lottery the probability of success is much smaller, for example, 0.00000000001. When modeling an index insurance product, we can use the Bernoulli distribution to simulate payouts for the next year in a specific area. The probability of a payout is often not equal to 50 percent but may be 15 percent, for example. In this case, the Bernoulli distribution within our Monte Carlo simulation model will generate a 1 in 15 percent of the scenarios and a 0 in 85 percent of the scenarios.

The Bernoulli distribution can be related, or linked, to other distributions in the model. For example, a second distribution can provide the actual payout amount in the case in which a payout occurs (see section 10.2.1.2.4.2).

Finally, a Bernoulli distribution is the same as a binomial distribution (see the next paragraph) when in the binomial distribution the number of events (or trials) is set at one.

10.2.1.2.2 Binomial Distribution. The binomial distribution is one of the most commonly used discrete distributions and it represents the outcome of multiple Bernoulli events, or trials. The best known example is the multiple coin toss problem discussed in section 10.1.3. The binomial distribution shows the distribution of the number of successes out of a certain number of trials along with the corresponding probability.

For example, if an employee of a health agency is randomly testing people in a country for a disease with a prevalence rate of 8 percent, the number of people in that survey who do have the disease will follow a binomial distribution. Or if a bank has outstanding loans and the annual default rate is 2 percent, the number of defaults during the next year will also follow a binomial distribution.

The parameters for the binomial distribution are the number of trials and the probability of success. Conventionally, these parameters are denoted as n and p, respectively. The binomial distribution in a Monte Carlo model samples how many successes (conventionally called s) there will be from the n trials.[12]

The binomial distribution can also help with an analysis of index insurance products. For example, in any given year or season an index insurance policy can result in a payout without any inventory damage caused by the named peril occurring (an example of insurer basis risk). Suppose we have reason to believe that the probability of such an event is 3 percent per year and remains the same over the next five years. We can use a binomial distribution to represent the probability distribution of the number of insurer basis risk events over the next five years. The number of years is the number of trials (n) and 3 percent is the probability of success (p).[13]

It is important to note that if we only want to model the probability of an insurer basis risk event in the next year, then we use a binomial distribution with just one trial, which is equivalent to a Bernoulli distribution. In this guide, all of the models focus on forecasting claims for the next season or year, so we use Bernoulli distributions (one trial), not binomial distributions (a series of trials).

10.2.1.2.3 Poisson Distribution. The Poisson distribution is also a discrete distribution, but unlike the Bernoulli and binomial distributions there is no probability of a trial succeeding or not. Instead, the Poisson distribution represents the count of independent events that happen according to a certain rate per **unit of exposure**. Units of exposure are often measures of time, so we might look at the number of automobile accidents in a specific city per year. The unit of exposure here is one year. The Poisson distribution can estimate how many accidents in the city might occur over the next five years. Units of exposure can be any continuum, such as volume, mass, or area. For example, we might look at the number of automobile accidents per intersection, where one intersection during one month of time is the unit of exposure. During this unit of exposure, a number of accidents can happen that can be simulated by the Poisson distribution.

The two parameters for a Poisson distribution are the rate (average number of events) per unit of exposure (lambda), and the exposure quantity (t).[14] In the car accident example, the rate per unit of exposure is 400 accidents per year (lambda) and the exposure quantity is five years (t). The Poisson distribution forecasts the number of events that could actually happen, called alpha.

Poisson event data are commonly referred to as count data. The Poisson distribution is useful for index insurance modeling of counts such as the number of typhoons occurring during the next year.

10.2.1.2.4 Beta Distribution. The beta distribution is the first continuous distribution discussed in this guide (the Bernoulli, binomial, and Poisson are all discrete). It is bounded by 0 on the left and 1 on the right. In other words, the beta distribution can only generate values greater than 0 and less than 1.

The beta distribution generally has two uses: (1) to model the uncertainty in a probability or proportion and (2) to model continuous variables that range from 0 to 1.

10.2.1.2.4.1 Use of the Beta Distribution #1: Modeling the uncertainty in a probability or proportion. The beta distribution models uncertainty in the true value of a probability or proportion.[15] Imagine that 10 cars are randomly selected in a large city and 3 of them are blue. How many cars in the city could now be estimated to be blue? A simple estimate is 30 percent, but with so few observations we should not overstate our certainty that 30 percent is the true proportion of blue cars in the city. With only 10 observations, actual values of 20 percent or 40 percent could also easily result in the same data (3 blue cars out of 10).

Risk Modeling for Appraising Named Peril Index Insurance Products
http://dx.doi.org/10.1596/978-1-4648-1048-0

This uncertainty about the probability or proportion can be very large when few data are available, which is fairly common for index insurance applications for which often only 10 to 30 years of historical data exist. The beta distribution provides a distribution of possible values for the probability that an index product will pay out during the next season.

The parameters of the beta distribution are conventionally represented by the Greek letters alpha and beta. Previous researchers have worked out various means of translating the data we usually work with into proper values of alpha and beta.[16] For example, we can estimate the probability of success (p) using a beta distribution with alpha = $s + 1$ and beta = $n - s + 1$, where s is the number of successes and n is the number of trials.

In the example of the 3 blue cars out of 10 randomly selected cars, our uncertainty about the actual proportion of blue cars in the city can be described by the blue line in figure 10.8. The peak of this distribution (the mode) is at 0.3 on the x-axis, which you probably suspected given that you saw 3 blue cars out of 10 cars. However, the distribution shows considerable uncertainty around what the true proportion is, and that even values as low as 0.10 and as high as 0.70 are possible. On the other hand, if we had seen 30 blue cars out of 100 randomly selected cars, the orange line beta distribution would have represented our uncertainty about the proportion of blue cars. In this case the uncertainty is quite a bit less because the estimate of the proportion was based on more data.

Turning to index insurance applications, suppose that we are again modeling insurer basis risk events, that is, situations in which the index product provides a payout despite there being no inventory damage attributable to the named peril. We have 10 years of historical data (n) and during those 10 years, an insurer

Figure 10.8 Probability Density Charts of Two Beta Distributions

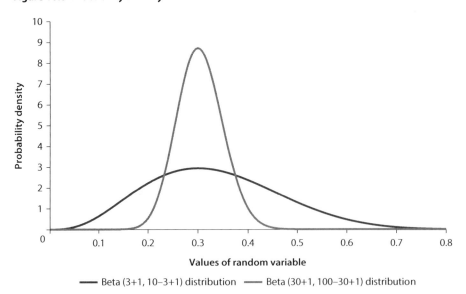

Beta (3+1, 10–3+1) distribution   Beta (30+1, 100–30+1) distribution

Risk Modeling for Appraising Named Peril Index Insurance Products
http://dx.doi.org/10.1596/978-1-4648-1048-0

basis risk event occurred in one year (s). A simple, first estimate of the probability of an insurer basis risk event is 10 percent (s/n). However, given our limited data set, we represent the uncertainty about the true probability as a beta distribution with alpha = 2 (that is, $s + 1 = 2$) and beta = 10 (that is, $n - s + 1 = 10$). If we do not use the beta distribution we ignore the uncertainty in the probability and can underestimate the overall risk.

10.2.1.2.4.2 Use of the Beta Distribution #2: Modeling continuous variables ranging from 0 to 1. The second potential use of the beta distribution is for modeling a continuous variable that can only vary from 0 to a maximum of 1. An example is the payout (as a percentage of the insured amount) that an index insurance product may produce next year. In fact, several of the example models that come with this guide use the beta distribution to simulate the payout ratios for cases in which there is a payout greater than 0 percent. The technique for determining the input parameters of the beta distribution based on the historical payout ratio for specific index products, called fitting distributions to data, is covered in section 10.2.2.1.

10.2.1.2.5 *Gamma Distribution.* The gamma distribution is another continuous distribution, but this one is bounded on the left by 0 and positively skewed without a right bound, meaning the right tail extends far to the right. A common application of the gamma distribution is in modeling the rate of Poisson events per unit of exposure, or the time required for a specific number of Poisson-distributed events to occur. In the insurance industry the gamma distribution is used to represent potential payout amounts in currency terms, for example, $400, rather than as a percentage of the sum insured, for example, 35 percent. The left-side bound at 0 corresponds to modeling payouts because only positive payout amounts are sensible. The long right-side tail represents the general behavior that, although most payouts will be of smaller amounts, a small number of payouts may be extremely large. Gamma distributions can also be used to represent trigger values, for example, 44 millimeters of rain during a crop season, because many triggers such as rainfall and degree hours can only have positive values.

There are different **parameterizations** of the gamma distribution, meaning that it can be calculated from functions that take different input parameters. A common parameterization requires two parameters: shape and scale. These are denoted by the Greek letters alpha and beta, respectively. The alpha parameter drives the shape of the distribution while the beta parameter drives its spread (scale). In practice, the larger the shape parameter (alpha), the more the gamma distribution tends to look like the normal distribution. With smaller values of alpha, the distribution looks like a much skewed distribution called the exponential. The scale parameter (beta) is directly proportional to its standard deviation. The bigger the scale parameter, the greater the variability in the distribution samples. A neat feature of the gamma distribution is that its **mean** is simply alpha times beta. This calculation is a quick way to check that the parameter values make sense compared with the historical data.

Risk Modeling for Appraising Named Peril Index Insurance Products
http://dx.doi.org/10.1596/978-1-4648-1048-0

As noted above, the gamma distribution can model payout amounts for index insurance when these are modeled in currency terms. The gamma distribution can also be used to model trigger values. However, the example models within this guide use historical payouts as a percentage of the insured amount (payout ratios). When handled in this fashion, the payouts are bounded by 0 and 1, with 1 being 100 percent. Thus, we use a beta distribution to model payouts in this guide (see chapter 16).

10.2.1.2.6 PERT Distribution. The PERT distribution is also a continuous distribution. It has three parameters: the minimum, most likely (mode), and maximum. This distribution is particularly useful for modeling experts' opinions about a quantity, such as the market size for a new product or the potential market share a new entrant can capture.

For example, when an insurance company plans to launch a new index product, there may be uncertainty about the number of bank branches that will purchase the product. Experts might indicate that they think the most likely number of bank branches that will purchase the product will be 50, but could be as low as 30 or as high as 100. Figure 10.9 shows the distribution for the PERT (minimum = 30, most likely = 50, maximum = 100), also written as PERT (30, 50, 100).

An important characteristic of the PERT distribution is that all values between the minimum and maximum are possible because it is a continuous distribution. For the bank branch example, we need to use Excel's ROUND function to make sure we do not get outcomes such as 45.7 branches enrolling, instead of 46.

As figure 10.9 also shows, values around the most likely value are sampled often while values close to the minimum of 30 and maximum of 100 are less likely to be sampled.

Figure 10.9 PERT (30, 50, 100)

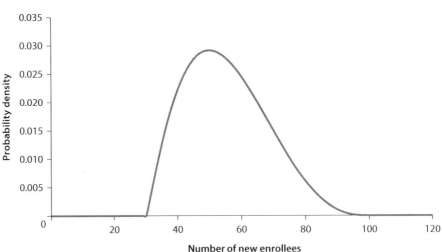

Note: PERT = program evaluation and review techniques.

Risk Modeling for Appraising Named Peril Index Insurance Products
http://dx.doi.org/10.1596/978-1-4648-1048-0

10.2.2 Distribution Parameters

Each of the distributions discussed, and every probability distribution, has certain parameters. The Bernoulli distribution has one (p). The binomial distribution has two (n and p) as does the Poisson (lambda and t), the beta (alpha and beta), and the normal (mean and standard deviation).

Where do the values for these parameters come from? In general, probability distributions are parameterized in two ways: expert opinion elicitation and **distribution fitting**. Expert opinion elicitation involves consulting the opinions of experts to quantify uncertainty.[17] Alternatively, historical data can be used to estimate model parameters using distribution fitting. Distribution fitting is discussed in the next section.

For further information on choosing parameters based on historical data or expert opinion the reader is encouraged to read the additional texts recommended at the start of this chapter, specifically Gelman (2013), Bolker (2008), and Law and Kelton (2006).

10.2.2.1 Distribution Fitting

Distribution fitting is used to represent historical data in the model to forecast future behavior. For example, the amount of money that the next customer in a store will spend may be modeled using the spending amounts of the last 100 people. In this case, we must have reason to believe that the historical spending data are credible for estimating the spending of the next person.

In the index insurance models in this guide, distribution fitting is used to identify the appropriate value of the distribution parameters for the index product payout ratios in the next year. In the case example, the payout is a proportion of the insured value—severe droughts result in 100 percent payouts and less severe droughts result in payouts of smaller percentages. The payout ratios are values from 0 (0 percent) to 1 (100 percent) and are continuous. The beta distribution, which also ranges from 0 to 1 and is continuous, is a reasonable choice. To use the beta distribution, we first need to estimate the values of the beta parameters alpha and beta.

To fit a distribution to data, historical data on the phenomenon of interest are needed. The process of fitting a distribution to the observed data is similar to trying on a number of different sizes and types of shirts to find the one that fits the best. For the case example, the historical data on payouts can be represented by a frequency graph (also called a histogram) of the different historical payout amounts that have occurred in the period covered by the historical data, as in figure 10.10.

Conceptually, the distribution can be manually fitted by choosing values for the beta parameters, for example, alpha = 1 and beta = 2, and using them to plot the curve of the corresponding beta distribution over the data (the blue histogram bars). Then the process can be repeated with different parameter values for the beta distribution (for example, alpha = 0.5, beta = 3) to see if the resulting curve matches the data better or worse than the first curve. If this process is repeated with different parameter values, a set of values that best mimicked the

Risk Modeling for Appraising Named Peril Index Insurance Products
http://dx.doi.org/10.1596/978-1-4648-1048-0

Figure 10.10 Frequency Graph of Historical Payout Amounts, Together with the Maximum Likelihood Estimation of the Fitted Beta Distribution

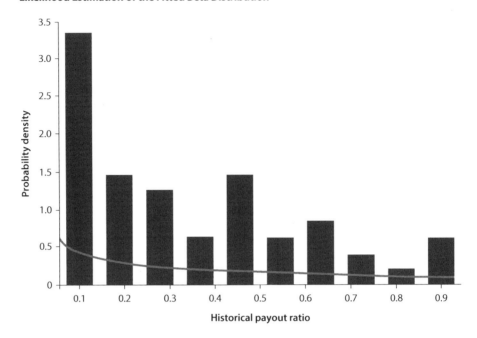

pattern would eventually emerge. Figure 10.10 is a beta distribution with alpha = 0.65 and beta = 1.07, represented by the orange curve.[18]

To fit the distribution, a judgment must be made of which curve (which parameters of the beta distribution) best approximate the data. There are different ways of calculating and judging the closeness of the curve to the data. Closeness is commonly determined by calculating the (joint) likelihood that the observed data came from the fitted distribution. Then a combination of parameters can be found that maximizes the chances that all the data points observed came from the fitted distribution and parameters. This process is called maximum likelihood estimation (MLE) and parameters from fitted distributions are called MLEs. Risk modeling software packages include automatic procedures to perform MLE fitting very quickly.

Multiple distributions may be appropriate for representing a given situation in a model. For example, some people prefer the gamma distribution to the lognormal distribution (which is another continuous distribution with a long tail to the right) for representing payouts. If there is no specific reason for choosing gamma over lognormal, the fits from both distributions can be compared using **goodness of fit** (GOF) statistical criteria.

A number of GOF statistics, such as the Anderson-Darling statistic and the Kolmogorov-Smirnov statistics, can help with selecting the best fitted distribution. However, these statistics do not take into account the complexity of candidate probability distributions (the number of parameters of the different distributions)

Risk Modeling for Appraising Named Peril Index Insurance Products
http://dx.doi.org/10.1596/978-1-4648-1048-0

that could be fitted to the data. In contrast, GOF statistics based on information criteria, such as the Akaike information criterion and the Bayesian information criterion, do penalize distributions for extra parameters.[19] For readers interested in learning more about information criteria, we recommend Gelman (2013) and Bolker (2008).

Different GOF statistics may return different conclusions about which distribution has the best fit. As we discussed in previous sections, it is therefore always necessary to also consider the key characteristics of the distribution (the type of variable, skewness, bounding, design for stochastic processes) as well as whether the distribution is commonly applied in the specific field (that is, industry practices).

10.2.2.2 Parameter Uncertainty

As discussed above, parameter uncertainty is the measure of the incompleteness of our knowledge (also called our lack of confidence or ignorance) about the true value of a parameter that cannot be readily observed. When a parameter is estimated, an idea of what the parameter might be is obtained, but the confidence around this estimate will depend on the amount of data that is available. With only a few observations, the uncertainty about the parameter is relatively high because many different values could result in those same observations.

Let us consider two examples in index insurance in which parameter uncertainty is relevant:

First, recall that when the distribution was fitted to the data in figure 10.10 MLEs were used to determine that the best fitting beta distribution parameters were alpha = 0.65 and beta = 1.07.

However, the same data could also have come from a beta distribution with alpha = 0.59 and beta = 1.18 or alpha = 0.55 and beta = 0.8. In other words, although alpha = 0.65 and beta = 1.07 are the MLEs of the beta distribution for this data, the exact values of both of these parameters are still uncertain.

Figure 10.11, where the best fit (based on MLEs) is the orange line and alternative fits are in green, shows this parameter uncertainty. There are actually an infinite number of alternative fits possible, but these other potential fits will be similar to the green lines. The data we have observed could have come from any of these alternative beta distributions. Figure 10.12 shows the uncertainty in the values of both the alpha and beta parameters of the fitted beta distribution. The uncertainty distributions of both of the variables are centered around the MLE of alpha and beta, which are equal to 0.65 and 1.07, respectively. Alternative values for the variables are, however, still possible. For example, even though the MLE of alpha is 0.65, its value could actually be 1, or an even higher value.

For the second example of parameter uncertainty, suppose we are modeling the chances of a drought occurring in the next year but do not know the probability of drought in a given year. Historical data might tell us that one drought year ($s = 2$) occurred in the past 10 years ($n = 10$). The best estimate of the probability of a drought occurring next year is 20 percent (s/n), which is also the MLE for the p parameter in a binomial distribution.

Risk Modeling for Appraising Named Peril Index Insurance Products
http://dx.doi.org/10.1596/978-1-4648-1048-0

Figure 10.11 Frequency Graph of Historical Payout Amounts, Together with the Maximum Likelihood Estimates of the Fitted Beta Distribution (Orange) and Alternative Fits Based on Parameter Uncertainty

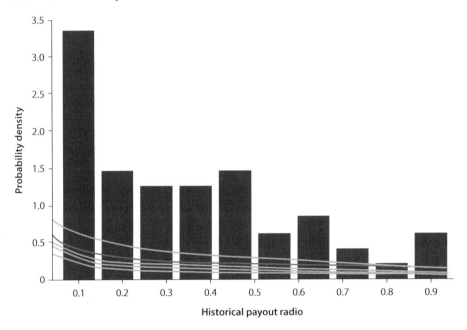

Figure 10.12 Parameter Uncertainty for Alpha and Beta

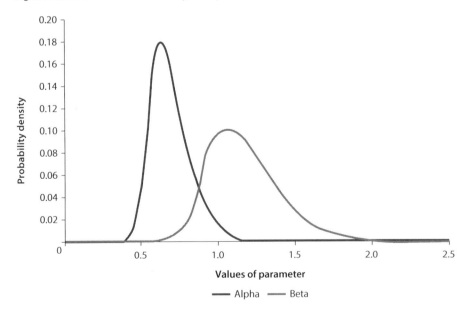

Risk Modeling for Appraising Named Peril Index Insurance Products
http://dx.doi.org/10.1596/978-1-4648-1048-0

With this information, we can model an uncertainty distribution for the parameter p with a beta distribution (that is, a continuous distribution that is bounded at 0 and 1). Using what is known in Bayesian statistics as a conjugate and uninformed prior,[20] we can then use the trials and successes in our historical data (trials, n, is the number of years of data, and successes, s, is the number of years in which a drought occurred) to compute the two parameters of the beta distribution as alpha = $s + 1$ and beta = $n - s + 1$. Using these two parameters within the beta distribution will provide the uncertainty distribution for the probability of a drought in the next year (the uncertainty around the true probability, p).

When the data are numerous, this distribution of parameter uncertainty will be relatively tight, which indicates that we have more confidence around what the true parameters are. It will be focused on a narrow range of possible values. When the data are few, the distribution will be broader, which indicates that we have less confidence about the true value. This is illustrated in figure 10.13 where the uncertainty is shown around the true probability p for two cases: (1) 10 samples with 2 successes (for example, 2 years of drought out of 10 years) and (2) 100 samples with 20 successes.

The modeling of the parameter uncertainty with the beta distribution is based on historical data and assumes that future patterns will be similar to those in the past. As a result, parameter uncertainty does not account for possible changes in the systems themselves over time (see section 9.3 and chapter 16). System changes relevant to index insurance may include climate change (which could change the frequency and severity of payouts) or increased resilience of a farmer's crop or livestock to weather risk due to breeding or management practices (which could

Figure 10.13 Tight vs. Broad Parameter Uncertainty

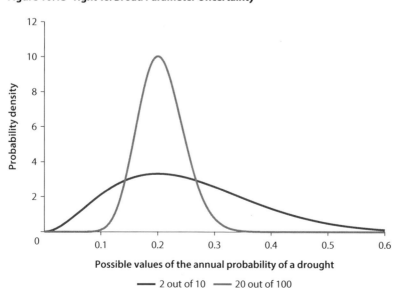

Risk Modeling for Appraising Named Peril Index Insurance Products
http://dx.doi.org/10.1596/978-1-4648-1048-0

change the actual losses, and therefore the amount of product design basis risk of the index product).

As can be seen in figure 10.13, when 2 drought years out of 10 years have been observed there is considerably more uncertainty around the true probability of a drought next year than when 100 years of historical data are available. However, in this example, one of the assumptions is that the annual probability of a drought does not change over time, which may or may not be a valid assumption. If the probability does change (for example, increase or decrease) over time, the distribution might be modified using time series methods.

If the drivers that cause droughts can be better understood, we may be able to better predict them and therefore reduce parameter uncertainty because we could explain why droughts have happened in the past (or not) and when they will likely happen again (Jewson and Brix 2005). Such unveiling and understanding of drivers is complicated, but would help index insurance with better pricing.

Whenever any parameter is estimated from historical data, especially in situations in which only limited data are available, parameter uncertainty can be important. The field of statistics (both classical statistics and Bayesian statistics) provides a variety of tools for estimating the relevant parameter uncertainty.

In the index insurance models in this guide, the probability of a payout per year per region includes parameter uncertainty. Parameter uncertainty in estimating the probability distribution of historical payouts could also have been included. However, it was not included because parameter uncertainty considerably slows down the speed of the Monte Carlo simulation models.[21] Therefore, if you use Monte Carlo models with limited amounts of historical data we encourage you to include parameter uncertainty. Alternatively, you can run the model twice, once with and once without parameter uncertainty, to determine whether including parameter uncertainty significantly affects the model's results and interpretations.

10.2.3 Modeling Relationships between Variables

So far this chapter has assumed that the probabilistic variables in the model are independent or uncorrelated. The price of oil and the number of wins of a professional sports team are uncorrelated. Knowing the price of oil will give one no advantage in predicting one's favorite team's wins.

Variables can also be correlated. A positive correlation means that as the value of one variable increases, the value of the other variable also tends to go up. Among children, age and height are positively correlated. As children age, they get taller and if we know a child's age we can make a more accurate guess as to the child's height. Negative correlation means the values of the two variables move in opposite directions. As one increases, the other tends to decrease, and vice versa. A statistical association between two or more variables is also called a correlation or a statistical relationship. It is important to note that correlation does not imply causation. Although two variables may be correlated, one does not necessarily cause the behavior of the other.

For example, imagine a single variable, Variable A, that represents an expert's estimate (and his or her uncertainty) of the number of bank branches in Region A that will purchase index insurance policies next year. Let us assume sales in Region A are expected to range between 30 and 100, with the most likely number of sales being 50. We can model Variable A with a PERT distribution that takes into account the most likely value for A (50) as well as the minimum (30) and maximum values for A (100). The most likely value is the peak of the PERT distribution and the minimum and maximum are the tails. If we draw values for A from this distribution, most will be around the most likely value but we will occasionally draw values close to the tails of the distribution.

Now imagine that we also offer index insurance in another nearby region, Region B. We can add a second variable in our model, Variable B, representing the number of bank branches in Region B that will purchase index insurance policies next year. In this case, we can use a PERT distribution for B with parameter values appropriate to Region B. Let's assume sales in Region B are expected to range between 50 and 200, with the most likely number of sales being 100.

Given the shapes of both PERT distributions, values closer to the maximum for Variable A and Variable B are relatively rare, and it is even rarer that we will draw high values for both variables in the same scenario of a Monte Carlo simulation. This assumption holds true as long as the two variables are uncorrelated (independent of each other). If, however, Variables A and B are strongly positively correlated, then when Variable A is high, Variable B will also tend to be high, and vice versa. Another way to say this is that when A and B are correlated, if sales in Region A are high (close to the estimated maximum of 100), we also expect high sales in Region B (closer to the estimated maximum of 200).

Even though it is rare to see a high value for Variable A, when we do, we are also likely to see a high value for Variable B. The same is true for extremely low values. As can be seen, the positive correlation between the variables, in this case the number of bank branches that purchase the product, can increase the risk to the insurance company because it increases the likelihood of extreme values, both positive and negative.

Analysts commonly describe correlations between variables in a probabilistic model using **Spearman's rank order correlation coefficient**, which is a metric that can vary between −1 and +1 and indicates the strength and direction of the correlation. Values closer to +1 or −1 indicate stronger positive or negative correlation, respectively. Negative values indicate negative correlation (the variables move in opposite directions), and positive values indicate positive correlation (the variables move in the same direction). One characteristic of the rank order correlation coefficient is that it assumes that the relationship between the variables is linear and the same throughout the range of the variables (for example, no wedge-shaped correlations). An alternative and more flexible way to represent correlations in a probabilistic model is to use **copulas**, which are used in the models in this guide.

Risk Modeling for Appraising Named Peril Index Insurance Products
http://dx.doi.org/10.1596/978-1-4648-1048-0

10.2.3.1 *Understanding Copulas*

To understand copulas, it is helpful to first work through an example of randomly sampling from a probability distribution. This method uses percentiles. Remember that if a student takes an academic test in school and her score is on the 90th percentile, her score is greater than 90 percent of the scores from the rest of the students in her class and also lower than 10 percent of the scores from the rest of the students. If her actual test score was 42 out of 50, that means that 90 percent of her class received lower scores than 42, and 10 percent received higher scores.[22] For any percentile x between 0 and 1 (remember that 1 is equal to 100 percent), we can find the corresponding test score, the score that is greater than x percent of the scores. This is also true of any probability distribution. Any value in the distribution can be related to the percentile, which is the percentage of the distribution that the specific value exceeds.

How are percentiles used to sample from a probability distribution? First, a number between 0 and 1 is randomly selected to serve as a percentile. The random number is drawn from a uniform distribution, which means that all values from 0 to 1 are equally likely to be drawn.[23] Second, the value that corresponds to that percentile in the probability distribution of interest is selected. For example, we randomly select 0.8 as the percentile from the gamma distribution with alpha = 5 and beta = 1 in figure 10.14. The corresponding value for the 80th percentile of the gamma distribution is 6.72.

Now this same method of sampling probability distributions can be applied to the situation of correlated variables within a probabilistic model. Let us return to our earlier example of Variable A and Variable B, which represent sales of index insurance products in two different regions, and use the method above to demonstrate how the value of one affects the other. First, we will look at the situation in which they are completely independent (zero correlation). Assume that they also both have PERT distributions. To start, we randomly draw a percentile

Figure 10.14 Generating a Random Value from a Gamma (5, 1) Distribution

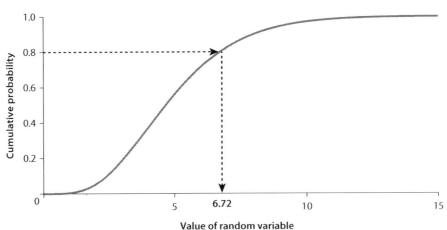

Risk Modeling for Appraising Named Peril Index Insurance Products
http://dx.doi.org/10.1596/978-1-4648-1048-0

from a uniform distribution bounded by 0 and 1, for example 0.8 (the 80th percentile), and select the corresponding value for A from its beta distribution, 66 in our example. Next, we draw a value for Variable B. Because Variables A and B are independent, the value we drew for Variable A has no impact on what we will draw for Variable B. For Variable B, we again randomly draw a percentile and select the corresponding value. We now have two random, independent values for A and B.

Second, let us take the situation in which Variable A and Variable B are strongly, positively correlated. In this case, if we randomly draw the 80th percentile for Variable A, we will also draw a large percentile for Variable B. In other words, the correlation between the variables restricts the range of possible percentiles for the second variable. The stronger the correlation between the variables, the narrower the range of possible percentiles for the second distribution becomes. The weaker the correlation between the variables, the wider the range of possible percentiles for the second distribution becomes.

In our example, Variable A and Variable B are strongly and positively correlated, and we have randomly drawn the 80th percentile (representing sales of 66) for Variable A. For Variable B, we will restrict the likely percentiles that can be picked, for example between the 75th and 85th percentiles. If A and B had been weakly correlated, the range of likely percentiles might stretch from the 65th to the 95th percentile.

A copula operates similarly to the example described above. It essentially restricts the percentile ranges of samples from the two distributions so that the resulting samples have the proper degree and direction of correlation. Correlations can exist not just between two variables (where there is one relationship) but also between multiple variables in a model. Fortunately, copulas have the ability to correlate many more than just two distributions. When multiple distributions are correlated, the numbers of relationships increase rapidly. For example, when there are three distributions, there are three relationships (between A and B, between A and C, and between B and C). When there are four distributions there are six relationships (A-B, A-C, A-D, B-C, B-D, C-D, or 3 + 2 + 1). When we are interested in the historical payout amounts for 10 nearby geographical areas, there will be a total of 45 relationships to consider (9 + 8 + ... + 1).[24]

Like probability distributions that can be fitted to data, copulas can also be fitted to data. When a copula is fitted to historical data, the strength of each of the relationships is based on the strength of the relationship that is displayed in the historical data. An advantage of fitting copulas to data is that it allows us to quickly and conveniently reflect relationships between variables based on historical patterns. A disadvantage is that, if relationships change over time, basing the correlations on historical data may not be valid.

The mathematics of both fitting and simulating copulas can be fairly complex, but fitting copulas and simulating from copulas is simple when using standard risk modeling software packages. For readers who are interested in learning more about the mathematics and applications of copulas, we recommend Cherubini, Luciano, and Vecchiato (2004; see the texts at the start of this chapter).

10.3 Key Outputs for Probabilistic Modeling

So far this chapter has looked at how and why we use probabilistic modeling as a tool to better understand index insurance products. It has also discussed how a Monte Carlo simulation based on a probability model results in an outcome that is itself also a probability distribution. The probabilistic models do not deliver only a simple number, but provide a more comprehensive and realistic view of the results. So what are some appropriate ways to summarize, interpret, and communicate the results from a probabilistic model?

10.3.1 General Metrics Used in Probabilistic Modeling

As an example, consider the histogram in figure 10.15 showing the hypothetical results from a model that estimates next year's total payout amount across 10 regions.

What does this histogram represent at the elementary level? Remember that when a Monte Carlo simulation model is run, at least 10,000 scenarios are generated that each represents a possible future outcome. Of course, we do not want to present a decision maker with 10,000 possible answers to the question "What will next year's claim amount be?" This is where the histogram comes in, because it provides a convenient overview of all the 10,000 possible outcomes of the Monte Carlo simulation. Many different metrics can help describe different aspects of this histogram, but we use four key metrics to interpret and summarize a histogram:

- The mean
- The spread, using percentiles such as the P5 and P95

Figure 10.15 Histogram Plot of Next Year's Total Payout Amount

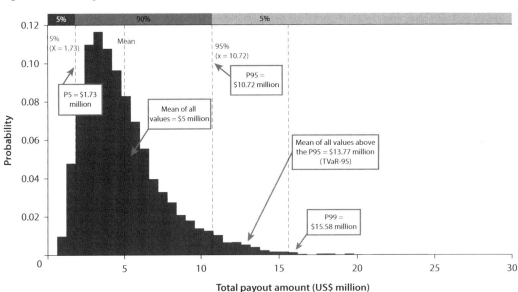

Note: P = percentile, for example, P5 = 5th percentile; TVaR = tail value at risk.

- The tail value at risk (TVaR)
- The probability of exceeding (or being less than) a certain threshold value

The mean of the outcome distribution (also called the expected value) tells us what the expected outcome is given all of the uncertainties and risks. It is the value one expects to get on average if an experiment is run many times. Going back to figure 10.15, the expected value of the total payout distribution is the average annual payout the insurer can expect to make over many years, which in this example is approximately US$5 million.

However, the mean outcome does not tell us anything about the uncertainty surrounding next year's payout amount. A common measure used to indicate the amount of uncertainty or randomness is the standard deviation.[25] A commonly used rule of thumb for understanding the standard deviation is that the mean plus or minus twice the standard deviation contains 95 percent of the range of outcomes. However, this rule only applies for normally (Gaussian) distributed variables. Therefore, this rule is not appropriate for the above distribution of annual payouts, nor for most resulting distributions that are used for index insurance.

Percentiles provide an easier way to describe the uncertainty around the expected outcome (that is, the spread of distributions). As discussed in section 10.2.3.1, any value in the distribution can be related to the percentile, which is the percentage of the distribution that the specific percentile value exceeds. Two common percentile values reported for Monte Carlo results are the P5 and the P95.[26] The P5 value will be on the left side of the distribution because the P5 value is greater than only 5 percent of values. The P95 is on the right side of the distribution because it is greater than 95 percent of the values. The P50 corresponds to the median, the value that separates the lower half of the values from the upper half.

Another way to think of percentiles is in terms of frequency. Again, the P95 value is greater than or equal to 95 percent of a distribution. This means that only 1 out of every 20 scenarios (5 percent of the values) resulted in values greater than the percentile amount. Figure 10.15 shows that the P95 for the payout amount distribution is $10.72 million, meaning that only 500 out of the 10,000 scenarios in the Monte Carlo model have claims that exceeded $10.72 million. We can also say that we expect to see values above the P95 only once every 20 years (500/10,000 = 1/20). Of course, such high payout amounts can occur multiple years in a row (each year having a 5 percent chance), but 1 in 20 years is the conventional way to describe and operationalize a probability of 5 percent. The P95 of a payout distribution is also known as the value at risk at the 95th percentile, or the VaR-95. A VaR value is always related to a certain time period, one year in our example. Therefore, when interpreting a VaR value it is important to always understand both the specific percentile it is reported at (P95 in our example) and the time period. VaR values for payout amounts with either higher percentiles or longer time periods will logically be higher.

The tail value at risk (TVaR), also called the **conditional value at risk** (CVaR), is another important and related metric for describing future possible payouts for index insurance. The TVaR is the expected value over a restricted portion of a distribution. In figure 10.15, the TVaR-95 is the expected value of the upper 5 percent of the distribution, that is, the mean of payouts that are greater than or equal to the P95 value (the VaR-95). In this example, the TVaR-95 is $13.77 million, which tells us that once in every 20 years we can expect an annual payout of this amount. As the histogram shows, payout values higher than $13.77 million are also possible. For example, the P99 of the payout distribution is $15.58 million, and logically the TVaR-99 will be even higher.

The fourth and final key metric this guide uses for summarizing probability distributions is the probability that a result is greater (or less) than a specific threshold. We can use any target value and identify the corresponding probability of the outcome being either lower or higher than this target value. For example, an insurer reviewing the payout distribution in figure 10.15 might want to know the probability that the payout amount in any given year will be greater than $15 million (which in this example is about 1.2 percent). Or the insurer might want to identify the probability of fund ruin, where the target value is the specific threshold of cash flows that, if not reached, will result in the ruin of the insurer's business.

Similar to finding the probability of an outcome greater than or less than a certain value, the probability of the result falling between two values can also be found by subtracting the percentile of the smaller value from the percentile of the larger. A classic application of this approach is to subtract the P2.5 from the P97.5 to get the values that bound the middle 95 percent of the distribution. This method is in essence the concept used to calculate 95 percent confidence intervals.

10.3.2 Outputs Used in Index Insurance Applications

So far this chapter has discussed four key metrics for summarizing an outcome from a probabilistic analysis. This section discusses five output metrics that are specifically used in financial and insurance applications:

- Probability of negative profits
- Required capital
- Economic value added (EVA)
- Sharpe ratio
- Return period

These output metrics are used in the example models explained in chapters 11 through 15 of this guide.

First, the **probability of negative profits** represents the probability that the insurer will experience a loss. Typically, the probability of a loss per week is different from the probability of a loss per year, so this metric also needs to be defined over a certain period. For the models in this guide, the probability is defined per year, but the probability can also be calculated over a multiple-year period.

In a Monte Carlo simulation model, the probability of a negative profit is calculated by simulating the annual profits and determining in what percentage of the scenarios the profits are negative. For example, if, after running 10,000 scenarios, 1,894 scenarios resulted in losses and the remainder in profit, the annual probability of a negative profit is estimated to be about 19 percent.

Second, **required capital** indicates how much capital must be held by the insurer to be confident (within a certain confidence level, for example, 95 percent) that the payouts and expenses can all be paid from the premium income and the required capital. For example, if the required capital at a 95 percent confidence level is $100,000, then in 19 out of 20 years (95 percent) the insurer will have more than sufficient capital to cover all payouts from premium income and the $100,000 in required capital. However, in 1 out of 20 years, the insurer will have to pay out all of its capital to cover the payouts. In other words, the required capital is a TVaR value (often based on the 95th percentile or higher) for how much capital the insurer needs to pay for claims within a certain period.

Two more index insurance–related outputs of a Monte Carlo simulation are discussed below: economic value added (EVA) and the Sharpe ratio. Both have required capital as one of their inputs. Because required capital is determined using a Monte Carlo simulation, two separate and sequential Monte Carlo simulations must be run to calculate these secondary metrics. The initial simulation estimates the required capital amount, given the variability in annual payouts by the insurer. In the example models, the output for this first Monte Carlo simulation is recorded as the "first simulation required capital." The next simulation calculates the secondary metrics using the value for "first simulation required capital." Wherever we use required capital to calculate a secondary metric in the models in this guide we indicate that two separate and sequential Monte Carlo simulations need to be performed.

Third, EVA is an estimate of the profits that the insurer can expect from the index insurance product in excess of the required rate of return. It is typically expressed as a percentage of the required capital, as follows:

$$\text{EVA} = (\text{Profits} - \text{Cost of capital})/\text{Required capital};$$

or more precisely,

$$\text{EVA} = (\text{Net premium income} - \text{Payout amounts} - \text{Required capital} \\ \times \text{Required return on capital})/\text{Required capital}.$$

Because the EVA depends on the payout amounts, which can vary greatly from year to year, the EVA can also vary greatly. Therefore, it is useful to report not only the expected EVA, but also the P5 and P95 of the EVA.

Fourth, the **Sharpe ratio**, also called the reward-to-variability ratio, can be used to gain an understanding of the performance of an investment by adjusting for

Risk Modeling for Appraising Named Peril Index Insurance Products
http://dx.doi.org/10.1596/978-1-4648-1048-0

its risks. More precisely, the Sharpe ratio is the excess in return per unit of risk, and is typically defined as follows:

Sharpe ratio = (Expected return on capital − Risk-free rate)/
Standard deviation of the return on capital.

Because the Sharpe ratio adjusts (that is, divides) the excess return (the return on the required capital that the insurer sets aside to cover potential payouts) by the standard deviation of the return on capital, investments with different risk profiles can be compared to understand which provides more excess return per unit of risk.

Fifth, the return period provides an indication of how frequently certain events can be expected to occur. It represents the average period until the next event happens over the long term. For example, the return period for an index insurance product payout of at least 50 percent of the insured amount might be 14.6 years. In this case, we expect that over the long term the product will pay out at least 50 percent once every 14.6 years. Of course, because this is an average metric, the product may pay out at least 50 percent more often, or there may be long periods in which it does not pay out at all because of year-to-year variability.

10.4 A Reminder on How to Use the Models in This Guide

It is important to keep in mind that probabilistic and deterministic model building is not a simple, automatic process. Every model, by definition, is a simplification of reality with assumptions, strengths, weaknesses, and limitations. Different individuals may end up with different models for the same problem because of differences in judgment, experience, and preferences.

This chapter provides some guidelines for choosing probability distributions for a given quantity. For the examples within this guide, we recommend using a beta distribution for representing and modeling payout ratios. However, the beta distribution cannot always be assumed to be the most appropriate distribution for this variable. When modeling payout ratios (which vary between 0 and 1), a Poisson distribution should never be used because a Poisson generates only discrete values such as 0, 1, 2, and so forth. However, depending on the data, a beta, gamma, or lognormal distribution could be appropriate.[27] Examining GOF statistics can help an analyst decide, but the type of variable, the skewness, bounding, and any special purpose of the distribution should also be considered in determining which distribution best represents the variable.

Sometimes models can be "wrong" because they violate basic principles of probability modeling (for example, using distributions in which the left tails extend below zero to simulate potential payouts), but there can often be several ways to build a correct model. Nevertheless, building accurate and useful Monte Carlo simulation models is not solely an "art." Building models requires expertise and knowledge of the different building blocks.

Risk Modeling for Appraising Named Peril Index Insurance Products
http://dx.doi.org/10.1596/978-1-4648-1048-0

The intent of this guide is to make you, the reader, an informed user of the probabilistic framework. Our models are not the ultimate, definitive models for index insurance. Rather than encouraging you to take up our models, add your data, and apply them blindly, we hope to help you develop the general skills necessary for developing, critiquing, and interpreting probabilistic models for index insurance modeling. You may very well need to adapt, rebuild, or enhance our models to suit your unique circumstances, data, and decision questions.

Finally, we want to again stress that clear and transparent communication of the assumptions behind any model you use or build is critical. Any simulation model you use to evaluate an index insurance product will have inherent assumptions, and you must clearly communicate to all relevant stakeholders these underlying hypotheses, assumptions, and potential limitations. Without this communication and understanding, stakeholders may not obtain the potential benefits (i.e., more informed decisions) of a probabilistic analysis of the index insurance product.

Notes

1. To be precise, a quantitative risk analysis does not have to be probabilistic, although many quantitative risk analyses use probabilistic modeling.

2. We define the term "on average," which is also referred to as "the mean," later in this chapter, but the reader can think of it as the average number of dots that one would get if one rolled a dice many times.

3. As discussed in section 10.3, numerous quantitative metrics can be used to describe the amount of uncertainty we may have about what could happen in the future.

4. The distribution for a single one of these events or trials is a Bernoulli distribution (see section 10.2.1.2.1).

5. See the references at the start of this chapter for more complete lists of probability distributions.

6. See section 10.2.1.2.1 for more information on the Bernoulli distribution.

7. Depending on the country, income distributions tend to be more or less skewed. The degree to which the income distribution is skewed is often summarized with a statistic called the Gini coefficient, which measures inequality. See http://data.worldbank.org/indicator/SI.POV.GINI.

8. The name PERT is an acronym for project evaluation and review techniques, a project management system for which the PERT distribution was developed to include uncertainty in project timelines. The PERT distribution is discussed in more detail later in this chapter.

9. This actually is only the case for discrete distributions and not for continuous distributions, as seen in the next section.

10. If a theoretically discrete variable takes extremely large values, we can treat it as continuous. For example, people disagree as to whether money is continuous or discrete, but risk models generally deal with very large values of money as continuous. Money at very high values behaves as if it were a continuous variable because the discrete steps (cents) are insignificantly small compared with the total values that

might be modeled. If millions of dollars are modeled, the values appear continuous. When values closer to one dollar are modeled, the values appear discrete.

11. Note that "success" does not always mean a "good" outcome. It just means the outcome that we are focusing on for our model. If we want to model the failure of a certain kind of factory equipment, our success, the thing we are modeling, may be the failure of the machine.

12. Some texts call each Monte Carlo scenario or iteration a trial, which can be confusing when you discuss Bernoulli distribution trials. This guide uses the term "scenario" for Monte Carlo iterations.

13. Remember, "success" is the occurrence of the outcome we are analyzing, in this case an insurer basis risk event. A basis risk event is not a positive outcome, but it is the one we are investigating.

14. There is only one input parameter in a Poisson distribution, which is the multiplication of lambda and t. In other words, the single rate input, lambda, can be normalized to any t exposure unit. If, for example, the lambda rate is 2 accidents per month, this rate can be normalized to 24 accidents per year, assuming that all calendar months have a rate of accidents of 2 per month.

15. When the beta distribution represents a probability, and the beta distribution is a parameter in another distribution (for example, the probability is used in a Bernoulli distribution), we call the fact that the probability itself is a distribution "parameter uncertainty." See section 10.2.2.2.

16. In fact, this research and the mathematics behind the beta distribution are part of Bayesian statistics. Bayesian statistics is a large and important field of statistics that is worth studying further but falls outside the scope of this guide.

17. Methods to elicit expert opinion are beyond the scope of this guide, but O'Hagan et al. (2006) and EFSA Guidance (2014) provide a thorough guide to expert elicitation methods. Available from http://eu.wiley.com/WileyCDA/WileyTitle/productCd-0470029994.html and http://www.efsa.europa.eu/en/efsajournal/pub/3734, respectively.

18. This process of iterative fitting is not necessary for a number of distributions for which maximum likelihood estimations (MLEs) are available, such as the gamma, normal, Poisson, binomial, and exponential distributions. However, conceptually we can still think of distribution fitting this way for these distributions.

19. Information criteria are commonly used in statistics and are based on the MLE of each of the distributions and also take into account the number of parameters within each distribution, to avoid overfitting the data to a distribution with many parameters.

20. For more information about Bayesian analysis and priors, see Gelman (2013).

21. Monte Carlo models that include parameter uncertainty are typically slower because during each iteration, the parameter values need to be reestimated, which commonly takes considerable computing power.

22. Of course, it could be that some students had a score of exactly 42. In situations in which percentiles describe continuous variables, however, this is not an issue because with continuous distributions the probability of an outcome of exactly 42 is zero.

23. A uniform distribution is a probability distribution in which all the values within its range have equal probability.

24. Often such multi-to-multi variable relationships are summarized in a correlation matrix that describes the correlations between all variables.

25. "Variance" is also often used, which is the standard deviation squared.

26. The P2.5 and P97.5 are also common, since the range of values between both percentiles provides the 95 percent confidence level.

27. The lognormal is another commonly used continuous distribution.

Bibliography

Bolker, B. M. 2008. *Ecological Models and Data in R*. Princeton, NJ: Princeton University Press. http://ms.mcmaster.ca/~bolker/emdbook/.

Brehm, P. J. 2007. *Enterprise Risk Analysis for Property & Liability Insurance Companies: A Practical Guide to Standard Models and Emerging Solutions*. New York: Guy Carpenter.

Cherubini, U., E. Luciano, and W. Vecchiato. 2004. *Copula Methods in Finance*. Hoboken, NJ: John Wiley & Sons.

EFSA (European Food Safety Authority). 2014. "Guidance on Expert Knowledge Elicitation in Food and Feed Safety Risk Assessment." *EFSA Journal* 12 (6): 3734.

Embrechts, P., F. Lindskog, and A. McNeil. 2003. "Modelling Dependence with Copulas and Applications to Risk Management." In *Handbook of Heavy Tailed Distributions in Finance*, edited by S. T. Rachev, 329–84. Amsterdam: Elsevier.

Forbes, C., and M. Evans. 2010. *Statistical Distributions*. 4th ed. Hoboken, NJ: Wiley. http://www.wiley.com/WileyCDA/WileyTitle/productCd-0470390638.html.

Gelman, A. 2013. *Bayesian Data Analysis*. 3rd ed. Boca Raton, FL: Chapman & Hall/CRC. http://www.stat.columbia.edu/~gelman/book/.

Grossi, P., H. Kunreuther, and C. C. Patel. 2005. *Catastrophe Modeling: A New Approach to Managing Risk*. New York: Springer Science Business Media.

Hertz, D. B. 1964. "Risk Analysis in Capital Investment." *Harvard Business Review*. 1964: 95–106.

Jewson, S., and A. Brix. 2005. *Weather Derivative Valuation: The Meteorological, Statistical, Financial, and Mathematical Foundations*. Cambridge: Cambridge University Press.

Law, A. M., and W. D. Kelton. 2006. *Simulation Modeling and Analysis*. 4th ed. New York: McGraw-Hill.

Lehman, D. E., H. Groenendaal, and G. Nolder. 2012. *Practical Spreadsheet Risk Modeling for Management*. Boca Raton, FL: Chapman & Hall/CRC.

ModelAssist. A Free and Comprehensive Quantitative Risk Analysis Training and Reference Software. http://www.epixanalytics.com/ModelAssist.html.

O'Hagan, A., C. E. Buck, A. Daneshkhah, J. R. Eiser, P. H. Garthwaite, D. J. Jenkinson, J. E. Oakley, and T. Rakow. 2006. *Uncertain Judgements: Eliciting Experts' Probabilities*. Hoboken, NJ: John Wiley & Sons.

Ragsdale, C. T. 2001. *Spreadsheet Modeling and Decision Analysis: A Practical Introduction to Management Science*. Cincinnati, OH: Southwestern College.

Tang, A., and E. A. Valdez. 2009. "Economic Capital and the Aggregation of Risks Using Copulas." University of New South Wales, Sydney, Australia.

Yan, J. 2006. "Multivariate Modeling with Copulas and Engineering Applications." In *Springer Handbook of Engineering Statistics*, edited by H. Pham, 973–90. London: Springer-Verlag.

CHAPTER 11

Evaluating the Base Index

11.1 Background and Objectives

Chapter 4 explained the data required for the key managerial questions for Base Index product design and evaluation during the pilot phase of launching an index insurance business line. It described eight steps in the analysis and decision-making process and provided interpretations of each of the decision metrics (figure 4.5).

The critical issue to remember about the Base Index is that because it provides such a high level of coverage, it is also very expensive and many policyholders will request a lower price—and lower coverage—product. However, it is extremely important that the insurer always produce a Base Index to explain to the policyholder the difference between complete coverage—that provided by the Base Index—and the coverage provided by other product options. Without this explicit comparison, policyholders often fall into the trap of expecting complete coverage even when they have purchased a lower coverage, less expensive product.

This chapter provides a step-by-step guide to using the probabilistic models that produce the decision metrics discussed in chapter 4 for evaluating the Base Index for product design basis risk. Using the Base Index's historical payout and historical inventory damage ratios for selected geographical areas within a market, the model simulates four key scenario parameters: payout ratios (Steps 14–18), inventory damage ratios (Steps 19–23), insured party basis risk ratios (Steps 24–29), and insurer basis risk ratios (Steps 30–35).

The model then uses these four groups of parameters to calculate key basis risk decision metrics, including return periods, return period ratios, the probability of no basis risk event occurring, and the magnitude of the expected basis risk events (Steps 36–44). These metrics allow the insurer to determine whether a particular Base Index needs improvement or if index insurance is not an appropriate risk management instrument for the prospective client.

At the end of this chapter, section 11.5 provides a brief discussion of how retrospective analysis can also be used to evaluate the Base Index for product design basis risk.

Table 11.1 Summary of Model Components for Evaluating the Base Index

Model component	Section	Excel sheet label	Steps	Description
Model inputs	11.2	MI_11.2_MODEL INPUTS	Steps 1–7	User-defined assumptions, relevant portfolio information, Base Index historical payout ratios, and historical inventory damage ratios are entered for all areas.
Model computations	11.3.1	MC_11.3.1&2_ DERIVED_INPUTS	Steps 8–10	Calculation of historical insured party basis risk ratios for each area. These **derived inputs** are used in Steps 24–29.
	11.3.2	MC_11.3.1&2_ DERIVED_INPUTS	Steps 11–13	Calculation of historical insurer basis risk ratios for each area. These derived inputs are used in Steps 30–35.
	11.3.3	MC_11.3.3_BI_ SCENARIOS	Steps 14–18	Simulation of scenario payout ratios for each area
	11.3.4	MC_11.3.4_DR_ SCENARIOS	Steps 19–23	Simulation of scenario inventory damage ratios for each area
	11.3.5	MC_11.3.5_INSD PARTY BASIS RISK	Steps 24–29	Simulation of scenario insured party basis risk amounts
	11.3.6	MC_11.3.6_INSR BASIS RISK	Steps 30–35	Simulation of scenario insurer basis risk amounts
	11.3.7	MC_11.3.7_DECISION METRICS	Steps 36–44	Calculation of product evaluation decision metrics
Model output	11.4	MO_11.4_MODEL OUTPUTS	None	Summary of product evaluation decision metrics

Table 11.1 provides a summary of the model components along with a guide to the sections in this chapter and the worksheet names in the accompanying Excel files.

This chapter uses the same case example of a product design and evaluation process as in part 1. Wherever a box is labeled "case example," screen shots of the model inputs, computations, or outputs for the case example are provided.

11.2 Model Inputs

For the Base Index product evaluation, the analyst starts by specifying the model inputs agreed upon with the insurance manager for the Base Index product evaluation (table 11.2).

Table 11.2 Model Inputs

Model component	Section	Excel sheet label	Steps	Description
Model inputs	11.2	MI_11.2_MODEL INPUTS	Steps 1–7	User defined assumptions, relevant portfolio information, Base Index historical payout ratios, and historical inventory damage ratios are entered for all areas.

11.2.1 Significant Payout and Damage Levels (Step 1)

The magnitude of the payout or damage that is being considered is among the user-defined assumptions used by the model. For the case example, the analyst specifies 10 percent inventory damage as a mild loss, 30 percent as a mild-to-medium loss, 50 percent as a medium loss, and 70 percent as a severe loss (case example box 11CB.1).

Case Example Box 11CB.1 Inputs—Step 1

STEP 1 : DEFINE SIGNIFICANT PAYOUT/DAMAGE LEVELS (%)

MILD IMPACT	10%
MILD-MEDIUM IMPACT	30%
MEDIUM IMPACT	50%
SEVERE IMPACT	70%

11.2.2 Prediction Interval (Step 2)

In Step 2, the analyst specifies the prediction interval based on the insurer's desired level of accuracy. The upper limit of the interval is used in calculating capital requirements. For example, if the insurer wants to hold capital at 99 percent tail value at risk (TVaR) (the payout amount for a 1-in-100 year event), the upper limit should be set at 99 percent. In the case example, the insurance manager and the analyst specify the upper limit as 95 percent (case example box 11CB.2). The prediction interval between the 5th (low) and 95th percentile is often called the 90 percent prediction interval.

Case Example Box 11CB.2 Inputs—Step 2

STEP 2 : INDICATE PREDICTION INTERVAL (%)

LOWER	5%
UPPER	95%

11.2.3 Total Sum Insured per Area (Step 3)

The total sum insured per area (case example box 11CB.3) will be used in simulating insured party and insurer basis risk amounts (during Steps 24–35).

Case Example Box 11CB.3 Inputs—Step 3

STEP 3 : ENTER TOTAL SUM INSURED PER AREA ($)

AREA A	AREA B	AREA C	AREA D	AREA E	AREA F	AREA G	AREA H	AREA I	AREA J
140,160	282,975	1,200,000	425,000	2,252,250	282,000	992,040	1,200,325	425,150	800,100

11.2.4 Historical Payout Ratios (Step 4)

Historical payout ratios for the Base Index (case example box 11CB.4) will be used for determining scenario payout ratios (Steps 14–18), basis risk amounts (Steps 24–35), and return periods (Steps 36–44).

Case Example Box 11CB.4 Inputs—Step 4

STEP 4 : ENTER BASE INDEX HISTORICAL PAYOUT RATIOS (%)

YEAR	AREA A	AREA B	AREA C	AREA D	AREA E	AREA F	AREA G	AREA H	AREA I	AREA J
1984	0.0%	0.0%	0.0%	0.0%	44.1%	0.0%	0.0%	0.0%	22.6%	90.4%
1985	0.0%	0.0%	0.0%	0.0%	0.0%	0.0%	0.0%	0.0%	0.0%	0.0%
1986	0.0%	0.0%	22.5%	0.0%	0.0%	0.0%	0.0%	0.0%	0.0%	7.5%
1987	0.0%	0.0%	0.0%	0.0%	22.5%	31.2%	0.0%	0.0%	0.0%	0.0%
1988	0.0%	0.0%	0.0%	47.5%	0.0%	0.0%	0.0%	0.0%	0.0%	0.0%
1989	0.0%	15.0%	0.0%	0.0%	7.5%	0.0%	0.0%	0.0%	0.0%	0.0%
1990	0.0%	0.0%	7.5%	100.0%	66.6%	0.0%	0.0%	0.0%	0.0%	2.5%
1991	0.0%	0.0%	0.0%	0.0%	0.0%	0.0%	0.0%	0.0%	0.0%	42.5%
1992	0.0%	0.0%	0.0%	50.0%	0.0%	0.0%	0.0%	0.0%	0.0%	86.0%
1993	0.0%	0.0%	0.0%	0.0%	0.0%	0.0%	0.0%	0.0%	0.0%	44.4%
1994	0.0%	0.0%	0.0%	0.0%	0.0%	0.0%	0.0%	0.0%	5.0%	96.0%
1995	0.0%	0.0%	0.0%	0.0%	0.0%	0.0%	0.0%	0.0%	0.0%	0.0%
1996	79.2%	0.0%	0.0%	0.0%	0.0%	5.8%	0.0%	0.0%	0.0%	27.5%
1997	0.0%	20.0%	0.0%	0.0%	0.0%	15.0%	0.0%	65.4%	0.0%	0.0%
1998	0.0%	0.0%	0.0%	0.0%	0.0%	0.0%	30.0%	0.0%	63.2%	0.0%
1999	0.0%	0.0%	0.0%	0.0%	2.5%	17.5%	2.5%	86.2%	0.0%	39.0%
2000	0.0%	0.0%	0.0%	0.0%	0.0%	0.0%	53.4%	0.0%	0.0%	0.0%
2001	0.0%	0.0%	0.0%	0.0%	0.0%	0.0%	0.0%	0.0%	0.0%	0.0%
2002	0.0%	0.0%	5.0%	0.0%	0.0%	0.0%	0.0%	0.0%	0.0%	0.0%
2003	0.0%	0.0%	0.0%	0.0%	0.0%	0.0%	0.0%	0.0%	29.0%	60.0%
2004	0.0%	0.0%	0.0%	19.2%	0.0%	0.0%	0.0%	0.0%	0.0%	0.0%
2005	0.0%	0.0%	0.0%	0.0%	0.0%	0.0%	0.0%	0.0%	0.0%	0.0%
2006	0.0%	0.0%	0.0%	2.5%	0.0%	0.0%	0.0%	0.0%	0.0%	39.4%
2007	0.0%	0.0%	0.0%	40.4%	0.0%	0.0%	0.0%	0.0%	0.0%	0.0%
2008	0.0%	0.0%	0.0%	0.0%	0.0%	0.0%	0.0%	0.0%	0.0%	17.5%
2009	0.0%	2.5%	0.0%	0.0%	0.0%	0.0%	0.0%	0.0%	32.8%	64.0%
2010	0.0%	0.0%	0.0%	0.0%	0.0%	0.0%	25.0%	61.2%	0.0%	0.0%
2011	2.5%	7.5%	0.0%	16.6%	0.0%	0.0%	0.0%	0.0%	0.0%	0.0%
2012	0.0%	5.0%	0.0%	0.0%	0.0%	2.5%	0.0%	0.0%	0.0%	0.0%
2013	0.0%	0.0%	0.0%	0.0%	9.0%	0.0%	0.0%	45.2%	0.0%	0.0%

11.2.5 Independent Historical Inventory Damage Data (Step 5)

Chapter 4 discussed the process for collecting independent historical inventory damage data and completing a qualitative classification of past damages for product design and evaluation. Based on data from multiple sources, the product design team rates the level of crop damage caused by the named peril—in each year for each geographical area—from 1 to 5, where 5 is the highest damages from drought and 1 represents mild damages from drought (case example box 11CB.5). In years with a rating of 1, farmers experienced up to a 20 percent loss in yields. In years with a rating of 2 the yield loss was 21 to 40 percent. In years with a rating of 3 the loss was 41 to 60 percent, and so on.

Case Example Box 11CB.5 Inputs—Step 5

STEP 5 : ENTER INDEPENDENT HISTORICAL INVENTORY DAMAGE CLASSIFICATIONS

YEAR	AREA A	AREA B	AREA C	AREA D	AREA E	AREA F	AREA G	AREA H	AREA I	AREA J
1984					3				3	5
1985							1			
1986		2	2							
1987					2	3		2		1
1988				3						
1989		2							1	
1990			2	5	5		1			
1991						1				4
1992				3				1		5
1993										3
1994							1		1	5
1995										
1996	5									
1997				1	1	1		3	1	
1998							2		3	
1999							2	5		3
2000							3	2		
2001										
2002			2			1				
2003		1							2	3
2004				2			1			
2005										
2006				2	1					2
2007				2						
2008										
2009				1		1			3	4
2010								5		
2011	2									
2012										
2013								3	1	

11.2.6 Historical Inventory Damage Ratios (Step 6)

The independent historical inventory damage data classifications are provided as categorical data, as shown in Step 5. The analyst then converts them into damage percentages using the midpoints of the damage ranges for each category (case example box 11CB.6). For example, a damage classification of 1 corresponds to the damage ratio 10 percent (midpoint between 0 and 20 percent), a damage classification of 2 corresponds to the damage ratio 30 percent (midpoint between 21 and 40 percent), and so on.

Note that in cases in which actual historical inventory damage ratios are available, the analyst should of course use these values for Step 6.

Later sections in this chapter provide estimates for the magnitude of insurer and insured party basis risk for the insurer to use in evaluating the quality of the Base Index.

Risk Modeling for Appraising Named Peril Index Insurance Products
http://dx.doi.org/10.1596/978-1-4648-1048-0

Case Example Box 11CB.6 Inputs—Step 6

STEP 6 : ENTER HISTORICAL INVENTORY DAMAGE RATIOS (%)

YEAR	AREA A	AREA B	AREA C	AREA D	AREA E	AREA F	AREA G	AREA H	AREA I	AREA J
1984	0.0%	0.0%	0.0%	0.0%	50.0%	0.0%	0.0%	0.0%	50.0%	90.0%
1985	0.0%	0.0%	0.0%	0.0%	0.0%	0.0%	10.0%	0.0%	0.0%	0.0%
1986	0.0%	30.0%	30.0%	0.0%	0.0%	0.0%	0.0%	0.0%	0.0%	0.0%
1987	0.0%	0.0%	0.0%	0.0%	30.0%	50.0%	0.0%	30.0%	0.0%	10.0%
1988	0.0%	0.0%	0.0%	50.0%	0.0%	0.0%	0.0%	0.0%	0.0%	0.0%
1989	0.0%	30.0%	0.0%	0.0%	0.0%	0.0%	0.0%	0.0%	10.0%	0.0%
1990	0.0%	0.0%	30.0%	90.0%	90.0%	0.0%	10.0%	0.0%	0.0%	0.0%
1991	0.0%	0.0%	0.0%	0.0%	0.0%	10.0%	0.0%	0.0%	0.0%	70.0%
1992	0.0%	0.0%	0.0%	50.0%	0.0%	0.0%	0.0%	10.0%	0.0%	90.0%
1993	0.0%	0.0%	0.0%	0.0%	0.0%	0.0%	0.0%	0.0%	0.0%	50.0%
1994	0.0%	0.0%	0.0%	0.0%	0.0%	0.0%	10.0%	0.0%	10.0%	90.0%
1995	0.0%	0.0%	0.0%	0.0%	0.0%	0.0%	0.0%	0.0%	0.0%	0.0%
1996	90.0%	0.0%	0.0%	0.0%	0.0%	0.0%	0.0%	0.0%	0.0%	0.0%
1997	0.0%	0.0%	0.0%	10.0%	10.0%	10.0%	0.0%	50.0%	10.0%	0.0%
1998	0.0%	0.0%	0.0%	0.0%	0.0%	0.0%	30.0%	0.0%	50.0%	0.0%
1999	0.0%	0.0%	0.0%	0.0%	0.0%	0.0%	30.0%	90.0%	0.0%	50.0%
2000	0.0%	0.0%	0.0%	0.0%	0.0%	0.0%	50.0%	30.0%	0.0%	0.0%
2001	0.0%	0.0%	0.0%	0.0%	0.0%	0.0%	0.0%	0.0%	0.0%	0.0%
2002	0.0%	0.0%	30.0%	0.0%	0.0%	10.0%	0.0%	0.0%	0.0%	0.0%
2003	0.0%	10.0%	0.0%	0.0%	0.0%	0.0%	0.0%	0.0%	30.0%	50.0%
2004	0.0%	0.0%	0.0%	30.0%	0.0%	0.0%	10.0%	0.0%	0.0%	0.0%
2005	0.0%	0.0%	0.0%	0.0%	0.0%	0.0%	0.0%	0.0%	0.0%	0.0%
2006	0.0%	0.0%	0.0%	30.0%	10.0%	0.0%	0.0%	0.0%	0.0%	30.0%
2007	0.0%	0.0%	0.0%	30.0%	0.0%	0.0%	0.0%	0.0%	0.0%	0.0%
2008	0.0%	0.0%	0.0%	0.0%	0.0%	0.0%	0.0%	0.0%	0.0%	0.0%
2009	0.0%	0.0%	0.0%	10.0%	0.0%	10.0%	0.0%	0.0%	50.0%	70.0%
2010	0.0%	0.0%	0.0%	0.0%	0.0%	0.0%	0.0%	90.0%	0.0%	0.0%
2011	30.0%	0.0%	0.0%	0.0%	0.0%	0.0%	0.0%	0.0%	0.0%	0.0%
2012	0.0%	0.0%	0.0%	0.0%	0.0%	0.0%	0.0%	0.0%	0.0%	0.0%
2013	0.0%	0.0%	0.0%	0.0%	0.0%	0.0%	0.0%	50.0%	10.0%	0.0%

Let's look at Area B from the case example. We can see from Step 6 that this area had three years with inventory damage events (30 percent in 1986, 30 percent in 1989, and 10 percent in 2003). But we know that the Base Index triggered five payouts (case example box 11CB.4). The Base Index triggered at least two unnecessary payouts.

A closer look shows that of the five years in which payouts were triggered, only one (1989) corresponds to a year in which inventory damage occurred. So, the index actually triggered four unnecessary payouts from the insurer to the insured party, all of which are examples of insurer basis risk.

That still leaves two years in which inventory damage occurred but no payout would have been triggered (1986 and 2003). In these cases, the insured party would have experienced inventory damage but received no payout, both examples of insured party basis risk.

11.2.7 Nonzero Historical Payout and Inventory Damage Ratios (Step 7)

In this step the analyst manually records all the nonzero values for the historical payout ratios and historical inventory damage ratios from Steps 4 to 6 (case example box 11CB.7). These inputs will be used in the simulation of payout ratios (Steps 14–18) and inventory damage ratios (Steps 19–23).

Case Example Box 11CB.7 Inputs—Step 7

STEP 7 : MANUALLY RECORD ALL NON-ZERO HISTORICAL PAYOUT RATIOS AND INVENTORY DAMAGE RATIOS (%)

HISTORICAL PAYOUT RATIOS	HISTORICAL INVENTORY DAMAGE RATIOS
79.2%	90.0%
2.5%	30.0%
15.0%	30.0%
20.0%	30.0%
2.5%	50.0%
7.5%	30.0%
5.0%	30.0%
22.5%	30.0%
7.5%	50.0%
5.0%	90.0%
47.5%	50.0%
100.0%	10.0%
50.0%	30.0%
19.2%	10.0%
2.5%	50.0%
40.4%	30.0%
16.6%	90.0%
44.1%	10.0%
22.5%	10.0%
7.5%	50.0%
66.6%	10.0%
2.5%	10.0%
9.0%	10.0%
31.2%	10.0%
5.8%	10.0%
15.0%	10.0%
17.5%	10.0%
2.5%	30.0%
30.0%	70.0%
2.5%	10.0%
53.4%	30.0%
25.0%	10.0%
65.4%	50.0%
86.2%	90.0%
61.2%	90.0%
45.2%	50.0%
22.6%	50.0%
63.2%	10.0%
5.0%	10.0%
29.0%	70.0%
32.8%	50.0%
90.4%	30.0%
7.5%	50.0%
2.5%	10.0%
42.5%	50.0%
86.0%	70.0%
44.4%	90.0%
96.0%	10.0%
27.5%	90.0%
39.0%	50.0%
60.0%	90.0%
39.4%	50.0%
17.5%	
64.0%	

11.3 Model Computations

The model completes seven sequential sets of computations for the Base Index product evaluation, starting with calculating the derived inputs—historical basis risk ratios (Steps 8–13)—then simulating four key scenario parameters (Steps 14–35), and finally determining the product evaluation decision metrics (Steps 36–44) (table 11.3).

Risk Modeling for Appraising Named Peril Index Insurance Products
http://dx.doi.org/10.1596/978-1-4648-1048-0

Table 11.3 Model Computations

Model component	Section	Excel sheet label	Steps	Description
Model computations	11.3.1	MC_11.3.1&2_ DERIVED INPUTS	Steps 8–10	Calculation of historical insured party basis risk ratios for each area. These derived inputs are used in section 11.3.5 (Steps 24–29).
	11.3.2	MC_11.3.1&2_ DERIVED INPUTS	Steps 11–13	Calculation of historical insurer basis risk ratios for each area. These derived inputs are used in section 11.3.6 (Steps 30–35).
	11.3.3	MC_11.3.3_BI_ SCENARIOS	Steps 14–18	Simulation of scenario payouts for each area
	11.3.4	MC_11.3.4_DR_ SCENARIOS	Steps 19–23	Simulation of scenario inventory damage ratios for each area
	11.3.5	MC_11.3.5_INSD PARTY BASIS RISK	Steps 24–29	Simulation of scenario insured party basis risk amounts
	11.3.6	MC_11.3.6_INSR BASIS RISK	Steps 30–35	Simulation of scenario insurer basis risk amounts
	11.3.7	MC_11.3.7_DECISION METRICS	Steps 36–44	Calculation of product evaluation decision metrics

11.3.1 Calculation of Historical Insured Party Basis Risk Ratios (Steps 8–10)

Table 11.4 Model Computations

Model component	Section	Excel sheet label	Steps	Description
Model Computations	11.3.1	MC_11.3.1&2_ DERIVED INPUTS	Steps 8–10	Calculation of historical insured party basis risk ratios for each area. These derived inputs are used in section 11.3.5 (Steps 24–29).

11.3.1.1 Overview

Insured party basis risk describes the scenario in which the payout amount is less than the farmer's actual losses caused by the named peril. In this case the farmer experiences an economic loss from the named peril but is not adequately compensated by the claim payout.

The insured party basis risk ratio (table 11.4) for the Base Index is calculated as follows (case example box 11CB.8):

Historical insured party = Max (0, [Historical inventory − Historical payout ratio]).
basis risk ratio   damage ratio
                                         Step 6   Step 4

Any time that the historical payout ratio is larger than the historical inventory damage ratio, the insured party basis risk is zero. In this situation, insurer basis risk will be greater than zero because the insurer will have paid out more than the actual losses (see section 11.3.2).

Risk Modeling for Appraising Named Peril Index Insurance Products
http://dx.doi.org/10.1596/978-1-4648-1048-0

11.3.1.2 Implementation in Excel (MC_11.3.1&.2_Derived Inputs)

Case Example Box 11CB.8 Computations—Step 8

STEP 8 : CALCULATE HISTORICAL INSURED PARTY BASIS RISK RATIOS (%)

YEAR	AREA A	AREA B	AREA C	AREA D	AREA E	AREA F	AREA G	AREA H	AREA I	AREA J
1984	0.0%	0.0%	0.0%	0.0%	5.9%	0.0%	0.0%	0.0%	27.4%	0.0%
1985	0.0%	0.0%	0.0%	0.0%	0.0%	0.0%	10.0%	0.0%	0.0%	0.0%
1986	0.0%	30.0%	7.5%	0.0%	0.0%	0.0%	0.0%	0.0%	0.0%	0.0%
1987	0.0%	0.0%	0.0%	0.0%	7.5%	18.8%	0.0%	30.0%	0.0%	10.0%
1988	0.0%	0.0%	0.0%	2.5%	0.0%	0.0%	0.0%	0.0%	0.0%	0.0%
1989	0.0%	15.0%	0.0%	0.0%	0.0%	0.0%	0.0%	0.0%	10.0%	0.0%
1990	0.0%	0.0%	22.5%	0.0%	23.4%	0.0%	10.0%	0.0%	0.0%	0.0%
1991	0.0%	0.0%	0.0%	0.0%	0.0%	10.0%	0.0%	0.0%	0.0%	27.5%
1992	0.0%	0.0%	0.0%	0.0%	0.0%	0.0%	0.0%	10.0%	0.0%	4.0%
1993	0.0%	0.0%	0.0%	0.0%	0.0%	0.0%	0.0%	0.0%	0.0%	5.8%
1994	0.0%	0.0%	0.0%	0.0%	0.0%	0.0%	10.0%	0.0%	5.0%	0.0%
1995	0.0%	0.0%	0.0%	0.0%	0.0%	0.0%	0.0%	0.0%	0.0%	0.0%
1996	10.8%	0.0%	0.0%	0.0%	0.0%	0.0%	0.0%	0.0%	0.0%	0.0%
1997	0.0%	0.0%	0.0%	10.0%	10.0%	0.0%	0.0%	0.0%	10.0%	0.0%
1998	0.0%	0.0%	0.0%	0.0%	0.0%	0.0%	0.0%	0.0%	0.0%	0.0%
1999	0.0%	0.0%	0.0%	0.0%	0.0%	0.0%	27.5%	3.8%	0.0%	11.0%
2000	0.0%	0.0%	0.0%	0.0%	0.0%	0.0%	0.0%	30.0%	0.0%	0.0%
2001	0.0%	0.0%	0.0%	0.0%	0.0%	0.0%	0.0%	0.0%	0.0%	0.0%
2002	0.0%	0.0%	25.0%	0.0%	0.0%	10.0%	0.0%	0.0%	0.0%	0.0%
2003	0.0%	10.0%	0.0%	0.0%	0.0%	0.0%	0.0%	0.0%	1.0%	0.0%
2004	0.0%	0.0%	0.0%	10.8%	0.0%	0.0%	10.0%	0.0%	0.0%	0.0%
2005	0.0%	0.0%	0.0%	0.0%	0.0%	0.0%	0.0%	0.0%	0.0%	0.0%
2006	0.0%	0.0%	0.0%	27.5%	10.0%	0.0%	0.0%	0.0%	0.0%	0.0%
2007	0.0%	0.0%	0.0%	0.0%	0.0%	0.0%	0.0%	0.0%	0.0%	0.0%
2008	0.0%	0.0%	0.0%	0.0%	0.0%	0.0%	0.0%	0.0%	0.0%	0.0%
2009	0.0%	0.0%	0.0%	10.0%	0.0%	10.0%	0.0%	0.0%	17.2%	6.0%
2010	0.0%	0.0%	0.0%	0.0%	0.0%	0.0%	0.0%	28.8%	0.0%	0.0%
2011	27.5%	0.0%	0.0%	0.0%	0.0%	0.0%	0.0%	0.0%	0.0%	0.0%
2012	0.0%	0.0%	0.0%	0.0%	0.0%	0.0%	0.0%	0.0%	0.0%	0.0%
2013	0.0%	0.0%	0.0%	0.0%	0.0%	0.0%	0.0%	4.8%	10.0%	0.0%

The table shows that three insured party basis risk events occurred in Area B in 1986, 1989, and 2003. For example, for 1986 the historical insured party basis risk ratio is

Historical insured party basis risk ratio = Max (0, [Historical inventory damage ratio − Historical payout ratio])

$$= \text{Max } (0, 30\% - 0\%)$$

$$= 30\%.$$

The same calculation is used for all 30 years and all 10 regions.

In Step 9 (no case example box provided) the model reorders the historical insured party basis risk ratios from the most recent year at the top to the least recent year at the bottom. The sorted years will be the key inputs for the model's determination of historical years with the largest insured party basis risk ratios in Step 41.

In Step 10, the analyst manually combines all the nonzero basis risk ratios from Step 8 into one list (case example box 11CB.9). In Step 24 the model will use only these values to fit a beta probability distribution for the simulation of insured party basis risk ratios.

Case Example Box 11CB.9 Computations—Step 10

STEP 10 : MANUALLY RECORD ALL NON-ZERO HISTORICAL INSURED PARTY BASIS RISK RATIOS FROM STEP 8 (%)

HISTORICAL BASIS RISK RATIOS
10.8%
27.5%
30.0%
15.0%
50.0%
7.5%
22.5%
25.0%
2.5%
10.0%
10.8%
10.0%
5.9%
7.5%
23.4%
10.0%
10.0%
18.8%
10.0%
10.0%
10.0%
10.0%
10.0%
10.0%
10.0%
16.6%
30.0%
10.0%
90.0%
28.8%
4.8%
27.4%
10.0%
10.0%
70.0%
1.0%
17.2%
10.0%
10.0%
4.0%
5.6%
11.0%
6.0%

11.3.2 Calculation of Historical Insurer Basis Risk Ratios (Steps 11–13)

11.3.2.1 Overview

Insurer basis risk describes the scenario in which the payout is greater than the actual losses the insured party experiences from the named peril (table 11.5). In this case the insurer suffers an economic loss because of unnecessary claims payments. The calculation for the historical insurer basis risk ratio for the Base Index is as follows:

$$\text{Historical insurer basis risk ratio} = \text{Max} \left(0, \left[\underset{\text{Step 6}}{\text{Historical payout ratio}} - \underset{\text{Step 4}}{\text{Historical inventory damage ratio}}\right]\right).$$

Risk Modeling for Appraising Named Peril Index Insurance Products
http://dx.doi.org/10.1596/978-1-4648-1048-0

Table 11.5 Model Computations

Model component	Section	Excel sheet label	Steps	Description
Model computations	11.3.2	MC_11.3.1&.2_ DERIVED INPUTS	Steps 11–13	Calculation of historical insurer basis risk ratios for each area. These derived inputs are used in section 11.3.6 (Steps 30–35).

The case example results are shown in case example box 11CB.10.

Any time the historical payout ratio is smaller than the historical inventory damage ratio, the insurer basis risk is zero.

11.3.2.2 Implementation in Excel (MC_11.3.1&.2_Derived Inputs)

Case Example Box 11CB.10 Computations—Step 11

STEP 11 : CALCULATE HISTORICAL INSURER BASIS RISK PAYOUT RATIOS (%)

YEAR	AREA A	AREA B	AREA C	AREA D	AREA E	AREA F	AREA G	AREA H	AREA I	AREA J
1984	0.0%	0.0%	0.0%	0.0%	0.0%	0.0%	0.0%	0.0%	0.0%	0.4%
1985	0.0%	0.0%	0.0%	0.0%	0.0%	0.0%	0.0%	0.0%	0.0%	0.0%
1986	0.0%	0.0%	0.0%	0.0%	0.0%	0.0%	0.0%	0.0%	0.0%	7.5%
1987	0.0%	0.0%	0.0%	0.0%	0.0%	0.0%	0.0%	0.0%	0.0%	0.0%
1988	0.0%	0.0%	0.0%	0.0%	0.0%	0.0%	0.0%	0.0%	0.0%	0.0%
1989	0.0%	0.0%	0.0%	0.0%	7.5%	0.0%	0.0%	0.0%	0.0%	0.0%
1990	0.0%	0.0%	0.0%	10.0%	0.0%	0.0%	0.0%	0.0%	0.0%	2.5%
1991	0.0%	0.0%	0.0%	0.0%	0.0%	0.0%	0.0%	0.0%	0.0%	0.0%
1992	0.0%	0.0%	0.0%	0.0%	0.0%	0.0%	0.0%	0.0%	0.0%	0.0%
1993	0.0%	0.0%	0.0%	0.0%	0.0%	0.0%	0.0%	0.0%	0.0%	0.0%
1994	0.0%	0.0%	0.0%	0.0%	0.0%	0.0%	0.0%	0.0%	0.0%	6.0%
1995	0.0%	0.0%	0.0%	0.0%	0.0%	0.0%	0.0%	0.0%	0.0%	0.0%
1996	0.0%	0.0%	0.0%	0.0%	0.0%	5.8%	0.0%	0.0%	0.0%	27.5%
1997	0.0%	20.0%	0.0%	0.0%	0.0%	5.0%	0.0%	15.4%	0.0%	0.0%
1998	0.0%	0.0%	0.0%	0.0%	0.0%	0.0%	0.0%	0.0%	13.2%	0.0%
1999	0.0%	0.0%	0.0%	0.0%	2.5%	17.5%	0.0%	0.0%	0.0%	0.0%
2000	0.0%	0.0%	0.0%	0.0%	0.0%	0.0%	3.4%	0.0%	0.0%	0.0%
2001	0.0%	0.0%	0.0%	0.0%	0.0%	0.0%	0.0%	0.0%	0.0%	0.0%
2002	0.0%	0.0%	0.0%	0.0%	0.0%	0.0%	0.0%	0.0%	0.0%	0.0%
2003	0.0%	0.0%	0.0%	0.0%	0.0%	0.0%	0.0%	0.0%	0.0%	10.0%
2004	0.0%	0.0%	0.0%	0.0%	0.0%	0.0%	0.0%	0.0%	0.0%	0.0%
2005	0.0%	0.0%	0.0%	0.0%	0.0%	0.0%	0.0%	0.0%	0.0%	0.0%
2006	0.0%	0.0%	0.0%	0.0%	0.0%	0.0%	0.0%	0.0%	0.0%	9.4%
2007	0.0%	0.0%	0.0%	10.4%	0.0%	0.0%	0.0%	0.0%	0.0%	0.0%
2008	0.0%	0.0%	0.0%	0.0%	0.0%	0.0%	0.0%	0.0%	0.0%	17.5%
2009	0.0%	2.5%	0.0%	0.0%	0.0%	0.0%	0.0%	0.0%	0.0%	0.0%
2010	0.0%	0.0%	0.0%	0.0%	0.0%	0.0%	25.0%	0.0%	0.0%	0.0%
2011	0.0%	7.5%	0.0%	16.6%	0.0%	0.0%	0.0%	0.0%	0.0%	0.0%
2012	0.0%	5.0%	0.0%	0.0%	0.0%	2.5%	0.0%	0.0%	0.0%	0.0%
2013	0.0%	0.0%	0.0%	0.0%	9.0%	0.0%	0.0%	0.0%	0.0%	0.0%

Step 11 shows that the Base Index generates four insurer basis risk events in Area B during the 30-year period.

Step 12 (no case example box provided) is similar to Step 9. The model reorders the insurer basis risk ratios from the most recent year to the least recent.

Risk Modeling for Appraising Named Peril Index Insurance Products
http://dx.doi.org/10.1596/978-1-4648-1048-0

Case Example Box 11CB.11 Computations—Step 13

STEP 13 : MANUALLY RECORD ALL NON-ZERO HISTORICAL INSURER BASIS RISK RATIOS FROM STEP 11 (%)

HISTORICAL BASIS RISK RATIOS
20.0%
2.5%
7.5%
5.0%
10.0%
2.5%
40.4%
16.6%
7.5%
2.5%
9.0%
5.8%
5.0%
17.5%
2.5%
2.5%
25.0%
15.4%
86.2%
13.2%
27.5%
0.4%
7.5%
2.5%
42.5%
6.0%
27.5%
10.0%
39.4%
17.5%

In Step 13, the analyst manually combines all the nonzero basis risk ratios from Step 11 into one list (case example box 11CB.11). These will be used in Step 30 to fit a beta probability distribution for the simulation of insurer basis risk ratios.

11.3.3 Simulation of Scenario Payout Ratios (Steps 14–18)
11.3.3.1 Overview
Based on the historical payout ratios (Step 4), the model simulates the scenario payout ratios (table 11.6) for the Base Index using estimates for three stochastic elements:

- *Frequency distribution* (Step 14): This distribution describes the frequency of payouts. Because most index insurance products will only pay out once a year (or season) and not multiple times, a Bernoulli distribution is the most appropriate for the frequency distribution. The frequency distribution describes the probability of a payout for each area based on the historical frequency of payouts.
- *Severity distribution* (Step 15): If a payout is made within a certain area, the percentage of the insured amount that needs to be paid out can vary widely. Some years the payout may be only 10 percent of the sum insured, while

Table 11.6 Model Computations

Model component	Section	Excel sheet label	Steps	Description
Model computations	11.3.3	MC_11.3.3_BI_ SCENARIOS	Steps 14–18	Simulation of scenario payout ratios for each area

in other years with more severe weather the payout may be closer to 100 percent. The severity distribution describes the variability in payout ratios for each area based on the historical severity of payouts.

- *Correlation function* (Steps 16–17): The occurrence of payouts in nearby areas or regions is typically codependent because of weather patterns. Severe weather and high payouts in one area often coincide with severe weather and high payouts in an adjoining area. The distribution—a copula in this case—describes the degree of correlation between payout ratios for each area based on the historical correlation of payouts.

Figure 11.1 summarizes the process for simulating scenario payout ratios from historical payout ratios for each area.

Figure 11.1 Generating Scenario Payout Ratios

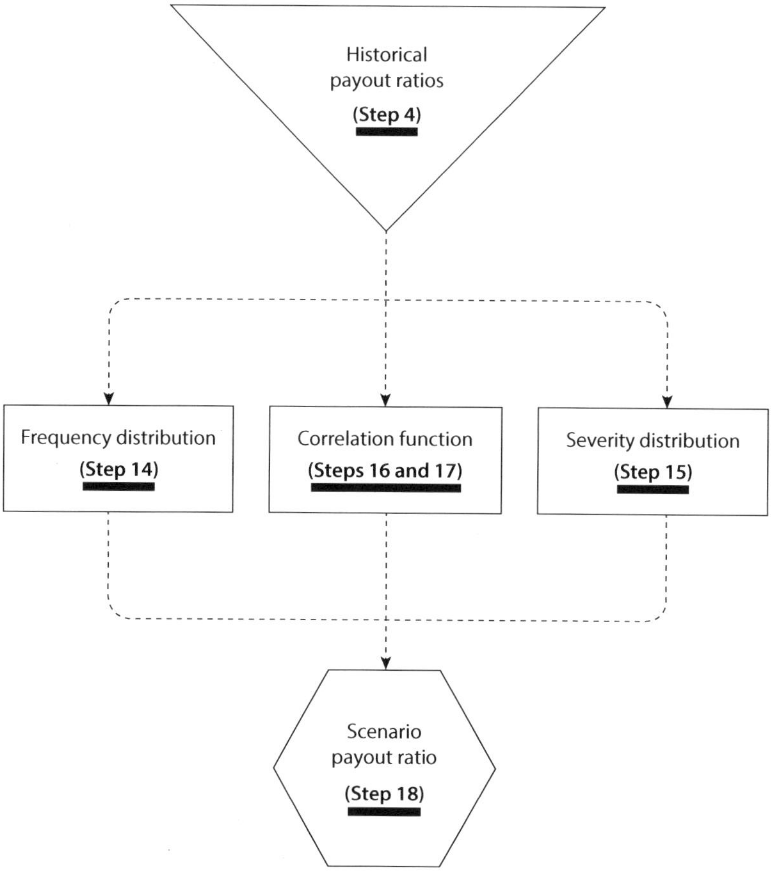

Risk Modeling for Appraising Named Peril Index Insurance Products
http://dx.doi.org/10.1596/978-1-4648-1048-0

Once the model estimates the frequency, severity, and correlation for each area, it simulates the payout ratios per area.

11.3.3.2 Implementation in Excel (MC_11.3.3_BI_Scenarios)

Case example boxes 11CB.12–11CB.14 show the simulation of scenario payout ratios for the case example.

Case Example Box 11CB.12 Computations—Step 14

STEP 14 : ENTER FREQUENCY

	AREA A	AREA B	AREA C	AREA D	AREA E	AREA F	AREA G	AREA H	AREA I	AREA J
SUCCESSES	2	5	3	7	6	5	4	4	5	13
TRIALS	30	30	30	30	30	30	30	30	30	30
ESTIMATE THE PROBABILITY	Beta(3;29)	Beta(6;26)	Beta(4;28)	Beta(8;24)	Beta(7;25)	Beta(6;26)	Beta(5;27)	Beta(5;27)	Beta(6;26)	Beta(14;18)
BERNOULLI OBJECT	Bernoulli(0,06)	Bernoulli(0,10)	Bernoulli(0,08)	Bernoulli(0,21)	Bernoulli(0,18)	Bernoulli(0,09)	Bernoulli(0,03)	Bernoulli(0,29)	Bernoulli(0,12)	Bernoulli(0,54)

Looking at Area B from the case example, case example box 11CB.4 shows that this area had five years with payouts greater than zero (payouts of 15 percent in 1989, 20 percent in 1997, 2.5 percent in 2009, 7.5 percent in 2011, and 5 percent in 2012) and hence 25 years with no payouts. Without taking uncertainty into account, the p parameter for this area would be the proportion of years with payouts to the total number of historical years.

Annual probability of a payout = Number of historical years with payouts/Total number of historical years

= 5/30

= 16.7%

However, because we do need to take uncertainty into account, the beta distribution is used to simulate the uncertainty in the annual probability of payouts.

Annual probability of a payout = (p) ~ beta distribution (alpha, beta)

= (p) ~ beta distribution (6, 26)

This simulation for Area B is shown in the Step 14 table as Beta (6;26), which is a beta distribution with alpha = 6 and beta = 26.

In Step 14, the model fits a beta distribution to the nonzero historical payout to estimate the annual probability of a payout that is greater than zero. This estimated probability is the parameter p, which is used in the Bernoulli distribution (frequency distribution).

With a large amount of data, this parameter could be estimated as a proportion of successes (number of years with a payment) to trials (total number of years).

Annual probability of a payout = Number of historical years with payouts/
Total number of historical years

However, because this sample is very small, we need to take uncertainty into account by estimating p for each scenario using a beta distribution. Thus, the annual probability of a payout is simulated as follows:

Annual probability of a payout = (p) ~ beta distribution (alpha, beta),
where
alpha = [Number of historical years with payouts > 0] + 1
beta = Number of historical years with no payouts + 1.

Case Example Box 11CB.13 Computations—Step 15

STEP 15 : INDICATE SEVERITY

	AREA A	AREA B	AREA C	AREA D	AREA E	AREA F	AREA G	AREA H	AREA I	AREA J
BETA OBJECT	Beta(0,65;1,07)	Beta(0,65;1,07)	Beta(0,65;1,07)	Beta(0,65;1,07)	Beta(0,65;1,07)	Beta(0,65;1,07)	Beta(0,65;1,07)	Beta(0,65;1,07)	Beta(0,65;1,07)	Beta(0,65;1,07)

In the case example, the number of nonzero historical payout ratios is very low for each area (between two and six). Therefore, instead of using only the data points for each area, the model assumes that the severity distribution for each area is the same as that for all areas. In other words, the case example model is assuming homogeneity of payout ratios for all of the areas. For each area the model fits a beta distribution using all 54 nonzero historical payout ratios (all 54 data points of all 10 areas). Each severity scenario that will be generated during the simulation process will come from this beta distribution for all nonzero payout ratios observed across all years in all areas.

This simulation for Area B is shown in the Step 15 table as Beta (0.65;1.07).

In Step 15, the model fits a beta distribution to the nonzero historical payout ratios to estimate payout severity (case example box 11CB.13). Other probability distributions can be used, but the beta distribution, which has a minimum of 0 and a maximum of 1, tends to fit data that ranges from 0 to 1 (that is, 100 percent).

Case Example Box 11CB.14 Computations—Steps 16–17

STEP 16A: CHOOSE COPULA

CHOSEN COPULA	T-COPULA

STEP 16B : DETERMINE COPULA MATRIX

	AREA A	AREA B	AREA C	AREA D	AREA E	AREA F	AREA G	AREA H	AREA I	AREA J
AREA A	100%	-6%	-5%	-8%	-7%	9%	-8%	-7%	-7%	4%
AREA B	-6%	100%	-10%	-11%	-7%	21%	-12%	28%	-9%	-21%
AREA C	-5%	-10%	100%	15%	17%	-10%	-9%	-10%	-10%	-14%
AREA D	-8%	-11%	15%	100%	55%	-15%	-13%	-16%	-15%	-5%
AREA E	-7%	-7%	17%	55%	100%	13%	-11%	-7%	4%	9%
AREA F	9%	21%	-10%	-15%	13%	100%	-10%	41%	-13%	-10%
AREA G	-8%	-12%	-9%	-13%	-11%	-10%	100%	10%	28%	-21%
AREA H	-7%	28%	-10%	-16%	-7%	41%	10%	100%	-14%	-9%
AREA I	-7%	-9%	-10%	-15%	4%	-13%	28%	-14%	100%	26%
AREA J	4%	-21%	-14%	-5%	9%	-10%	-21%	-9%	26%	100%
Degrees of freedom	5									

STEP 17: DETERMINE COPULA FOR FUNCTION

COPULA	0.19	0.81	0.87	0.71	0.39	0.20	0.81	0.93	0.96	0.83

Steps 16–17 fit a copula to the historical payout ratios to estimate the correlation between annual payouts in each area (case example box 11CB.14).

In Step 16A the model determines the best-fitting copula for the historical payout ratios. Different copulas can be used in this step. In quantitative finance the two commonly used copulas are the normal (or Gaussian) copula and the t copula (see chapter 10 and Cherubini, Luciano, and Vecchiato [2004]). However, because of the long-tail nature of risks insured through named peril index insurance, the use of the normal copula would not be appropriate. We instead do recommend using either the t copula (see chapter 10) or other copulas with the ability to capture tail dependence (see Cherubini, Luciano, and Vecchiato [2004] for more details about tail dependence and the difference between alternative copulas). In Step 16B, the model estimates the parameters of the copula from the historical payout ratio data.

Finally, in Step 17, the model simulates the copulas.

It is important to note that the greater the correlation between the areas, the greater the total amount that the insurer may have to pay out in a season for all areas together. In other words, higher correlation causes higher risk to the insurer (and possibly reinsurer).

Potentially higher payouts caused by highly correlated exposure will mean that the insurer must hold more required capital, which involves greater cost. In these circumstances, finding areas with less correlated exposure or obtaining additional reinsurance can help the insurer reduce the costs of the required capital.

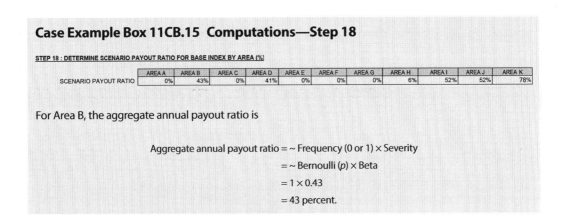

Case Example Box 11CB.15 Computations—Step 18

STEP 18 : DETERMINE SCENARIO PAYOUT RATIO FOR BASE INDEX BY AREA (%)

	AREA A	AREA B	AREA C	AREA D	AREA E	AREA F	AREA G	AREA H	AREA I	AREA J	AREA K
SCENARIO PAYOUT RATIO	0%	43%	0%	41%	0%	0%	0%	6%	52%	52%	78%

For Area B, the aggregate annual payout ratio is

$$\text{Aggregate annual payout ratio} = \sim \text{Frequency (0 or 1)} \times \text{Severity}$$
$$= \sim \text{Bernoulli } (p) \times \text{Beta}$$
$$= 1 \times 0.43$$
$$= 43 \text{ percent.}$$

In Step 18, the simulation incorporates all three stochastic elements discussed above (case example box 11CB.15):

- The frequency of payouts for each area (Step 14)
- The severity of payouts for each area (Step 15)
- The correlation between payouts in all areas (Steps 16–17)

Step 18 combines all three elements to simulate annual payout ratios for each of the areas.

The model generates a copula that represents the correlation between and among all the different areas (Step 17). Values picked from this copula will determine the frequency value for each area (case example box 11CB.16).

Case Example Box 11CB.16 Determining Area Level Scenario Frequency and Severity Values

For Area B, Step 17 picked the 81st percentile from the copula, so the model selects the 81st percentile value from the frequency distribution (Bernoulli) for Area B (Step 14). This value is 1, indicating a payout is expected to occur.

The model also generates a severity value for Area B from the severity distribution (beta distribution), which equals 0.43 in the example (Step 15).

Note that only the frequency value, and not the severity value, is determined by the copula.

Step 18 combines the frequency and severity distributions into an aggregate payout ratio simulation for each area.

$$\text{Aggregate annual payout ratio} = \sim \text{Frequency (0 or 1)} \times \text{Severity}$$
$$= \sim \text{Bernoulli } (p) \times \text{Beta}$$
$$\text{Step 14} \qquad \text{Step 15}$$

The scenario payout ratios for each area are calculated in the same way.

Note that whenever the frequency distribution (Bernoulli distribution) simulates a 0, meaning there is no payout expected, we ignore the value of the severity distribution (beta distribution). This makes sense conceptually because if no payout occurs then the payout's magnitude does not matter. Mathematically, we can see that multiplying the frequency value (zero) by any severity value will produce a payout ratio of zero. Taking this a bit further, if we know that the payout ratio for an area is zero, then we also know that the frequency (Bernoulli) distribution generated a zero.

11.3.4 Simulation of Scenario Inventory Damage Ratios (Steps 19–23)
11.3.4.1 Overview

This set of model computations simulates the scenario inventory damage ratios for the Base Index (table 11.7). Later in this chapter, the model compares the scenario inventory damage ratios to the scenario payout ratios (Steps 14–18) to evaluate the basis risk of the Base Index.

Table 11.7 Model Computations

Model component	Section	Excel sheet label	Steps	Description
Model computations	11.3.4	MC_11.3.4_DR_SCENARIOS	Steps 19–23	Simulation of scenario inventory damage ratios for each area

Risk Modeling for Appraising Named Peril Index Insurance Products
http://dx.doi.org/10.1596/978-1-4648-1048-0

11.3.4.2 *Implementation in Excel (MC_11.3.4_DR_Scenarios)*

The steps for simulating the scenario inventory damage ratios (Step 19–23; case example box 11CB.17) are similar to those for simulating the payout ratios (Steps 14–18) but use different model inputs. Instead of using nonzero historical payout ratios, the model uses nonzero historical inventory damage ratios. Here the focus is on simulating inventory damage caused by the named perils rather than on simulating the payouts triggered by the Base Index.

Case Example Box 11CB.17 Computations—Steps 19–23

STEP 19 : ENTER FREQUENCY

	AREA A	AREA B	AREA C	AREA D	AREA E	AREA F	AREA G	AREA H	AREA I	AREA J
SUCCESSES	2	3	3	8	5	5	7	7	8	10
TRIALS	30	30	30	30	30	30	30	30	30	30
ESTIMATE THE PROBABILITY	Beta(3,29)	Beta(4,28)	Beta(4,28)	Beta(9,23)	Beta(6,26)	Beta(6,26)	Beta(8,24)	Beta(8,24)	Beta(9,23)	Beta(11,21)
BERNOULLI OBJECT	Bernoulli(0.04)	Bernoulli(0.13)	Bernoulli(0.22)	Bernoulli(0.18)	Bernoulli(0.20)	Bernoulli(0.17)	Bernoulli(0.34)	Bernoulli(0.20)	Bernoulli(0.34)	Bernoulli(0.40)

STEP 20 : INDICATE SEVERITY

	AREA A	AREA B	AREA C	AREA D	AREA E	AREA F	AREA G	AREA H	AREA I	AREA J
BETA OBJECT	Beta(1,03;1,45)	Beta(1,03;1,45)	Beta(1,03;1,45)	Beta(1,03;1,45)	Beta(1,03;1,45)	Beta(1,03;1,45)	Beta(1,03;1,45)	Beta(1,03;1,45)	Beta(1,03;1,45)	Beta(1,03;1,45)

STEP 21A: CHOOSE COPULA

CHOSEN COPULA	T-COPULA

STEP 21B : DETERMINE COPULA MATRIX

	AREA A	AREA B	AREA C	AREA D	AREA E	AREA F	AREA G	AREA H	AREA I	AREA J
AREA A	100%	-7%	-8%	-11%	-8%	-8%	-10%	-11%	-11%	-15%
AREA B	-7%	100%	34%	15%	10%	-10%	-13%	-14%	2%	-12%
AREA C	-8%	34%	100%	32%	42%	1%	-5%	-15%	-16%	-21%
AREA D	-11%	-15%	32%	100%	56%	-12%	-4%	-16%	-17%	1%
AREA E	-8%	10%	42%	56%	100%	20%	-1%	-6%	14%	7%
AREA F	-8%	-10%	1%	-12%	20%	100%	-14%	13%	-1%	1%
AREA G	-10%	-13%	-5%	-4%	-1%	-14%	100%	28%	9%	-5%
AREA H	-11%	-14%	-15%	-16%	-6%	13%	28%	100%	-13%	-5%
AREA I	-11%	2%	-16%	-17%	14%	-1%	9%	-13%	100%	40%
AREA J	-15%	-12%	-21%	1%	7%	1%	-5%	-5%	40%	100%
Degrees of freedom	5									

STEP 22: DETERMINE COPULA FOR FUNCTION

COPULA FUNCTION	0.10	0.40	0.54	0.26	0.81	0.89	0.14	0.77	0.89	0.93

STEP 23 : DETERMINE SCENARIO DAMAGE RATIO BY AREA (%)

SCENARIO DAMAGE RATIO	0%	0%	0%	0%	55%	16%	0%	84%	79%	15%

11.3.5 Simulation of Scenario Insured Party Basis Risk Amounts (Steps 24–29)

11.3.5.1 *Overview*

The simulation of scenario insured party basis risk amounts quantifies the insured party basis risk losses for the Base Index (table 11.8).

Table 11.8 Model Computations

Model component	Section	Excel sheet label	Steps	Description
Model computations	11.3.5	MC_11.3.5_INSD PARTY BASIS RISK	Steps 24–29	Simulation of scenario insured party basis risk amounts

11.3.5.2 *Implementation in Excel (MC_11.3.5_Insd Party Basis Risk)*

The process for simulating scenario insured party basis risk amounts is similar to that for simulating scenario payout ratios (Steps 14–18) but with two key differences.

First, the model's main inputs are the nonzero historical insured party basis risk ratios (Step 10) instead of the nonzero historical payout ratios.

Second, Steps 28 and 29 simulate monetary amounts for insured party basis risk rather than just a ratio.

Case example box 11CB.18 shows the simulation of scenario insured party basis risk amounts for the case example.

Case Example Box 11CB.18 Computations—Steps 24–29

STEP 24 : ENTER FREQUENCY

	AREA A	AREA B	AREA C	AREA D	AREA E	AREA F	AREA G	AREA H	AREA I	AREA J
SUCCESSES	2	3	3	5	5	4	5	6	7	6
TRIALS	30	30	30	30	30	30	30	30	30	30
ESTIMATE THE PROBABILITY	Beta(3,29)	Beta(4,28)	Beta(4,28)	Beta(6,26)	Beta(6,26)	Beta(5,27)	Beta(6,26)	Beta(7,25)	Beta(8,24)	Beta(7,25)
BERNOULLI OBJECT	Bernoulli(0,10)	Bernoulli(0,08)	Bernoulli(0,05)	Bernoulli(0,12)	Bernoulli(0,17)	Bernoulli(0,24)	Bernoulli(0,14)	Bernoulli(0,29)	Bernoulli(0,22)	Bernoulli(0,11)

STEP 25 : INDICATE SEVERITY

BETA OBJECT	Beta(1,08,4,63)	Beta(1,08,4,63)	Beta(1,08,4,63)	Beta(1,08,4,63)	Beta(1,08,4,63)	Beta(1,08,4,63)	Beta(1,08,4,63)	Beta(1,08,4,63)	Beta(1,08,4,63)	Beta(1,08,4,63)

STEP 26 : CHOOSE COPULA

CHOSEN COPULA	T-COPULA

STEP 26B : DETERMINE COPULA MATRIX

	AREA A	AREA B	AREA C	AREA D	AREA E	AREA F	AREA G	AREA H	AREA I	AREA J
AREA A	100%	-7%	-7%	-9%	-9%	-9%	9%	-10%	11%	-9%
AREA B	-7%	100%	11%	-11%	-11%	-11%	-12%	-12%	1%	-12%
AREA C	-7%	11%	100%	-11%	47%	20%	10%	-12%	-13%	-12%
AREA D	-9%	-11%	-11%	100%	31%	0%	-3%	-14%	10%	-7%
AREA E	-9%	-11%	47%	31%	100%	8%	12%	2%	12%	-6%
AREA F	-9%	-11%	20%	0%	8%	100%	-14%	33%	5%	58%
AREA G	-9%	-12%	10%	-3%	12%	-14%	100%	-6%	-12%	16%
AREA H	10%	12%	-12%	-14%	2%	33%	-6%	100%	-14%	10%
AREA I	-11%	1%	-13%	10%	12%	5%	-12%	-14%	100%	-7%
AREA J	-9%	-12%	-12%	-7%	-6%	58%	16%	10%	-7%	100%
Degrees of freedom	4									

STEP 27: DETERMINE COPULA FOR FUNCTION

COPULA FUNCTION	0.42	0.58	0.70	0.52	0.69	0.44	0.28	0.83	0.77	0.63

STEP 28 : DETERMINE SCENARIO INSURED PARTY BASIS RISK AMOUNTS BY AREA ($)

SCENARIO BASIS RISK AMOUNT	-	-		-	148,846	-	-	186,609	24,774	-

STEP 29: DETERMINE SCENARIO PORTFOLIO BASIS RISK AMOUNT ($)

SCENARIO BASIS RISK AMOUNT	360,229

In the case example, the scenario insured party basis risk amounts for Areas E ($148,846), H ($186,609), and I ($24,774) sum to the total insured party basis risk amount of $360,229.

In Step 28, the model calculates insured party basis risk amounts for each area by multiplying the insured party basis risk ratios (Steps 8–10) by the total sum insured per area (Step 3). In Step 29, the model sums the basis risk amounts for all the areas to give a scenario total basis risk amount. The greater the frequency and severity of insured party basis risk events (that is, false negatives), the greater the amount of insured party basis risk.

11.3.6 Simulation of Scenario Insurer Basis Risk Amounts (Steps 30–35)
11.3.6.1 Overview
The simulation of scenario insurer basis risk amounts quantifies the insurer basis risk losses for the Base Index (table 11.9).

Risk Modeling for Appraising Named Peril Index Insurance Products
http://dx.doi.org/10.1596/978-1-4648-1048-0

Table 11.9 Model Computations

Model component	Section	Excel sheet label	Steps	Description
Model computations	11.3.6	MC_11.3.6_INSR BASIS RISK	Steps 30–35	Simulation of scenario insurer basis risk amounts

11.3.6.2 Implementation in Excel (MC_11.3.6_Insurer Basis Risk)

The steps for simulating the scenario insurer basis risk amounts (case example box 11CB.19) are similar to those for simulating insured party basis risk amounts (Steps 24–29) but use different model inputs. The input values are the nonzero historical insurer basis risk ratios (Step 13).

The reader is referred back to Steps 24–29 for further details on the modeling.

Case Example Box 11CB.19 Computations—Steps 30–35

STEP 30 : ENTER FREQUENCY

	AREA A	AREA B	AREA C	AREA D	AREA E	AREA F	AREA G	AREA H	AREA I	AREA J
SUCCESSES	0	4	0	3	3	4	3	1	1	8
TRIALS	30	30	30	30	30	30	30	30	30	30
ESTIMATE THE PROBABILITY	Beta(1,31)	Beta(5,27)	Beta(1,31)	Beta(4,28)	Beta(4,28)	Beta(5,27)	Beta(4,28)	Beta(2,30)	Beta(2,30)	Beta(9,23)
BERNOULLI OBJECT	Bernoulli(0,01)	Bernoulli(0,12)	Bernoulli(0,04)	Bernoulli(0,13)	Bernoulli(0,13)	Bernoulli(0,12)	Bernoulli(0,07)	Bernoulli(0,07)	Bernoulli(0,05)	Bernoulli(0,20)

STEP 31 : INDICATE SEVERITY

| BETA OBJECT | Beta(0,79,3,73) | Beta(0,79,3,73) | Beta(0,79,3,73) | Beta(0,79,3,73) | Beta(0,79,3,73) | Beta(0,79,3,73) | Beta(0,79,3,73) | Beta(0,79,3,73) | Beta(0,79,3,73) | Beta(0,79,3,73) |

STEP 32A : CHOOSE COPULA

CHOSEN COPULA	T-COPULA

STEP 32B : DETERMINE COPULA MATRIX

	AREA A	AREA B	AREA C	AREA D	AREA E	AREA F	AREA G	AREA H	AREA I	AREA J
AREA A	100%	0%	0%	0%	0%	0%	0%	0%	0%	0%
AREA B	0%	100%	0%	18%	-9%	20%	-6%	91%	-6%	-13%
AREA C	0%	0%	100%	0%	0%	0%	0%	0%	0%	0%
AREA D	0%	18%	0%	100%	-10%	10%	-7%	-6%	-6%	-11%
AREA E	0%	-9%	0%	-10%	100%	11%	-6%	-6%	-6%	-13%
AREA F	0	20%	0%	-10%	11%	100%	-6%	22%	-4%	12%
AREA G	0	6%	0%	-7%	-6%	-6%	100%	-4%	-4%	9%
AREA H	0	91%	0%	-6%	-6%	22%	-4%	100%	-3%	-8%
AREA I	0	-6%	0%	-6%	-6%	-4%	-4%	-3%	100%	-8%
AREA J	0	-13%	0%	-11%	-13%	12%	-9%	-8%	-8%	100%

Degrees of freedom: 3

STEP 33: DETERMINE COPULA FOR FUNCTION

COPULA FUNCTION	0.64	0.90	0.64	0.83	0.88	0.91	0.50	0.82	0.17	0.16

STEP 34 : DETERMINE SCENARIO INSURER BASIS RISK AMOUNT BY AREA

SCENARIO BASIS RISK AMOUNT	-	52,322	-	20,786	-	27,799	-	-	-	-

STEP 35: DETERMINE SCENARIO PORTFOLIO INSURER BASIS RISK AMOUNT

SCENARIO BASIS RISK AMOUNT	100,907

In the case example, the basis risk amounts for Areas B ($52,322), D ($20,786), and F ($27,799) sum to the total insurer basis risk amount of $100,907.

11.3.7 Calculation of Product Evaluation Decision Metrics (Steps 36–44)

At this point the model has simulated four key scenario parameters (payout ratios, inventory damage ratios, insured party basis risk amounts, and insurer basis risk amounts) for evaluating the Base Index. Based on these parameters, the model then calculates a number of important metrics that help gauge the level of basis risk inherent in the Base Index (table 11.10).

Table 11.10 Model Computations

Model component	Section	Excel sheet label	Steps	Description
Model computations	11.3.7	MC_11.3.7_DECISION METRICS	Steps 36–44	Calculation of product evaluation decision metrics

11.3.7.1 Expected Return Periods for Inventory Damage and the Base Index

11.3.7.1.1 Overview. The expected return period for inventory damage is the expected frequency at which inventory damage caused by the named peril occurs at specific damage levels (for example, damage to 10 percent of the inventory, 30 percent of the inventory, 50 percent of the inventory, and 70 percent of the inventory). The expected return period for the Base Index is the frequency at which the Base Index makes a payout at specific payout levels.

Figure 11.2 provides an overview of how the model estimates the expected return periods for both inventory damage and the Base Index.

Figure 11.2 Generating Expected Return Periods for Inventory Damage and the Base Index

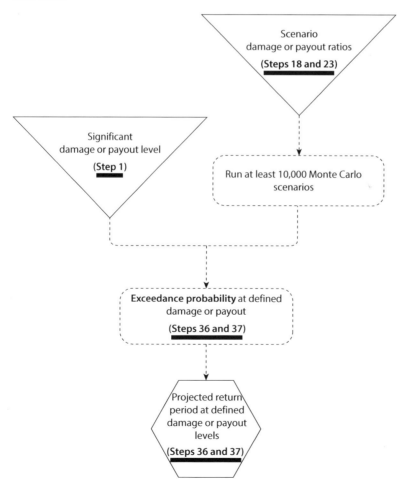

Risk Modeling for Appraising Named Peril Index Insurance Products
http://dx.doi.org/10.1596/978-1-4648-1048-0

11.3.7.1.2 Implementation in Excel. Case example box 11CB.20 shows the simulation of expected return periods for inventory damage events and Base Index payouts.

Case Example Box 11CB.20 Computations—Steps 36–37

STEP 36 : CALCULATE PROJECTED INVENTORY DAMAGE RETURN PERIODS

				AREA A	AREA B	AREA C	AREA D	AREA E	AREA F	AREA G	AREA H	AREA I	AREA J
EXCEEDANCE PROBABILITY	@	10%	DAMAGE LEVEL	8%	11%	11%	25%	17%	16%	22%	22%	24%	30%
EXCEEDANCE PROBABILITY	@	30%	DAMAGE LEVEL	5%	8%	8%	17%	11%	12%	16%	16%	17%	21%
EXCEEDANCE PROBABILITY	@	50%	DAMAGE LEVEL	3%	5%	5%	11%	7%	7%	10%	10%	11%	13%
EXCEEDANCE PROBABILITY	@	70%	DAMAGE LEVEL	2%	2%	2%	5%	3%	4%	5%	5%	5%	6%
RETURN PERIOD	@	10%	DAMAGE LEVEL	13	9	9	4	6	6	5	4	4	3
RETURN PERIOD	@	30%	DAMAGE LEVEL	18	13	12	6	9	9	6	6	6	5
RETURN PERIOD	@	50%	DAMAGE LEVEL	30	20	19	9	14	14	10	10	9	8
RETURN PERIOD	@	70%	DAMAGE LEVEL	62	40	42	19	29	27	22	20	19	17

STEP 37 : CALCULATE BASE INDEX RETURN PERIODS

				AREA A	AREA B	AREA C	AREA D	AREA E	AREA F	AREA G	AREA H	AREA I	AREA J
EXCEEDANCE PROBABILITY	@	10%	PAYOUT LEVEL	7%	14%	9%	19%	17%	14%	12%	12%	15%	34%
EXCEEDANCE PROBABILITY	@	30%	PAYOUT LEVEL	5%	9%	6%	13%	11%	10%	8%	9%	10%	23%
EXCEEDANCE PROBABILITY	@	50%	PAYOUT LEVEL	3%	6%	4%	8%	7%	6%	6%	6%	6%	15%
EXCEEDANCE PROBABILITY	@	70%	PAYOUT LEVEL	2%	3%	2%	5%	4%	4%	3%	3%	3%	8%
RETURN PERIOD	@	10%	PAYOUT LEVEL	14	7	11	5	6	7	9	8	7	3
RETURN PERIOD	@	30%	PAYOUT LEVEL	20	11	16	8	9	11	12	12	10	4
RETURN PERIOD	@	50%	PAYOUT LEVEL	30	17	24	12	14	16	18	18	16	7
RETURN PERIOD	@	70%	PAYOUT LEVEL	52	30	43	22	26	27	33	34	29	12

For Area B in the case example, inventory damage was greater than 10 percent (mild damage) in 1,100 of the 10,000 Monte Carlo scenarios (not shown box steps, the model automatically counts these).

Exceedance probability = Number of scenarios with inventory damage > significant damage level/

Total number of scenarios

= 1,100/10,000

= 11 percent

At the 10 percent damage level the exceedance probability is 11 percent for Area B. In other words, there is an 11 percent probability that the inventory damage level will be greater than 10 percent in Area B.

In the case example, the inventory damage return period for Area B at the 10 percent damage level is nine.

Return period = 1/Exceedance probability

= 1/11 percent

= 9

In Area B, the next 10 percent or greater damage level is expected to occur in nine years. In other words, we expect that once in every nine years, the inventory damage level in Area B will be greater than 10 percent.

In Step 36, at least 10,000 scenario inventory damage ratios (Monte Carlo simulations) are generated for each significant damage level (Step 1) and area. The proportion of the 10,000 scenarios with damage ratios greater than each significant damage level (10 percent, 30 percent, 50 percent, and 70 percent) is the exceedance probability:

Exceedance probability = Number of scenarios with inventory damage > significant damage level/

Total number of scenarios.

Also in Step 36, the model calculates the inventory damage return period for each damage level and area as

$$\text{Return period} = 1/\text{Exceedance probability.}$$

In Step 37, the model calculates the exceedance probabilities and expected return periods for Base Index payouts for each of the four significant payout levels and areas using the same equations as used in Step 36.

11.3.7.2 Return Period Ratio

11.3.7.2.1 Overview. The return period ratio shows the level of insurer or insured party basis risk for each significant damage or payout level and area. When this ratio is equal to 1, the Base Index triggers a payout at the same frequency as the occurrence of actual inventory damage events. When the ratio is greater than 1, the Base Index triggers a payout more frequently than the occurrence of insured events (insurer basis risk). When the ratio is between 0 and 1, the Base Index triggers payouts less frequently than the occurrence of actual insured events (insured party basis risk).

11.3.7.2.2 Implementation in Excel (MC_11.3.7_Decison Metrics). The return period ratio metric is calculated as

$$\text{Return period ratio} = \text{Inventory damage return period/Base Index return period.}$$

Case example box 11CB.21 shows the calculation of the return period ratios.

Case Example Box 11CB.21 Computations—Step 38

STEP 38 : CALCULATE RETURN PERIOD RATIOS

				AREA A	AREA B	AREA C	AREA D	AREA E	AREA F	AREA G	AREA H	AREA I	AREA J
RETURN PERIOD RATIO	@	10%	DAMAGE/PAYOUT LEVEL	0.93	1.25	0.83	0.76	0.99	0.86	0.53	0.55	0.60	1.14
RETURN PERIOD RATIO	@	30%	DAMAGE/PAYOUT LEVEL	0.93	1.15	0.78	0.73	0.98	0.82	0.52	0.54	0.59	1.13
RETURN PERIOD RATIO	@	50%	DAMAGE/PAYOUT LEVEL	0.99	1.21	0.81	0.77	1.02	0.87	0.57	0.55	0.61	1.18
RETURN PERIOD RATIO	@	70%	DAMAGE/PAYOUT LEVEL	1.18	1.33	0.99	0.88	1.08	0.98	0.66	0.57	0.67	1.41

In the case example, the inventory damage return period at the 10 percent damage level was nine years for Area B. The Base Index return period at the 10 percent damage level was seven years for Area B. Inventory damage attributable to the named peril occurs once in every nine years, but the Base Index pays once in every seven years. The index is paying more frequently than is necessary, thus leading to insurer basis risk.

The return period ratio is 1.25.

Return period ratio = Inventory damage return period/Base Index return period

        = 9.0507/7.2366

        = 1.25

The Base Index return period ratio is greater than 1, which confirms the presence of insurer basis risk.

Risk Modeling for Appraising Named Peril Index Insurance Products
http://dx.doi.org/10.1596/978-1-4648-1048-0

11.3.7.3 *Insured Party Basis Risk Statistics*

11.3.7.3.1 Overview. When the return period ratio is between 0 and 1, the Base Index is triggering payouts less frequently than actual inventory damage events, indicating the presence of insured party basis risk.

However, the return period ratio does not tell us whether the Base Index is triggering in the right years and for the right amounts. Even with a return period ratio of 1, the Base Index may still have insured party basis risk. This section explains the calculation of additional statistics that further describe the Base Index's insured party basis risk.

Figure 11.3 provides an overview of how the model simulates the probability of having no insured party basis risk events and the expected insured party basis risk amount (Steps 39–40).

Figure 11.4 provides an overview of how the model determines the historical years with the largest insured party basis risk ratios (Step 41).

Figure 11.3 Generating Probability of Having No Insured Party Basis Risk Event and Expected Insured Party Basis Risk Amount

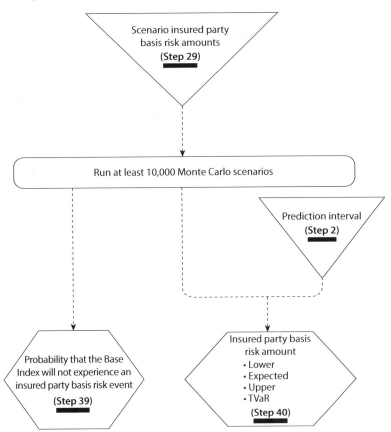

Note: TVaR = tail value at risk.

Figure 11.4 Generating Historical Years with the Largest Insured Party Basis Risk Ratios

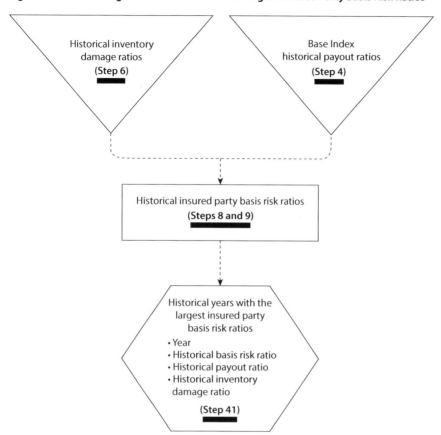

11.3.7.3.2 Implementation in Excel (MC_11.3.7_Decison Metrics). In Step 39 (case example box 11CB.22), the model runs at least 10,000 scenarios for each area based on the scenario insured party basis risk amounts and calculates the proportion of the scenarios in which the insured party basis risk amount was zero. This value indicates the percentage of years when no insured party basis risk events are expected for each area. Put differently, this figure is the probability that no insured party basis risk event will occur during the next risk period for each of the areas.

In Step 40, the model uses the same 10,000 scenarios to determine the expected amount of insured party basis risk for the portfolio (all geographical areas). This amount is reflected in currency terms as well as a percentage of the total sum insured. Based on the prediction interval selected in Step 2, the model also calculates the appropriate percentile and TVaR values. These values indicate the expected magnitude of the Base Index's insured party basis risk. Note that when the percentage of years with no insured party basis risk is higher, the magnitude of the basis risk is lower and vice versa.

These insured party basis risk metrics also provide a good starting point for an insurer that is pricing the Base Index, as discussed in detail in chapter 12.

Risk Modeling for Appraising Named Peril Index Insurance Products
http://dx.doi.org/10.1596/978-1-4648-1048-0

Case Example Box 11CB.22 Computations—Steps 39 and 40

STEP 39: CALCULATE PROBABILITY THE BASE INDEX WILL NOT EXPERIENCE AN INSURED PARTY BASIS RISK EVENT.

AREA A	AREA B	AREA C	AREA D	AREA E	AREA F	AREA G	AREA H	AREA I	AREA J
90%	88%	88%	81%	81%	84%	82%	79%	74%	78%

STEP 40 : CALCULATE PROJECTED INSURED PARTY BASIS RISK AMOUNT

	AMOUNT	% OF TOTAL
LOWER	0	0%
EXPECTED	276,655	3%
UPPER	978,750	12%
TVaR	1,310,579	16%

Step 39 shows that Area B has an 88 percent chance of having no insured party basis risk event in the next risk period.

Step 40 shows that the expected insured party basis risk amount is $276,655, which is 3 percent of the portfolio's total sum insured. The prediction interval for the case example is 90 percent (Step 2), so the model also shows the 5th and 95th percentiles and the TVaR 95 percent. The TVaR 95 percent tells us that for a 1-in-20 year event, the insured party basis risk amount for all the areas is expected to be as high as $1,310,579.

Note: TVaR = tail value at risk.

In addition to the insured party basis risk metrics discussed above, memorable years in which the Base Index would have failed to trigger or triggered inadequate payouts will be of interest to the prospective policyholder. A product that fails to trigger in years that are considered catastrophic has low client value and should not be promoted. Case example box 11CB.23 shows the calculation of the historical years with the largest insured party basis risk ratios.

In Step 9, the model reordered the insured party basis risk ratios from the most recent to least recent year for each area.

In Step 41, the model now selects the years with the largest insured party basis risk ratios. In areas where this value—the largest basis risk ratio—is repeated across multiple years, the model selects the most recent of these years. The most recent year events are chosen because prospective policyholders are more likely to remember these than older events. Next, the model selects each year's corresponding historical payout ratio and historical inventory damage ratio.

Case Example Box 11CB.23 Computations—Step 41

STEP 41 : CALCULATE HISTORICAL YEARS WITH LARGEST INSURED PARTY BASIS RISK RATIOS

	AREA A	AREA B	AREA C	AREA D	AREA E	AREA F	AREA G	AREA H	AREA I	AREA J
HISTORICAL YEAR WITH LARGEST INSURED PARTY BASIS RISK RATIO	2011	1986	2002	2006	1990	1987	1999	2000	1984	1991
BASIS RISK RATIO	28%	30%	25%	28%	23%	19%	28%	30%	27%	28%
HISTORICAL PAYOUT RATIO	3%	0%	5%	3%	67%	31%	3%	0%	23%	43%
HISTORICAL INVENTORY DAMAGE RATIO	30%	30%	30%	30%	90%	50%	30%	30%	50%	70%

For Area B in the case example, the largest historical basis risk ratio was 30 percent, which occurred in 1986. In that year, if the Base Index contract had been in place, the insured party would have suffered inventory damage of about 30 percent but the index would not have triggered.

Risk Modeling for Appraising Named Peril Index Insurance Products
http://dx.doi.org/10.1596/978-1-4648-1048-0

The insurance manager can use these years as examples when explaining the limitations of the coverage provided by the Base Index to the policyholder.

11.3.7.4 Insurer Basis Risk Statistics

11.3.7.4.1 Overview. Next the model calculates the metrics for insurer basis risk. These metrics provide more detail about the amount of payouts the insurer can expect as a result of insurer basis risk (case example box 11CB.24).

Case Example Box 11CB.24 Computations—Steps 42–44

STEP 42: CALCULATE PROBABILITY THE BASE INDEX WILL NOT EXPERIENCE AN INSURER BASIS RISK EVENT.

AREA A	AREA B	AREA C	AREA D	AREA E	AREA F	AREA G	AREA H	AREA I	AREA J
97%	84%	97%	87%	88%	84%	88%	94%	94%	77%

STEP 43 : CALCULATE PROJECTED INSURER BASIS RISK AMOUNT

	AMOUNT	% OF TOTAL
LOWER	-	0%
EXPECTED	159,939	2%
UPPER	709,878	9%
TVaR	1,009,740	13%

STEP 44 : CALCULATE HISTORICAL YEARS WITH LARGEST INSURER BASIS RISK RATIOS

	AREA A	AREA B	AREA C	AREA D	AREA E	AREA F	AREA G	AREA H	AREA I	AREA J
HISTORICAL YEAR WITH LARGEST INSURER BASIS RISK RATIO	1984	1997	1984	2011	2013	1999	2010	1997	1998	1996
BASIS RISK RATIO	0%	20%	0%	17%	9%	18%	25%	15%	13%	28%
HISTORICAL PAYOUT RATIO	0%	20%	0%	17%	9%	18%	25%	65%	63%	28%
HISTORICAL INVENTORY DAMAGE RATIO	0%	0%	0%	0%	0%	0%	0%	50%	50%	0%

For the case example, there is an 84 percent probability of Area B having no insurer basis risk event in the next risk period. For the whole portfolio, the expected insurer basis risk value is $159,939 (that is, 2 percent of the sum insured for the portfolio). The tail value at risk indicates that the insurer basis risk is expected to be $1,009,740 (13 percent of portfolio value) once every 20 years. The largest insurer basis risk amount in Area B—20 percent of the insured amount—occurred most recently in 1997 when the Base Index would have triggered a 20 percent payout despite no inventory damage caused by the named peril.

Note: TVaR = tail value at risk.

11.3.7.4.2 Implementation in Excel (MC_11.3.7_DECISION METRICS). The steps for calculating the insurer basis risk statistics are similar to those for calculating the insured party basis risk statistics (Steps 39–41) but use different model inputs. Instead of using scenario insured party basis risk amounts, the model now uses scenario insurer basis risk amounts. Please refer to Steps 39–41 for a detailed explanation of the process.

11.4 Model Outputs

The model output sheet summarizes the product evaluation decision metrics (table 11.11) for the Base Index produced in Steps 36–44, including the following:

- Inventory damage return periods for each area
- Base Index return periods for each area
- Return period ratios for each area

Risk Modeling for Appraising Named Peril Index Insurance Products
http://dx.doi.org/10.1596/978-1-4648-1048-0

Table 11.11 Model Outputs

Model component	Section	Excel sheet label	Steps	Description
Model outputs	11.4	MO_11.4_MODEL OUTPUTS	None	Summary of product evaluation decision metrics.

Box 11.1 Overview of Calculations for the Base Index Product Evaluation Metrics

Scenario metrics (one Monte Carlo scenario)

- *Historical insured party basis risk ratio* = Max (0, [Historical inventory damage ratio − Historical payout ratio])
- *Historical insurer basis risk ratio* = Max (0, [Historical payout ratio − Historical inventory damage ratio])
- *Annual probability of a payout* = Number of historical years with payouts/Total number of historical years
- *Annual probability of a payout* = (p) ~ beta distribution (alpha, beta)
- *Size of basis risk* ~ beta distribution, based on fit to empirical data
- *Correlation of basis risk* ~ t copula, based on fit to empirical data, where

  alpha = [Number of historical years with payouts > 0] + 1

  beta = Number of historical years with no payouts + 1
- *Aggregate annual payout ratio per area*

  ~ Frequency (0 or 1) × Severity

  ~ Bernoulli (p) × beta

Metrics based on at least 10,000 Monte Carlo scenarios

- *Exceedance probability* = (Number of scenarios with inventory damage > significant damage level)/Total number of scenarios
- *Return period* = 1/Exceedance probability
- *Return period ratio* = Inventory damage return period/Base Index return period
- *Probability that no insured party basis risk event will occur during the next risk period* = Number of scenarios where basis risk = 0/Total number of scenarios

---

- Probability that the Base Index will not experience an insured party or insurer basis risk event in the next risk period for each area
- Expected amount of insured party and insurer basis risk for the portfolio
- Historical years with largest insured party and insurer basis risk events for each area

The insurance manager uses these metrics in chapter 4 to answer the key managerial questions for evaluating the Base Index (see box 11.1). See case example box 11CB.25 for outputs.

Case Example Box 11CB.25 Outputs

INVENTORY DAMAGE RETURN PERIODS

				AREA A	AREA B	AREA C	AREA D	AREA E	AREA F	AREA G	AREA H	AREA I	AREA J
RETURN PERIOD	@	10%	DAMAGE LEVEL	13	9	9	4	6	6	5	4	4	3
RETURN PERIOD	@	30%	DAMAGE LEVEL	18	13	12	6	9	9	6	6	6	5
RETURN PERIOD	@	50%	DAMAGE LEVEL	30	20	19	9	14	14	10	10	9	8
RETURN PERIOD	@	70%	DAMAGE LEVEL	62	40	42	19	29	27	22	20	19	17

BASE INDEX RETURN PERIODS

				AREA A	AREA B	AREA C	AREA D	AREA E	AREA F	AREA G	AREA H	AREA I	AREA J
RETURN PERIOD	@	10%	PAYOUT LEVEL	14	7	11	5	6	7	9	8	7	3
RETURN PERIOD	@	30%	PAYOUT LEVEL	20	11	16	8	9	11	12	12	10	4
RETURN PERIOD	@	50%	PAYOUT LEVEL	30	17	24	12	14	16	18	18	16	7
RETURN PERIOD	@	70%	PAYOUT LEVEL	52	30	43	22	26	27	33	34	29	12

RETURN PERIOD RATIOS

				AREA A	AREA B	AREA C	AREA D	AREA E	AREA F	AREA G	AREA H	AREA I	AREA J
RETURN PERIOD RATIO	@	10%	DAMAGE/PAYOUT LEVEL	0.93	1.25	0.83	0.76	0.99	0.86	0.53	0.55	0.60	1.14
RETURN PERIOD RATIO	@	30%	DAMAGE/PAYOUT LEVEL	0.93	1.15	0.78	0.73	0.98	0.82	0.52	0.54	0.59	1.13
RETURN PERIOD RATIO	@	50%	DAMAGE/PAYOUT LEVEL	0.99	1.21	0.81	0.77	1.02	0.87	0.57	0.55	0.61	1.18
RETURN PERIOD RATIO	@	70%	DAMAGE/PAYOUT LEVEL	1.18	1.33	0.99	0.88	1.08	0.98	0.66	0.57	0.67	1.41

PROBABILITY THAT THE BASE INDEX WILL NOT EXPERIENCE AN INSURED PARTY BASIS RISK EVENT

AREA A	AREA B	AREA C	AREA D	AREA E	AREA F	AREA G	AREA H	AREA I	AREA J
90%	88%	86%	81%	81%	84%	82%	79%	74%	78%

PROJECTED INSURED PARTY BASIS RISK AMOUNT

	AMOUNT	% OF TOTAL SUM INSURED
LOWER	0	0%
EXPECTED	276,655	3%
UPPER	978,750	12%
TVaR	1,310,579	16%

HISTORICAL YEARS WITH LARGEST INSURED PARTY BASIS RISK RATIOS

	AREA A	AREA B	AREA C	AREA D	AREA E	AREA F	AREA G	AREA H	AREA I	AREA J
HISTORICAL YEARS WITH LARGEST INSURED PARTY BASIS RISK RATIO	2011	1986	2002	2006	1990	1987	1999	2000	1984	1991
BASIS RISK RATIO	28%	30%	25%	28%	23%	19%	28%	30%	27%	28%
HISTORICAL INVENTORY DAMAGE RATIO	3%	0%	5%	3%	67%	31%	3%	0%	23%	43%

PROBABILITY THAT THE BASE INDEX WILL NOT EXPERIENCE AN INSURER BASIS RISK EVENT

AREA A	AREA B	AREA C	AREA D	AREA E	AREA F	AREA G	AREA H	AREA I	AREA J
97%	84%	97%	87%	88%	94%	92%	94%	94%	72%

PROJECTED INSURER BASIS RISK STATISTICS AMOUNT

	AMOUNT	% OF TOTAL SUM INSURED
LOWER		0%
EXPECTED	159,939	2%
UPPER	709,878	9%
TVaR	1,009,740	13%

HISTORICAL YEARS WITH LARGEST INSURER BASIS RISK RATIOS

	AREA A	AREA B	AREA C	AREA D	AREA E	AREA F	AREA G	AREA H	AREA I	AREA J
HISTORICAL YEARS WITH LARGEST INSURED PARTY BASIS RISK RATIO	1984	1997	1984	2011	2013	1999	2010	1997	1998	1996
BASIS RISK RATIO	0%	20%	0%	17%	9%	18%	25%	15%	13%	28%
HISTORICAL PAYOUT RATIO	0%	20%	0%	17%	9%	18%	25%	65%	63%	28%
HISTORICAL INVENTORY DAMAGE RATIO	0%	0%	0%	0%	0%	0%	0%	50%	50%	0%

Note: TVaR = tail value at risk.

11.5 Alternative Modeling Approach: Retrospective Analysis

This chapter provides a step-by-step guide to using probabilistic models to evaluate the Base Index for product design basis risk. Chapter 16 discusses two additional probabilistic modeling approaches for calculating these metrics.

This section briefly describes a different type of nonprobabilistic analysis that is also used in index insurance product design and evaluation: **retrospective analysis**. A retrospective analysis can be used to evaluate the Base Index for basis risk. The key inputs to the retrospective analysis are the historical payout ratios and historical inventory damage ratios also used in the probabilistic approach (Steps 4 and 6). In the probabilistic approach, these inputs were used to simulate projected future values for both ratios, which were then compared to evaluate the basis risk of the Base Index.

The retrospective approach does not require simulation of any projected future values. Instead, historical inventory damage ratios are simply compared to historical payout ratios. The analysis is based only on historical values. The model tests the predictive power of the Base Index in retrospect. First, the model identifies the years for each area where the inventory damage ratio and payout ratios were both high, meaning that the Base Index correctly triggered a high payout that corresponded to high inventory damage caused by the named peril (case example box 11CB.26).

Risk Modeling for Appraising Named Peril Index Insurance Products
http://dx.doi.org/10.1596/978-1-4648-1048-0

Case Example Box 11CB.26 Review of Base Index Performance for Historical Events with Greater than 50 Percent Damage Level

For the case example, we set the level for a high inventory damage ratio as 50 percent and greater and the level for a high payout ratio as 30 percent and greater. Looking back at the historical inventory damage ratios in Step 6, we see that out of the 300 data points (that is, 10 areas for 30 years), 23 have damage ratios of at least 50 percent. The total number of historical events with damage ratios greater than 50 percent is 23 for the case example.

  When these 23 data points are compared with the corresponding points for the historical payout ratios, we see that 22 of them also triggered payouts of at least 30 percent. These are the years for which the Base Index correctly triggered a high payout that corresponded to high inventory damage caused by the named peril. Only one historical event with a high damage level—Area I in 1984—triggered a payout of less than 30 percent.

Second, the model identifies the years for each area in which the inventory damage ratio and payout ratio were both low, meaning that the Base Index correctly triggered a low payout that corresponded to low inventory damage caused by the named peril (case example box 11CB.27).

The results of this analysis can be shown in a classification matrix, as in table 11.12.

Using the classification matrix, the basis risk metrics can be calculated for the Base Index as in case example box 11CB.28.

Based on these metrics from the retrospective analysis, the insurer can conclude whether the Base Index's level of product design basis risk is acceptable. A good source of advice on acceptable levels for each metric is international reinsurers that have supported the writing of index products in different markets around the world.

Case Example Box 11CB.27 Review of Base Index Payouts of at Least 30 Percent

Looking back at the historical payout ratios for the case example in Step 4, out of the 300 data points, 25 have payout ratios of at least 30 percent. These are the total number of years with historical payouts greater than 30 percent.

  When these 25 data points are compared with the corresponding points for historical inventory damage ratios, we see that 22 of them also have inventory damage ratios greater than 50 percent. These are the years for which the Base Index correctly triggered a low payout that corresponded to low inventory damage caused by the named peril. Three high payouts—for Area G in 1998, Area J in 2006, and Area D in 2007—corresponded with historical events with damage levels less than 50 percent.

Table 11.12 Retrospective Classification Matrix for the Base Index

	Historical payout ratios of at least 30 percent	Historical payout ratios of less than 30 percent	Total
Historical events with damage ratios of at least 50 percent	22	1	23
Historical events with damage ratios of less than 50 percent	3	274	277
Total	25	275	300

Case Example Box 11CB.28 Calculation of Risk Metrics

Probability of Base Index triggering correctly

= [Number of high historical payout ratios that correspond to high historical damage ratios

+ number of low historical payout ratios that correspond to low historical damage ratios]

/Total data points

= [22 + 274]/300

= 99 percent

Probability of Base Index triggering insufficient payout when inventory damage occurs (insured party basis risk)

= Number of low historical payout ratios that correspond to high historical damage ratios

/Total number of historical events with high damage ratios

= 1/23

= 4 percent

Probability of Base Index triggering payout unnecessarily (insurer basis risk)

= Number of high historical payout ratios that correspond to low historical damage ratios

/Total number of historical events with low damage ratios

= 3/277

= 1 percent

Inventory damage return period = Total number of data points/Total number of historical events with high damage ratios

= 300/23

= 13 years

Base Index return period = Total number of data points/Total number of high historical payout ratios

= 300/25

= 12 years

From the above calculations of the metrics, we can conclude that if the Base Index had been in place during the past 30 years, it would have triggered payouts correctly 99 percent of the time. In 4 percent of cases, it would have triggered insufficient payouts when the policyholder experienced inventory damage of more than 50 percent from the named peril (low insured party basis risk). The insurer would have made a payout of at least 30 percent when the inventory damage was less than 50 percent in only 1 percent of cases (suggesting a fairly low insurer basis risk). Furthermore, the inventory damage return period and the Base Index return period are very similar, which confirms an overall high level of accuracy.

Because of limited data per area, the retrospective approach is best applied to a whole portfolio rather than to individual areas. Unfortunately, this portfolio-level approach does not provide the information necessary to improve the index structure for specific areas.

A clear limitation of the retrospective approach is that it only considers how the Base Index would have performed during the past 30 years. Although this approach provides some limited insight into the risks associated with index insurance products, probabilistic modeling provides far more. For example, a retrospective analysis cannot estimate the TVaR metric of basis risk that probabilistic models do.

Bibliography

Brehm, P. J. 2007. *Enterprise Risk Analysis for Property & Liability Insurance Companies: A Practical Guide to Standard Models and Emerging Solutions*. New York: Guy Carpenter.

Cherubini, U., E. Luciano, and W. Vecchiato. 2004. *Copula Methods in Finance*. Hoboken, NJ: John Wiley & Sons.

Crouhy, M., D. Galai, and R. Mark. 2006. *The Essentials of Risk Management*. New York: McGraw-Hill.

Embrechts, P., F. Lindskog, and A. McNeil. 2003. "Modelling Dependence with Copulas and Applications to Risk Management." In *Handbook of Heavy Tailed Distributions in Finance*, edited by S. T. Rachev, 329–84. Amsterdam: Elsevier.

Grossi, P., H. Kunreuther, and C. C. Patel. 2005. *Catastrophe Modeling: A New Approach to Managing Risk*. New York: Springer Science Business Media.

Lam, J. 2003. *Enterprise Risk Management: From Incentives to Controls*. Hoboken, NJ: Wiley.

Law, A. M., and W. D. Kelton. 2006. *Simulation Modeling and Analysis*. 4th ed. New York: McGraw-Hill.

Lehman, D. E., H. Groenendaal, and G. Nolder. 2012. *Practical Spreadsheet Risk Modeling for Management*. Boca Raton, FL: Chapman & Hall/CRC.

Morsink, K., D. Clarke, and S. Mapfumo. 2016. "How to Measure Whether Index Insurance Provides Reliable Protection." Policy Research Working Paper 7744, World Bank, Washington, DC.

Ragsdale, C. T. 2001. *Spreadsheet Modeling and Decision Analysis: A Practical Introduction to Management Science*. Cincinnati, OH: Southwestern College.

Tang, A., and E. A. Valdez. 2009. "Economic Capital and the Aggregation of Risks Using Copulas." University of New South Wales, Sydney, Australia.

Yan, J. 2006. "Multivariate Modeling with Copulas and Engineering Applications." In *Springer Handbook of Engineering Statistics*, edited by H. Pham, 973–90. London: Springer-Verlag.

CHAPTER 12

Pricing the Base Index

12.1 Background and Objectives

Chapter 5 explained the key managerial questions for Base Index product pricing during the pilot phase of launching an index insurance business line. It explained a series of steps for determining the price for a portfolio-priced Base Index under three situations:

- The policy is not reinsured
- The policy is reinsured through proportional reinsurance only
- The policy is reinsured through a combination of nonproportional reinsurance and proportional reinsurance

This chapter provides a step-by-step guide to using the probabilistic models that produce the decision metrics discussed in chapter 5. Using the Base Index's historical payout ratios for the portfolio, the model simulates the scenario portfolio payout amount (steps 8–12) and then estimates decision metrics for different Base Index portfolio-priced premium rates with no reinsurance (Steps 13–18), with proportional reinsurance only (Steps 19–24), and with proportional and nonproportional reinsurance (Steps 25–30). Based on these metrics the insurer can determine the portfolio-priced premium rate for the Base Index that best meets the profit objectives and risk tolerance of the insurer.

In addition to providing metrics for portfolio pricing the Base Index, the model in this chapter also calculates the equitable premiums for each of the geographical areas (Steps 31–38). The insurer will repeat the pricing process with any later Redesigned Indexes or prototype products.

Table 12.1 provides a summary of the model components along with a guide to the sections in this chapter and the worksheets in the accompanying Excel files.

12.2 Model Inputs

The analyst starts by specifying the model inputs agreed upon with the insurance manager for pricing the Base Index (table 12.2).

Table 12.1 Summary of Model Components for Pricing the Base Index

Model component	Section	Excel sheet label	Steps	Description
Model inputs	12.2	MI_12.2_MODEL INPUTS	Steps 1–7	User-defined assumptions, relevant portfolio and insurer information, historical payout ratios, and reinsurance terms are entered.
Model computations	12.3.1	MC_12.3.1__PAYOUT_SCENARIOS	Steps 8–12	Simulation of scenario payout amounts
	12.3.2	MC_12.3.2_NO REINSURANCE	Steps 13–18	Calculation of product pricing decision metrics for no reinsurance
	12.3.3	MC_12.3.3_PR REINSURANCE	Steps 19–24	Calculation of product pricing decision metrics for proportional reinsurance only
	12.3.4	MC_12.3.4_PR & NP REINSURANCE	Steps 25–30	Calculation of product pricing decision metrics for proportional and nonproportional reinsurance
	12.3.5	MC_12.3.5_EQUITABLE PREMIUMS	Steps 31–38	Calculation of equitable premium metrics for each geographical area
Model outputs	12.4	MO_12.5_MODEL OUTPUT	None	Summary of pricing decision metrics for no reinsurance, proportional reinsurance only, and proportional and nonproportional reinsurance, plus equitable premium rates for each geographical area

Table 12.2 Model Inputs

Model component	Section	Excel sheet label	Steps	Description
Model inputs	12.2	MI_12.2_MODEL INPUTS	Steps 1–7	User defined assumptions, relevant portfolio and insurer information, historical payout ratios, and reinsurance terms are entered.

12.2.1 Exposed Units (Step 1)

The portfolio pricing depends on the total sum insured per insured area, known as the **exposed units** per area. This input is calculated from the number of insured units and the average unit size (AUS; the average sum insured per unit) for each area (case example box 12CB.1).

In cases in which the policyholder has high uncertainty about the average unit size per area, this uncertainty can be specified as a probability distribution. The most appropriate distribution for this operation is a project evaluation and review techniques (PERT) distribution for which the input parameters are the minimum, most likely, and maximum values (see chapter 10).

Case Example Box 12CB.1 Inputs—Step 1

STEP 1 : ENTER EXPOSED UNITS

	AREA A	AREA B	AREA C	AREA D	AREA E	AREA F	AREA G	AREA H	AREA I	AREA J
# OF INSURED UNITS	1,168	3,773	7,500	4,250	21,450	3,000	8,267	12,635	3,865	7,620
UNIT SIZE ($)	120	75	160	100	105	94	120	95	110	105
EXPOSED UNITS ($)	140,160	282,975	1,200,000	425,000	2,252,250	282,000	992,040	1,200,325	425,150	800,100

12.2.2 Internal Insurer Assumptions (Step 2)
The analyst next specifies inputs based on internal insurer data (case example box 12CB.2).

- Total sum insured ($): Total for all geographical areas.
- Starting fund value ($): The accumulated net premiums from previous risk periods and any start-up funds for the index insurance business line.
- Expense loading (as a percentage of premiums): Selling, general, and administrative costs. These costs will differ from company to company. For a new product line, the insurer can use rates from a comparable class in its portfolio or from data collected from other companies writing the same class of business. Reinsurers may also give some guidance based on international experience.
- Target profit margin (%): The profit margin that the insurer is targeting for the business line.
- Required return on capital (%): The return that the insurer's shareholders require to keep their capital in this business line. Please note that this is an effective rate per risk period and not per year.
- Risk-free rate (%): The interest an investor would expect from a risk-free investment. Typically, the cost of the interest rate on a three-month U.S. Treasury bill is used as a proxy.
- Prediction interval (%).

12.2.3 Premium Rates (Step 3)
The analyst next inputs the portfolio gross premium rates to be evaluated by the model (case example box 12CB.3). The expense costs (as specified in Step 2) will be subtracted before arriving at net premium rates.

Case Example Box 12CB.2 Inputs—Step 2

STEP 2 : ENTER INSURER ASSUMPTIONS

TOTAL SUM INSURED ($)	8,000,000
STARTING FUND VALUE ($)	50,000
EXPENSE LOADING (%)	15%
TARGET PROFIT MARGIN (%)	10%
CAPITAL (%)	5%
RISK FREE RATE (%)	2%

PREDICTION INTERVAL (%)

LOWER	5%
UPPER	95%

Risk Modeling for Appraising Named Peril Index Insurance Products
http://dx.doi.org/10.1596/978-1-4648-1048-0

Case Example Box 12CB.3 Inputs—Step 3

STEP 3 : ENTER PORTFOLIO GROSS PREMIUM RATES TO BE EVALUATED (%)

SENARIO #	GROSS PREMIUM RATE
1	3%
2	4%
3	5%
4	6%
5	7%
6	8%
7	9%
8	10%
9	11%
10	12%

12.2.4 Historical Payout Ratios (Step 4)

The historical payout ratios for the Base Index (case example box 12CB.4) will be used in the simulation of payout ratios in steps 8–12.

12.2.5 Nonzero Historical Payout Ratios (Step 5)

In this step (no case example box provided) the analyst manually records all the nonzero values for the historical payout ratios from Step 4. These inputs will be used in the simulation of payout ratios (Steps 8–12).

Case Example Box 12CB.4 Inputs—Step 4

STEP 4 : ENTER HISTORICAL PAYOUT RATIOS (%)

YEAR	AREA A	AREA B	AREA C	AREA D	AREA E	AREA F	AREA G	AREA H	AREA I	AREA J
1984	0.0%	0.0%	0.0%	0.0%	44.1%	0.0%	0.0%	0.0%	22.6%	90.4%
1985	0.0%	0.0%	0.0%	0.0%	0.0%	0.0%	0.0%	0.0%	0.0%	0.0%
1986	0.0%	0.0%	22.5%	0.0%	0.0%	0.0%	0.0%	0.0%	0.0%	7.5%
1987	0.0%	0.0%	0.0%	0.0%	22.5%	31.2%	0.0%	0.0%	0.0%	0.0%
1988	0.0%	0.0%	0.0%	47.5%	0.0%	0.0%	0.0%	0.0%	0.0%	0.0%
1989	0.0%	15.0%	0.0%	0.0%	7.5%	0.0%	0.0%	0.0%	0.0%	0.0%
1990	0.0%	0.0%	7.5%	100.0%	66.6%	0.0%	0.0%	0.0%	0.0%	2.5%
1991	0.0%	0.0%	0.0%	0.0%	0.0%	0.0%	0.0%	0.0%	0.0%	42.5%
1992	0.0%	0.0%	0.0%	50.0%	0.0%	0.0%	0.0%	0.0%	0.0%	86.0%
1993	0.0%	0.0%	0.0%	0.0%	0.0%	0.0%	0.0%	0.0%	0.0%	44.4%
1994	0.0%	0.0%	0.0%	0.0%	0.0%	0.0%	0.0%	0.0%	5.0%	96.0%
1995	0.0%	0.0%	0.0%	0.0%	0.0%	0.0%	0.0%	0.0%	0.0%	0.0%
1996	79.2%	0.0%	0.0%	0.0%	0.0%	5.8%	0.0%	0.0%	0.0%	27.5%
1997	0.0%	20.0%	0.0%	0.0%	0.0%	15.0%	0.0%	65.4%	0.0%	0.0%
1998	0.0%	0.0%	0.0%	0.0%	0.0%	0.0%	30.0%	0.0%	63.2%	0.0%
1999	0.0%	0.0%	0.0%	0.0%	2.5%	17.5%	2.5%	86.2%	0.0%	39.0%
2000	0.0%	0.0%	0.0%	0.0%	0.0%	0.0%	53.4%	0.0%	0.0%	0.0%
2001	0.0%	0.0%	0.0%	0.0%	0.0%	0.0%	0.0%	0.0%	0.0%	0.0%
2002	0.0%	0.0%	5.0%	0.0%	0.0%	0.0%	0.0%	0.0%	0.0%	0.0%
2003	0.0%	0.0%	0.0%	0.0%	0.0%	0.0%	0.0%	0.0%	29.0%	60.0%
2004	0.0%	0.0%	0.0%	19.2%	0.0%	0.0%	0.0%	0.0%	0.0%	0.0%
2005	0.0%	0.0%	0.0%	0.0%	0.0%	0.0%	0.0%	0.0%	0.0%	0.0%
2006	0.0%	0.0%	0.0%	2.5%	0.0%	0.0%	0.0%	0.0%	0.0%	39.4%
2007	0.0%	0.0%	0.0%	40.4%	0.0%	0.0%	0.0%	0.0%	0.0%	0.0%
2008	0.0%	0.0%	0.0%	0.0%	0.0%	0.0%	0.0%	0.0%	0.0%	17.5%
2009	0.0%	2.5%	0.0%	0.0%	0.0%	0.0%	0.0%	0.0%	32.8%	64.0%
2010	0.0%	0.0%	0.0%	0.0%	0.0%	0.0%	25.0%	61.2%	0.0%	0.0%
2011	2.5%	7.5%	0.0%	16.6%	0.0%	0.0%	0.0%	0.0%	0.0%	0.0%
2012	0.0%	5.0%	0.0%	0.0%	0.0%	2.5%	0.0%	0.0%	0.0%	0.0%
2013	0.0%	0.0%	0.0%	0.0%	9.0%	0.0%	0.0%	45.2%	0.0%	0.0%

12.2.6 Proportional Reinsurance Terms (Step 6)

The analyst specifies the percentage of the risk that will be ceded to the reinsurer under a potential proportional reinsurance arrangement (case example box 12CB.5).

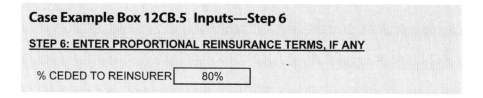

Case Example Box 12CB.5 Inputs—Step 6

STEP 6: ENTER PROPORTIONAL REINSURANCE TERMS, IF ANY

% CEDED TO REINSURER   80%

12.2.7 Nonproportional Reinsurance Terms (Step 7)

The analyst specifies several parameters for a potential nonproportional reinsurance arrangement (case example box 12CB.6).

The *treaty retention* is the amount of claim exposure that the insurer will retain. None of the payout amounts less than the treaty retention amount specified by the user will be covered by the reinsurer.

The *aggregate loss limit* is the upper limit of exposure that the reinsurer will cover. For any claims between the treaty retention and the aggregate loss limit, the reinsurer will cover a percentage of the losses (the percentage carried by the reinsurer under nonproportional treaty).

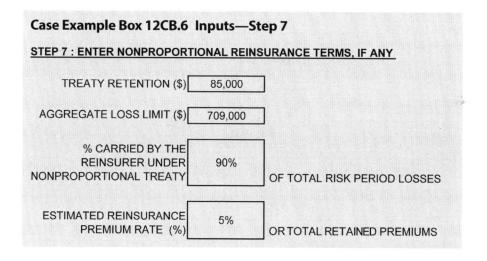

Case Example Box 12CB.6 Inputs—Step 7

STEP 7 : ENTER NONPROPORTIONAL REINSURANCE TERMS, IF ANY

TREATY RETENTION ($)   85,000

AGGREGATE LOSS LIMIT ($)   709,000

% CARRIED BY THE REINSURER UNDER NONPROPORTIONAL TREATY   90%   OF TOTAL RISK PERIOD LOSSES

ESTIMATED REINSURANCE PREMIUM RATE (%)   5%   OR TOTAL RETAINED PREMIUMS

Finally, the reinsurer will charge the insurer a reinsurance premium that is a percentage of the retained premium income.

12.3 Model Computations

The model completes five sets of computations for pricing the Base Index, starting with simulating the key scenario parameters—payout amounts for the Base Index (Steps 8–12)—then producing product pricing decision metrics for the portfolio-priced premiums under the three reinsurance scenarios (Steps 13–30), and finally determining the equitable premiums for each geographical area (Steps 31–38) (see table 12.3).

Remember that the insurer will repeat these pricing computations with any later Redesigned Indexes or prototype products.

12.3.1 Simulation of Scenario Portfolio Payout Amount (Steps 8–12)
12.3.1.1 Overview
Based on the historical payout ratios (Step 4), the model simulates the scenario payout ratios for the Base Index using estimates for three stochastic elements: frequency, severity, and correlation.

12.3.1.2 Implementation in Excel (MC_12.3.1_PAYOUT_SCENARIOS)
Steps 8–12 (table 12.4) for simulating the scenario portfolio payout amount are similar to Steps 14–18 in section 11.3.3 but with one key difference. In chapter 11, the model calculates only the payout ratios. In this chapter, however, Steps 11 and 12 calculate monetary amounts for the payouts by area and for the total portfolio rather than just ratios.

The reader is referred back to section 11.3.3 for further details on the modeling.

Table 12.3 Model Computations

Model component	Section	Excel sheet label	Steps	Description
Model computations	12.3.1	MC_12.3.1_PAYOUT_SCENARIOS	Steps 8–12	Simulation of scenario payout amounts
	12.3.2	MC_12.3.2_NO REINSURANCE	Steps 13–18	Calculation of product pricing decision metrics for no reinsurance
	12.3.3	MC_12.3.3_PR REINSURANCE	Steps 19–24	Calculation of product pricing decision metrics for proportional reinsurance only
	12.3.4	MC_12.3.4_PR & NP REINSURANCE	Steps 25–30	Calculation of product pricing decision metrics for proportional and nonproportional reinsurance
	12.3.5	MC_12.3.5_EQUITABLE PREMIUMS	Steps 31–38	Calculation of equitable premium metrics for each geographical area

Table 12.4 Model Computations

Model component	Section	Excel sheet label	Steps	Description
Model computations	12.3.1	MC_12.3.1_PAYOUT_SCENARIOS	Steps 8–12	Simulation of scenario payout amounts

Case example box 12CB.7 shows the simulation of the scenario portfolio payout amount for the case example.

12.3.2 Calculation of Product Pricing Decision Metrics—No Reinsurance (Steps 13–18)

At this point the model has simulated the scenario portfolio payout amounts. Based on these scenario payouts, the model now calculates decision metrics that estimate the financial results for the insurer under a number of different premium rates and in three reinsurance situations (table 12.5). First, the model addresses the scenario in which the Base Index is not reinsured.

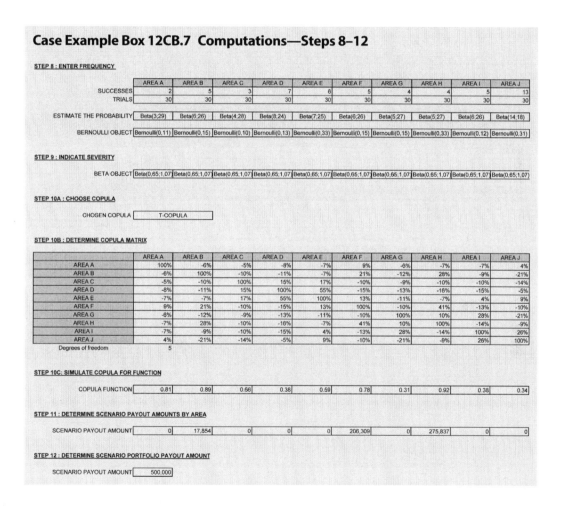

Case Example Box 12CB.7 Computations—Steps 8–12

STEP 8 : ENTER FREQUENCY

	AREA A	AREA B	AREA C	AREA D	AREA E	AREA F	AREA G	AREA H	AREA I	AREA J
SUCCESSES	2	5	3	7	6	5	4	4	5	13
TRIALS	30	30	30	30	30	30	30	30	30	30
ESTIMATE THE PROBABILITY	Beta(3;29)	Beta(6;26)	Beta(4;28)	Beta(8;24)	Beta(7;25)	Beta(6;26)	Beta(5;27)	Beta(5;27)	Beta(6;26)	Beta(14;18)
BERNOULLI OBJECT	Bernoulli(0,11)	Bernoulli(0,15)	Bernoulli(0,10)	Bernoulli(0,13)	Bernoulli(0,33)	Bernoulli(0,15)	Bernoulli(0,15)	Bernoulli(0,33)	Bernoulli(0,12)	Bernoulli(0,31)

STEP 9 : INDICATE SEVERITY

	AREA A	AREA B	AREA C	AREA D	AREA E	AREA F	AREA G	AREA H	AREA I	AREA J
BETA OBJECT	Beta(0,65;1,07)	Beta(0,65;1,07)	Beta(0,65;1,07)	Beta(0,65;1,07)	Beta(0,65;1,07)	Beta(0,65;1,07)	Beta(0,65;1,07)	Beta(0,65;1,07)	Beta(0,65;1,07)	Beta(0,65;1,07)

STEP 10A : CHOOSE COPULA

CHOSEN COPULA	T-COPULA

STEP 10B : DETERMINE COPULA MATRIX

	AREA A	AREA B	AREA C	AREA D	AREA E	AREA F	AREA G	AREA H	AREA I	AREA J
AREA A	100%	-6%	-5%	-8%	-7%	9%	-6%	-7%	-7%	4%
AREA B	-6%	100%	-10%	-11%	-7%	21%	-12%	28%	-9%	-21%
AREA C	-5%	-10%	100%	15%	17%	-10%	-9%	-10%	-10%	-14%
AREA D	-8%	-11%	15%	100%	55%	-15%	-13%	-16%	-15%	-5%
AREA E	-7%	-7%	17%	55%	100%	13%	-11%	-7%	4%	9%
AREA F	9%	21%	-10%	-15%	13%	100%	-10%	41%	-13%	-10%
AREA G	-6%	-12%	-9%	-13%	-11%	-10%	100%	10%	28%	-21%
AREA H	-7%	28%	-10%	-16%	-7%	41%	10%	100%	-14%	-9%
AREA I	-7%	-9%	-10%	-15%	4%	-13%	28%	-14%	100%	26%
AREA J	4%	-21%	-14%	-5%	9%	-10%	-21%	-9%	26%	100%
Degrees of freedom	5									

STEP 10C: SIMULATE COPULA FOR FUNCTION

COPULA FUNCTION	0.81	0.89	0.66	0.38	0.59	0.78	0.31	0.92	0.38	0.34

STEP 11 : DETERMINE SCENARIO PAYOUT AMOUNTS BY AREA

SCENARIO PAYOUT AMOUNT	0	17,854	0	0	0	206,309	0	275,837	0	0

STEP 12 : DETERMINE SCENARIO PORTFOLIO PAYOUT AMOUNT

SCENARIO PAYOUT AMOUNT	500,000

Table 12.5 Model Computations

Model component	Section	Excel sheet label	Steps	Description
Model computations	12.3.2	MC_12.3.2_NO REINSURANCE	Steps 13–18	Calculation of product pricing decision metrics for no reinsurance

Risk Modeling for Appraising Named Peril Index Insurance Products
http://dx.doi.org/10.1596/978-1-4648-1048-0

12.3.2.1 Expected Losses and Required Capital

12.3.2.1.1 Overview. Figure 12.1 provides an overview of how the model simulates the **expected losses** and required capital based on the scenario portfolio payout amount (Step 12). The portfolio payout amount is the same as losses for the insurer because with no reinsurance the insurer will need to pay all claims.

12.3.2.1.2 Implementation in Excel (MC_12.3.2_NO REINSURANCE). Case example box 12CB.8 shows the steps in which the model estimates the expected portfolio losses and required capital.

In Step 13, the model inserts the value for the scenario portfolio payout amount from Step 12 as the scenario losses. Remember, because no reinsurer is involved, the portfolio payout amount is the same as the losses for the insurer.

In Step 14, the model generates at least 10,000 scenario loss amounts (Monte Carlo scenarios) for the portfolio and determines the expected losses for the next risk period. Based on the prediction interval selected in Step 2, the model also calculates the appropriate percentile and tail value at risk (TVaR) values. These values indicate the expected magnitude of the insurer's losses.

Figure 12.1 Generating Expected Losses and Required Capital

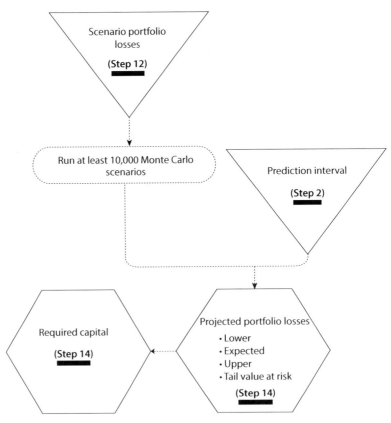

Note: TVaR = tail value at risk.

Case Example Box 12CB.8 Computations—Steps 13 and 14

STEP 13 : SHOW SCENARIO PORTFOLIO LOSSES

	500,000

STEP 14 : CALCULATE PROJECTED PORTFOLIO LOSSES AND REQUIRED CAPITAL

LOWER	0%
EXPECTED	619,287
UPPER	2,038,858
TVaR	2,488,867

REQUIRED CAPITAL	1,869,580

REQUIRED CAPITAL   (1st simulation) | 1,869,580 |

> After a first simulation, copy the value (value only) from the Required Capital cell to the Required Capital (1st simulation) cell.

In the case example, the expected losses for the next risk period are $619,287. The prediction interval for the case example is 90 percent, so the model also shows the 5th and 95th percentiles and the tail value at risk (TVaR) 95 percent. The TVaR 95 percent tells us that for a 1-in-20 year event, the losses are expected to be as high as $2,488,867.

In the case example, the required capital is $1,869,580.

$$\text{Required capital} = \text{TVaR losses} - \text{Expected losses}$$
$$= \$2,488,867 - \$619,287$$
$$= \$1,869,580$$

The insurer should keep $1,869,580 in reserve (as required capital) to stay solvent in case of a 1-in-20 year event (TVaR 95 percent).

Also in Step 14, the model uses the same 10,000 scenarios to calculate the required capital for the portfolio. The required capital is the amount of capital that the insurer will need to keep in reserve to be sure that it can make the payouts for extreme events, defined as the total claim that is expected once every 20 years (that is, TVaR).

$$\text{Required capital} = \text{TVaR losses} - \text{Expected losses}$$

Remember, the model—and its calculation of required capital (see section 10.3.2)–– assumes that the index insurance product that is evaluated is the only product that the insurer offers (see section 9.3). In reality, the insurer would most likely have several lines of business, and the capital allocated to each business line will be a function of the overall capital required for the whole firm. The guide follows this simplistic approach because each company will have unique business and asset compositions, and each market will have different regulatory requirements. Following a **monoline insurance** approach allows us to demonstrate the principles underlying probabilistic modeling without introducing too much complexity.

12.3.2.2 Combined Ratios and Profit Margins

12.3.2.2.1 Overview. In this section the model compares combined ratios and profit margins across different premium rates; later sections compare them across alternative reinsurance situations. Profit margins and combined ratios are useful in both product development and financial reporting. Profit margin measures the percentage of the insurance premium that the insurer actually keeps in earnings. The calculation of the combined ratio and profit margin is shown in figure 12.2.

Figure 12.2 Generating Expected Combined Ratios and Profit Margins

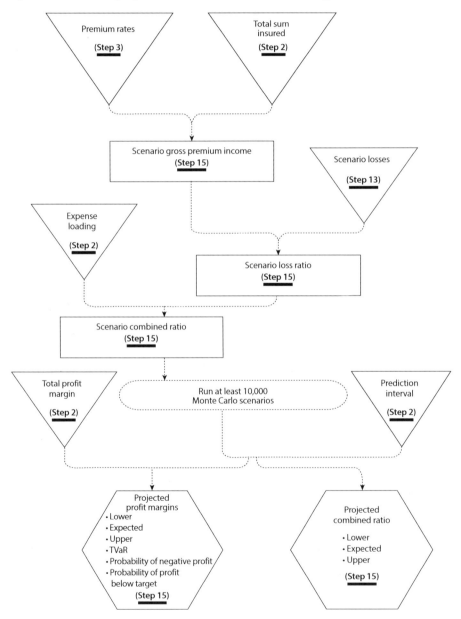

Note: TVaR = tail value at risk.

12.3.2.2.2 Implementation in Excel (MC_12.3.2_NO REINSURANCE). In Step 15 (case example box 12CB.9), the model first calculates the scenario gross premium income for each premium rate (Step 3) and the total portfolio sum insured (Step 2).

Scenario gross premium income = Premium rate × Total portfolio sum insured
(Step 3)   (Step 2)

Case Example Box 12CB.9 Computations—Step 15

STEP 15 : CALCULATE COMBINED RATIO AND PROFIT MARGIN

ITERATION #	GROSS PREMIUM RATE (%)	GROSS PREMIUM INCOME ($)	SCENARIO COMBINED RATIO (%)	SCENARIO PROFIT MARGIN (%)	PROJECTED COMBINED RATIO (%)				PROJECTED PROFIT MARGIN (%)			PROBABILITY OF NEGATIVE PROFIT (%)	PROBABILITY OF PROFIT BELOW TARGET (%)
					Lower	Expected	Upper	TVaR	Lower	Expected	Upper		
1	3%	240,000	223%	-123%	15%	273%	865%	1087%	-766%	-173%	85%	66%	68%
2	4%	320,000	171%	-71%	15%	209%	652%	804%	-553%	-109%	85%	60%	63%
3	5%	400,000	140%	-40%	15%	170%	525%	646%	-426%	-70%	85%	55%	58%
4	6%	480,000	119%	-19%	15%	144%	440%	541%	-341%	-44%	85%	50%	53%
5	7%	560,000	104%	-4%	15%	126%	379%	466%	-280%	-26%	85%	46%	49%
6	8%	640,000	93%	7%	15%	112%	334%	409%	-234%	-12%	85%	41%	45%
7	9%	720,000	84%	16%	15%	101%	298%	366%	-199%	-1%	85%	38%	42%
8	10%	800,000	78%	23%	15%	92%	270%	331%	-170%	8%	85%	34%	38%
9	11%	880,000	72%	28%	15%	85%	247%	302%	-147%	15%	85%	31%	35%
10	12%	960,000	67%	33%	15%	80%	227%	278%	-128%	20%	85%	28%	32%

For the case example, the gross premium income for the 10 percent premium rate is $800,000.

Scenario gross premium income = Premium rate × Total portfolio sum insured

= 10 percent × 8,000,000

= $800,000

The scenario loss ratio for the 10 percent premium rate is 62.5 percent (not shown in Step 15 table).

Scenario loss ratio = Scenario losses/Scenario gross premium income

= 500,000/800,000

= 62.5 percent

The scenario combined ratio for the 10 percent premium rate is 77.5 percent.

Scenario combined ratio = Scenario loss ratio + Expense loading

= 62.5 percent + 15 percent

= 77.5 percent

For the case example, the scenario profit margin for the 10 percent premium rate is 22.5 percent.

Scenario profit margin = 100 percent − Scenario combined ratio

= 100 percent − 77.5 percent

= 22.5 percent

For the 10 percent premium rate in the case example, the probability of a negative profit is 34 percent.

Probability of a negative profit = ~ 3,400 of the 10,000 Monte Carlo scenarios

= 34 percent

For the 10 percent premium rate in the case example, the probability of a profit of less than the target profit margin is 38 percent.

Probability of a profit below the target profit margin = ~ 3,800 of the 10,000 Monte Carlo scenarios

= 38 percent

Note: TVaR = tail value at risk.

Risk Modeling for Appraising Named Peril Index Insurance Products
http://dx.doi.org/10.1596/978-1-4648-1048-0

Also in Step 15, the model calculates the scenario loss ratio for each premium rate using the scenario losses (Step 13) and the gross premium income.

$$\text{Scenario loss ratio} = \text{Scenario losses/Scenario gross premium income}$$
(Step 13)

Next, Step 15 calculates the scenario combined ratio for each premium rate using the scenario loss ratio and expense loading.

$$\text{Scenario combined ratio} = \text{Scenario loss ratio} + \text{Expense loading}$$
(Step 2)

Next, Step 15 calculates the scenario profit margin for each premium rate from the scenario combined ratio.

$$\text{Scenario profit margin} = 100 \text{ percent} - \text{Scenario combined ratio}$$
(Step 15)

At this point, the model generates at least 10,000 Monte Carlo combined ratio scenarios for each of the 10 possible premium rates and determines the expected combined ratio for the next risk period (92 percent for the 10 percent premium rate in the case example). Based on the prediction interval selected in Step 2, the model also calculates the appropriate percentile and TVaR values for the combined ratio.

Using the same 10,000 scenarios, the model next calculates the profit margins for each of the 10 premium rates and determines the expected profit margin for the next risk period (8 percent for the 10 percent premium rate in the case example), along with the appropriate percentiles.

Finally, the model calculates the probability of a negative profit and the probability of a profit of less than the target profit margin (Step 2) for each of the premium rates.

$$\text{Probability of a negative profit} = \text{percent of Monte Carlo scenarios in which the scenario profits are lower than \$0}$$

$$\begin{aligned} \text{Probability of a profit below} \\ \text{the target profit margin} \end{aligned} = \text{percent of Monte Carlo scenarios in which the scenario profits are lower than the target profit margin}$$
(Step 2)

12.3.2.3 Probability of Fund Ruin

12.3.2.3.1 Overview. The probability of fund ruin (figure 12.3) is another important metric for the insurer when considering pricing for the Base Index. This probability indicates the likelihood that the capital fund available to cover the product risk will be exhausted over a specified time frame. The model considers a one-year or one-growing-season period.

Figure 12.3 Generating Probability of Fund Ruin

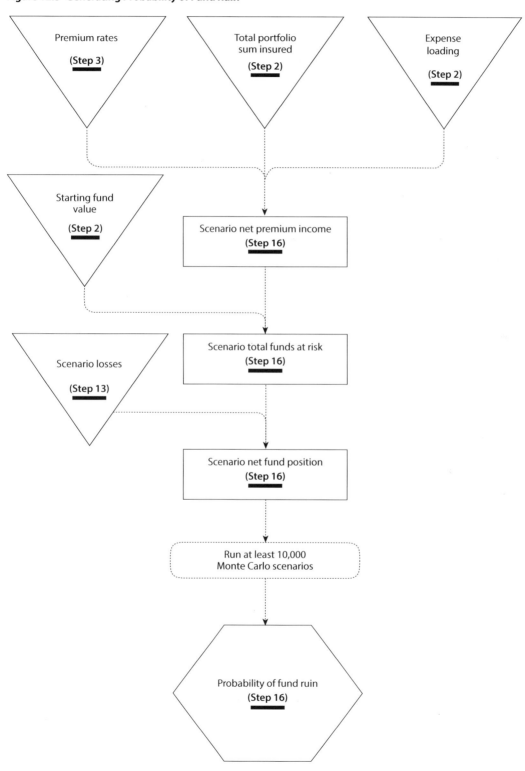

Risk Modeling for Appraising Named Peril Index Insurance Products
http://dx.doi.org/10.1596/978-1-4648-1048-0

Implementation in Excel (MC_12.3.2_NO REINSURANCE)
In Step 16 (case example box 12CB.10), the model calculates the net premium rate from the gross premium rate and the expense loading.

Scenario net premium rate = Scenario gross premium rate × (1 – Expense loading)
                              (Step 3)   (Step 2)

Case Example Box 12CB.10 Computations—Step 16

STEP 16 : CALCULATE PROBABILITY OF FUND RUIN

ITERATION #	GROSS PREMIUM RATE (%)	NET PREMIUM RATE (%)	TOTAL FUNDS AT RISK ($)	SCENARIO NET FUND POSITION ($)	PROBABILITY OF FUND RUIN (%)
1	3%	2.6%	254,000	-246,000	62%
2	4%	3.4%	322,000	-178,000	56%
3	5%	4.3%	390,000	-110,000	51%
4	6%	5.1%	458,000	-42,000	47%
5	7%	6.0%	526,000	26,000	42%
6	8%	6.8%	594,000	94,000	39%
7	9%	7.7%	662,000	162,000	35%
8	10%	8.5%	730,000	230,000	32%
9	11%	9.4%	798,000	298,000	29%
10	12%	10.2%	866,000	366,000	26%

For the case example, the scenario net premium rate for the 10 percent gross premium rate is 8.5 percent:

Scenario net premium rate = Scenario gross premium rate × (1–Expense loading)
= 10 percent × (1 – 0.15)
= 8.5 percent

The scenario net premium income for the 10 percent gross premium rate is $680,000 (not shown in Step 16 table).

Scenario net premium income = Scenario net premium rate × Total sum insured
= 8.5 percent × 8,000,000
= $680,000

In the case example, the total funds at risk for the 10 percent premium rate are $730,000.

Scenario total funds at risk = Scenario net premium income + Starting fund value
= 680,000 + 50,000
= $730,000

For the case example, the scenario net fund position for the 10 percent premium rate is $230,000.

Scenario net fund position = Total funds at risk – Scenario losses
= 730,000 – 500,000
= $230,000

The net premium rates will be used in Step 35 when estimating the capital return.

Also in Step 16, the model calculates the scenario **net premium income** for each premium rate from the net premium rates and the total portfolio sum insured.

$$\text{Scenario net premium income} = \text{Scenario net premium rate} \times \text{Total sum insured}$$
$$(\text{Step 3}) \qquad\qquad (\text{Step 3}) \qquad\qquad (\text{Step 2})$$

Also in Step 16, the model calculates the **total funds at risk** for each premium rate from the net premium income and the starting fund value (Step 2). This value is the maximum amount of exposure that the insurer is willing to take during a risk period.

$$\text{Scenario total funds at risk} = \text{Scenario net premium income} + \text{Starting fund value}$$
$$(\text{Step 2})$$

Step 16 next calculates the scenario **net fund position** for each premium rate from the scenario losses (Step 13) and the total funds at risk.

$$\text{Scenario net fund position} = \text{Scenario total funds at risk} - \text{Scenario losses}$$
$$(\text{Step 13})$$

At this point, the model generates at least 10,000 scenario net fund positions for each premium rate. The proportion of the 10,000 scenarios with fund positions less than zero (32 percent for the 10 percent premium rate in the case example) is the probability of fund ruin.

12.3.2.4 Economic Value Added
12.3.2.4.1 Overview. Another metric for the insurer to evaluate when deciding premium rates is the economic value added (EVA). EVA is the profit earned by the firm minus the cost of financing the firm's capital (figure 12.4). The insurer behind the risk-taking activity establishes the capital requirement. For the EVA to be positive, the profit from the index insurance product will need to more than cover the costs of the capital required for issuing the index insurance product. Specifically, EVA is the difference between the value derived from selling the product (the premium income) and the cost of doing so, including expenses, potential payouts, and financing costs of the required capital. In this guide, the EVA is expressed as a percentage of required capital.

Implementation in Excel (MC_12.3.2_NO REINSURANCE)
In Step 17 (case example box 12CB.11), the model calculates the net premium income as in Step 16. Next, the model calculates the scenario capital charge.

$$\text{Scenario capital charge} = \text{Required capital} \times \text{Required return on capital}$$
$$(\text{Step 14}) \qquad\qquad (\text{Step 2})$$

Figure 12.4 Generating Potential Economic Value Added

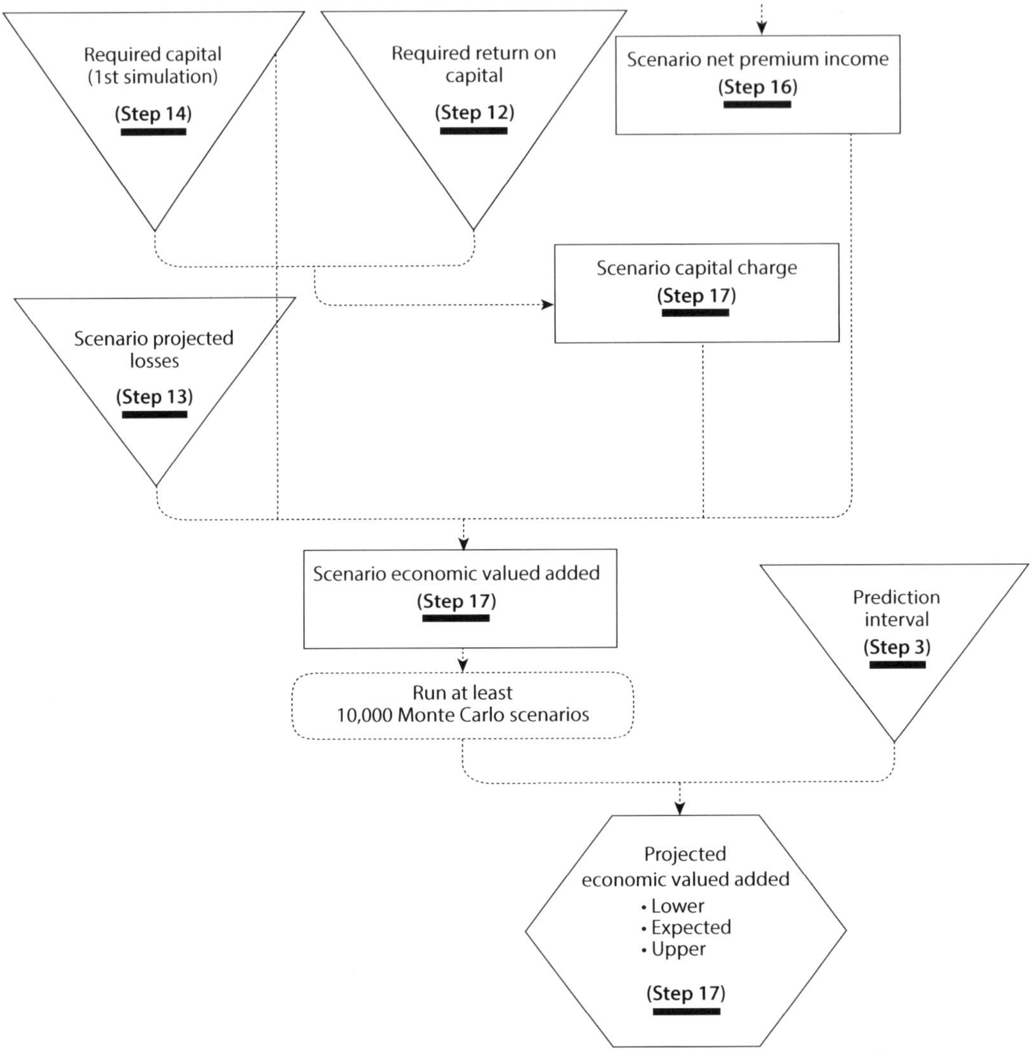

Case Example Box 12CB.11 Computations—Step 17

STEP 17 : CALCULATE ECONOMIC VALUE ADDED

ITERATION #	GROSS PREMIUM RATE (%)	NET PREMIUM RATE (%)	NET PREMIUM INCOME ($)	CAPITAL CHARGE ($)	SCENARIO EVA (%)	PROJECTED EVA (%)		
						Lower	Expected	Upper
1	3%	2.6%	204,000	93,479	-21%	-103%	-27%	6%
2	4%	3.4%	272,000	93,479	-17%	-100%	-24%	10%
3	5%	4.3%	340,000	93,479	-14%	-96%	-20%	13%
4	6%	5.1%	408,000	93,479	-10%	-92%	-16%	17%
5	7%	6.0%	476,000	93,479	-6%	-89%	-13%	20%
6	8%	6.8%	544,000	93,479	-3%	-85%	-9%	24%
7	9%	7.7%	612,000	93,479	1%	-82%	-5%	28%
8	10%	8.5%	680,000	93,479	5%	-78%	-2%	31%
9	11%	9.4%	748,000	93,479	8%	-74%	2%	35%
10	12%	10.2%	816,000	93,479	12%	-71%	6%	39%

box continues next page

Risk Modeling for Appraising Named Peril Index Insurance Products
http://dx.doi.org/10.1596/978-1-4648-1048-0

Case Example Box 12CB.11 Computations—Step 17 *(continued)*

The capital charge for the 10 percent premium rate is $93,479 in the case example.

$$\text{Scenario capital charge} = \text{Required capital} \times \text{Required return on capital}$$
$$= \$1,869,580 \times 5 \text{ percent}$$
$$= \$93,479$$

In the case example, the EVA for the 10 percent premium rate is 4.6 percent.

$$\text{Scenario EVA} = (\text{Scenario net premium income} - \text{Scenario losses} - \text{Scenario capital charge})/\text{Required capital}$$
$$= (\$680,000 - \$500,000 - \$93,479)/\$1,869,580$$
$$= 4.6 \text{ percent}$$

Note: EVA = economic value added.

If the insurer were free to invest the required capital it would have expected to generate gains equal to the capital charge. But because the insurer must hold the required capital, it incurs the capital charge as an opportunity cost.

Next, Step 17 calculates the scenario EVA for each premium.

Scenario EVA = (Scenario net premium – Scenario losses – Scenario capital charge)/
income   Required capital
(Step 16)   (Step 13)   (Step 14)

The EVA indicates the profit earned by the product less the cost of financing the required capital, as a percentage of the capital required.

Based on these calculations, the model generates at least 10,000 scenario EVA results for each premium rate and determines the expected EVA for the next risk period (–2 percent for the 10 percent premium rate in the case example), along with the appropriate percentile values for the EVA.

12.3.2.5 The Sharpe Ratio

12.3.2.5.1 Overview. The Sharpe ratio (figure 12.5) provides the insurer with an estimate of how much risk is being taken to get a certain return. Imagine that the insurer has two investment alternatives, both with a 15 percent expected return. The Sharpe ratios for these investments will clearly show if one has a higher risk than the other. A negative Sharpe ratio indicates an investment with an expected negative return per unit of risk assumed, while a positive Sharpe ratio indicates an investment with an expected positive return per unit of risk assumed.

Implementation in Excel (MC_12.3.2_NO REINSURANCE)

In Step 18 (case example box 12CB.12), the model first calculates scenario return on capital for each premium rate from the net premium income (Step 16), the scenario losses (Step 13), and the required capital (Step 14).

Scenario return on capital = (Scenario net premium income – Scenario losses)/
(Step 16)   (Step 13)
Required capital
(Step 14)

Risk Modeling for Appraising Named Peril Index Insurance Products
http://dx.doi.org/10.1596/978-1-4648-1048-0

Figure 12.5 Generating Sharpe Ratios

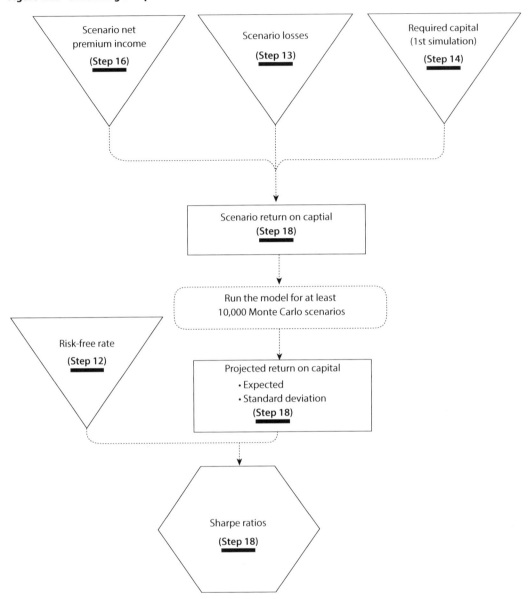

Based on these calculations, the model generates at least 10,000 Monte Carlo scenario returns on capital for each premium rate and determines the expected return on capital for the next risk period (3 percent for the 10 percent premium rate in the case example) as well as the standard deviation of the return on capital (36 percent).

Note that for all premium levels considered, the standard deviation of the return on capital is the same. The standard deviations are all the same because

Case Example Box 12CB.12 Computations—Step 18

STEP 18 : CALCULATE SHARPE RATIO

ITERATION #	GROSS PREMIUM RATE (%)	SCENARIO RETURN ON CAPITAL (%)	PROJECTED RETURN ON CAPITAL (%)		SHARPE RATIO
			Expected	Standard Deviation	
1	3%	-16%	-22%	36%	-0.68
2	4%	-12%	-19%	36%	-0.58
3	5%	-9%	-15%	36%	-0.47
4	6%	-5%	-11%	36%	-0.37
5	7%	-1%	-8%	36%	-0.27
6	8%	2%	-4%	36%	-0.17
7	9%	6%	0%	36%	-0.07
8	10%	10%	3%	36%	0.03
9	11%	13%	7%	36%	0.14
10	12%	17%	11%	36%	0.24

The scenario return on capital for the 10 percent premium rate is 9.6 percent (rounded up to 10 percent) for the case example.

Scenario return on capital = (Scenario net premium income – Scenario losses)/Required capital

= ($680,000 – $500,000)/$1,869,580

= 9.6 percent

For the case example, the Sharpe ratio is 0.027 (rounded up to 3 percent) for the 10 percent premium rate. Although positive, this ratio is less than those for the 11 percent and 12 percent premium rates because of the lower expected return.

Sharpe ratio = (Expected return on capital – Risk-free rate)/Standard deviation of the expected return on capital

= (3 percent – 2 percent)/36 percent

= 2.7 percent

the actual premium levels are assumed not to change the risk of the insured units. Although the expected returns will increase with higher premiums, the standard deviation (that is, the spread around the expected returns) does not change.

Next, the model calculates the Sharpe ratio from the expected return on capital, the risk-free rate (Step 2), and the standard deviation for the return on capital.

Sharpe ratio = (Expected return on capital – Risk-free rate)/Standard deviation of
the return on capital

(Step 2)

A positive Sharpe ratio indicates an investment with an expected positive return per unit of risk assumed. Premium rates with higher Sharpe ratios are

Risk Modeling for Appraising Named Peril Index Insurance Products
http://dx.doi.org/10.1596/978-1-4648-1048-0

preferred because the higher the Sharpe ratio, the greater the expected return on the capital invested relative to the amount of risk taken.

These metrics are also calculated for situations with proportional and nonproportional insurance in the following sections.

12.3.3 Calculation of Product Pricing Decision Metrics—Proportional Reinsurance Only (Steps 19–24)

12.3.3.1 Overview

The preceding sections discussed the generation of pricing decision metrics for the Base Index for the scenario with no reinsurance. Now we will review the same process for the scenario with proportional reinsurance only (table 12.6 and figure 12.6).

The objective of this process is to evaluate the effect of proportional reinsurance arrangements. Reinsurance can reduce the premium rates of an index insurance product because the reinsurance firm may need to set aside less required capital than the insurer would have because the reinsurer's portfolio is highly diversified. In addition, the reinsurer may have a lower cost of capital or other operational costs that are lower.

There are two main differences between the current proportional reinsurance only and the previously evaluated no reinsurance situations:

First, the scenario losses (Step 13) will be reduced by the percentage ceded to the reinsurer (Step 6; "net PR" means "net proportional reinsurance").

$$\underset{\text{(Step 13)}}{\text{Scenario retained claims (net PR)}} = \text{Scenario losses} \times (1 - \underset{\text{(Step 6)}}{\text{percent ceded to reinsurer})}$$

Second, the insurer passes along a portion of the premium income with the risk ceded to the reinsurer.

$$\text{Scenario gross premium income (net PR)} = \underset{\text{(Step 15)}}{\text{Scenario gross premium income}} \times \underset{\text{(Step 6)}}{(1 - \text{percent ceded to reinsurer})}$$

This guide assumes that the insurer makes no profit on the ceded risk. Therefore, the percentage of the insured amount that is ceded to the reinsurer represents a reduction in the sum insured. This conservative approach recognizes that reinsurance market prices are very volatile with more favorable terms when the market is soft (that is, high liquidity) than when it is hard (that is, low liquidity).[1]

Table 12.6 Model Computations

Model component	Section	Excel sheet label	Steps	Description
Model computations	12.3.3	MC_12.3.3_PR REINSURANCE	Steps 19–24	Calculation of product pricing decision metrics for proportional reinsurance only

Figure 12.6 Generating Product Pricing Decision Metrics (Proportional Reinsurance Only)

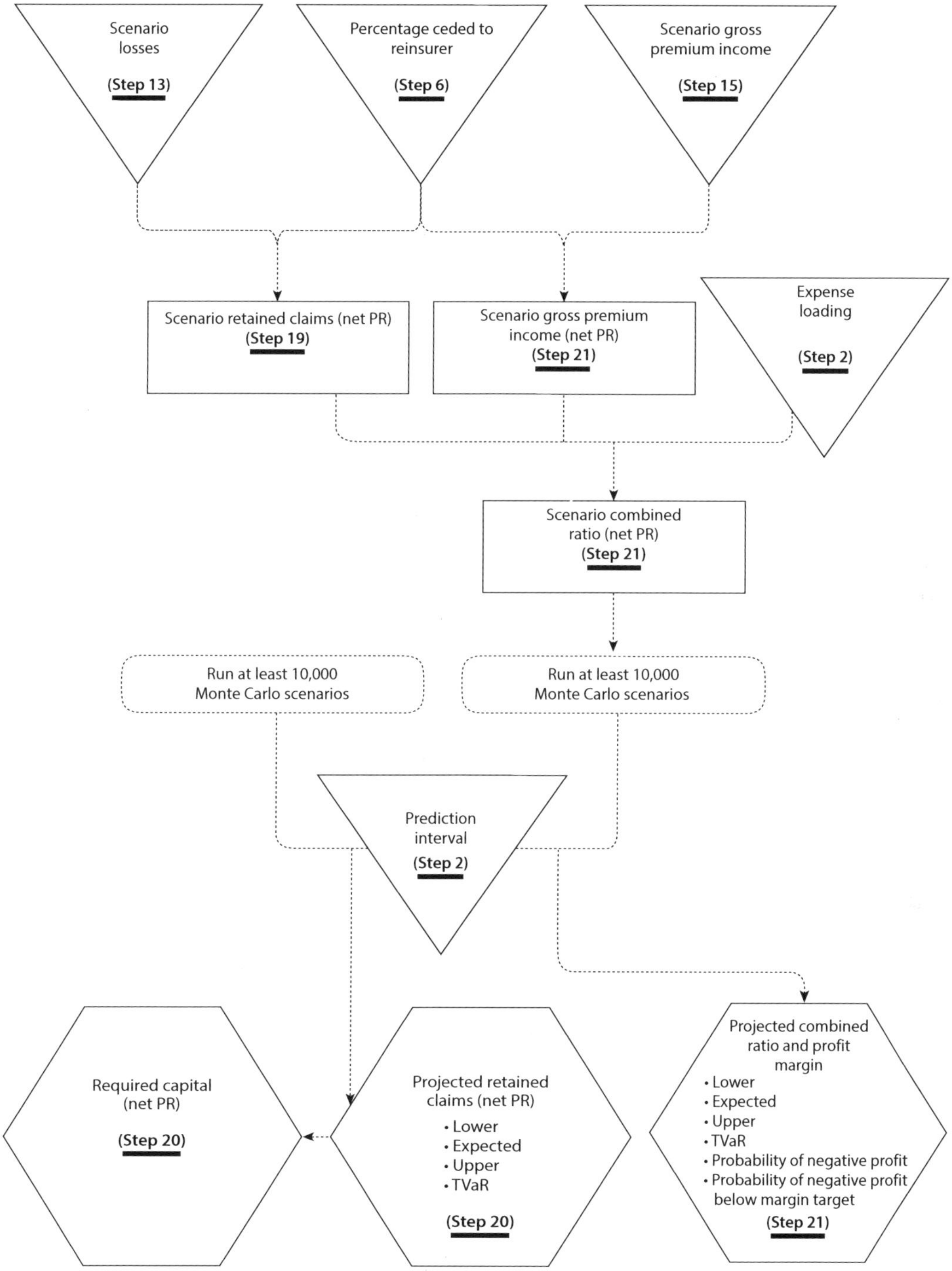

Scenario
losses
(Step 13)

Percentage ceded to
reinsurer
(Step 6)

Scenario gross
premium income
(Step 15)

Scenario retained claims (net PR)
(Step 19)

Scenario gross premium
income (net PR)
(Step 21)

Expense
loading
(Step 2)

Scenario combined
ratio (net PR)
(Step 21)

Run at least 10,000
Monte Carlo scenarios

Run at least 10,000
Monte Carlo scenarios

Prediction
interval
(Step 2)

Required capital
(net PR)

(Step 20)

Projected retained
claims (net PR)
• Lower
• Expected
• Upper
• TVaR

(Step 20)

Projected combined
ratio and profit
margin
• Lower
• Expected
• Upper
• TVaR
• Probability of negative profit
• Probability of negative profit
  below margin target
(Step 21)

Note: PR = proportional reinsurance; TVaR = tail value at risk.

Risk Modeling for Appraising Named Peril Index Insurance Products
http://dx.doi.org/10.1596/978-1-4648-1048-0

12.3.3.2 Implementation in Excel (MC_12.3.3.1_PR REINSURANCE)

The modeling process for the proportional reinsurance only scenario is very similar to that for the no reinsurance situation (Steps 13–18) but uses scenario retained claims net of proportional reinsurance in place of scenario losses.

In Step 19 the model calculates the scenario retained claims (net PR) (case example box 12CB.13) from the scenario losses and the percentage ceded to the insurer. These are the claim payouts for which the insurer is responsible.

In Step 20 (case example box 12CB.14), the model generates at least 10,000 scenario retained claims (net PR) for the portfolio and determines the expected

---

Case Example Box 12CB.13 Computations—Step 19

STEP 19 : SHOW SCENARIO PORTFOLIO LOSSES (NET PR)

$$\boxed{100,000}$$

For the case example, with 80 percent of the risk ceded to the reinsurer (step 6), the scenario losses for the portfolio are reduced from $500,000 to $100,000.

Scenario retained claims (net PR) = Scenario losses × (1 − percent ceded to reinsurer)

$$= 500,000 \times (1 - 80 \text{ percent})$$

$$= \$100,000$$

Note: PR = proportional reinsurance.

Case Example Box 12CB.14 Computations—Step 20

STEP 20 : CALCULATE PROJECTED LOSSES AND REQUIRED CAPITAL

LOWER	-
EXPECTED	123,857
UPPER	407,772
TVaR	497,772

REQUIRED CAPITAL	373,915
REQUIRED CAPITAL (1st simulation)	373,915

After a first simulation, copy the value (value only) from the Required Capital cell to the Required Capital (1st simulation) cell.

For the case example, with proportional reinsurance (PR) the expected retained claims for the next risk period are reduced to $123,857 (from $619,287) and the required capital to $373,915 (from $1,869,580). Note that the required capital is therefore reduced by 80 percent compared with the previously evaluated no reinsurance situation, which is exactly the percentage ceded to the proportional reinsurer.

Required capital (net PR) = TVaR retained claims (net PR) − Expected retained claims (net PR)

$$= \$497,772 - \$123,857$$

$$= \$373,915$$

Note: TVaR = tail value at risk.

---

retained claims (net PR) for the next risk period. Based on the prediction interval selected in Step 2, the model also calculates the appropriate percentile and TVaR values of the retained claims.

Also in Step 20, the model uses the same 10,000 scenarios to calculate the required capital (net PR).

Required capital (net PR) = TVaR retained claims (net PR) − Expected retained claims (net PR)

In Step 21, the model simulates the combined ratios and profit margins for each premium rate (case example box 12CB.15). The process is similar to Step 15, but uses gross premium income (net PR) rather than gross premium income.

The remaining steps for determining the pricing decision metrics for the proportional reinsurance situation (Steps 22–24) are similar to the no reinsurance situation (Steps 16–18) but use the scenario losses (net PR) and gross premium income (net PR) formulas where appropriate.

Case Example Box 12CB.15 Computations—Step 21

STEP 21 : CALCULATE COMBINED RATIO AND PROFIT MARGIN

ITERATION #	GROSS PREMIUM RATE (%)	GROSS PREMIUM INCOME ($)	SCENARIO COMBINED RATIO (%)	SCENARIO PROFIT MARGIN (%)	PROJECTED COMBINED RATIO (%)				PROJECTED PROFIT MARGIN (%)			PROBABILITY OF NEGATIVE PROFIT (%)	PROBABILITY OF PROFIT BELOW TARGET (%)
					Lower	Expected	Upper	TVaR	Lower	Expected	Upper		
1	3%	48,000	223%	-123%	15%	273%	865%	1067%	-766%	-173%	85%	66%	68%
2	4%	64,000	171%	-71%	15%	209%	652%	804%	-553%	-109%	85%	60%	63%
3	5%	80,000	140%	-40%	15%	170%	525%	646%	-426%	-70%	85%	55%	58%
4	6%	96,000	119%	-19%	15%	144%	440%	541%	-341%	-44%	85%	50%	53%
5	7%	112,000	104%	-4%	15%	126%	379%	466%	-280%	-26%	85%	46%	49%
6	8%	128,000	93%	7%	15%	112%	334%	409%	-234%	-12%	85%	41%	45%
7	9%	144,000	84%	16%	15%	101%	298%	366%	-199%	-1%	85%	38%	42%
8	10%	160,000	78%	23%	15%	92%	270%	331%	-170%	8%	85%	34%	38%
9	11%	176,000	72%	28%	15%	85%	247%	302%	-147%	15%	85%	31%	35%
10	12%	192,000	67%	33%	15%	80%	227%	278%	-128%	20%	85%	28%	32%

For the case example, the gross premium income (net PR) for the 10 percent premium rate is $160,000.

Gross premium income (net PR) = Gross premium income × (1 − Percentage ceded to reinsurer)

= $800,000 × (1 − 80 percent)

= $160,000

Note: PR = proportional reinsurance; TVaR = tail value at risk.

12.3.4 Calculation of Product Pricing Decision Metrics—Proportional and Nonproportional Reinsurance (Steps 25–30)

12.3.4.1 Overview

In this section the model calculates the product pricing metrics for the scenario in which the Base Index has both proportional and nonproportional reinsurance (table 12.7 and figure 12.7).

Table 12.7 Model Computations

Model component	Section	Excel sheet label	Steps	Description
Model computations	12.3.4	MC_12.3.4_PR & NP REINSURANCE	Steps 25–30	Calculation of product pricing decision metrics for proportional and nonproportional reinsurance

Risk Modeling for Appraising Named Peril Index Insurance Products
http://dx.doi.org/10.1596/978-1-4648-1048-0

Figure 12.7 Generating Product Pricing Decision Metrics (Proportional and Nonproportional Reinsurance)

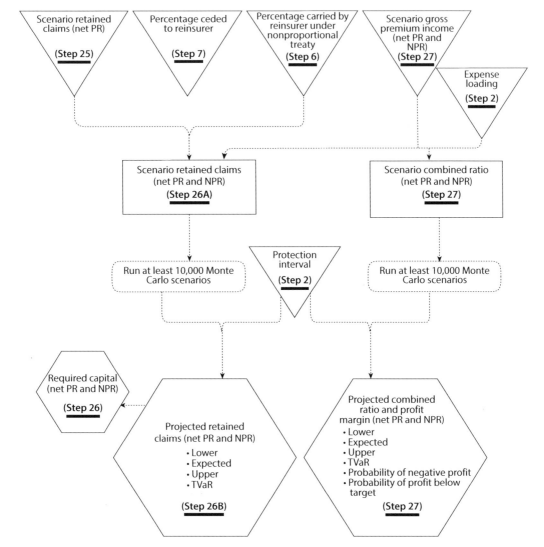

Note: NPR = nonproportional reinsurance; PR = proportional reinsurance; TVaR = tail value at risk.

There are two main differences between the proportional and nonproportional reinsurance situation and the no reinsurance situation:

First, the scenario losses and gross premium income are again reduced by the (proportional reinsurance) percentage that is ceded to the reinsurance company (Step 6). In addition, the reinsurance company will pay a set percentage of the nonceded claims between the treaty retention and the aggregate loss limit (Step 7).

When the losses are less than the treaty retention, the reinsurance policy will not pay the insurer anything on the nonceded claims.

For nonceded claims that are between the treaty retention and the aggregate loss limit, the insurer's payout will be as follows (NPR = nonproportional reinsurance):

Scenario reinsurance payout (net PR and NPR) (Step 19)	=	(Scenario losses net PR – Treaty retention) (Step 7)	×	Percent carried by the reinsurer under nonproportional treaty. (Step 7)

For any nonceded losses that are higher than the aggregate loss limit, the reinsurance will pay out nothing.

The insurer's net retained claims will be

Scenario retained claims (net PR and NPR) = Scenario retained claims net PR –
(Step 19)   Reinsurance payout net PR and NPR.

Second, the nonproportional reinsurance will have direct costs to the insurer, specifically, the reinsurance premium rate, which is typically specified as a percentage of the total premium amount. This cost will influence the insurer's profit and loss metrics directly.

Gross premium income = [Gross premium × (1 – Percent ceded to × (1 – Expense
(net PR and NPR)   income   reinsurer)]   loading)
                          (Step 15)   (Step 6)   (Step 2)

                          – nonproportional reinsurance premium rate]

12.3.4.2 Implementation in Excel (MC_12.3.4_PR & NP REINSURANCE)

The modeling process for the proportional and nonproportional reinsurance situation is again very similar to that for the no reinsurance situation (Steps 13–18) but uses scenario retained claims net of proportional and nonproportional reinsurance in place of scenario losses.

In Step 25 (case example box 12CB.16), the model calculates the scenario retained claims (net PR) from the scenario payout amount (Step 12) and the percentage ceded to the insurer (Step 6). This process (and the resulting value) is identical to Step 19 for the proportional reinsurance only scenario.

In Step 26A, the model calculates the scenario retained claims (net PR and NPR).

Scenario reinsurance payout (net PR and NPR) (Step 19)	=	(Scenario retained claims net PR – Treaty retention) (Step 7)	×	Percent carried by the reinsurer under nonproportional treaty (Step 12)

Scenario retained claims = Scenario retained – Scenario reinsurance
(net PR and NPR)   claims net PR   payout
                          (Step 19)

Risk Modeling for Appraising Named Peril Index Insurance Products
http://dx.doi.org/10.1596/978-1-4648-1048-0

Case Example Box 12CB.16 Computations—Steps 25 and 26

STEP 25 : SHOW SCENARIO RETAINED CLAIMS (NET PR)

100,000

STEP 26A : CALCULATE SCENARIO RETAINED CLAIMS (NET PR AND NPR)

SCENARIO LOSSES (NET PR)	100,000
TREATY RETENTION	85,000
AGGREGATE LOSS LIMIT	709,000
SCENARIO REINSURANCE PAYOUT	13,500
SCENARIO RETAINED CLAIMS (NET PR AND NPR)	86,500

STEP 26B : CALCULATE PROJECTED RETAINED CLAIMS AND REQUIRED CAPITAL (NET PR AND NPR)

LOWER	0
EXPECTED	62,861
UPPER	117,277
TVaR	128,124
REQUIRED CAPITAL	65,263
REQUIRED CAPITAL (1st simulation)	65,263

After a first simulation, copy the value (value only) from the Required Capital cell to the Required Capital (1st simulation) cell.

In the case example, the scenario reinsurance payout for the portfolio is $13,500 and the scenario retained claims (net PR and NPR) are $86,500.

Scenario reinsurance payout (net PR and NPR) = (Scenario retained claims net PR – Treaty retention) × Percent carried by the reinsurer under nonproportional treaty

$$= (100,000 - 85,000) \times 90 \text{ percent}$$

$$= \$13,500$$

Scenario retained claims (net PR and NPR) = Scenario retained claims net PR – Scenario reinsurance payout

$$= 100,000 - 13,500$$

$$= \$86,500$$

For the case example, with both proportional and nonproportional reinsurance the expected retained claims for the next risk period are reduced to $62,861 (from $123,857 with proportional reinsurance only in Step 20) and the required capital to $65,263 (from $373,915 in Step 20). The reason for this large reduction in the required capital is that whenever claims are higher than the treaty retention, the reinsurer starts to cover the costs of a percentage of the payouts. This can greatly reduce the risk and the TVaR, and therefore the required capital for the insurer.

Required capital (net PR and NPR) = TVaR retained claims net PR and NPR – Expected retained claims net PR and NPR

$$= 128,124 - 62,861$$

$$= \$65,263$$

Note: NPR = nonproportional reinsurance; PR = proportional reinsurance; TVaR = tail value at risk.

In Step 26B, the model generates at least 10,000 scenario retained claims (net PR and NPR) for the portfolio and determines the expected retained claims (net PR and NPR) for the next risk period. Based on the prediction interval selected in Step 2, the model also calculates the appropriate percentile and TVaR values of the retained claims.

Also in Step 26B, the model uses the same 10,000 scenarios to calculate the required capital (net PR and NPR).

Required capital = TVaR retained claims − Expected retained

(net PR and NPR)   (net PR and NPR)   claims (net PR and NPR)

In Step 27, the model simulates the combined ratio and profit margin for each premium rate (case example box 12CB.17). The process is the same as for Step 15, but uses gross premium income (net PR and NPR) in place of gross premium income.

The remaining steps for determining the pricing decision metrics for the proportional and nonproportional reinsurance situation (Steps 28–30) are the same as for the no reinsurance situation (Steps 16–18), but use the scenario retained claims and gross premium income that are net of PR and NPR instead.

See box 12.1 for a recap of the formulas used in the preceding text.

Case Example Box 12CB.17 Computations—Step 27

STEP 27 : CALCULATE COMBINED RATIO AND PROFIT MARGIN

ITERATION #	GROSS PREMIUM RATE (%)	GROSS PREMIUM INCOME ($)	SCENARIO COMBINED RATIO (%)	SCENARIO PROFIT MARGIN (%)	PROJECTED COMBINED RATIO (%)				PROJECTED PROFIT MARGIN (%)			PROBABILITY OF NEGATIVE PROFIT (%)	PROBABILITY OF PROFIT BELOW TARGET (%)
					Lower	Expected	Upper	TVaR	Lower	Expected	Upper		
1	3%	38,400	240%	-140%	15%	179%	320%	348%	-221%	-79%	85%	70%	71%
2	4%	51,200	184%	-84%	15%	138%	244%	265%	-144%	-38%	85%	65%	67%
3	5%	64,000	150%	-50%	15%	113%	198%	215%	-98%	-13%	85%	60%	63%
4	6%	76,800	128%	-28%	15%	97%	168%	182%	-68%	3%	85%	56%	59%
5	7%	89,600	112%	-12%	15%	85%	146%	158%	-46%	15%	85%	52%	55%
6	8%	102,400	99%	1%	15%	76%	130%	140%	-30%	24%	85%	42%	52%
7	9%	115,200	90%	10%	15%	70%	117%	126%	-17%	30%	85%	20%	44%
8	10%	128,000	83%	17%	15%	64%	107%	115%	-7%	36%	85%	10%	23%
9	11%	140,800	76%	24%	15%	60%	98%	106%	2%	40%	85%	4%	12%
10	12%	153,600	71%	29%	15%	56%	91%	98%	9%	44%	85%	1%	6%

For the case example, the gross premium income (net PR and NPR) for the 10 percent premium rate is $128,000.

Scenario gross premium income (net PR and NPR) = [Scenario gross premium income × (1 − Percent ceded to reinsurer)]

× (1 − Expense loading − Nonproportional reinsurance premium rate)

= [$800,000 × (1 − 80 percent)] × (1 − 15 percent − 5 percent)

= $128,000

Box 12.1 Summary of Key Formulas Used in the Chapter

Scenario metrics (one Monte Carlo scenario)

- Retained claims (net PR) = Losses × (1 − Percent ceded to reinsurer)
- Reinsurance payout (net PR and NPR) = [Retained claims (net PR) − Treaty retention] × Percent carried by the reinsurer under proportional treaty
- Retained claims (net PR and NPR) = Retained claims (net PR) − Reinsurance payout
- Gross premium income = Premium rate × Total portfolio sum insured
- Gross premium income (net PR) = Gross premium income × (1 − Percent ceded to reinsurer)
- Gross premium income (net PR and NPR) = [Gross premium income × (1 − Percent ceded to reinsurer)] × (1 − Expense loading − Nonproportional reinsurance premium rate)
- Loss ratio = Losses/Gross premium income
- Combined ratio = Loss ratio + Expense loading
- Profit margin = 1 − Combined ratio
- Net premium rate = Gross premium rate × (1 − Expense loading)
- Net premium income = Net premium rate × Total sum insured
- Total funds at risk = Net premium income + Starting fund value
- Net fund position = Total funds at risk − Losses

Metrics based on at least 10,000 Monte Carlo scenarios

- Required capital = TVaR losses − Expected losses
- Required capital (net PR) = TVaR retained claims (net PR) − Expected retained claims (net PR)
- Required capital (net PR and NPR) = TVaR retained claims (net PR and NPR) − Expected retained claims (net PR and NPR)
- Probability of a negative profit = Percentage of scenarios in which the scenario profits are less than $0
- Probability of a profit below the target profit margin = Percentage of scenarios in which the scenario profits are less than the target profit margin
- Probability of fund ruin = Percentage of scenarios in which the scenario net fund positions are less than $0
- EVA = (Net premium income − Losses − Capital charge)/Required capital
- Return on capital = (Net premium income − Losses)/Required capital

Note: EVA = economic value added; NPR = nonproportional reinsurance; PR = proportional reinsurance; TVaR = tail value at risk.

12.3.5 Calculation of Equitable Premiums Metrics (Steps 31–38)

The preceding sections discussed the generation of pricing decision metrics for the Base Index to help the insurer select the best portfolio-priced premium rate for the entire portfolio of geographical areas. However, each geographical area covered by a portfolio-priced index product in reality has a different risk profile (for example, less rain or more extreme maximum temperatures), which corresponds with a different premium rate. The premium rates that are specific to each area in the portfolio are called equitable premium rates.

An equitable premium for each area takes into account the relative riskiness of each area. Areas that are riskier require the insurance company to have more capital available on hand and should therefore have higher premiums than the less risky areas.

To calculate the equitable premium rate for each area (table 12.8), the model first simulates the payout amounts by area as in Steps 8–11. Recall that in Step 12, the model sums the payout amounts for all areas to produce the total portfolio payout amount. However, because we are now looking at individual areas, this additional step is not needed. Instead, we will use the payout amounts for each area.

In this guide, equitable premiums are calculated as follows:

$$\text{Equitable premium rate} = \frac{\{[APPIU + EROC \times (RCPIU)]/AUS\}}{(1 - Total\ expense\ loading)},$$

where APPIU = average payout per insured unit,

EROC = expected return on capital,

RCPIU = required capital per insured unit,

and AUS = average unit size (Step 1).

To make the logic easier to follow, we will first explain how the APPIU, RCPIU, and EROC are calculated before explaining the calculation of the equitable premium rate for each area.

12.3.5.1 Components APPIU and RCPIU

12.3.5.1.1 Overview. Figure 12.8 provides an overview of how the model generates the APPIU and RCPIU from the scenario payout amounts by area.

12.3.5.1.2 Implementation in Excel (MC_12.3.5_EQUITABLE PREMIUMS). In Step 31, the model first generates at least 10,000 scenario payout amounts for each area and determines the average (expected) payout amount for each

Table 12.8 Model Computations

Model component	Section	Excel sheet label	Steps	Description
Model computations	12.3.5	MC_12.3.5_EQUITABLE PREMIUMS	Steps 31–38	Calculation of equitable premium metrics for each geographical area

Risk Modeling for Appraising Named Peril Index Insurance Products
http://dx.doi.org/10.1596/978-1-4648-1048-0

Figure 12.8 Generating APPIU and RCPIU for Each Area

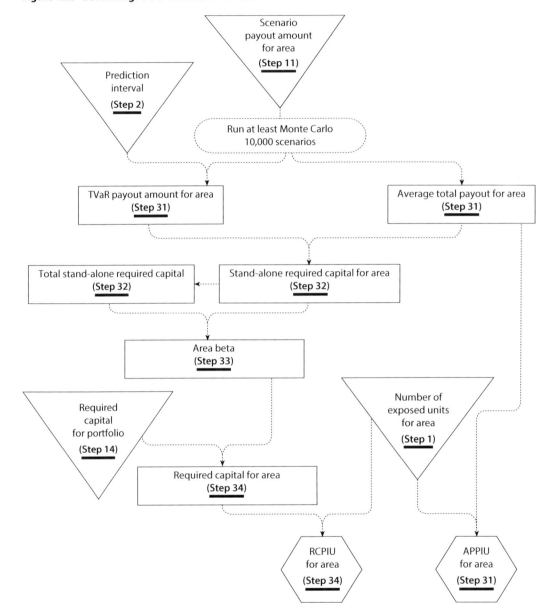

Note: APPIU = average payout per insured unit; RCPIU = required capital per insured unit; TVaR = tail value at risk.

(case example box 12CB.18). Based on the prediction interval selected in Step 2, the model also calculates the appropriate TVaR of the payout amount for each of the areas. The expected payout per area and the TVaR of the payout per area are both used in Step 32 to calculate an area's stand-alone required capital.

Also in Step 31, the model calculates the APPIU for each area.

Risk Modeling for Appraising Named Peril Index Insurance Products
http://dx.doi.org/10.1596/978-1-4648-1048-0

Case Example Box 12CB.18 Computations—Step 31

STEP 31 : CALCULATE AVERAGE PAYOUT PER INSURED UNIT ($)

	AREA A	AREA B	AREA C	AREA D	AREA E	AREA F	AREA G	AREA H	AREA I	AREA J
EXPECTED PAYOUT AMOUNT FOR AREA	5,124	20,598	58,362	38,266	181,837	20,948	56,145	74,290	31,116	132,600
APPIU	4.39	5.46	7.78	9.00	8.48	6.98	6.79	5.88	8.05	17.40

For Area B in the case example, the APPIU is $5.46.

APPIU for area = Average payout amount for area/Number of exposed units for area

$= 20{,}598/3{,}773$

$= \$5.46$

Note: APPIU = average payout per insured unit.

APPIU for area = Average payout amount for area/
Number of insured units for area
(Step 1)

In Step 32 (case example box 12CB.19), the model calculates the stand-alone required capital for each area.

Case Example Box 12CB.19 Computations—Steps 32–34

STEP 32 : CALCULATE PORTFOLIO STAND ALONE REQUIRED CAPITAL ($)

	AREA A	AREA B	AREA C	AREA D	AREA E	AREA F	AREA G	AREA H	AREA I	AREA J
STAND ALONE REQUIRED CAPITAL FOR AREA	81,290	198,800	779,630	308,511	1,621,737	202,522	667,255	844,747	307,278	586,156
PORTFOLIO STAND ALONE REQUIRED CAPITAL	5,597,927									

STEP 33 : CALCULATE AREA BETA

	AREA A	AREA B	AREA C	AREA D	AREA E	AREA F	AREA G	AREA H	AREA I	AREA J
BETA	1.5%	3.6%	13.9%	5.5%	29.0%	3.6%	11.9%	15.1%	5.5%	10.5%

STEP 34 : CALCULATE REQUIRED CAPITAL PER INSURED UNIT ($)

	AREA A	AREA B	AREA C	AREA D	AREA E	AREA F	AREA G	AREA H	AREA I	AREA J
REQUIRED CAPITAL FOR AREA	27,149	66,395	260,378	103,035	541,622	67,638	222,847	282,125	102,624	195,762
RCPIU FOR AREA	23.24	17.60	34.72	24.24	25.25	22.55	26.98	22.33	26.55	25.69

For the case example, the stand-alone required capital for Area B is $198,800.

Stand-alone required capital for area = TVaR payout amount for area − Average payout amount for area

$= 219{,}398 - 20{,}598$

$= \$198{,}800$

The portfolio stand-alone required capital for the portfolio is $5,597,927

Portfolio stand-alone capital $= 81{,}290 + 198{,}800 + 779{,}630 + 308{,}511 + 1{,}621{,}737 + 202{,}522 + 667{,}255 + 844{,}747 +$
$307{,}278 + 586{,}156$

$= \$5{,}597{,}927$

box continues next page

Risk Modeling for Appraising Named Peril Index Insurance Products
http://dx.doi.org/10.1596/978-1-4648-1048-0

Case Example Box 12CB.19 Computations—Steps 32–34 *(continued)*

For the case example, the beta for Area B is 3.5513 percent (rounded to 3.6 percent in the Step 33 table).

Area beta = Stand-alone required capital for area/Total stand-alone required capital for portfolio

$$= 198,800/5,597,927$$

$$= 3.5513 \text{ percent}$$

For the case example the required capital for Area B is $66,395.

Required capital for area = Required capital for portfolio × Area beta

$$= 1,869,580 \times 3.5513 \text{ percent}$$

$$= \$66,395$$

The RCPIU for Area B is $17.60.

RCPIU for area = Required capital for area/Number of exposed units for area

$$= \$66,395/3,773$$

$$= \$17.60$$

Note: RCPIU = required capital per insured unit.

Stand-alone required = TVaR payout amount − Expected payout amount
capital for area   for area   for area
(Step 31)   (Step 31)

Also in Step 32, the model calculates the total stand-alone required capital for the portfolio by summing the stand-alone required capital for all of the geographical areas.

The total stand-alone required capital for the portfolio will always be higher than the required capital under portfolio pricing (Step 14). With portfolio pricing, the required capital is lower because of diversification.

Step 33 calculates the beta for each area.

Area beta = Stand-alone required capital for area/Total stand-alone required capital
for portfolio

(Step 32)   (Step 32)

This beta value represents the equitable proportion of the portfolio's total stand-alone required capital that is allocated to each area in light of its relative riskiness.

Step 34 calculates the required capital for each area.

Required capital for area = Required capital for portfolio × Area beta

(Step 14)   (Step 33)

Also in Step 34, the model calculates the RCPIU for each area.

RCPIU for area = Required capital for area/Number of exposed units for area

(Step 1)

12.3.5.2 Component EROC

12.3.5.2.1 Overview. Another important input to calculation of equitable premiums per area is the EROC, the expected return on capital. Figure 12.9

Figure 12.9 Generating EROC for Each Area

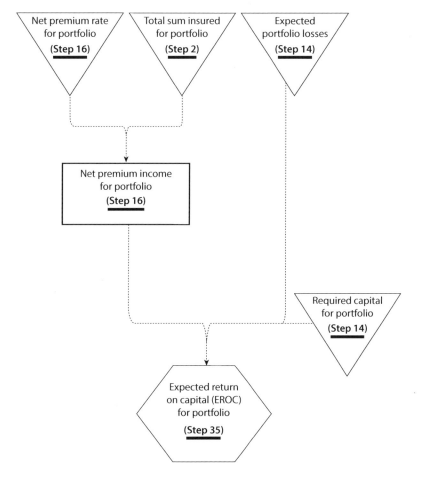

Risk Modeling for Appraising Named Peril Index Insurance Products
http://dx.doi.org/10.1596/978-1-4648-1048-0

provides an overview of how the model generates the EROC from the scenario payout amounts by area.

Case Example Box 12CB.20 Computations—Step 35

STEP 35 : CALCULATE EXPECTED RETURN ON CAPITAL

GROSS PREMIUM RATE (%)	NET PREMIUM RATE (%)	NET PREMIUM INCOME ($)	EXPECTED PORTFOLIO LOSSES ($)	EXPECTED PORTFOLIO RETURN ON CAPITAL (%)
3%	2.6%	204,000	619,287	-22%
4%	3.4%	272,000	619,287	-19%
5%	4.3%	340,000	619,287	-15%
6%	5.1%	408,000	619,287	-11%
7%	6.0%	476,000	619,287	-8%
8%	6.8%	544,000	619,287	-4%
9%	7.7%	612,000	619,287	0%
10%	8.5%	680,000	619,287	3%
11%	9.4%	748,000	619,287	7%
12%	10.2%	816,000	619,287	11%

For the case example, the expected return on capital (EROC) for the portfolio at the 10 percent premium rate is 3.2474 percent (rounded up to 3 percent).

EROC for portfolio = (Net premium income for portfolio − Expected portfolio losses)/Required capital for portfolio

= (680,000 − 619,287)/1,869,580

= 3.2474 percent

Using the 10 percent premium rate increases shareholder value for the insurer because the EROC is positive.

12.3.5.2.2 Implementation in Excel (MC_12.3.5_EQUITABLE PREMIUMS). In Step 35, the model calculates the EROC (case example box 12CB.20).

EROC for portfolio = (Net premium income − Expected portfolio/Required capital
                        for portfolio   losses)   for portfolio
                        (Step 16)   (Step 14)   (Step 14)

12.3.5.3 Equitable Premium Rates

12.3.5.3.1 Overview. Figure 12.10 provides an overview of how the model generates the equitable premium rates for each area from the APPIU, RCPIU, EROC, and AUS.

Risk Modeling for Appraising Named Peril Index Insurance Products
http://dx.doi.org/10.1596/978-1-4648-1048-0

Figure 12.10 Generating Equitable Premium Rates for Each Area

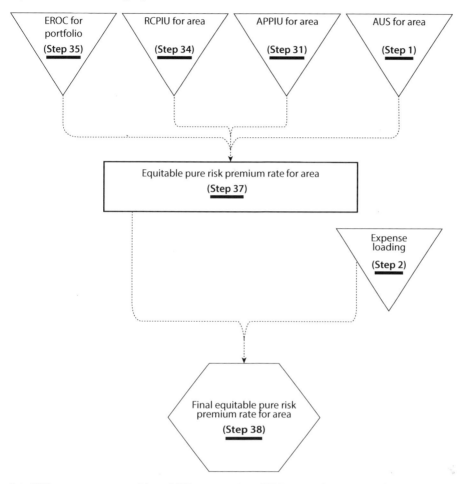

Note: APPIU = average payout per unit insured; AUS = average unit size; EROC = expected return on capital; RCPIU = required capital per insured unit.

12.3.5.3.2 Implementation in Excel (MC_12.3.5_EQUITABLE PREMIUMS). In Step 36A (case example box 12CB.21), the model calculates the expected return on capital per unit for each area and portfolio-priced premium rate.

$$\text{EROC per unit for area} = \underset{\text{(Step 34)}}{\text{RCPIU for area}} \times \underset{\text{(Step 35)}}{\text{EROC for portfolio}}$$

In Step 36B the model then calculates the equitable pure risk premium income per unit for each area and portfolio-priced premium rate.

$$\underset{\text{income per unit for area}}{\text{Equitable pure risk premium}} = \underset{\text{(Step 31)}}{\text{APPIU for area}} + \underset{\text{(Step 36A)}}{\text{EROC per unit for area}}$$

Risk Modeling for Appraising Named Peril Index Insurance Products
http://dx.doi.org/10.1596/978-1-4648-1048-0

Case Example Box 12CB.21 Computations—Steps 36 and 37

STEP 36A : CALCULATE EXPECTED RETURN ON CAPITAL PER UNIT ($)

GROSS PREMIUM RATE (%)	AREA A	AREA B	AREA C	AREA D	AREA E	AREA F	AREA G	AREA H	AREA I	AREA J
3%	-5.16	-3.91	-7.71	-5.39	-5.61	-5.01	-5.99	-4.96	-5.90	-5.71
4%	-4.32	-3.27	-6.45	-4.50	-4.69	-4.19	-5.01	-4.15	-4.93	-4.77
5%	-3.47	-2.63	-5.19	-3.62	-3.77	-3.37	-4.03	-3.34	-3.97	-3.84
6%	-2.63	-1.99	-3.92	-2.74	-2.85	-2.55	-3.05	-2.52	-3.00	-2.90
7%	-1.78	-1.35	-2.66	-1.86	-1.94	-1.73	-2.07	-1.71	-2.03	-1.97
8%	-0.94	-0.71	-1.40	-0.98	-1.02	-0.91	-1.09	-0.90	-1.07	-1.03
9%	-0.09	-0.07	-0.14	-0.09	-0.10	-0.09	-0.11	-0.09	-0.10	-0.10
10%	0.75	0.57	1.13	0.79	0.82	0.73	0.88	0.73	0.86	0.83
11%	1.60	1.21	2.39	1.67	1.74	1.55	1.86	1.54	1.83	1.77
12%	2.45	1.85	3.65	2.55	2.66	2.37	2.84	2.35	2.79	2.70

STEP 36B: CALCULATE EQUITABLE PURE RISK PREMIUM INCOME PER UNIT ($)

GROSS PREMIUM RATE (%)	AREA A	AREA B	AREA C	AREA D	AREA E	AREA F	AREA G	AREA H	AREA I	AREA J
3%	-0.78	1.55	0.07	3.62	2.87	1.97	0.80	0.92	2.15	11.70
4%	0.07	2.19	1.33	4.50	3.79	2.79	1.78	1.73	3.12	12.63
5%	0.91	2.83	2.60	5.38	4.71	3.61	2.76	2.54	4.08	13.56
6%	1.76	3.47	3.86	6.26	5.62	4.43	3.75	3.36	5.05	14.50
7%	2.61	4.11	5.12	7.15	6.54	5.25	4.73	4.17	6.02	15.43
8%	3.45	4.75	6.38	8.03	7.46	6.07	5.71	4.98	6.98	16.37
9%	4.30	5.39	7.65	8.91	8.38	6.89	6.69	5.79	7.95	17.30
10%	5.14	6.03	8.91	9.79	9.30	7.71	7.67	6.60	8.91	18.24
11%	5.99	6.67	10.17	10.67	10.22	8.53	8.65	7.42	9.88	19.17
12%	6.83	7.31	11.43	11.55	11.13	9.35	9.63	8.23	10.84	20.10

STEP 37 : CALCULATE EQUITABLE PURE RISK PREMIUM RATE (%)

GROSS PREMIUM RATE (%)	AREA A	AREA B	AREA C	AREA D	AREA E	AREA F	AREA G	AREA H	AREA I	AREA J
3%	-0.65%	2.07%	0.04%	3.62%	2.73%	2.10%	0.67%	0.97%	1.96%	11.14%
4%	0.06%	2.92%	0.83%	4.50%	3.61%	2.97%	1.49%	1.82%	2.83%	12.03%
5%	0.76%	3.77%	1.62%	5.38%	4.48%	3.85%	2.30%	2.68%	3.71%	12.92%
6%	1.47%	4.63%	2.41%	6.26%	5.36%	4.72%	3.12%	3.53%	4.59%	13.81%
7%	2.17%	5.48%	3.20%	7.15%	6.23%	5.59%	3.94%	4.39%	5.47%	14.70%
8%	2.88%	6.33%	3.99%	8.03%	7.11%	6.46%	4.75%	5.24%	6.35%	15.59%
9%	3.58%	7.19%	4.78%	8.91%	7.98%	7.33%	5.57%	6.10%	7.22%	16.48%
10%	4.29%	8.04%	5.57%	9.79%	8.85%	8.21%	6.39%	6.95%	8.10%	17.37%
11%	4.99%	8.89%	6.36%	10.67%	9.73%	9.08%	7.21%	7.81%	8.98%	18.26%
12%	5.69%	9.75%	7.15%	11.55%	10.60%	9.95%	8.02%	8.66%	9.86%	19.15%

In the case example, the expected return on capital (EROC) per unit for Area B at the 10 percent portfolio-priced premium rate is $0.57.

$$\text{EROC per unit for area} = \text{RCPIU for area} \times \text{EROC for portfolio}$$

$$= \$17.60 \times 3.2474 \text{ percent}$$

$$= \$0.57$$

The equitable pure risk premium income per unit for Area B at the 10 percent portfolio-priced premium rate is $6.03.

$$\text{Equitable pure risk premium income per unit for area} = \text{APPIU for area} + \text{EROC per unit for area}$$

$$= 5.46 + 0.57$$

$$= \$6.03$$

In the case example, the equitable pure risk premium rate for Area B at the 10 percent portfolio-priced premium rate is 8.04 percent.

$$\text{Equitable pure risk premium rate for area} = \text{Equitable pure risk premium income per unit for area/AUS for area}$$

$$= 6.03/75$$

$$= 8.04 \text{ percent}$$

In Step 37, the model calculates the equitable pure risk premium for each area and portfolio-priced premium rate.

Equitable pure risk premium = Equitable pure risk premium/AUS for area
rate for area   income per unit for area
(Step 36B)   (Step 1)

In Step 38 (case example box 12CB.22), the model calculates the final equitable premium rate for each area and each portfolio-priced premium rate.

Final equitable premium = Equitable pure risk/(100 percent − Expense loading)
rate for area   premium rate for area
(Step 37)   (Step 2)

The same process is followed in calculating equitable rates at different portfolio premium levels and for each geographical area, A to J. This result means that Area B is less risky than the average of the other areas.

See box 12.2 for a summary of the calculations illustrated in figure 12.10.

Case Example Box 12CB.22 Computations—Step 38

STEP 38 : CALCULATE FINAL EQUITABLE PREMIUM RATE (%)

GROSS PREMIUM RATE (%)	AREA A	AREA B	AREA C	AREA D	AREA E	AREA F	AREA G	AREA H	AREA I	AREA J
3%	-0.76%	2.43%	0.05%	4.26%	3.21%	2.47%	0.79%	1.14%	2.30%	13.10%
4%	0.07%	3.44%	0.98%	5.29%	4.24%	3.50%	1.75%	2.14%	3.34%	14.15%
5%	0.90%	4.44%	1.91%	6.33%	5.27%	4.52%	2.71%	3.15%	4.37%	15.20%
6%	1.73%	5.44%	2.84%	7.37%	6.30%	5.55%	3.67%	4.16%	5.40%	16.24%
7%	2.55%	6.45%	3.77%	8.41%	7.33%	6.58%	4.63%	5.16%	6.43%	17.29%
8%	3.38%	7.45%	4.69%	9.44%	8.36%	7.60%	5.59%	6.17%	7.47%	18.34%
9%	4.21%	8.46%	5.62%	10.48%	9.39%	8.63%	6.56%	7.17%	8.50%	19.39%
10%	5.04%	9.46%	6.55%	11.52%	10.42%	9.66%	7.52%	8.18%	9.53%	20.43%
11%	5.87%	10.46%	7.48%	12.56%	11.45%	10.68%	8.48%	9.19%	10.57%	21.48%
12%	6.70%	11.47%	8.41%	13.59%	12.48%	11.71%	9.44%	10.19%	11.60%	22.53%

In the case example, the final equitable premium rate for Area B at the 10 percent portfolio-priced premium rate is 9.46 percent.

Final equitable premium rate for area = Equitable pure risk premium rate for area/(100 percent − Expense loading)

= 8.04 percent/(100 percent − 15 percent)

= 9.46 percent

In this case the insurer charges a 10 percent premium rate for the product across all areas of the portfolio, but the equitable premium rate for Area B is actually 9.46 percent.

Box 12.2 Overview of Calculations for the Equitable Premiums Metrics

Metrics based on at least 10,000 Monte Carlo scenarios

$$\text{Equitable premium rate} = \frac{\{[APPIU + EROC \times (RCPIU)]/AUS\}}{(1 - Total\ expense\ loading)},$$

box continues next page

Box 12.2 **Overview of Calculations for the Equitable Premiums Metrics** *(continued)*
where

APPIU = average payout per insured unit,

EROC = expected return on capital,

RCPIU = required capital per insured unit,

and AUS = average unit size.

- APPIU for area = Average payout amount for area/Number of insured units for area
- Stand-alone required capital for area = TVaR payout amount for area − Expected payout amount for area
- Area beta = Stand-alone required capital for area/Total stand-alone required capital for portfolio
- Required capital for area = Required capital for portfolio × Area beta
- RCPIU for area = Required capital for area/Number of insured units for area
- EROC for portfolio = (Net premium income for portfolio − Expected portfolio losses)/Required capital for portfolio
- EROC per unit for area = RCPIU for area × EROC for portfolio
- Equitable pure risk premium income per unit for area = APPIU for area + EROC per unit for area
- Equitable pure risk premium rate for area = Equitable pure risk premium income per unit for area/AUS for area
- Final equitable premium rate for area = Equitable pure risk premium rate for area/(100 percent − Expense loading)

Note: TVaR = tail value at risk.

12.4 Model Outputs

The model output sheet (table 12.9 and case example box 12CB.23) summarizes the product pricing metrics for the Base Index that were calculated in Steps 8–38. These include the following for each portfolio-priced premium rate under the no reinsurance, proportional reinsurance only, and proportional reinsurance and nonproportional reinsurance situations:

- Losses
- Required capital
- Combined ratios
- Profit margins
- Probability of fund ruin
- EVA
- Sharpe ratio

For each geographical area and at each portfolio-priced premium rate:

- Equitable premium rates

Table 12.9 Model Outputs

Model component	Section	Excel sheet label	Steps	Description
Model outputs	12.4	MO_12.4_MODEL OUTPUTS	None	Summary of pricing decision metrics for no reinsurance, proportional reinsurance only, and proportional and nonproportional reinsurance, and equitable premium rates for each geographical area

Case Example Box 12CB.23 Outputs

PORTFOLIO PRICED WITH NO REINSURANCE

PORTFOLIO PRICED WITH PROPORTIONAL REINSURANCE

PORTFOLIO PRICED WITH PROPORTIONAL AND NON-PROPORTIONAL REINSURANCE

FINAL EQUITABLE PREMIUM RATES

Note: EVA = economic value added; TVaR = tail value at risk.

The insurance manager uses these metrics in chapter 5 to answer the key managerial questions for pricing the Base Index.

The insurer will produce these same pricing metrics for any later Redesigned Indexes or prototype products by repeating the same pricing process.

Note

1. In reality insurers and reinsurers may have different costs of capital, for example, because of different degrees of risk and diversification.

Risk Modeling for Appraising Named Peril Index Insurance Products
http://dx.doi.org/10.1596/978-1-4648-1048-0

Bibliography

Brehm, P. J. 2007. *Enterprise Risk Analysis for Property & Liability Insurance Companies: A Practical Guide to Standard Models and Emerging Solutions*. New York: Guy Carpenter.

Cherubini, U., E. Luciano, and W. Vecchiato. 2004. *Copula Methods in Finance*. Hoboken, NJ: John Wiley & Sons.

Crouhy, M., D. Galai, and R. Mark. 2006. *The Essentials of Risk Management*. New York: McGraw-Hill.

Embrechts, P., F. Lindskog, and A. McNeil. 2003. "Modelling Dependence with Copulas and Applications to Risk Management." In *Handbook of Heavy Tailed Distributions in Finance*, edited by S. T. Rachev, 329–84. Amsterdam: Elsevier.

Grossi, P., H. Kunreuther, and C. C. Patel. 2005. *Catastrophe Modeling: A New Approach to Managing Risk*. New York: Springer Science Business Media.

Harrison, C. M. 2004. *Reinsurance Principles and Practices*. Malvern, PA: American Institute for Chartered Property Casualty Underwriters/Insurance Institute of America.

Lam, J. 2003. *Enterprise Risk Management: From Incentives to Controls*. Hoboken, NJ: Wiley.

Law, A. M., and W. D. Kelton. 2006. *Simulation Modeling and Analysis*. 4th ed. New York: McGraw-Hill.

Lehman, D. E., H. Groenendaal, and G. Nolder. 2012. *Practical Spreadsheet Risk Modeling for Management*. Boca Raton, FL: Chapman & Hall/CRC.

Ragsdale, C. T. 2001. *Spreadsheet Modeling and Decision Analysis: A Practical Introduction to Management Science*. Cincinnati, OH: Southwestern College.

Tang, A., and E. A. Valdez. 2009. "Economic Capital and the Aggregation of Risks Using Copulas." University of New South Wales, Sydney, Australia.

Yan, J. 2006. "Multivariate Modeling with Copulas and Engineering Applications." In *Springer Handbook of Engineering Statistics*, edited by H. Pham, 973–90. London: Springer-Verlag.

CHAPTER 13

Evaluating the Redesigned Index

13.1 Background and Objectives

Chapter 6 explains the key managerial questions for the evaluation of the Redesigned Index during the pilot phase of launching an index insurance business line. It outlines a series of steps for determining and explaining the differences in the level of coverage provided by the Base and the Redesigned Indexes.

As also discussed in earlier chapters, an objective of a Redesigned Index is typically to provide the policyholder with a lower-cost alternative to the Base Index. While the Base Index provides the highest level of coverage possible against inventory damage caused by the named peril, the Redesigned Index provides a lower level of coverage and so has a lower cost. The implied deductible is the difference in coverage between the Base Index and the Redesigned Index. It is the amount of risk that the policyholder chooses to retain and not transfer to the insurance company.

It is extremely important that the insurer always produce a Base Index to explain to the policyholder the difference between complete coverage—that provided by the Base Index—and the coverage provided by the Redesigned Index. Without this explicit comparison, policyholders often fall into the trap of expecting complete coverage even when they have purchased a less expensive product that provides lower coverage.

This chapter provides a step-by-step guide to using the probabilistic models that produce the decision metrics discussed in chapter 6. The model simulates three key scenario parameters:

- The payout ratios for the Base Index (Steps 10–14)
- The payout ratios for the Redesigned Index (Steps 15–19)
- The implied deductible amounts (Steps 20–25)

The model then uses these three parameters to calculate key Redesigned Index product evaluation decision metrics, including return periods, return period ratios,

Table 13.1 Summary of Model Components for Evaluating the Redesigned Index

Model component	Section	Excel sheet label	Steps	Description
Model input	13.2	MI_13.2_MODEL INPUTS	Steps 1–6	User-defined assumptions, relevant portfolio information, and Base Index and Redesigned Index historical payout ratios are entered for all areas.
Model computations	13.3.1	MC_13.3.1_DERIVED INPUTS	Steps 7–9	Calculation of historical implied deductible ratios. These derived inputs are used for Steps 20–25.
Model computations	13.3.2	MC_13.3.2_BI_SCENARIOS	Steps 10–14	Simulation of scenario payout ratios for the Base Index for each area
Model computations	13.3.3	MC_13.3.3_RI_SCENARIOS	Steps 15–19	Simulation of scenario payout ratios for the Redesigned Index for each area
Model computations	13.3.4	MC_13.3.4_IMPL-DED_SCENARIOS	Steps 20–25	Simulation of scenario implied deductible amounts for each area and for the portfolio
Model computations	13.3.5	MC_13.3.5_DECISION METRICS	Steps 26–31	Calculation of product evaluation decision metrics
Model output	13.4	MO_13.4_MODEL OUTPUT	None	Summary of product evaluation decision metrics

the probability of no implied deductible event occurring, and the magnitude of the expected implied deductibles (Steps 26–31). These metrics allow the insurer to understand and clearly explain to the policyholder the differences in level of coverage between the Redesigned Index and the Base Index. The insurer will repeat the product evaluation process with any later prototype products.

Table 13.1 provides a summary of the model components along with a guide to the sections in this chapter and the worksheets in the accompanying Excel files.

Section 11.5 provides a brief discussion of how retrospective analysis can also be used to evaluate the Redesigned Index.

13.2 Model Inputs

The analyst starts by specifying the model inputs (table 13.2) agreed upon with the insurance manager for the evaluation of the Redesigned Index.

13.2.1 Significant Payout Levels (Step 1)

The significant payout level inputs are the same as those specified in section 11.2.1. However, in this section the purpose of the inputs is to facilitate the

Table 13.2 Model Inputs

Model component	Section	Excel sheet label	Steps	Description
Model input	13.2	MI_13.2_MODEL INPUTS	Steps 1–6	User defined assumptions, relevant portfolio information, and Base Index and Redesigned Index historical payout ratios are entered for all areas.

generation and comparison of return periods for both the Base Index and the Redesigned Indexes.

Four damage levels are evaluated (case example box 13CB.1) because an index may provide insufficient coverage at mild and mild-to-medium impact levels but sufficient coverage for higher damage levels and vice versa. For a policyholder that is most concerned with covering medium-to-severe damage, the ability of the Redesigned Index to make appropriate payments at the higher damage levels will be most relevant for evaluating the product.

Case Example Box 13CB.1 Inputs—Step 1

STEP 1 : DEFINE SIGNIFICANT PAYOUT/DAMAGE LEVELS (%)

MILD IMPACT	10%
MILD-MEDIUM IMPACT	30%
MEDIUM IMPACT	50%
SEVERE IMPACT	70%

13.2.2 Prediction Interval (Step 2)

The prediction interval inputs (case example box 13CB.2) are the same as those specified in section 11.2.2 and will be used for the implied deductible metrics for the Redesigned Index in Steps 26–31.

Case Example Box 13CB.2 Inputs—Step 2

STEP 2 : INDICATE PREDICTION INTERVAL (%)

LOWER	5%
UPPER	95%

13.2.3 Total Sum Insured per Area (Step 3)

The total sum insured per area (case example box 13CB.3) will be used for generating the implied deductible amounts in Steps 20–25.

Case Example Box 13CB.3 Inputs—Step 3

STEP 3 : ENTER TOTAL SUM INSURED PER AREA

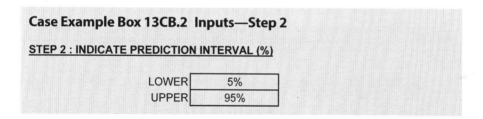

AREA A	AREA B	AREA C	AREA D	AREA E	AREA F	AREA G	AREA H	AREA I	AREA J
140,160	282,975	1,200,000	425,000	2,252,250	282,000	992,040	1,200,325	425,150	800,100

13.2.4 Base Index Historical Payout Ratios (Step 4)

The Base Index historical payout ratios (case example box 13CB.4) will be used for simulating return periods for the Base Index (Steps 10–14) and simulating implied deductible amounts for the Redesigned Index (Steps 20–25).

Case Example Box 13CB.4 Inputs—Step 4

STEP 4 : ENTER BASE INDEX HISTORICAL PAYOUT RATIOS

YEAR	AREA A	AREA B	AREA C	AREA D	AREA E	AREA F	AREA G	AREA H	AREA I	AREA J
1984	0.0%	0.0%	0.0%	0.0%	44.1%	0.0%	0.0%	0.0%	22.6%	90.4%
1985	0.0%	0.0%	0.0%	0.0%	0.0%	0.0%	0.0%	0.0%	0.0%	0.0%
1986	0.0%	0.0%	22.5%	0.0%	0.0%	0.0%	0.0%	0.0%	0.0%	7.5%
1987	0.0%	0.0%	0.0%	0.0%	22.5%	31.2%	0.0%	0.0%	0.0%	0.0%
1988	0.0%	0.0%	0.0%	47.5%	0.0%	0.0%	0.0%	0.0%	0.0%	0.0%
1989	0.0%	15.0%	0.0%	0.0%	7.5%	0.0%	0.0%	0.0%	0.0%	0.0%
1990	0.0%	0.0%	7.5%	100.0%	66.6%	0.0%	0.0%	0.0%	0.0%	2.5%
1991	0.0%	0.0%	0.0%	0.0%	0.0%	0.0%	0.0%	0.0%	0.0%	42.5%
1992	0.0%	0.0%	0.0%	50.0%	0.0%	0.0%	0.0%	0.0%	0.0%	86.0%
1993	0.0%	0.0%	0.0%	0.0%	0.0%	0.0%	0.0%	0.0%	0.0%	44.4%
1994	0.0%	0.0%	0.0%	0.0%	0.0%	0.0%	0.0%	0.0%	5.0%	96.0%
1995	0.0%	0.0%	0.0%	0.0%	0.0%	0.0%	0.0%	0.0%	0.0%	0.0%
1996	79.2%	0.0%	0.0%	0.0%	0.0%	5.8%	0.0%	0.0%	0.0%	27.5%
1997	0.0%	20.0%	0.0%	0.0%	0.0%	15.0%	0.0%	65.4%	0.0%	0.0%
1998	0.0%	0.0%	0.0%	0.0%	0.0%	0.0%	30.0%	0.0%	63.2%	0.0%
1999	0.0%	0.0%	0.0%	0.0%	2.5%	17.5%	2.5%	86.2%	0.0%	39.0%
2000	0.0%	0.0%	0.0%	0.0%	0.0%	0.0%	53.4%	0.0%	0.0%	0.0%
2001	0.0%	0.0%	0.0%	0.0%	0.0%	0.0%	0.0%	0.0%	0.0%	0.0%
2002	0.0%	0.0%	5.0%	0.0%	0.0%	0.0%	0.0%	0.0%	0.0%	0.0%
2003	0.0%	0.0%	0.0%	0.0%	0.0%	0.0%	0.0%	0.0%	29.0%	60.0%
2004	0.0%	0.0%	0.0%	19.2%	0.0%	0.0%	0.0%	0.0%	0.0%	0.0%
2005	0.0%	0.0%	0.0%	0.0%	0.0%	0.0%	0.0%	0.0%	0.0%	0.0%
2006	0.0%	0.0%	0.0%	2.5%	0.0%	0.0%	0.0%	0.0%	0.0%	39.4%
2007	0.0%	0.0%	0.0%	40.4%	0.0%	0.0%	0.0%	0.0%	0.0%	0.0%
2008	0.0%	0.0%	0.0%	0.0%	0.0%	0.0%	0.0%	0.0%	0.0%	17.5%
2009	0.0%	2.5%	0.0%	0.0%	0.0%	0.0%	0.0%	0.0%	32.8%	64.0%
2010	0.0%	0.0%	0.0%	0.0%	0.0%	0.0%	25.0%	61.2%	0.0%	0.0%
2011	2.5%	7.5%	0.0%	16.6%	0.0%	0.0%	0.0%	0.0%	0.0%	0.0%
2012	0.0%	5.0%	0.0%	0.0%	0.0%	2.5%	0.0%	0.0%	0.0%	0.0%
2013	0.0%	0.0%	0.0%	0.0%	9.0%	0.0%	0.0%	45.2%	0.0%	0.0%

13.2.5 Redesigned Index Historical Payout Ratios (Step 5)

The Redesigned Index historical payout ratios (case example box 13CB.5) will be used for determining the implied deductible amounts (Steps 20–25) and the expected return period for the Redesigned Index (Steps 26 and 27).

13.2.6 Nonzero Historical Payout Ratios (Step 6)

In Step 6 (case example box 13CB.6) the analyst manually records all the non-zero values for the historical payout ratios from Steps 4 and 5. These inputs will

Case Example Box 13CB.5 Inputs—Step 5

STEP 5 : ENTER REDESIGNED INDEX HISTORICAL PAYOUT RATIOS

YEAR	AREA A	AREA B	AREA C	AREA D	AREA E	AREA F	AREA G	AREA H	AREA I	AREA J
1984	0.0%	0.0%	0.0%	0.0%	0.0%	0.0%	0.0%	0.0%	0.0%	80.4%
1985	0.0%	0.0%	0.0%	0.0%	0.0%	0.0%	0.0%	0.0%	0.0%	0.0%
1986	0.0%	0.0%	10.0%	0.0%	0.0%	0.0%	0.0%	0.0%	0.0%	0.0%
1987	0.0%	0.0%	0.0%	0.0%	0.0%	0.0%	0.0%	0.0%	0.0%	0.0%
1988	0.0%	0.0%	0.0%	35.0%	0.0%	0.0%	0.0%	0.0%	0.0%	0.0%
1989	0.0%	2.5%	0.0%	0.0%	0.0%	0.0%	0.0%	0.0%	0.0%	0.0%
1990	0.0%	0.0%	0.0%	72.5%	16.6%	0.0%	0.0%	0.0%	0.0%	0.0%
1991	0.0%	0.0%	0.0%	0.0%	0.0%	0.0%	0.0%	0.0%	0.0%	30.0%
1992	0.0%	0.0%	0.0%	50.0%	0.0%	0.0%	0.0%	0.0%	0.0%	76.0%
1993	0.0%	0.0%	0.0%	0.0%	0.0%	0.0%	0.0%	0.0%	0.0%	34.4%
1994	0.0%	0.0%	0.0%	0.0%	0.0%	0.0%	0.0%	0.0%	0.0%	86.0%
1995	0.0%	0.0%	0.0%	0.0%	0.0%	0.0%	0.0%	0.0%	0.0%	0.0%
1996	29.2%	0.0%	0.0%	0.0%	0.0%	0.0%	0.0%	0.0%	0.0%	15.0%
1997	0.0%	7.5%	0.0%	0.0%	0.0%	2.5%	0.0%	15.4%	0.0%	0.0%
1998	0.0%	0.0%	0.0%	0.0%	0.0%	0.0%	17.5%	0.0%	13.2%	0.0%
1999	0.0%	0.0%	0.0%	0.0%	0.0%	5.0%	0.0%	36.2%	15.0%	29.0%
2000	0.0%	0.0%	0.0%	0.0%	0.0%	0.0%	3.4%	0.0%	0.0%	0.0%
2001	0.0%	0.0%	0.0%	0.0%	0.0%	0.0%	0.0%	0.0%	0.0%	0.0%
2002	0.0%	0.0%	0.0%	0.0%	0.0%	0.0%	0.0%	0.0%	0.0%	0.0%
2003	0.0%	0.0%	0.0%	0.0%	0.0%	0.0%	0.0%	0.0%	0.0%	50.0%
2004	0.0%	0.0%	0.0%	0.0%	0.0%	0.0%	0.0%	0.0%	0.0%	0.0%
2005	0.0%	0.0%	0.0%	0.0%	0.0%	0.0%	0.0%	0.0%	0.0%	0.0%
2006	0.0%	0.0%	0.0%	0.0%	0.0%	0.0%	0.0%	0.0%	0.0%	29.4%
2007	0.0%	0.0%	0.0%	0.0%	0.0%	0.0%	0.0%	0.0%	0.0%	0.0%
2008	0.0%	0.0%	0.0%	0.0%	0.0%	0.0%	0.0%	0.0%	0.0%	5.0%
2009	0.0%	0.0%	0.0%	0.0%	0.0%	0.0%	0.0%	0.0%	0.0%	54.0%
2010	0.0%	0.0%	0.0%	0.0%	0.0%	0.0%	12.5%	11.2%	0.0%	0.0%
2011	0.0%	0.0%	0.0%	0.0%	0.0%	0.0%	0.0%	0.0%	0.0%	0.0%
2012	0.0%	0.0%	0.0%	0.0%	0.0%	0.0%	0.0%	0.0%	0.0%	39.0%
2013	0.0%	0.0%	0.0%	0.0%	0.0%	0.0%	0.0%	0.0%	0.0%	0.0%

Case Example Box 13CB.6 Inputs—Step 6

STEP 6 : MANUALLY RECORD ALL NON-ZERO HISTORICAL PAYOUT RATIOS FOR THE BASE AND REDESIGNED INDEXES

BASE INDEX	REDESIGNED INDEX
79.2%	29.2%
3%	2.5%
15%	7.5%
20%	10.0%
3%	35.0%
8%	72.5%
5%	50.0%
23%	16.6%
8%	2.5%
5%	5.0%
48%	17.5%
100%	3.4%
50%	12.5%
19.2%	15.4%
2.5%	36.2%
40.4%	11.2%
16.6%	13.2%
44.1%	15.0%
22.5%	80.4%
8%	30.0%
66.6%	76.0%
2.5%	34.4%
9.0%	86.0%
31.2%	15.0%
5.8%	29.0%
15.0%	50.0%
17.5%	29.4%
2.5%	5.0%
30.0%	54.0%
2.5%	
53.4%	
25%	
65%	
86%	
61%	
45%	
23%	
63%	
5%	
29%	
33%	
90%	
8%	
3%	
43%	
86%	
44%	
96%	
28%	
39%	
60%	
39%	
18%	
64%	

For the case example, about half of the payouts for the Base Index (25 out of 54) would not have been made with the Redesigned Index in place. This should not come as a surprise, given that the Redesigned Index provides less coverage and is less expensive.

be used in the simulation of scenario payout ratios for the Base Index (Steps 10–14) and the Redesigned Index (Steps 15–19).

Note that the two columns of figures cannot be compared row-by-row and should be considered as two separate tables because the product parameters are different. However, we can make some broad conclusions based on the figures.

13.3 Model Computations

The model completes five sets of computations for evaluating the Redesigned Index (table 13.3), starting with calculating the derived inputs—historical implied deductible ratios (Steps 7–9)—then simulating the three key scenario parameters (Steps 10–25), and finally producing the product evaluation decision metrics (Steps 26–31).

Remember, the insurer will repeat the product evaluation computations for any later prototype products.

Table 13.3 Model Computations

Model component	Section	Excel sheet label	Steps	Description
Model computations	13.3.1	MC_13.3.1_DERIVED INPUTS	Steps 7–9	Calculation of historical implied deductible ratios. These derived inputs are used for Steps 20–25.
	13.3.2	MC_13.3.2_BI_SCENARIOS	Steps 10–14	Simulation of scenario payout ratios for the Base Index for each area
	13.3.3	MC_13.3.3_RI_SCENARIOS	Steps 15–19	Simulation of scenario payout ratios for the Redesigned Index for each area
	13.3.4	MC_13.3.4_IMPL-DED_SCENARIOS	Steps 20–25	Simulation of scenario implied deductible amounts for each area and for the portfolio
	13.3.5	MC_13.3.5_DECISION METRICS	Steps 26–31	Calculation of product evaluation decision metrics

13.3.1 Calculation of Historical Implied Deductible Ratios (Steps 7–9)
13.3.1.1 Overview
The historical implied deductible ratio (table 13.4) is the difference between the historical payout ratios for the Base and Redesigned Indexes.

Historical implied = Max (0, Base Index historical − Redesigned Index historical
deductible ratio   payout ratio   payout ratio)
(Step 4)   (Step 5)

The implied deductible ratio can only be zero or positive. It is the reduction in payouts that results from redesigning the Base Index.

Table 13.4 Model Computations

Model component	Section	Excel sheet label	Steps	Description
Model computations	13.3.1	MC_13.3.1_DERIVED INPUTS	Steps 7–9	Calculation of historical implied deductible ratios. These derived inputs are used for Steps 20–25.

13.3.1.2 Implementation in Excel (MC_13.3.1_Derived Inputs)

In Step 7, the model calculates the implied deductible ratio for each year and for each area (case example box 13CB.7).

In Step 8 (no case example box), the model reorders the historical implied deductible ratios for all areas from Step 7, from the most recent year at the top to the least recent year at the bottom. The model will use these derived inputs in Step 31 when it selects the historical years with the largest implied deductibles.

In Step 9 (case example box 13CB.8), the analyst manually combines all of the nonzero historical implied deductible ratios from Step 7 into one column.

Case Example Box 13CB.7 Computations—Step 7

STEP 7 : CALCULATE HISTORICAL IMPLIED DEDUCTIBLE RATIOS

YEAR	AREA A	AREA B	AREA C	AREA D	AREA E	AREA F	AREA G	AREA H	AREA I	AREA J
1984	0.0%	0.0%	0.0%	0.0%	44.1%	0.0%	0.0%	0.0%	22.6%	10.0%
1985	0.0%	0.0%	0.0%	0.0%	0.0%	0.0%	0.0%	0.0%	0.0%	0.0%
1986	0.0%	0.0%	12.5%	0.0%	0.0%	0.0%	0.0%	0.0%	0.0%	7.5%
1987	0.0%	0.0%	0.0%	0.0%	22.5%	31.2%	0.0%	0.0%	0.0%	0.0%
1988	0.0%	0.0%	0.0%	12.5%	0.0%	0.0%	0.0%	0.0%	0.0%	0.0%
1989	0.0%	12.5%	0.0%	0.0%	7.5%	0.0%	0.0%	0.0%	0.0%	0.0%
1990	0.0%	0.0%	7.5%	27.5%	50.0%	0.0%	0.0%	0.0%	0.0%	2.5%
1991	0.0%	0.0%	0.0%	0.0%	0.0%	0.0%	0.0%	0.0%	0.0%	12.5%
1992	0.0%	0.0%	0.0%	0.0%	0.0%	0.0%	0.0%	0.0%	0.0%	10.0%
1993	0.0%	0.0%	0.0%	0.0%	0.0%	0.0%	0.0%	0.0%	0.0%	10.0%
1994	0.0%	0.0%	0.0%	0.0%	0.0%	0.0%	0.0%	0.0%	5.0%	10.0%
1995	0.0%	0.0%	0.0%	0.0%	0.0%	0.0%	0.0%	0.0%	0.0%	0.0%
1996	50.0%	0.0%	0.0%	0.0%	0.0%	5.8%	0.0%	0.0%	0.0%	12.5%
1997	0.0%	12.5%	0.0%	0.0%	0.0%	12.5%	0.0%	50.0%	0.0%	0.0%
1998	0.0%	0.0%	0.0%	0.0%	0.0%	0.0%	12.5%	0.0%	50.0%	0.0%
1999	0.0%	0.0%	0.0%	0.0%	2.5%	12.5%	2.5%	50.0%	0.0%	10.0%
2000	0.0%	0.0%	0.0%	0.0%	0.0%	0.0%	50.0%	0.0%	0.0%	0.0%
2001	0.0%	0.0%	0.0%	0.0%	0.0%	0.0%	0.0%	0.0%	0.0%	0.0%
2002	0.0%	0.0%	5.0%	0.0%	0.0%	0.0%	0.0%	0.0%	0.0%	0.0%
2003	0.0%	0.0%	0.0%	0.0%	0.0%	0.0%	0.0%	0.0%	29.0%	10.0%
2004	0.0%	0.0%	0.0%	19.2%	0.0%	0.0%	0.0%	0.0%	0.0%	0.0%
2005	0.0%	0.0%	0.0%	0.0%	0.0%	0.0%	0.0%	0.0%	0.0%	0.0%
2006	0.0%	0.0%	0.0%	2.5%	0.0%	0.0%	0.0%	0.0%	0.0%	10.0%
2007	0.0%	0.0%	0.0%	40.4%	0.0%	0.0%	0.0%	0.0%	0.0%	0.0%
2008	0.0%	0.0%	0.0%	0.0%	0.0%	0.0%	0.0%	0.0%	0.0%	12.5%
2009	0.0%	2.5%	0.0%	0.0%	0.0%	0.0%	0.0%	0.0%	32.8%	10.0%
2010	0.0%	0.0%	0.0%	0.0%	0.0%	0.0%	12.5%	50.0%	0.0%	0.0%
2011	2.5%	7.5%	0.0%	16.6%	0.0%	0.0%	0.0%	0.0%	0.0%	0.0%
2012	0.0%	5.0%	0.0%	0.0%	0.0%	2.5%	0.0%	0.0%	0.0%	0.0%
2013	0.0%	0.0%	0.0%	0.0%	9.0%	0.0%	0.0%	45.2%	0.0%	0.0%

For the case example, there are five historical years in Area B that have positive implied deductible ratios. These years are 1989 (12.5 percent), 1997 (12.5 percent), 2009 (2.5 percent), 2011 (7.5 percent), and 2012 (5 percent). In these five historical years, the insured party would have assumed additional risk as a result of choosing the Redesigned Index rather than the Base Index. For example, in 1997, the implied deductible was 12.5 percent.

Historical implied deductible ratio = Max (0, Base Index historical payout ratio − Redesigned Index historical payout ratio)

= Max (0, 20 percent − 7.5 percent)

= 12.5 percent

Case Example Box 13CB.8 Computations—Step 9

STEP 9 : MANUALLY RECORD ALL NON-ZERO HISTORICAL IMPLIED DEDUCTIBLE RATIOS FROM STEP 7

HISTORICAL IMPLIED DEDUC. RATIOS
50.0%
2.5%
12.5%
12.5%
2.5%
7.5%
5.0%
12.5%
7.5%
5.0%
12.5%
27.5%
19.2%
2.5%
40.4%
16.6%
44.1%
22.5%
7.5%
50.0%
2.5%
9.0%
31.2%
5.8%
12.5%
12.5%
2.5%
12.5%
2.5%
50.0%
12.5%
50.0%
50.0%
50.0%
45.2%
22.6%
50.0%
5.0%
29.0%
32.8%
10.0%
7.5%
2.5%
12.5%
10.0%
10.0%
10.0%
12.5%
10.0%
10.0%
10.0%
12.5%
10.0%

The model will use these derived inputs in Steps 20–25 for the simulation of implied deductible amounts.

13.3.2 Simulation of Scenario Payout Ratios for the Base Index (Steps 10–14)
13.3.2.1 Overview
The model's simulation of the scenario payout ratios for the Base Index for each area (table 13.5) incorporates three stochastic elements (frequency, severity, and correlation) just as in section 11.3.3.

Table 13.5 Model Computations

Model component	Section	Excel sheet label	Steps	Description
Model computations	13.3.2	MC_13.3.2_BI_SCENARIOS	Steps 10–14	Simulation of scenario payout ratios for the Base Index for each area

13.3.2.2 Implementation in Excel (MC_13.3.2_BI_SCENARIOS)
Steps 10–14 for simulating the scenario payout ratios for the Base Index (case example box 13CB.9) are exactly the same as Steps 14–18 in section 11.3.3. The reader is referred back to section 11.3.3 for further details on the modeling.

Case Example Box 13CB.9 Computations—Steps 10–14

STEP 10 : DETERMINE FREQUENCY

	AREA A	AREA B	AREA C	AREA D	AREA E	AREA F	AREA G	AREA H	AREA I	AREA J
SUCCESSES	2	5	3	7	6	5	4	4	5	13
TRIALS	30	30	30	30	30	30	30	30	30	30
ESTIMATE THE PROBABILITY	Beta(3;29)	Beta(6;26)	Beta(4;28)	Beta(8;24)	Beta(7;25)	Beta(6;26)	Beta(5;27)	Beta(5;27)	Beta(6;26)	Beta(14;18)
BERNOULLI OBJECT	Bernoulli(0.13)	Bernoulli(0.13)	Bernoulli(0.26)	Bernoulli(0.24)	Bernoulli(0.25)	Bernoulli(0.21)	Bernoulli(0.08)	Bernoulli(0.08)	Bernoulli(0.20)	Bernoulli(0.45)

STEP 11 : DETERMINE SEVERITY

	AREA A	AREA B	AREA C	AREA D	AREA E	AREA F	AREA G	AREA H	AREA I	AREA J
BETA OBJECT	Beta(0.65;1.07)	Beta(0.65;1.07)	Beta(0.65;1.07)	Beta(0.65;1.07)	Beta(0.65;1.07)	Beta(0.65;1.07)	Beta(0.65;1.07)	Beta(0.65;1.07)	Beta(0.65;1.07)	Beta(0.65;1.07)

STEP 12A : CHOOSE COPULA

CHOSEN COPULA: T-COPULA

STEP 12B : DETERMINE COPULA MATRIX

	AREA A	AREA B	AREA C	AREA D	AREA E	AREA F	AREA G	AREA H	AREA I	AREA J
AREA A	100%	-6%	-5%	-8%	-7%	9%	-6%	-7%	-7%	4%
AREA B	-6%	100%	-10%	-11%	-7%	21%	-12%	28%	-9%	-21%
AREA C	-5%	-10%	100%	15%	17%	-10%	-9%	-10%	-10%	-14%
AREA D	-8%	-11%	15%	100%	55%	-15%	-13%	-16%	-15%	-5%
AREA E	-7%	-7%	17%	55%	100%	13%	-11%	-7%	4%	9%
AREA F	9%	21%	-10%	-15%	13%	100%	-10%	41%	-13%	-10%
AREA G	-6%	-12%	-9%	-13%	-11%	-10%	100%	10%	28%	-21%
AREA H	-7%	28%	-10%	-16%	-7%	41%	10%	100%	-14%	-9%
AREA I	-7%	-9%	-10%	-15%	4%	-13%	28%	-14%	100%	26%
AREA J	4%	-21%	-14%	-5%	9%	-10%	-21%	-9%	26%	100%
Degrees of freedom	5									

STEP 13: DETERMINE COPULA FUNCTION

	AREA A	AREA B	AREA C	AREA D	AREA E	AREA F	AREA G	AREA H	AREA I	AREA J
COPULA FUNCTION	0.24	0.86	0.08	0.39	0.58	0.65	0.71	0.89	0.30	0.55

STEP 14 : DETERMINE SCENARIO PAYOUT RATIO FOR BASE INDEX

	AREA A	AREA B	AREA C	AREA D	AREA E	AREA F	AREA G	AREA H	AREA I	AREA J
SCENARIO PAYOUT RATIO	0%	0%	0%	0%	0%	0%	0%	6%	0%	41%

13.3.3 Simulation of Scenario Payout Ratios for the Redesigned Index (Steps 15–19)

13.3.3.1 Overview

The purpose of determining the scenario payout ratios for the Redesigned Index (table 13.6) is to compare them to those for the Base Index. In this way, the model evaluates and quantifies the implied deductible assumed by the insured party when selecting the Redesigned Index.

Table 13.6 Model Computations

Model component	Section	Excel sheet label	Steps	Description
Model computations	13.3.3	MC_13.3.3_RI_SCENARIOS	Steps 15–19	Simulation of scenario payout ratios for the Redesigned Index for each area

13.3.3.2 Implementation in Excel (MC_13.3.3_RI_SCENARIOS)

Steps 15–19 for simulating the scenario payout ratios for the Redesigned Index (case example box 13CB.10) are similar to Steps 10–14 but use the historical payout ratios for the Redesigned Index (Step 5) as inputs.

The reader is again referred back to section 11.3.3 for further details on the modeling.

Case Example Box 13CB.10 Computations—Steps 15–19

STEP 15 : DETERMINE FREQUENCY

	AREA A	AREA B	AREA C	AREA D	AREA E	AREA F	AREA G	AREA H	AREA I	AREA J
SUCCESSES	1	2	1	3	1	2	3	3	2	11
TRIALS	30	30	30	30	30	30	30	30	30	30
ESTIMATE THE PROBABILITY	Beta(2;30)	Beta(3;29)	Beta(2;30)	Beta(4;28)	Beta(2;30)	Beta(3;29)	Beta(4;28)	Beta(4;28)	Beta(3;29)	Beta(12;20)
BERNOULLI OBJECT	Bernoulli(0,06)	Bernoulli(0,08)	Bernoulli(0,09)	Bernoulli(0,12)	Bernoulli(0,03)	Bernoulli(0,07)	Bernoulli(0,13)	Bernoulli(0,09)	Bernoulli(0,04)	Bernoulli(0,58)

STEP 16 : DETERMINE SEVERITY

	AREA A	AREA B	AREA C	AREA D	AREA E	AREA F	AREA G	AREA H	AREA I	AREA J
BETA OBJECT	Beta(0,91;2,11)	Beta(0,91;2,11)	Beta(0,91;2,11)	Beta(0,91;2,11)	Beta(0,91;2,11)	Beta(0,91;2,11)	Beta(0,91;2,11)	Beta(0,91;2,11)	Beta(0,91;2,11)	Beta(0,91;2,11)

STEP 17A : CHOOSE COPULA

CHOSEN COPULA: T-COPULA

STEP 17B : DETERMINE COPULA MATRIX

	AREA A	AREA B	AREA C	AREA D	AREA E	AREA F	AREA G	AREA H	AREA I	AREA J
AREA A	100%	-4%	-3%	-6%	-3%	-5%	-5%	-5%	-5%	-1%
AREA B	-4%	100%	-4%	-8%	-4%	39%	-7%	31%	-6%	-15%
AREA C	-3%	-4%	100%	-6%	-3%	-5%	-5%	-5%	-5%	-11%
AREA D	-6%	-8%	-6%	100%	76%	-8%	-9%	-9%	-8%	9%
AREA E	-3%	-4%	-3%	76%	100%	-5%	-5%	-5%	-5%	-11%
AREA F	-5%	39%	-5%	-8%	-5%	100%	-7%	96%	85%	3%
AREA G	-5%	-7%	-5%	-9%	-5%	-7%	100%	9%	49%	-18%
AREA H	-5%	31%	-5%	-9%	-5%	96%	9%	100%	84%	0%
AREA I	-5%	-6%	-5%	-8%	-5%	65%	49%	64%	100%	-1%
AREA J	-1%	-15%	-11%	9%	-11%	3%	-18%	0%	-1%	100%
Degrees of freedom	3									

STEP 18: DETERMINE COPULA FUNCTION

	AREA A	AREA B	AREA C	AREA D	AREA E	AREA F	AREA G	AREA H	AREA I	AREA J
COPULA FUNCTION	0.45	0.98	0.49	0.75	0.94	0.74	0.05	0.48	0.47	0.17

STEP 19 : DETERMINE SCENARIO PAYOUT RATIO FOR REDESIGNED INDEX (%)

	AREA A	AREA B	AREA C	AREA D	AREA E	AREA F	AREA G	AREA H	AREA I	AREA J
SCENARIO PAYOUT RATIO	0%	56%	0%	0%	0%	0%	0%	0%	0%	0%

box continues next page

> **Case Example Box 13CB.10 Computations—Steps 15–19** *(continued)*
>
> Comparing the results of Steps 10 and 15 for the case example, we can see that the frequency of payouts for the Redesigned Index is less than for the Base Index. These results make sense because the Redesigned Index provides a lower level of coverage. With the Redesigned Index, the insured party retains more risk than with the Base Index. In other words, some inventory damage caused by named peril events that would be covered by the Base Index will not trigger for the Redesigned Index.
>
> For example, in Area B, the Base Index triggers five payouts but the Redesigned Index triggers only two. The missing three payouts are part of the Redesigned Index's implied deductible. On seeing the lower level of coverage provided by the Redesigned Index, the insured party may decide to purchase an index product that provides more coverage, such as the more expensive Base Index.

13.3.4 Simulation of Scenario Implied Deductible Amounts (Steps 20–25)

13.3.4.1 *Overview*

The main objective of generating the scenario portfolio implied deductible amount (table 13.7) is to quantify the Redesigned Index's implied deductible.

Table 13.7 Model Computations

Model component	Section	Excel sheet label	Steps	Description
Model computations	13.3.4	MC_13.3.4_IMPL-DED_ SCENARIOS	Steps 20–25	Simulation of scenario implied deductible amounts for each area and for the portfolio

13.3.4.2 *Implementation in Excel (MC_13.3.4_IMPL_DED_SCENARIOS)*

Steps 20–25 for simulating the scenario portfolio implied deductible amount (case example box 13CB.11) are similar to Steps 10–14. However, there are two main differences between the calculations:

First, these steps use the historical implied deductible ratios for the Redesigned Index as inputs (Step 9), rather than the historical payout ratios for the Base Index.

Second, Steps 24 and 25 calculate monetary amounts for the payouts by area and for the total portfolio rather than just ratios.

The reader is referred back to section 11.3.3 for further details on the modeling.

13.3.5 Calculation of Product Evaluation Decision Metrics (Steps 26–31)

At this point the model has simulated three key scenario parameters (payout ratios for the Base Index and the Redesigned Index as well as the implied deductible amounts) for the evaluation of the Redesigned Index. Based on these three parameters, the model now calculates a number of important metrics that help determine the level of coverage provided by the Redesigned Index compared with the Base Index (table 13.8).

Risk Modeling for Appraising Named Peril Index Insurance Products
http://dx.doi.org/10.1596/978-1-4648-1048-0

Case Example Box 13CB.11   Computations—Steps 20–25

STEP 20 : DETERMINE FREQUENCY

	AREA A	AREA B	AREA C	AREA D	AREA E	AREA F	AREA G	AREA H	AREA I	AREA J
SUCCESSES	2	5	3	7	6	5	4	4	5	13
TRIALS	30	30	30	30	30	30	30	30	30	30
ESTIMATE THE PROBABILITY	Beta(3,29)	Beta(6,26)	Beta(4,28)	Beta(8,24)	Beta(7,25)	Beta(6,26)	Beta(5,27)	Beta(5,27)	Beta(6,26)	Beta(14,16)
BERNOULLI OBJECT	Bernoulli(0,11)	Bernoulli(0,23)	Bernoulli(0,10)	Bernoulli(0,15)	Bernoulli(0,22)	Bernoulli(0,21)	Bernoulli(0,13)	Bernoulli(0,13)	Bernoulli(0,10)	Bernoulli(0,51)

STEP 21 : DETERMINE SEVERITY

	AREA A	AREA B	AREA C	AREA D	AREA E	AREA F	AREA G	AREA H	AREA I	AREA J
BETA OBJECT	Beta(1,17;5,07)	Beta(1,17;5,07)	Beta(1,17;5,07)	Beta(1,17;5,07)	Beta(1,17;5,07)	Beta(1,17;5,07)	Beta(1,17;5,07)	Beta(1,17;5,07)	Beta(1,17;5,07)	Beta(1,17;5,07)

STEP 22A : CHOOSE COPULA

CHOSEN COPULA	T-COPULA

STEP 22B : DETERMINE COPULA MATRIX

	AREA A	AREA B	AREA C	AREA D	AREA E	AREA F	AREA G	AREA H	AREA I	AREA J
AREA A	100%	-6%	-6%	-6%	-7%	10%	-5%	-8%	-8%	29%
AREA B	-6%	100%	-12%	-3%	-7%	13%	-11%	22%	-9%	-28%
AREA C	-6%	-12%	100%	14%	27%	-11%	-9%	-12%	-12%	2%
AREA D	-6%	-3%	14%	100%	24%	-14%	-11%	-16%	-16%	-28%
AREA E	-7%	-7%	27%	24%	100%	19%	-10%	-6%	8%	1%
AREA F	10%	13%	-11%	-14%	19%	100%	-8%	26%	-13%	-8%
AREA G	-5%	-11%	-9%	-11%	-10%	-8%	100%	5%	8%	-21%
AREA H	-8%	22%	-12%	-16%	-6%	26%	5%	100%	-15%	-13%
AREA I	-8%	-9%	-12%	-16%	8%	-13%	8%	-15%	100%	16%
AREA J	29%	-28%	2%	-28%	1%	-8%	-21%	-13%	16%	100%
Degrees of freedom	5									

STEP 23: DETERMINE COPULA FUNCTION

	AREA A	AREA B	AREA C	AREA D	AREA E	AREA F	AREA G	AREA H	AREA I	AREA J
COPULA FUNCTION	0.27	0.72	0.73	0.51	0.96	0.91	0.81	0.81	0.01	0.00

STEP 24 : DETERMINE SCENARIO IMPLIED DEDUCTIBLE AMOUNTS BY AREA ($)

	AREA A	AREA B	AREA C	AREA D	AREA E	AREA F	AREA G	AREA H	AREA I	AREA J
SCENARIO IMPLIED DEDUCTIBLE AMOUNT	0	0	0	0	603,966	7,751	0	0	0	0

STEP 25: DETERMINE SCENARIO PORTFOLIO IMPLIED DEDUCTIBLE AMOUNT ($)

SCENARIO IMPLIED DEDUCTIBLE AMOUNT	611,718

For the case example, the scenario portfolio implied deductible amount is $611,718. This amount is the sum of the implied deductible amounts for Areas E ($603,966) and F ($7,751).

Table 13.8 Model Computations

Model component	Section	Excel sheet label	Steps	Description
Model computations	13.3.5	MC_13.3.5_DECISION METRICS	Steps 26–31	Calculation of product evaluation decision metrics

13.3.5.1 Expected Return Periods for the Base and Redesigned Indexes

13.3.5.1.1 Overview. Figure 13.1 provides an overview of how the model generates the expected return periods for the Base and Redesigned Indexes, which is similar to the process explained in section 11.3.7.1.

13.3.5.1.2 Implementation in Excel (MC_13.3.5_DECISION METRICS). Step 26, in which the return period is simulated for the Base Index (case example box 13CB.12), is exactly the same as Step 37 in section 11.3.7.1.

The reader is referred to section 11.3.7.1 for further details on the modeling.

Figure 13.1 Generating Return Periods for the Base and Redesigned Indexes

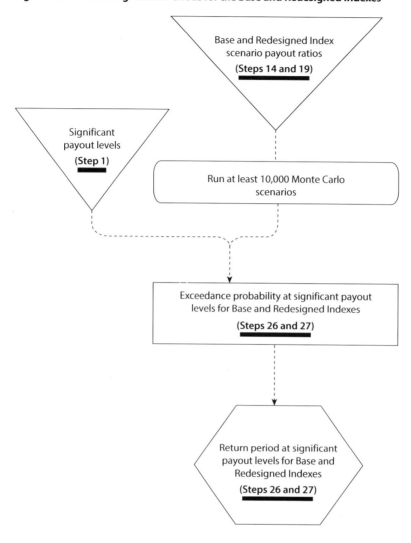

Case Example Box 13CB.12 Computations—Steps 26 and 27

STEP 26 : CALCULATE BASE INDEX RETURN PERIODS

				AREA A	AREA B	AREA C	AREA D	AREA E	AREA F	AREA G	AREA H	AREA I	AREA J
EXCEEDANCE PROBABILITY	@	10%	PAYOUT LEVEL	7%	15%	10%	19%	17%	14%	12%	12%	14%	33%
EXCEEDANCE PROBABILITY	@	30%	PAYOUT LEVEL	5%	10%	7%	13%	11%	10%	8%	8%	10%	23%
EXCEEDANCE PROBABILITY	@	50%	PAYOUT LEVEL	3%	7%	4%	9%	8%	7%	6%	6%	7%	15%
EXCEEDANCE PROBABILITY	@	70%	PAYOUT LEVEL	2%	4%	2%	5%	4%	3%	3%	3%	4%	8%
RETURN PERIOD	@	10%	PAYOUT LEVEL	14	7	10	5	6	7	8	8	7	3
RETURN PERIOD	@	30%	PAYOUT LEVEL	21	10	15	8	9	10	12	12	10	4
RETURN PERIOD	@	50%	PAYOUT LEVEL	32	15	23	12	13	15	18	18	15	7
RETURN PERIOD	@	70%	PAYOUT LEVEL	61	27	47	21	24	29	32	32	27	12

STEP 27 : CALCULATE REDESIGNED INDEX RETURN PERIODS

				AREA A	AREA B	AREA C	AREA D	AREA E	AREA F	AREA G	AREA H	AREA I	AREA J
EXCEEDANCE PROBABILITY	@	10%	PAYOUT LEVEL	5%	7%	5%	10%	5%	7%	9%	9%	7%	29%
EXCEEDANCE PROBABILITY	@	30%	PAYOUT LEVEL	3%	4%	3%	6%	3%	4%	5%	5%	4%	17%
EXCEEDANCE PROBABILITY	@	50%	PAYOUT LEVEL	1%	2%	1%	3%	1%	2%	3%	3%	2%	8%
EXCEEDANCE PROBABILITY	@	70%	PAYOUT LEVEL	0%	1%	0%	1%	0%	1%	1%	1%	1%	3%
IMPLIED RETURN PERIOD	@	10%	PAYOUT LEVEL	22	13	21	10	20	14	11	11	14	3
IMPLIED RETURN PERIOD	@	30%	PAYOUT LEVEL	39	24	37	17	37	25	19	19	26	6
IMPLIED RETURN PERIOD	@	50%	PAYOUT LEVEL	85	50	73	34	87	52	39	39	55	12
IMPLIED RETURN PERIOD	@	70%	PAYOUT LEVEL	294	145	263	106	217	159	110	103	189	38

Risk Modeling for Appraising Named Peril Index Insurance Products
http://dx.doi.org/10.1596/978-1-4648-1048-0

In Step 27, the model calculates the exceedance probabilities and expected return periods for Redesigned Index payouts for each significant payout level and area (case example box 13CB.12).

13.3.5.2 Return Period Ratio (Step 28)

13.3.5.2.1 Overview. The return period ratio shows the level of implied deductible for specific payout levels for each of the areas in the portfolio. When this ratio is equal to 1, the Redesigned Index triggers a payout at the same expected frequency as the Base Index. When the ratio is between 0 and 1, the Redesigned Index triggers payouts less frequently than the Base Index (implied deductible). We expect this outcome because the lower cost Redesigned Index provides less coverage than the Base Index.

13.3.5.2.2 Implementation in Excel (MC_13.3.5_DECISION METRICS). Step 28 is similar to Step 38 in section 11.3.7.2 but uses the return periods for the Base Index and Redesigned Index (case example box 13CB.13). In Step 28, the model calculates the return period ratio for each area and payout level.

$$\text{Return period ratio} = \frac{\text{Expected return period}}{\text{for Base Index}} / \frac{\text{Expected return period for}}{\text{Redesigned Index}}$$
$$\text{(Step 26)} \qquad\qquad \text{(Step 27)}$$

Case Example Box 13CB.13 Computations—Step 28

STEP 28 : CALCULATE RETURN PERIOD RATIOS

				AREA A	AREA B	AREA C	AREA D	AREA E	AREA F	AREA G	AREA H	AREA I	AREA J
RETURN PERIOD RATIO	@	10%	PAYOUT LEVEL	0.64	0.60	0.49	0.53	0.30	0.49	0.79	0.77	0.48	0.87
RETURN PERIOD RATIO	@	30%	PAYOUT LEVEL	0.54	0.41	0.41	0.44	0.23	0.39	0.63	0.62	0.41	0.73
RETURN PERIOD RATIO	@	50%	PAYOUT LEVEL	0.38	0.30	0.31	0.34	0.15	0.29	0.45	0.45	0.27	0.53
RETURN PERIOD RATIO	@	70%	PAYOUT LEVEL	0.21	0.19	0.18	0.20	0.11	0.18	0.29	0.31	0.17	0.31

13.3.5.3 Implied Deductible Statistics (Steps 29–31)

13.3.5.3.1 Overview. When the return period ratio is between 0 and 1, the Redesigned Index is triggering payouts at a lower expected frequency than the Base Index, indicating an implied deductible. We expect this outcome because the lower cost Redesigned Index provides less coverage than the Base Index.

However, the return period ratio does not tell us whether the Redesigned Index is triggering in the right years and for the right amounts. This section explains the calculation of three additional metrics that further describe the Redesigned Index's implied deductible: the probability of having no implied deductible amounts in the next risk period, the expected amount of the implied deductible, and historical years with the largest implied deductible amounts.

Figure 13.2 Generating Probability of No Implied Deductible Event and Expected Implied Deductible Amounts

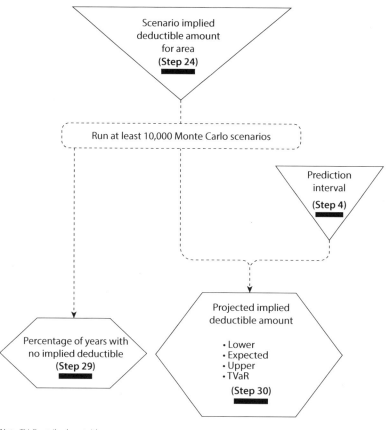

Note: TVaR = tail value at risk.

Figure 13.2 provides an overview of how the model generates the first two metrics: the probability of having no implied deductible and the amount of the implied deductible.

Figure 13.3 provides an overview of how the model generates the historical years with the largest implied deductible amounts.

13.3.5.3.2 Implementation in Excel (MC_13.3.5_DECISION METRICS). Steps 29–31 are similar to Steps 39–41 in section 11.3.7.2, but use the scenario implied deductible amounts (Step 24) instead of the insured party basis risk amounts.

In Step 29, the model generates at least 10,000 scenarios for each area based on the scenario implied deductible amounts and calculates the proportion of the scenarios in which the implied deductible was zero (case example box 13CB.14). This figure indicates the percentage of years in which no implied deductible is expected for each area. Expressed differently,

Risk Modeling for Appraising Named Peril Index Insurance Products
http://dx.doi.org/10.1596/978-1-4648-1048-0

Figure 13.3 Generating Historical Years with Largest Implied Deductible Amount

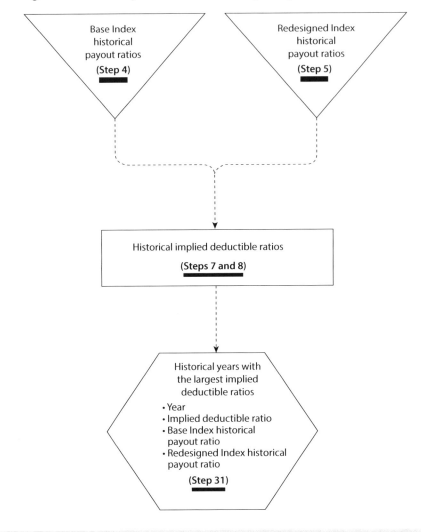

Case Example Box 13CB.14 Computations—Steps 29 and 30

STEP 29: CALCULATE PERCENTAGE OF YEARS WITH NO IMPLIED DEDUCTIBLE

AREA A	AREA B	AREA C	AREA D	AREA E	AREA F	AREA G	AREA H	AREA I	AREA J
91%	80%	87%	75%	78%	81%	64%	64%	81%	55%

STEP 30 : CALCULATE PROJECTED IMPLIED DEDUCTIBLE AMOUNT

	AMOUNT	% OF SUM INSURED
LOWER	0	0%
EXPECTED	309,342	4%
UPPER	990,402	12%
TVaR	1,283,575	16%

For the case example, in Area B there is an 80 percent chance of having no implied deductible in the next risk period. Because we know that higher percentages of years with no implied deductible correspond with a lower magnitude of implied deductible, we can tell that the implied deductible amount for Area A (91 percent of years with no implied deductible) will be the lowest of all the areas, and the amount for Area J (55 percent) will likely be the highest. The Redesigned Index affects the different areas in different ways.

box continues next page

> **Case Example Box 13CB.14 Computations—Steps 29 and 30** *(continued)*
>
> For the portfolio as a whole, the expected implied deductible amount is $309,342, which is 4 percent of the total portfolio sum insured. This figure means that in the next risk period, the policyholder can expect to miss out on $309,342 in payouts that it would have received from the Base Index. For a 1-in-20-year event, the implied deductible amount is expected to be as high as $1,283,575 (that is, TVaR 95 percent of the implied deductible).
>
> *Note:* TVaR = tail value at risk.

this figure is the probability that no implied deductible will occur during the next risk period.

In Step 30, the model uses the same 10,000 scenarios to determine the expected amount of the implied deductible for the portfolio (all geographical areas). This amount is reflected in currency terms and as a percentage of the total sum insured. Based on the prediction interval selected in Step 2, the model also calculates the appropriate percentile and the tail value at risk. The values of these metrics indicate the expected magnitude of the Redesigned Index's implied deductible. Note that when the percentage of years with no implied deductible for an area is higher, the magnitude of the implied deductible is lower and vice versa.

In addition to the metrics related to the implied deductible amounts, memorable years in which the Redesigned Index would have failed to trigger or would have triggered payouts smaller than those for the Base Index will be of interest to the prospective policyholder.

In Step 8, the model reordered the historical implied deductible ratios from the most recent to least recent year for each area.

In Step 31, the model now selects the years with the largest implied deductible ratios (case example box 13CB.15). In areas where this value—the largest implied deductible ratio—is repeated across multiple years, the model selects the most recent of these years. The most recent year events are chosen because prospective policyholders are more likely to remember these than older events. Next, the model selects each year's corresponding Base Index and Redesigned Index payout ratios. The insurance manager will use these years as examples when explaining to the policyholder the limitations of the coverage provided by the Redesigned Index in comparison to the Base Index.

Case Example Box 13CB.15 Computations—Step 31

STEP 31 : CALCULATE HISTORICAL YEARS WITH LARGEST IMPLIED DEDUCTIBLE RATIOS

	AREA A	AREA B	AREA C	AREA D	AREA E	AREA F	AREA G	AREA H	AREA I	AREA J
HISTORICAL YEAR WITH LARGEST IMPLIED DEDUCTIBLE RATIO	1996	1989	1986	2007	1990	1987	2000	2010	1998	2008
IMPLIED DEDUCTIBLE RATIO	50%	12.50%	13%	40%	50%	31%	50%	50%	50%	13%
BASE INDEX PAYOUT RATIO	79%	15%	23%	40%	67%	31%	53%	61%	63%	18%
REDESIGNED INDEX PAYOUT RATIO	29%	2.5%	10%	0%	17%	0%	3%	11%	13%	5%

For Area B in the case example, the largest historical implied deductible ratio was 12.5 percent, which occurred in 1989. In that year, the Base Index would have triggered a 15 percent payout but the Redesigned Index would have triggered only a 2.5 percent payout.

Risk Modeling for Appraising Named Peril Index Insurance Products
http://dx.doi.org/10.1596/978-1-4648-1048-0

13.4 Model Outputs

The model output sheet summarizes the product evaluation decision metrics (box 13.1; case example box 13CB.16) for the Redesigned Index produced in Steps 7–31. These include the following:

- Base Index and Redesigned Index return periods for each area
- Return period ratios for each area
- Probability that the Redesigned Index will have no implied deductible in the next risk period for each area
- The expected amount of the implied deductible for the portfolio
- Historical years with largest implied deductible events for each area

---

Box 13.1 Overview of Calculations for the Redesigned Index Product Evaluation Metrics

Derived inputs

- *Historical implied deductible ratio* = Max (0, Base Index historical payout ratio − Redesigned Index historical payout ratio)

Metrics based on at least 10,000 Monte Carlo scenarios

- *Return period ratio* = Expected return period for Base Index/Expected return period for Redesigned Index

---

Case Example Box 13CB.16 Outputs

BASE INDEX RETURN PERIODS

				AREA A	AREA B	AREA C	AREA D	AREA E	AREA F	AREA G	AREA H	AREA I	AREA J
RETURN PERIOD	@	10%	PAYOUT LEVEL	14	7	10	5	6	7	8	8	7	3
RETURN PERIOD	@	30%	PAYOUT LEVEL	21	10	15	8	9	10	12	12	10	4
RETURN PERIOD	@	50%	PAYOUT LEVEL	32	15	23	12	13	15	18	18	15	7
RETURN PERIOD	@	70%	PAYOUT LEVEL	61	27	47	21	24	29	32	32	27	12

REDESIGNED INDEX RETURN PERIODS

				AREA A	AREA B	AREA C	AREA D	AREA E	AREA F	AREA G	AREA H	AREA I	AREA J
IMPLIED RETURN PERIOD	@	10%	PAYOUT LEVEL	22	13	21	10	20	14	11	11	14	3
IMPLIED RETURN PERIOD	@	30%	PAYOUT LEVEL	39	24	37	17	37	25	19	19	25	6
IMPLIED RETURN PERIOD	@	50%	PAYOUT LEVEL	85	50	73	34	87	52	39	39	55	12
IMPLIED RETURN PERIOD	@	70%	PAYOUT LEVEL	294	145	263	106	217	159	110	103	159	38

RETURN PERIOD RATIOS

				AREA A	AREA B	AREA C	AREA D	AREA E	AREA F	AREA G	AREA H	AREA I	AREA J
RETURN PERIOD RATIO	@	10%	PAYOUT LEVEL	0.64	0.50	0.49	0.53	0.30	0.49	0.79	0.77	0.48	0.87
RETURN PERIOD RATIO	@	30%	PAYOUT LEVEL	0.54	0.41	0.41	0.44	0.23	0.39	0.63	0.62	0.41	0.73
RETURN PERIOD RATIO	@	50%	PAYOUT LEVEL	0.38	0.30	0.31	0.34	0.16	0.29	0.45	0.45	0.27	0.53
RETURN PERIOD RATIO	@	70%	PAYOUT LEVEL	0.21	0.19	0.18	0.20	0.11	0.18	0.29	0.31	0.17	0.31

PERCENTAGE OF YEARS WITH NO IMPLIED DEDUCTIBLE

91%	80%	87%	75%	76%	81%	84%	84%	81%	55%

PROJECTED IMPLIED DEDUCTIBLE AMOUNT

	AMOUNT	% OF SUM INSURED
LOWER	0	0%
EXPECTED	309.342	4%
UPPER	990.402	12%
TVaR	1.263.575	18%

HISTORICAL YEARS WITH LARGEST IMPLIED DEDUCTIBLE RATIOS

	AREA A	AREA B	AREA C	AREA D	AREA E	AREA F	AREA G	AREA H	AREA I	AREA J
HISTORICAL YEAR WITH LARGEST IMPLIED DEDUCTIBLE RATIO	1996	1989	1986	2007	1990	1987	2000	2010	1996	2008
IMPLIED DEDUCTIBLE RATIO	50%	12.5%	13%	40%	50%	31%	50%	50%	50%	13%
BASE INDEX PAYOUT RATIO	79%	15%	23%	40%	67%	31%	53%	61%	63%	18%
REDESIGNED INDEX PAYOUT RATIO	29%	2.5%	10%	0%	17%	0%	3%	11%	13%	5%

Note: TVaR = tail value at risk.

The insurance manager uses these metrics in chapter 6 to answer the key managerial questions for evaluating the Redesigned Index.

The insurer will produce these same outputs for any later prototype products by repeating the same product evaluation process.

13.5 Alternative Modeling Approach: Retrospective Analysis

Section 11.5 detailed how to use retrospective analysis to evaluate the Base Index for basis risk. A retrospective approach can also be used to evaluate the Redesigned Index's implied deductible.

In this case the retrospective approach compares the Base Index historical payout ratios (Step 4) and the Redesigned Index historical payout ratios (Step 5). All of the analysis is based only on historical values.

The reader is referred to section 11.5 for further details on the modeling.

Bibliography

Brehm, P. J. 2007. *Enterprise Risk Analysis for Property & Liability Insurance Companies: A Practical Guide to Standard Models and Emerging Solutions*. New York: Guy Carpenter.

Cherubini, U., E. Luciano, and W. Vecchiato. 2004. *Copula Methods in Finance*. Hoboken, NJ: John Wiley & Sons.

Crouhy, M., D. Galai, and R. Mark. 2006. *The Essentials of Risk Management*. New York: McGraw-Hill.

Embrechts, P., F. Lindskog, and A. McNeil. 2003. "Modelling Dependence with Copulas and Applications to Risk Management." In *Handbook of Heavy Tailed Distributions in Finance*, edited by S. T. Rachev, 329–84. Amsterdam: Elsevier.

Grossi, P., H. Kunreuther, and C. C. Patel. 2005. *Catastrophe Modeling: A New Approach to Managing Risk*. New York: Springer Science Business Media.

Lam, J. 2003. *Enterprise Risk Management: From Incentives to Controls*. Hoboken, NJ: Wiley.

Law, A. M., and W. D. Kelton. 2006. *Simulation Modeling and Analysis*. 4th ed. New York: McGraw-Hill.

Lehman, D. E., H. Groenendaal, and G. Nolder. 2012. *Practical Spreadsheet Risk Modeling for Management*. Boca Raton, FL: Chapman & Hall/CRC.

Morsink, K., D. Clarke, and S. Mapfumo. 2016. "How to Measure Whether Index Insurance Provides Reliable Protection." Policy Research Working Paper 7744, World Bank, Washington, DC.

Ragsdale, C. T. 2001. *Spreadsheet Modeling and Decision Analysis: A Practical Introduction to Management Science*. Cincinnati, OH: Southwestern College.

Tang, A., and E. A. Valdez. 2009. "Economic Capital and the Aggregation of Risks Using Copulas." University of New South Wales, Sydney, Australia.

Yan, J. 2006. "Multivariate Modelling with Copulas and Engineering Applications." In *Springer Handbook of Engineering Statistics*, edited by H. Pham, 973–90. London: Springer-Verlag.

.

CHAPTER 14

Detailed Market Analysis

14.1 Background and Objectives

Chapter 7 explained the key managerial questions for a detailed analysis of the broader market for index insurance beyond the pilot phase of launching an index insurance business line. For the market analysis, the insurer designs and prices a Base Index and a set of Redesigned Indexes—prototype products—which are evaluated (chapters 4 and 6) and priced (chapter 5) using the same process as in the pilot phase. The objective of the detailed market analysis is to identify the specific market segments that provide the highest expected volumes and profit for the investment of the insurer's resources, as well as to identify the product coverage and price combinations preferred by these market segments.

This chapter provides a step-by-step guide to using the probabilistic models that produce the decision metrics for the market analysis discussed in chapter 7.

Table 14.1 provides a summary of the model components along with a guide to the sections in this chapter and the worksheets in the accompanying Excel files.

14.2 Model Inputs

The analyst starts by specifying the model inputs agreed upon with the insurance manager for the detailed market analysis (table 14.2).

14.2.1 Internal Insurer Assumptions (Step 1)

The analyst first specifies inputs based on the following internal insurer data (case example box 14CB.1):

- Target loss ratio (percentage): The target loss ratio (minimum, most likely, and maximum) can be based on expert opinion (for example, the insurer's experience from other areas or regions) or on an area-specific analysis like that for the equitable premium rates in section 12.3.5. In addition, the target loss ratio may be part of the insurer's overall risk appetite strategy. In general, we do not advise using the minimum or maximum loss ratio from the pilot phase because

Table 14.1 Summary of Model Components for the Detailed Market Analysis

Model component	Section	Excel sheet label	Steps	Description
Model input	14.2	MI_14.2_MODEL INPUTS	Steps 1–2	Internal insurer assumptions and data from external market research are entered for all areas.
Model computations	14.3	MC_14.3_MODEL_ COMPUTATIONS	Steps 3–7	Calculation of detailed market analysis decision metrics
Model outputs	14.4	MO_14.4_MODEL OUTPUTS	None	Summary of detailed market analysis decision metrics

Table 14.2 Model Inputs

Model component	Section	Excel sheet label	Steps	Description
Model input	14.2	MI_14.2_MODEL INPUTS	Steps 1–2	Internal insurer assumptions and data from external market research are entered for all areas.

Case Example Box 14CB.1 Inputs—Step 1

STEP 1 : ENTER INSURER ASSUMPTIONS

TARGET LOSS RATIO (%)
MINIMUM	13%
EXPECTED	79%
MAXIMUM	114%

TARGET PROFIT MARGIN (%) 10%

REQUIRED RETURN ON CAPITAL (%) 5%

RISK-FREE RATE (%) 2%

PREDICTION INTERVAL (%)
LOWER	5%
UPPER	95%

EXPENSE LOADING (%)

MARKET SEGMENT	FIRM SIZE		
	Small	Medium	Large
Rural Banks	20%	15%	10%
MFIs	20%	15%	10%
Seed Companies	20%	15%	10%
Agribusinesses	20%	15%	10%
NGOs	20%	15%	10%

Note: MFI = microfinance institution; NGO = nongovernmental organization.

this is an annual loss ratio, which will typically have high variability. In this chapter the objective is to examine the viability of an index insurance product, which requires looking at the loss ratio over a longer period than one year to understand the trend. As a starting point, we recommend using the 25th and 75th percentile of the pilot phase loss ratio as the minimum and maximum for the detailed market analysis, implying a decision horizon of four to five years.
- Target profit margin (percentage) (section 12.2.2).
- Required return on capital (section 12.2.2).
- Risk-free rate (section 12.2.2).
- Prediction interval: Remember, the upper limit of the interval is used in calculating the capital requirements. For example, if the insurer wants to hold capital at 99 percent tail value at risk (TVaR; the payout amount for a 1-in-100 year event), the upper limit should be set at 99 percent. In the case example, the insurance manager and the analyst specify the upper limit as the 95th percentile.
- Expense loading for each market segment and firm size.

The insurer can use its experience during the pilot phase to set these values. Reinsurers may also give some guidance based on international experience.

14.2.2 External Research on the Market (Step 2)

The remaining inputs are based on in-depth research on the market, for example, obtained from a specialist research firm (case example box 14CB.2).

- Number of firms in market by size and market segment.
- Modal portfolio size by firm size and market segment. The modal portfolio size is the average insurable amount per firm, which is specified for each market segment and firm size. The analyst must estimate the most likely minimum and maximum average insurable amount per firm. These input parameters will be used for project evaluation and review techniques (PERT) distributions to represent uncertainty about the average insurable amount per firm.
- Premium rates for each prototype product.
- Most popular prototype for each market segment and size.
- Number of firms that are expected to purchase the most popular prototype by firm size and market segment. The analyst must estimate the most likely, minimum, and maximum number of firms. These input parameters will be used for PERT distributions to represent uncertainty about the number of firms that will purchase the product.

The above list includes data that are generally needed to estimate market and market segment demand. If the available market and demand data come in a different format, the probabilistic model will have to be adjusted to take into account this alternative data.

Case Example Box 14CB.2 Inputs—Step 2

In the case example, the insurer hires an international consulting firm to complete a detailed value chain study and stakeholder interviews on the preferred prototype option for each market segment by size of firm.

The Base Prototype provides the highest level of coverage (and highest premium rate at 10 percent), and is the most popular option for nongovernmental organizations of all sizes. The Redesigned Prototype 1 provides coverage for events with at least mild-to-medium severity levels (6 percent premium rate) and is the most popular option for rural banks, microfinance institutions, and agribusinesses of all sizes. The Redesigned Prototype 2 covers only the most severe events (4 percent premium rate) and is the most popular option for seed companies of all sizes.

STEP 2: ENTER MARKET RESEARCH DATA

A) SUMMARY OF MARKET INFORMATION

NUMBER OF FIRMS					
	Rural Banks	MFIs	Seed Companies	Agribusinesses	NGOs
Small	10	5	12	15	8
Medium	5	3	6	6	5
Large	2	0	3	2	3

MODAL PORTFOLIO SIZE					
	Rural Banks	MFIs	Seed Companies	Agribusinesses	NGOs
Small	$ 1,000,000	$ 1,000,000	$ 1,000,000	$ 2,500,000	$ 500,000
Medium	$ 2,500,000	$ 2,500,000	$ 7,500,000	$ 7,500,000	$ 1,000,000
Large	$ 5,000,000	$ 5,000,000	$ 10,000,000	$ 15,000,000	$ 2,500,000

B) PRODUCT DEMAND INFORMATION

SMALL FIRMS					
Premium Rates	Rural Banks	MFIs	Seed Companies	Agribusinesses	NGOs
Base Prototype	10%	10%	10%	10%	10%
Redesigned Prototype 1	6%	6%	6%	6%	6%
Redesigned Prototype 2	4%	4%	4%	4%	4%
Most Popular Prototype (per market segment)	Redesigned Prototype 1	Redesigned Prototype 1	Redesigned Prototype 2	Redesigned Prototype 1	Base Prototype
Minimum Uptake	2	3	5	3	2
Most Likely Uptake	6	4	5	4	3
Maximum Uptake	8	4	6	5	5
Total Firms	10	5	12	15	8

MEDIUM FIRMS					
Premium Rates	Rural Banks	MFIs	Seed Companies	Agribusinesses	NGOs
Base Prototype	10%	10%	10%	10%	10%
Redesigned Prototype 1	6%	6%	6%	6%	6%
Redesigned Prototype 2	4%	4%	4%	4%	4%
Most Popular Prototype (per market segment)	Redesigned Prototype 1	Redesigned Prototype 1	Redesigned Prototype 2	Redesigned Prototype 1	Base Prototype
Minimum Uptake	2	2	2	2	2
Most Likely Uptake	3	2	4	4	2
Maximum Uptake	4	2	5	6	4
Total Firms	5	3	6	6	5

LARGE FIRMS					
Premium Rates	Rural Banks	MFIs	Seed Companies	Agribusinesses	NGOs
Base Prototype	10%	10%	10%	10%	10%
Redesigned Prototype 1	6%	6%	6%	6%	6%
Redesigned Prototype 2	4%	4%	4%	4%	4%
Most Popular Prototype (per market segment)	Redesigned Prototype 1	Redesigned Prototype 1	Redesigned Prototype 2	Redesigned Prototype 1	Base Prototype
Minimum Uptake	1	0	1	1	1
Most Likely Uptake	1	0	2	2	2
Maximum Uptake	2	0	3	2	3
Total Firms	2	0	3	2	3

Note: MFI = microfinance institution; NGO = nongovernmental organization.

14.3 Model Computations

The model completes one set of computations to produce the detailed market analysis decision metrics (table 14.3).

14.3.1 Premium Incomes (Step 3)
14.3.1.1 Overview
Figure 14.1 provides an overview of how the model generates the expected premium income for the most popular prototype for each market segment and firm size.

Table 14.3 Model Computations

Model component	Section	Excel sheet label	Steps	Description
Model computations	14.3	MC_14.3_MODEL COMPUTATIONS	Steps 3–7	Calculation of detailed market analysis decision metrics

Figure 14.1 Generating Expected Premium Incomes

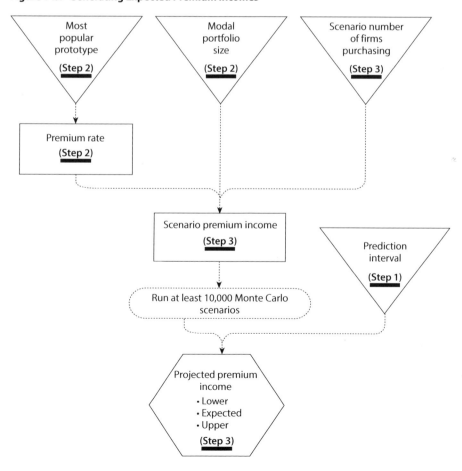

14.3.1.2 Implementation in Excel (MC_14_MODEL_COMPUTATIONS)

In Step 3, the model determines the scenario number of firms purchasing the prototype product for each market segment and firm size using a PERT distribution (case example box 14CB.3). The PERT distribution accounts for uncertainty about the number of firms that will actually purchase the index product.

Scenario number of firms purchasing = PERT(Minimum number of firms, Most likely number of firms, Maximum number of firms) (Step 2)

Also in Step 3, the model calculates the premium income for the most popular prototype option for each market segment and firm size,

Scenario premium = Modal portfolio × Premium rate × Scenario
of firms purchasing   size   number
                 (Step 2)   (Step 2)   (Step 3)

Case Example Box 14CB.3 Computations—Step 3

STEP 3: CALCULATE PROJECTED PREMIUM INCOME

FIRM SIZE	MARKET SEGMENT	MODAL PORTFOLIO SIZE ($)	MOST POPULAR PROTOTYPE	GROSS PREMIUM RATE (%)	ITERATION # OF FIRMS PURCHASING	SCENARIO PREMIUM INCOME ($)	PROJECTED PREMIUM INCOME ($)		
							Lower	Expected	Upper
SMALL	Rural Banks	$ 1,000,000	Redesigned Prototype 1	6%	6	$ 360,000	$ 240,000	$ 339,984	$ 420,000
	MFIs	$ 1,000,000	Redesigned Prototype 1	6%	4	$ 240,000	$ 240,000	$ 237,924	$ 240,000
	Seed Companies	$ 1,000,000	Redesigned Prototype 2	4%	5	$ 200,000	$ 200,000	$ 201,328	$ 200,000
	Agribusinesses	$ 2,500,000	Redesigned Prototype 1	6%	4	$ 600,000	$ 450,000	$ 600,840	$ 750,000
	NGOs	$ 500,000	Base Prototype	10%	3	$ 150,000	$ 100,000	$ 158,735	$ 200,000
MEDIUM	Rural Banks	$ 2,500,000	Redesigned Prototype 1	6%	3	$ 450,000	$ 300,000	$ 450,150	$ 600,000
	MFIs	$ 2,500,000	Redesigned Prototype 1	6%	2	$ 300,000	$ 300,000	$ 300,000	$ 300,000
	Seed Companies	$ 7,500,000	Redesigned Prototype 2	4%	3	$ 900,000	$ 900,000	$ 1,150,680	$ 1,500,000
	Agribusinesses	$ 7,500,000	Redesigned Prototype 1	6%	5	$ 2,250,000	$ 1,350,000	$ 1,800,990	$ 2,250,000
	NGOs	$ 1,000,000	Base Prototype	10%	3	$ 300,000	$ 200,000	$ 224,000	$ 300,000
LARGE	Rural Banks	$ 5,000,000	Redesigned Prototype 1	6%	1	$ 300,000	$ 300,000	$ 310,020	$ 300,000
	MFIs	$ 5,000,000	Redesigned Prototype 1	6%		$ -	$ -	$ -	$ -
	Seed Companies	$ 10,000,000	Redesigned Prototype 2	4%	3	$ 1,200,000	$ 400,000	$ 798,680	$ 1,200,000
	Agribusinesses	$ 15,000,000	Redesigned Prototype 1	6%	1	$ 900,000	$ 1,800,000	$ 1,772,010	$ 1,800,000
	NGOs	$ 2,500,000	Base Prototype	10%	3	$ 750,000	$ 250,000	$ 499,500	$ 750,000

In the case example, the scenario number of medium seed companies purchasing is three.

Scenario number of firms purchasing = PERT(Minimum number of firms, Most likely number of firms, Maximum number

of firms)

= PERT(2, 4, 5)

= 3

The scenario premium income for medium seed companies is $900,000.

Scenario premium income = Modal portfolio size × Premium rate × Scenario number of firms purchasing

= $7,500,000 × 4 percent × 3

= $900,000

Note: MFI = microfinance institution; NGO = nongovernmental organization.

At this point, Step 3 generates at least 10,000 scenario premium income amounts for each market segment and firm size and determines the expected premium income for each ($1,150,680 for medium seed companies in the case example). Based on the prediction interval selected in Step 1, the model also calculates the appropriate percentile values.

14.3.2 Expected Losses and Required Capital (Step 4)
14.3.2.1 Overview
Figure 14.2 provides an overview of how the model generates the expected losses and required capital for the most popular prototype for each market segment and firm size.

Figure 14.2 Generating Expected Losses and Required Capital

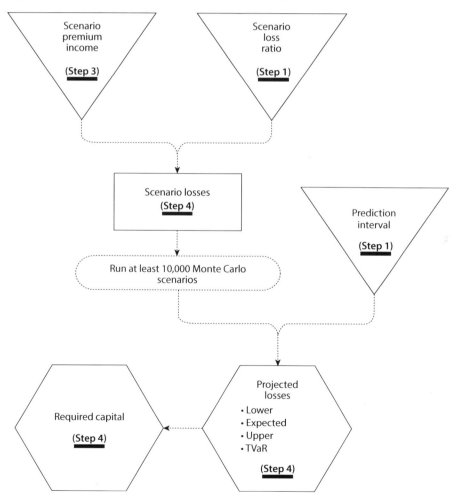

Note: TVaR = tail value at risk.

Risk Modeling for Appraising Named Peril Index Insurance Products
http://dx.doi.org/10.1596/978-1-4648-1048-0

14.3.2.2 Implementation in Excel (MC_14.3_MODEL COMPUTATIONS)

Step 4 is similar to Steps 13 and 14 in section 12.3.2.1, but uses scenario loss ratios to calculate the scenario losses rather than historical payout ratios.

In Step 4, the model determines the scenario loss ratio for each market segment and firm size using a PERT distribution (case example box 14CB.4).

Scenario loss = PERT(Minimum target, Most likely target, Maximum target
ratio   loss ratio   loss ratio   loss ratio)
                       (Step 1)   (Step 1)   (Step 1)

Case Example Box 14CB.4 Computations—Step 4

STEP 4 : CALCULATE PROJECTED LOSSES AND REQUIRED CAPITAL

FIRM SIZE	MARKET SEGMENT	SCENARIO PREMIUM INCOME ($)	SCENARIO LOSS RATIO (%)	SCENARIO LOSSES ($)	PROJECTED LOSSES ($)				REQUIRED CAPITAL (values copied from 1st simulation)	REQUIRED CAPITAL (1st simulation)
					Lower	Expected	Upper	TVaR		
SMALL	Rural Banks	$ 360,000	81%	$ 293,037	$ 120,419	$ 250,908	$ 391,980	$ 425,949	$ 175,041	$ 175,041
	MFIs	$ 240,000	59%	$ 140,879	$ 96,393	$ 175,727	$ 245,972	$ 254,096	$ 78,369	$ 78,369
	Seed Companies	$ 200,000	73%	$ 145,052	$ 82,427	$ 147,884	$ 206,200	$ 215,653	$ 67,768	$ 67,768
	Agribusinesses	$ 600,000	78%	$ 465,950	$ 241,359	$ 443,643	$ 637,312	$ 692,499	$ 248,856	$ 248,856
	NGOs	$ 150,000	68%	$ 101,501	$ 58,664	$ 117,439	$ 165,918	$ 202,622	$ 85,183	$ 85,183
MEDIUM	Rural Banks	$ 450,000	66%	$ 296,845	$ 173,439	$ 333,439	$ 485,926	$ 545,286	$ 211,846	$ 211,846
	MFIs	$ 300,000	67%	$ 202,432	$ 122,870	$ 221,223	$ 306,022	$ 317,942	$ 96,719	$ 96,719
	Seed Companies	$ 900,000	74%	$ 662,208	$ 440,867	$ 851,861	$ 1,281,944	$ 1,398,333	$ 546,473	$ 546,473
	Agribusinesses	$ 2,250,000	77%	$ 1,740,169	$ 655,337	$ 1,326,719	$ 2,077,966	$ 2,275,498	$ 948,778	$ 948,778
	NGOs	$ 300,000	57%	$ 170,472	$ 86,806	$ 164,962	$ 271,023	$ 295,726	$ 130,765	$ 130,765
LARGE	Rural Banks	$ 300,000	51%	$ 154,216	$ 122,051	$ 228,473	$ 317,577	$ 403,678	$ 175,206	$ 175,206
	MFIs	$ -	69%	$ -	$ -	$ -	$ -	$ -	$ -	$ -
	Seed Companies	$ 1,200,000	56%	$ 674,334	$ 264,113	$ 588,167	$ 907,474	$ 1,069,432	$ 481,265	$ 481,265
	Agribusinesses	$ 900,000	90%	$ 809,717	$ 690,479	$ 1,310,472	$ 1,835,175	$ 1,909,636	$ 599,164	$ 599,164
	NGOs	$ 750,000	59%	$ 444,443	$ 167,947	$ 369,754	$ 572,421	$ 676,836	$ 307,082	$ 307,082

In the case example, the scenario loss ratio for medium seed companies is 74 percent.

Scenario loss ratio = PERT(Minimum target loss ratio, Most likely target loss ratio, Maximum target loss ratio)

= PERT(13 percent, 79 percent, 14 percent)

= 73.5787 percent

The scenario losses for medium seed companies are $662,208.

Scenario losses = Scenario premium income × Scenario loss ratio

= 900,000 × 73.5787 percent

= $662,208

In the case example, the required capital for medium seed companies is $546,473.

Required capital = TVaR losses − Expected losses

= $1,398,334 − $851,861

= $546,473

The insurer should keep $546,473 in reserve to stay solvent in case of a 1-in-20 year event (TVaR 95 percent).

Note: MFI = microfinance institution; NGO = nongovernmental organization; TVaR = tail value at risk.

Also in Step 4, the model calculates the scenario losses for each market segment and firm size.

$$\text{Scenario losses} = \text{Scenario premium income} \times \text{Scenario loss ratio}$$
$$(\text{Step 3})$$

At this point, Step 4 generates at least 10,000 scenario losses for each market segment and firm size and determines the expected losses for each ($851,861 for medium seed companies). Based on the prediction interval selected in Step 1, the model also calculates the appropriate percentile and TVaR values.

Finally, Step 4 uses the same 10,000 scenarios to calculate the required capital for the portfolio.

$$\text{Required capital} = \text{TVaR losses} - \text{Expected losses}$$

14.3.3 Combined Ratios and Profit Margins (Step 5)
14.3.3.1 Overview
Figure 14.3 provides an overview of how the model generates the combined ratio and profit margin for the most popular prototype for each market segment and firm size.

14.3.3.2 Implementation in Excel (MC_14.3_MODEL_COMPUTATIONS)
Step 5 is similar to Step 15 in section 12.3.2.2, but uses the scenario loss ratio based on the PERT distribution (Step 4) to calculate the scenario combined ratio.

In Step 5 (case example box 14CB.5), the model first calculates the scenario combined ratio for each market segment and firm size.

$$\text{Scenario combined ratio} = \text{Scenario loss ratio} + \text{Expense loading}$$
$$(\text{Step 4}) \qquad (\text{Step 1})$$

Also in Step 5, the model calculates the scenario profit margin for each market segment and firm size.

$$\text{Scenario profit margin} = 100 \text{ percent} - \text{Scenario combined ratio}$$

At this point, Step 5 generates at least 10,000 scenario combined ratios for each market segment and firm size and determines the expected combined ratio for each (89 percent for medium seed companies in the case example). Based on the prediction interval selected in Step 1, the model also calculates the appropriate percentile values.

Step 5 also generates at least 10,000 scenario profit margins for each market segment and firm size and determines the expected profit margin (11 percent for

Risk Modeling for Appraising Named Peril Index Insurance Products
http://dx.doi.org/10.1596/978-1-4648-1048-0

Figure 14.3 Generating Expected Combined Ratios and Profit Margins

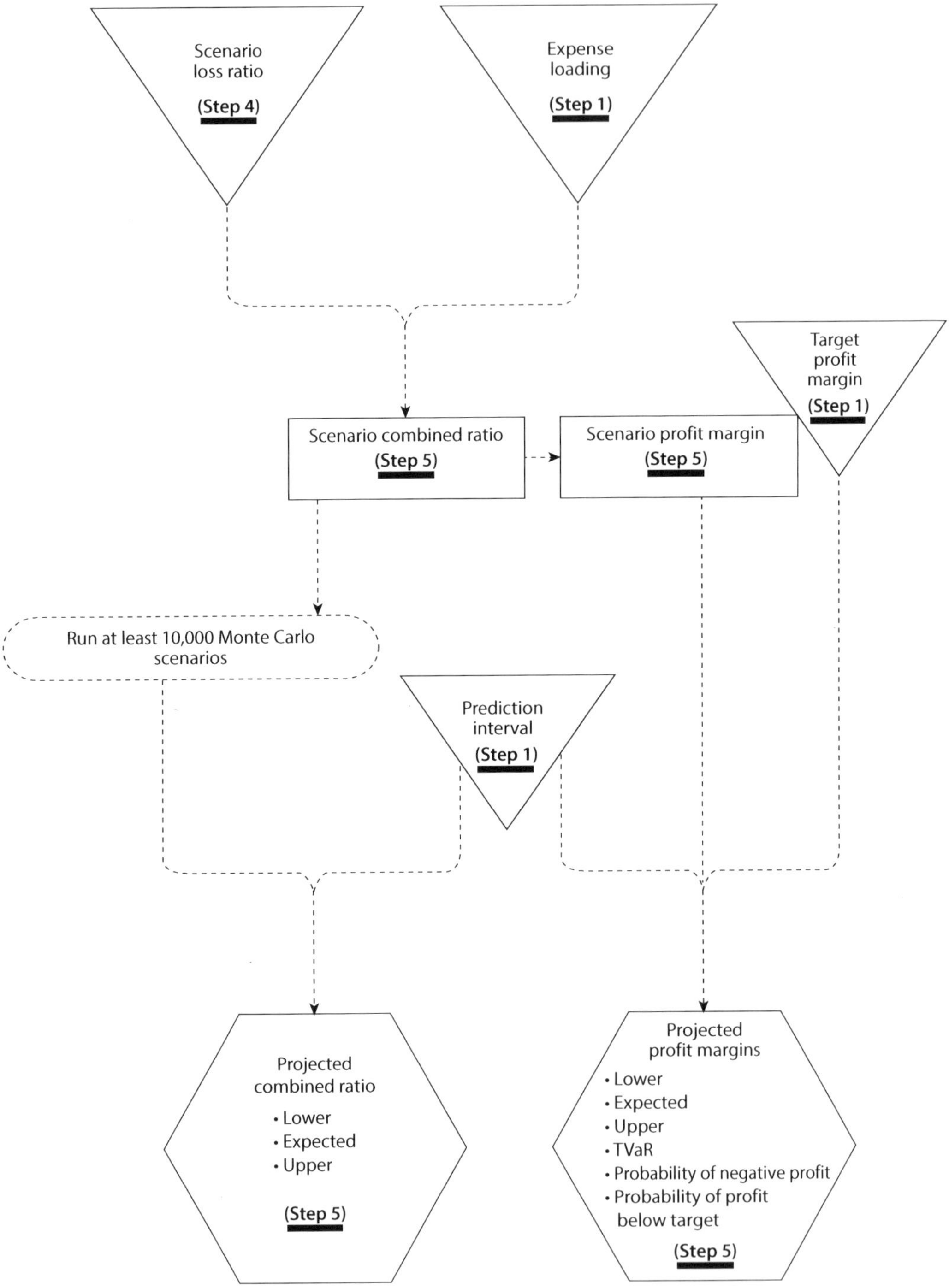

Note: TVaR = tail value at risk.

Case Example Box 14CB.5 Computations—Step 5

STEP 5 : CALCULATE PROJECTED COMBINED RATIO AND PROFIT MARGIN

FIRM SIZE	MARKET SEGMENT	SCENARIO LOSS RATIO (%)	EXPENSE LOADING (%)	SCENARIO COMBINED RATIO (%)	SCENARIO PROFIT MARGIN (%)	PROJECTED COMBINED RATIO (%)			PROJECTED PROFIT MARGIN			PROBABILITY OF NEGATIVE PROFIT (%)	PROBABILITY OF PROFIT BELOW TARGET (%)
						Lower	Expected	Upper	Lower	Expected	Upper		
SMALL	Rural Banks	81%	20%	101%	-1%	61%	94%	122%	-22%	6%	39%	41%	60%
	MFIs	59%	20%	79%	21%	61%	94%	123%	-23%	6%	39%	40%	59%
	Seed Companies	73%	20%	93%	7%	61%	93%	122%	-22%	7%	39%	40%	58%
	Agribusinesses	78%	20%	98%	2%	62%	94%	122%	-22%	6%	38%	40%	59%
	NGOs	68%	20%	88%	12%	62%	94%	123%	-23%	6%	38%	41%	60%
MEDIUM	Rural Banks	66%	15%	81%	19%	56%	89%	117%	-17%	11%	44%	31%	51%
	MFIs	67%	15%	82%	18%	56%	89%	117%	-17%	11%	44%	31%	50%
	Seed Companies	74%	15%	89%	11%	56%	89%	117%	-17%	11%	44%	31%	50%
	Agribusinesses	77%	15%	92%	8%	56%	89%	117%	-17%	11%	44%	30%	50%
	NGOs	57%	15%	72%	28%	56%	89%	117%	-17%	11%	44%	30%	50%
LARGE	Rural Banks	51%	10%	61%	39%	50%	84%	112%	-12%	16%	49%	22%	40%
	MFIs	69%	10%	79%	21%	52%	84%	112%	-12%	16%	48%	22%	40%
	Seed Companies	56%	10%	66%	34%	51%	84%	112%	-12%	16%	49%	22%	40%
	Agribusinesses	90%	10%	100%	0%	52%	84%	112%	-12%	16%	48%	21%	41%
	NGOs	59%	10%	69%	31%	52%	84%	113%	-13%	16%	48%	22%	41%

For the case example, the scenario combined ratio for medium seed companies is 89 percent.

$$\text{Scenario combined ratio} = \text{Scenario loss ratio} + \text{Expense loading}$$
$$= 74 \text{ percent} + 15 \text{ percent}$$
$$= 89 \text{ percent}$$

The scenario profit margin for medium seed companies is 11 percent.

$$\text{Scenario profit margin} = 100 \text{ percent} - \text{Scenario combined ratio}$$
$$= 100 \text{ percent} - 89 \text{ percent}$$
$$= 11 \text{ percent}$$

The probability of a negative profit is 31 percent.

$$\text{Probability of a negative profit} = \text{Number of scenarios with profit} < 0 / \text{Total number of scenarios}$$
$$= 3{,}100/10{,}000$$
$$= 31 \text{ percent}$$

The probability of a profit below the target profit margin is 50 percent.

Probability of a profit below the target profit margin = Number of scenarios with profit margin < Target profit margin/ Total number of scenarios

(Step 1)

$$= 5{,}000/10{,}000$$
$$= 50 \text{ percent}$$

Note: MFI = microfinance institution; NGO = nongovernmental organization.

medium seed companies in the case example) and appropriate percentile values for each.

Finally, Step 5 calculates the probability of a negative profit and the probability of a profit below the target profit margin (Step 1) for each market segment and firm size.

Probability of a negative profit = Number of scenarios with profit < 0 /Total number of scenarios

Probability of a profit below = Number of scenarios < Target profit margin/
the target profit margin   with profit margin   Total number of scenarios
(Step 1)

14.3.4 Economic Value Added (Step 6)

14.3.4.1 Overview

Economic value added (EVA) measures the flow of economic value created from a business, taking into account the costs of the firm's capital. EVA is the difference between the value derived from selling the product and the cost of doing so. The reader is referred to section 12.3.2.4 for more detail on EVA.

Figure 14.4 provides an overview of how the model generates the EVA for the most popular prototype for each market segment and firm size.

14.3.4.2 Implementation in Excel (MC_14.3_MODEL COMPUTATIONS)

In Step 6 (case example box 14CB.6), the model calculates the capital charge and expense amount for each of the market segments.

Scenario capital charge = Scenario required capital × Required return on capital
(Step 4)   (Step 1)

Scenario expense amount = Expense loading × Scenario premium income
(Step 1)   (Step 3)

Also in Step 6, the model calculates the scenario EVA.

	(Scenario		Scenario	
Scenario =	premium −	Scenario −	expense −	Capital charge)/
EVA	income	losses	amount	Required capital
	(Step 3)	(Step 4)		(Step 4)

At this point, Step 6 generates at least 10,000 scenario EVA results for each market segment and firm size and determines the expected EVA for each (18 percent for medium seed companies in the case example). Based on the prediction interval selected in Step 1, the model also calculates the appropriate percentile values of the EVA.

Figure 14.4 Generating Projected Values for Economic Value Added (EVA) Metrics

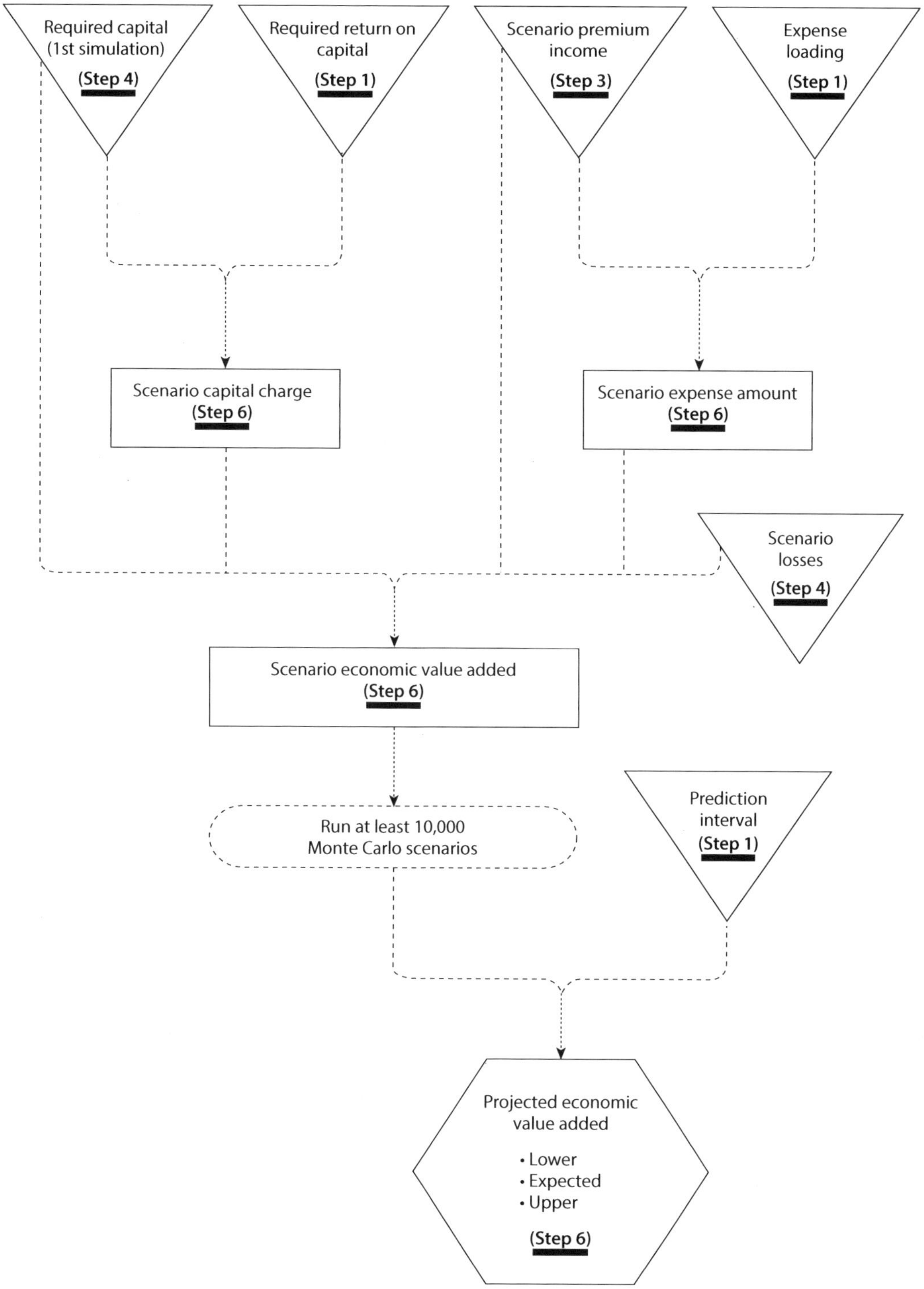

Case Example Box 14CB.6 Computations—Step 6

STEP 6 : CALCULATIE ECONOMIC VALUE ADDED

FIRM SIZE	MARKET SEGMENT	SCENARIO PREMIUM INCOME ($)	SCENARIO LOSSES ($)	SCENARIO EXPENSE AMOUNT ($)	CAPITAL CHARGE ($)	SCENARIO EVA (%)	PROJECTED EVA (%)		
							Lower	Expected	Upper
SMALL	Rural Banks	$ 360,000	$ 218,803	$ 72,000	$ 8,752	35%	-49%	7%	73%
	MFIs	$ 240,000	$ 128,215	$ 48,000	$ 3,918	76%	-74%	14%	114%
	Seed Companies	$ 200,000	$ 188,060	$ 40,000	$ 3,388	-46%	-71%	14%	111%
	Agribusinesses	$ 600,000	$ 546,269	$ 120,000	$ 12,443	-32%	-58%	10%	88%
	NGOs	$ 200,000	$ 205,071	$ 40,000	$ 4,259	-58%	-47%	6%	69%
MEDIUM	Rural Banks	$ 450,000	$ 296,570	$ 67,500	$ 10,592	36%	-42%	18%	90%
	MFIs	$ 300,000	$ 192,855	$ 45,000	$ 4,836	59%	-58%	30%	132%
	Seed Companies	$ 900,000	$ 572,817	$ 135,000	$ 27,324	30%	-42%	18%	89%
	Agribusinesses	$ 1,800,000	$ 1,383,301	$ 270,000	$ 47,439	10%	-37%	17%	81%
	NGOs	$ 200,000	$ 125,620	$ 30,000	$ 6,538	29%	-34%	14%	72%
LARGE	Rural Banks	$ 300,000	$ 282,544	$ 30,000	$ 8,760	-12%	-27%	24%	83%
	MFIs	$ -	$ -	$ -	$ -		0%	0%	0%
	Seed Companies	$ 800,000	$ 588,229	$ 80,000	$ 24,063	22%	-25%	22%	80%
	Agribusinesses	$ 1,800,000	$ 1,982,424	$ 180,000	$ 29,958	-65%	-41%	42%	138%
	NGOs	$ 750,000	$ 644,890	$ 75,000	$ 15,354	5%	-26%	21%	78%

In the case example, the scenario capital charge for medium seed companies is $27,324.

Scenario capital charge = Scenario required capital × Required return on capital

= $546,473 × 5 percent

= $27,324

The scenario expense amount for medium seed companies is $135,000.

Scenario expense amount = Expense loading × Scenario premium income

= 15 percent × 900,000

= $135,000

The scenario EVA for medium seed companies is 30 percent.

Scenario EVA = (Scenario premium income − Scenario losses − Scenario expense amount − Scenario capital charge)/ Required capital

= (900,000 − 572,817 − 135,000 − 27,324)/546,473

= 30 percent

Note: MFI = microfinance institution; NGO = nongovernmental organization.

14.3.5 Sharpe Ratio (Step 7)
14.3.5.1 Overview
Figure 14.5 provides an overview of how the model generates the Sharpe ratios for only the most popular prototype for each market segment and firm size.

14.3.5.2 Implementation in Excel (MC_14.3_MODEL COMPUTATIONS)
Step 7 is similar to Step 18 in section 12.3.2.5, but includes the scenario expense amount in the calculation of the scenario return on capital.

In Step 7 (case example box 14CB.7), the model calculates the scenario return on capital for each market segment and firm size.

Figure 14.5 Generating Sharpe Ratios

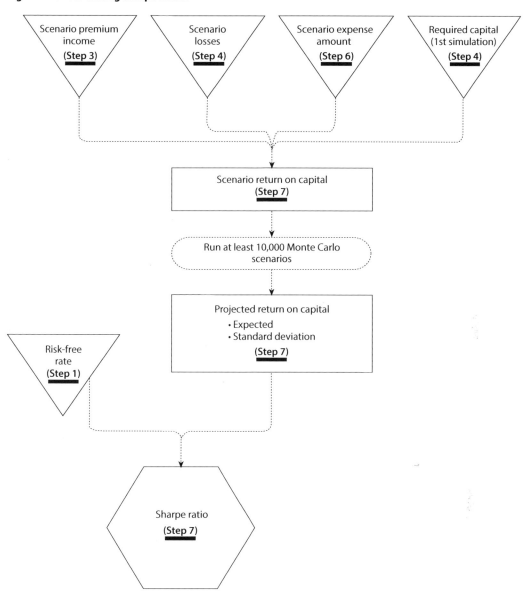

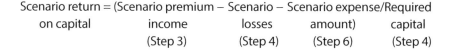

$$\text{Scenario return on capital} = \frac{(\text{Scenario premium income (Step 3)} - \text{Scenario losses (Step 4)} - \text{Scenario expense amount (Step 6)})}{\text{Required capital (Step 4)}}$$

At this point, the model generates at least 10,000 Monte Carlo scenario returns on capital for each market segment and firm size and determines the expected return on capital for each (23 percent for medium seed companies in the case example) as well as the standard deviation of the return on capital (40 percent).

Risk Modeling for Appraising Named Peril Index Insurance Products
http://dx.doi.org/10.1596/978-1-4648-1048-0

Case Example Box 14CB.7 Computations—Step 7

STEP 7 : CALCULATE THE SHARPE RATIO

FIRM SIZE	MARKET SEGMENT	SCENARIO PREMIUM INCOME ($)	SCENARIO EXPENSE AMOUNT ($)	SCENARIO LOSSES ($)	SCENARIO PROFITS ($)	SCENARIO RETURN ON CAPITAL (%)	PROJECTED RETURN ON CAPITAL		SHARPE RATIO
							Expected	Standard Deviation	
SMALL	Rural Banks	$ 360,000	$ 72,000	$ 218,803	$ 69,197	40%	12%	37%	0.27
	MFIs	$ 240,000	$ 48,000	$ 128,215	$ 63,785	81%	19%	57%	0.29
	Seed Companies	$ 200,000	$ 40,000	$ 188,060	$ (28,060)	-41%	19%	55%	0.31
	Agribusinesses	$ 600,000	$ 120,000	$ 546,269	$ (66,269)	-27%	15%	45%	0.29
	NGOs	$ 200,000	$ 40,000	$ 205,071	$ (45,071)	-53%	11%	36%	0.26
MEDIUM	Rural Banks	$ 450,000	$ 67,500	$ 296,570	$ 85,930	41%	23%	40%	0.53
	MFIs	$ 300,000	$ 45,000	$ 192,855	$ 62,145	64%	35%	58%	0.57
	Seed Companies	$ 900,000	$ 135,000	$ 572,817	$ 192,183	35%	23%	40%	0.53
	Agribusinesses	$ 1,800,000	$ 270,000	$ 1,383,301	$ 146,699	15%	22%	36%	0.54
	NGOs	$ 200,000	$ 30,000	$ 125,620	$ 44,380	34%	19%	33%	0.53
LARGE	Rural Banks	$ 300,000	$ 30,000	$ 282,544	$ (12,544)	-7%	29%	34%	0.79
	MFIs	$ -	$ -	$ -	$ -				
	Seed Companies	$ 800,000	$ 80,000	$ 588,229	$ 131,771	27%	27%	33%	0.77
	Agribusinesses	$ 1,800,000	$ 180,000	$ 1,982,424	$ (362,424)	-60%	47%	55%	0.83
	NGOs	$ 750,000	$ 75,000	$ 644,890	$ 30,110	10%	26%	32%	0.76

The scenario return on capital for medium seed companies is 35 percent for the case example.

Scenario return on capital = (Scenario premium income – Scenario losses – Scenario expense amount)/Required capital

= (900,000 – 572,817 – 135,000)/546,473

= 35 percent

For the case example, medium seed companies have a Sharpe ratio of 0.53.

Sharpe ratio = (Expected return on capital – Risk-free rate)/Standard deviation of expected return on capital

= (23 percent – 2 percent)/40 percent

= 0.53

Note: MFI = microfinance institution; NGO = nongovernmental organization.

Finally, the model calculates the Sharpe ratio.

Sharpe ratio = (Expected return – Risk-free)/Standard deviation of expected
on capital   rate   return on capital
(Step 1)

A positive Sharpe ratio indicates an investment with an expected positive return per unit of risk assumed. Premium rates with higher Sharpe ratios are preferred because the higher the Sharpe ratio, the greater the expected return on the capital invested relative to the amount of risk taken.

As a reminder, all metrics within this guide, including the Sharpe ratio, are calculated for the specific index product and do not take into account other products the insurer has in the market. In general, the insurer should also evaluate how the Sharpe ratio of its overall product portfolio is affected by the new index product.

See box 14.1 for a summary of the market analysis calculations.

Box 14.1 Overview of Calculations for the Detailed Market Analysis Metrics

Scenario metrics (one Monte Carlo scenario)
- Number of firms purchasing = PERT(Minimum number of firms, Most likely number of firms, Maximum number firms)
- Premium income = Modal portfolio size × Premium rate × Scenario number of firms purchasing
- Loss ratio = PERT(Minimum target loss ratio, Most likely target loss ratio, Maximum target loss ratio)
- Scenario losses = Scenario premium income × Scenario loss ratio
- Scenario combined ratio = Scenario loss ratio + Expense loading
- Scenario profit margin = 100 percent − Scenario combined ratio
- Capital charge = Scenario required capital × Required return on capital
- Scenario expense amount = Expense loading × Scenario premium income
- Scenario EVA = (Scenario premium income − Scenario losses − Scenario expense amount − Capital charge)/Required capital
- Scenario return on capital = (Scenario premium income − Scenario losses − Scenario expense amount)/Required capital

Metrics based on at least 10,000 Monte Carlo scenarios
- Premium income
- Losses
- Required capital = TVaR losses − Expected losses
- Combined ratio
- Profit margin
- Probability of a negative profit = Number of scenarios with profit < 0/Total number of scenarios
- Probability of profit below the target profit margin = Number of scenarios with profit margin < target profit margin/Total number of scenarios
- Economic value added
- Return on capital
- Sharpe ratio = (Expected return on capital − Risk-free rate)/Standard deviation of return on capital

Note: EVA = economic value added; PERT = project evaluation and review techniques; TVaR = tail value at risk.

14.4 Model Outputs (MO_14.4_MODEL OUTPUTS)

The model output sheet (case example box 14CB.8) summarizes the detailed market analysis decision metrics for the Redesigned Index produced in Steps 3–7 (table 14.4). These include the following:

- Premium income
- Projected losses

Risk Modeling for Appraising Named Peril Index Insurance Products
http://dx.doi.org/10.1596/978-1-4648-1048-0

- Projected combined ratio
- Projected profit margins
- Probability of negative profit
- Probability of profit below target
- EVA
- Sharpe ratios

Case Example Box 14CB.8 Outputs

FIRM SIZE	MARKET SEGMENT	PROJECTED PREMIUM INCOME ($)			PROJECTED LOSSES ($)			PROJECTED COMBINED RATIO (%)			PROJECTED PROFIT MARGIN (%)			PROBABILITY OF NEGATIVE PROFIT (%)	PROBABILITY OF PROFIT BELOW TARGET (%)	PROJECTED EVA			SHARPE RATIO
		Lower	Expected	Upper	Lower	Expected	Upper	Lower	Expected	Upper	Lower	Expected	Upper			5%	Expected	95%	
SMALL	Rural Banks	240,000	339,984	420,000	120,419	250,908	391,980	61%	94%	122%	-22%	6%	39%	41%	60%	-49%	7%	73%	0.27
	MFIs	240,000	237,924	240,000	96,393	176,727	245,972	61%	94%	123%	-23%	6%	39%	40%	59%	-74%	14%	114%	0.29
	Seed Companies	200,000	201,328	200,000	82,427	147,684	206,200	61%	93%	122%	-22%	7%	39%	40%	58%	-71%	14%	111%	0.31
	Agribusinesses	450,000	600,840	750,000	241,359	443,643	637,312	62%	94%	122%	-22%	6%	38%	40%	59%	-58%	10%	88%	0.29
	NGOs	100,000	158,735	200,000	58,664	117,439	185,918	62%	94%	123%	-23%	6%	38%	41%	60%	-47%	6%	69%	0.26
MEDIUM	Rural Banks	300,000	450,150	600,000	173,439	333,439	485,926	58%	89%	117%	-17%	11%	44%	31%	51%	-42%	18%	90%	0.53
	MFIs	300,000	300,000	300,000	122,870	221,223	306,022	56%	89%	117%	-17%	11%	44%	31%	50%	-58%	30%	132%	0.57
	Seed Companies	900,000	1,150,560	1,500,000	440,867	851,861	1,281,944	56%	89%	117%	-17%	11%	44%	31%	50%	-42%	18%	89%	0.53
	Agribusinesses	1,350,000	1,800,960	2,250,000	655,337	1,326,718	2,077,966	56%	89%	117%	-17%	11%	44%	30%	50%	-37%	17%	81%	0.54
	NGOs	200,000	224,000	300,000	86,806	164,962	271,023	58%	89%	117%	-17%	11%	44%	30%	50%	-34%	14%	72%	0.53
LARGE	Rural Banks	300,000	310,020	300,000	122,051	228,473	317,577	50%	84%	112%	-12%	16%	46%	22%	40%	-27%	24%	82%	0.79
	MFIs	-	-	-	-	-	-	52%	84%	112%	-12%	16%	46%	22%	40%	0%	0%	0%	
	Seed Companies	400,000	798,680	1,200,000	264,113	588,167	907,474	51%	84%	112%	-12%	16%	49%	22%	40%	-25%	22%	90%	0.77
	Agribusinesses	1,800,000	1,772,010	1,800,000	690,479	1,310,472	1,835,175	52%	84%	112%	-12%	10%	46%	21%	41%	-41%	42%	138%	0.83
	NGOs	250,000	499,500	750,000	187,947	369,754	572,421	52%	84%	113%	-13%	10%	46%	22%	41%	-26%	21%	78%	0.76

Note: EVA = economic value added; MFI = microfinance institution; NGO = nongovernmental organization.

Table 14.4 Model Outputs

Model component	Section	Excel sheet label	Steps	Description
Model outputs	14.4	MO_14.4_MODEL OUTPUTS	None	Summary of detailed market analysis decision metrics

The insurance manager uses these metrics in chapter 7 to answer the key managerial questions for a detailed analysis of the broader market for index insurance beyond the pilot phase.

Bibliography

Brehm, P. J. 2007. *Enterprise Risk Analysis for Property & Liability Insurance Companies: A Practical Guide to Standard Models and Emerging Solutions.* New York: Guy Carpenter.

Cherubini, U., E. Luciano, and W. Vecchiato. 2004. *Copula Methods in Finance.* Hoboken, NJ: John Wiley & Sons.

Crouhy, M., D. Galai, and R. Mark. 2006. *The Essentials of Risk Management.* New York: McGraw-Hill.

Embrechts, P., F. Lindskog, and A. McNeil. 2003. "Modelling Dependence with Copulas and Applications to Risk Management." In *Handbook of Heavy Tailed Distributions in Finance*, edited by S. T. Rachev, 329–84. Amsterdam: Elsevier.

Grossi, P., H. Kunreuther, and C. C. Patel. 2005. *Catastrophe Modeling: A New Approach to Managing Risk.* New York: Springer Science Business Media.

Lam, J. 2003. *Enterprise Risk Management: From Incentives to Controls*. Hoboken, NJ: Wiley.

Law, A. M., and W. D. Kelton. 2006. *Simulation Modeling and Analysis*. 4th ed. New York: McGraw-Hill.

Lehman, D. E., H. Groenendaal, and G. Nolder. 2012. *Practical Spreadsheet Risk Modeling for Management*. Boca Raton, FL: Chapman & Hall/CRC.

Ragsdale, C. T. 2001. *Spreadsheet Modeling and Decision Analysis: A Practical Introduction to Management Science*. Cincinnati, OH: Southwestern College.

Tang, A., and E. A. Valdez. 2009. "Economic Capital and the Aggregation of Risks Using Copulas." University of New South Wales, Sydney, Australia.

Yan, J. 2006. "Multivariate Modelling with Copulas and Engineering Applications." In *Springer Handbook of Engineering Statistics*, edited by H. Pham, 973–90. London: Springer-Verlag.

CHAPTER 15

Value of Index Insurance

15.1 Background and Objectives

Chapter 8 explained the key managerial questions for evaluating the value of index insurance for a specific market segment—financial service providers such as microfinance institutions, commercial banks, and agribusinesses that provide financing to smallholder farmers. The objective of the analysis is to determine the extent to which the named peril index insurance prototype product can reduce the service provider's losses during years with high defaults, as well as the maximum price the service provider will be willing to pay for this reduction in losses (that is, the value of the index insurance).

This chapter provides a step-by-step guide (table 15.1) to using the probabilistic models that produce the decision metrics discussed in chapter 8. The model simulates two key scenario parameters: the gross default rate (Steps 10–16) and net default rate for the prototype product (Steps 17–23).

The model then uses these parameters to calculate the value of index insurance decision metrics (Steps 24–30). These metrics allow the insurer to clearly explain to the policyholder the degree to which the named peril affects the default rates and the relative benefits of purchasing the index insurance prototype product.

The model in this chapter relies on two key assumptions: First, the quality of the analysis depends on the reliability of the historical default rate data. The calculation of the value of index insurance will not be reliable if the default data are not reliable (for example, missing data points in certain geographical areas or years). However, the analysis can still be directionally useful as long as the insurer and the financial service provider both understand and appreciate the limitations of the data.

Second, the analysis assumes that the effect of the named peril on the financial service provider's portfolio is felt at the end of the risk period, for example, an agricultural loan that is payable as a bullet payment at the end of the season. This assumption is violated if loan repayments are made weekly or monthly, and the peril is one such as typhoons over a six-month period. In these cases, the default data should relate to repayment soon after the occurrence of the event (for example, 30 days or 60 days after a typhoon), and the data processing becomes more complicated. Such analysis is beyond the scope of this guide.

15.2 Model Inputs

The analyst starts by specifying the model inputs agreed upon with the insurance manager (table 15.2) for the value of index insurance analysis.

15.2.1 Data from the Policyholder (Steps 1–5)

The analyst first specifies inputs based on internal data obtained from the prospective policyholder (case example box 15CB.1):

- Target maximum annual default rate (percent). This metric provides an indication of the financial service provider's risk tolerance.
- The financial service provider's cost of capital (percent).
- Debt recovery expense (percentage of nonperforming loans). These are the costs incurred by the financier to try to recover debt.
- Prediction interval (percent).
- Historical default rates by geographic area (restructures and write-offs). Ideally, more than 10 years of data for each area should be available.
- Distribution of loans by geographic area (percent).

Table 15.1 Summary of Model Components for the Value of Index Insurance

Model component	Section	Excel sheet label	Steps	Description
Model input	15.2	MI_15.2_MODEL INPUTS	Steps 1–7	Data from the prospective policyholder and historical payout ratios for the prototype product are entered.
Model computations	15.3.1	MC_15.3.1_DERIVED INPUTS	Steps 8–9	Calculation of historical net default rates for each area. These derived inputs are used for Steps 24–30.
	15.3.2	MC_15.3.2_GROSS NPL SCENARIOS	Steps 10–16	Simulation of scenario gross default rates for each area and the portfolio.
	15.3.3	MC_15.3.3_NET NPL SCENARIOS	Steps 17–23	Simulation of scenario net default rates for each area and the portfolio.
	15.3.4	MC_15.3.4_DECISION METRICS	Steps 24–30	Calculation of value of index insurance decision metrics.
Model outputs	15.4	MO_15.4_MODEL OUTPUTS	None	Summary of value of index insurance decision metrics.

Table 15.2 Model Inputs

Model component	Section	Excel sheet label	Steps	Description
Model input	15.2	MI_15.2_Model Inputs	Steps 1–7	Data from the prospective policyholder and historical payout ratios for the prototype product are entered.

Case Example Box 15CB.1 Inputs—Steps 1–5

In the case example, the prospective policyholder discussed in this chapter is a large agribusiness interested in Redesigned Prototype 1 (6 percent premium rate). The agribusiness provides the insurer with 10 years of default data for 10 geographical areas.

STEP 1 : ENTER TARGET MAXIMUM DEFAULT RATE

TARGET MAXIMUM DEFAULT RATE	4%

STEP 2 : ENTER FINANCING COST PARAMETERS

COST OF CAPITAL (%)	5%
DEBT RECOVERY EXPENSE (%)	20%

STEP 3 : INDICATE PREDICTION INTERVAL (%)

LOWER	5%
UPPER	95%

STEP 4 : ENTER GROSS DEFAULT RATES (%)

YEAR	AREA A	AREA B	AREA C	AREA D	AREA E	AREA F	AREA G	AREA H	AREA I	AREA J
2004	2%	3%	1%	3%	2%	15%	3%	3%	4%	1%
2005	2%	2%	1%	1%	8%	2%	3%	2%	4%	1%
2006	2%	3%	2%	1%	2%	3%	3%	2%	4%	1%
2007	5%	4%	1%	2%	2%	2%	25%	3%	27%	34%
2008	0%	2%	1%	16%	2%	20%	3%	34%	4%	27%
2009	9%	3%	4%	2%	2%	4%	4%	5%	4%	5%
2010	1%	15%	1%	2%	1%	3%	3%	2%	10%	3%
2011	1%	3%	1%	4%	3%	2%	5%	1%	4%	5%
2012	1%	3%	1%	2%	10%	1%	3%	2%	3%	4%
2013	1%	3%	2%	5%	2%	3%	3%	2%	3%	4%

STEP 5: ENTER LOAN DISBURSEMENT DISTRIBUTION (%)

AREA A	AREA B	AREA C	AREA D	AREA E	AREA F	AREA G	AREA H	AREA I	AREA J
10%	10%	10%	10%	10%	10%	10%	10%	10%	10%

15.2.2 Historical Payout Ratios for the Prototype Product (Step 6)

The historical payout ratios are those for the prototype product the insurer will evaluate (case example box 15CB.2).

15.2.3 Nonzero Gross Default Rates (Step 7)

In Step 7 (no case example box), the analyst manually records all the nonzero values for gross default rates from Step 4. These figures will be used in Step 10 to fit a probability distribution to the nonzero historical gross default rates.

Case Example Box 15CB.2 Inputs—Step 6

In the case example, the insurer uses the historical payout ratios for Redesigned Prototype 1.

STEP 6 : ENTER HISTORICAL PAYOUT RATIOS (%)

YEAR	AREA A	AREA B	AREA C	AREA D	AREA E	AREA F	AREA G	AREA H	AREA I	AREA J
2004	0.0%	0.0%	0.0%	0.0%	0.0%	15.0%	0.0%	0.0%	0.0%	0.0%
2005	0.0%	0.0%	0.0%	0.0%	4.0%	0.0%	0.0%	0.0%	0.0%	0.0%
2006	0.0%	0.0%	0.0%	0.0%	0.0%	0.0%	0.0%	0.0%	0.0%	0.0%
2007	0.0%	0.0%	0.0%	0.0%	0.0%	0.0%	23.0%	0.0%	22.0%	23.0%
2008	0.0%	0.0%	0.0%	13.0%	0.0%	19.0%	0.0%	31.0%	0.0%	24.0%
2009	5.0%	0.0%	2.0%	0.0%	0.0%	0.0%	0.0%	0.0%	0.0%	0.0%
2010	0.0%	11.0%	0.0%	0.0%	0.0%	0.0%	0.0%	0.0%	7.0%	0.0%
2011	0.0%	0.0%	0.0%	0.0%	0.0%	0.0%	0.0%	0.0%	0.0%	0.0%
2012	0.0%	0.0%	0.0%	0.0%	7.0%	0.0%	0.0%	0.0%	0.0%	0.0%
2013	0.0%	0.0%	0.0%	1.0%	0.0%	0.0%	0.0%	0.0%	0.0%	0.0%

15.3 Model Computations

The model completes four main sets of computations (table 15.3) to analyze the value of index insurance for the prototype product, starting with calculating the derived inputs—net default rates (Steps 8–9)—then simulating the two key scenario parameters (Steps 10–23), and finally producing the value of index insurance decision metrics (Steps 24–30).

15.3.1 Calculation of Historical Net Default Rates (Steps 8–9)
15.3.1.1 Overview
The historical net default rate (table 15.4) is the amount of default risk that the policyholder would have retained if the prototype policy had been in place in the past. It is the default risk that is not linked to the named peril and so not covered by the policy. It is calculated as follows:

Historical net default rate = Max (0,[Historical gross default rate − Historical payout ratio]).

                              Step 4   Step 6

Insurance is meant to indemnify losses and not enrich the insured. The value of the historical net default rate cannot be less than zero because that would be an enrichment of the insured.

Table 15.3 Model Computations

Model component	Section	Excel sheet label	Steps	Description
Model computations	15.3.1	MC_15.3.1_DERIVED_INPUTS	Steps 8–9	Calculation of historical net default rates for each area. These derived inputs are used for Steps 24–30.
Model computations	15.3.2	MC_15.3.2_GROSS NPL SCENARIOS	Steps 10–16	Simulation of scenario gross default rates for each area and the portfolio
Model computations	15.3.3	MC_15.3.3_NET NPL SCENARIOS	Steps 17–23	Simulation of scenario net default rates for each area and the portfolio
Model computations	15.3.4	MC_15.3.4_DECISION METRICS	Steps 24–30	Calculation of value of index insurance decision metrics

Table 15.4 Model Computations

Model component	Section	Excel sheet label	Steps	Description
Model computations	15.3.1	MC_15.3.1_DERIVED INPUTS	Steps 8–9	Calculation of historical net default rates for each area. These derived inputs are used for Steps 24–30.

15.3.1.2 Implementation in Excel (MC_15.3.1_DERIVED INPUTS)
In Step 8 (case example box 15CB.3), the model calculates the historical net default rate for each area and year.

Case Example Box 15CB.3 Computations—Step 8

STEP 8 : CALCULATE NET DEFAULT RATES

YEAR	AREA A	AREA B	AREA C	AREA D	AREA E	AREA F	AREA G	AREA H	AREA I	AREA J
2004	2%	3%	1%	3%	2%	0%	3%	3%	4%	1%
2005	2%	2%	1%	1%	4%	2%	3%	2%	4%	1%
2006	2%	3%	2%	1%	2%	3%	3%	2%	4%	1%
2007	5%	4%	1%	2%	2%	2%	2%	3%	5%	11%
2008	0%	2%	1%	3%	2%	1%	3%	3%	4%	3%
2009	4%	3%	2%	2%	2%	4%	4%	5%	4%	5%
2010	1%	4%	1%	2%	1%	3%	3%	2%	3%	3%
2011	1%	3%	1%	4%	3%	2%	5%	1%	4%	5%
2012	1%	3%	1%	2%	3%	1%	3%	2%	3%	4%
2013	1%	3%	2%	4%	2%	3%	3%	2%	3%	4%

For Area B in the case example, the historical net default rate is 3 percent for 2009.

Historical net default rate = Max(0,[Historical gross default rate – Historical payout ratio])

= Max(0,[3 percent – 0 percent])

= 3 percent

In Step 9 (no case example box), the analyst manually records all the nonzero values for historical net default rates from Step 8. These figures will be used in Step 17 to fit a probability distribution to the nonzero historical net default rates.

15.3.2 Simulation of Scenario Gross Default Rates (Steps 10–16)

15.3.2.1 Overview

The purpose of determining the scenario gross default rates (table 15.5), which illustrate the situation in which the policyholder has no index insurance coverage, is to compare them with the net default rates, which describe the situation in which the policyholder has purchased the prototype index product.

15.3.2.2 Implementation in Excel (MC_15.3.2_GROSS NPL SCENARIOS)

Steps 10–16 (case example box 15CB.4) for simulating the scenario gross default rates are similar to Steps 14–18 in section 11.3.3. However, there are two main differences between the calculations. First, Steps 10–16 use the historical nonzero gross default rates from the policyholder (Step 7), rather than the historical payout ratios for the Base Index. Second, Step 16 calculates a weighted average of the default rates for all areas using the distribution of loans by geographic area (Step 5) as weights.

$$\begin{array}{c}\text{Scenario}\\\text{gross}\\\text{portfolio}\\\text{default rate}\end{array} = \begin{array}{c}\text{Scenario gross}\\\text{default rate for Area}\\\text{A} \times \text{Distribution of}\\\text{loans for Area A}\\\text{(Step 15)}\end{array} + \begin{array}{c}\text{Scenario gross}\\\text{default rate for Area}\\\text{B} \times \text{Distribution of}\\\text{loans for Area B}\\\text{(Step 15)}\end{array} + \begin{array}{c}\text{... Scenario gross}\\\text{default rate for Area}\\\text{N} \times \text{Distribution}\\\text{of loans for Area N}\\\text{(Step 15)}\end{array}$$

The reader is referred back to section 11.3.3 for further detail on the modeling.

Risk Modeling for Appraising Named Peril Index Insurance Products
http://dx.doi.org/10.1596/978-1-4648-1048-0

Table 15.5 Model Computations

Model component	Section	Excel sheet label	Steps	Description
Model computations	15.3.2	MC_15.3.2_GROSS NPL SCENARIOS	Steps 10–16	Simulation of scenario gross default rates for each area and the portfolio

Case Example Box 15CB.4 Computations—Steps 10–16

STEP 10 : DETERMINE FREQUENCY

	AREA A	AREA B	AREA C	AREA D	AREA E	AREA F	AREA G	AREA H	AREA I	AREA J
SUCCESSES	9	10	10	10	10	10	10	10	10	10
TRIALS	10	10	10	10	10	10	10	10	10	10
ESTIMATE THE PROBABILITY	Beta(10;2)	Beta(11;1)	Beta(11;1)	Beta(11;1)	Beta(11;1)	Beta(11;1)	Beta(11;1)	Beta(11;1)	Beta(11;1)	Beta(11;1)
BERNOULLI OBJECT	Bernoulli(0,95)	Bernoulli(0,87)	Bernoulli(0,81)	Bernoulli(0,94)	Bernoulli(0,88)	Bernoulli(0,93)	Bernoulli(0,84)	Bernoulli(0,98)	Bernoulli(0,99)	Bernoulli(0,95)

STEP 11 : DETERMINE SEVERITY

	AREA A	AREA B	AREA C	AREA D	AREA E	AREA F	AREA G	AREA H	AREA I	AREA J
BETA OBJECT	Beta(1,08;20,95)	Beta(1,08;20,95)	Beta(1,08;20,95)	Beta(1,08;20,95)	Beta(1,08;20,95)	Beta(1,08;20,95)	Beta(1,08;20,95)	Beta(1,08;20,95)	Beta(1,08;20,95)	Beta(1,08;20,95)

STEP 12 : CHOOSE COPULA

CHOSEN COPULA   T-COPULA

STEP 13 : DETERMINE COPULA MATRIX

	AREA A	AREA B	AREA C	AREA D	AREA E	AREA F	AREA G	AREA H	AREA I	AREA J
AREA A	1.00	-0.12	0.77	-0.37	-0.19	-0.24	0.37	-0.22	0.30	0.12
AREA B	-0.12	1.00	-0.16	-0.21	-0.32	-0.20	-0.02	-0.20	0.25	-0.13
AREA C	0.77	-0.16	1.00	-0.18	-0.26	-0.17	-0.16	-0.10	-0.22	-0.22
AREA D	-0.37	-0.21	-0.18	1.00	-0.24	0.78	-0.15	0.95	-0.17	0.52
AREA E	-0.19	-0.32	-0.26	-0.24	1.00	-0.33	-0.18	-0.19	-0.26	-0.25
AREA F	-0.24	-0.20	-0.17	0.78	-0.33	1.00	-0.21	0.80	-0.20	0.31
AREA G	0.37	-0.02	-0.16	-0.15	-0.18	-0.21	1.00	-0.11	0.96	0.75
AREA H	-0.22	-0.20	-0.10	0.95	-0.19	0.80	-0.11	1.00	-0.11	0.57
AREA I	0.30	0.25	-0.22	-0.17	-0.26	-0.20	0.96	-0.11	1.00	0.71
AREA J	0.12	-0.13	-0.22	0.52	-0.25	0.31	0.75	0.57	0.71	1.00

Degrees of freedom   2

STEP 14: DETERMINE COPULA FUNCTION

COPULA FUNCTION	0.535	0.849	0.225	0.325	0.045	0.607	0.878	0.269	0.902	0.733

STEP 15 : DETERMINE SCENARIO GROSS DEFAULT RATES BY AREA (%)

SCENARIO DEFAULT RATE	3.6%	1.0%	11.2%	2.6%	0.0%	7.2%	4.7%	2.5%	0.9%	2.9%

STEP 16 : DETERMINE SCENARIO GROSS PORTFOLIO DEFAULT RATE (%)

SCENARIO DEFAULT RATE   3.67%

In the case example the scenario gross default rate is 3.67 percent.

Scenario portfolio gross default rate = Scenario gross default rate for Area A × Distribution of loans for Area A

+ Scenario gross default rate for Area B × Distribution of loans for Area B

+ ... Scenario gross default rate for Area J × Distribution of loans for Area J

= 3.6 percent ×10 percent + 1.0 percent ×10 percent + 11.2 percent ×10 percent

+ 2.6 percent × 10 percent

+ 0.0 percent × 10 percent + 7.2 percent × 10 percent + 4.7 percent × 10 percent

+ 2.5 percent × 10 percent

+ 0.9 percent ×10 percent + 2.9 percent ×10 percent

= 3.67 percent

15.3.3 Simulation of Scenario Net Default Rates (Steps 17–23)
15.3.3.1 Overview

The scenario net default rates (table 15.6) provide information on the policy-holder's defaults in the situation in which it is covered by the prototype index product. These are compared with the gross default rates for the situation without coverage to determine the value of the index insurance.

15.3.3.2 Implementation in Excel (MC_15.3.3_NET NPL SCENARIOS)

Steps 17–23 for simulating the scenario net default rates (case example box 15CB.5) are similar to Steps 10–16 but use the historical nonzero net default rates (Step 9) as inputs.

The reader is referred back to section 11.3.3 for further detail on the modeling.

Table 15.6 Model Computations

Model component	Section	Excel sheet label	Steps	Description
Model computations	15.3.3	MC_15.3.3_NET NPL SCENARIOS	Steps 17–23	Simulation of scenario net default rates for each area and the portfolio

Case Example Box 15CB.5 Computations—Steps 17–23

STEP 17 : DETERMINE FREQUENCY

	AREA A	AREA B	AREA C	AREA D	AREA E	AREA F	AREA G	AREA H	AREA I	AREA J
SUCCESSES	9	10	10	10	10	9	10	10	10	10
TRIALS	10	10	10	10	10	10	10	10	10	10
ESTIMATE THE PROBABILITY	Beta(10;2)	Beta(11;1)	Beta(11;1)	Beta(11;1)	Beta(11;1)	Beta(10;2)	Beta(11;1)	Beta(11;1)	Beta(11;1)	Beta(11;1)
BERNOULLI OBJECT	Bernoulli(0.65)	Bernoulli(0.97)	Bernoulli(0.93)	Bernoulli(0.96)	Bernoulli(0.91)	Bernoulli(0.87)	Bernoulli(0.92)	Bernoulli(0.92)	Bernoulli(0.99)	Bernoulli(0.96)

STEP 18 : DETERMINE SEVERITY

	AREA A	AREA B	AREA C	AREA D	AREA E	AREA F	AREA G	AREA H	AREA I	AREA J
BETA OBJECT	Beta(3.81;138.03)	Beta(3.81;138.03)	Beta(3.81;138.03)	Beta(3.81;138.03)	Beta(3.81;138.03)	Beta(3.81;138.03)	Beta(3.81;138.03)	Beta(3.81;138.03)	Beta(3.81;138.03)	Beta(3.81;138.03)

STEP 19 : CHOOSE COPULA

CHOSEN COPULA	T-COPULA

STEP 20 : DETERMINE COPULA MATRIX

	AREA A	AREA B	AREA C	AREA D	AREA E	AREA F	AREA G	AREA H	AREA I	AREA J
AREA A	1.00	0.44	0.20	-0.38	-0.06	0.31	-0.26	0.57	0.67	0.61
AREA B	0.44	1.00	0.00	0.00	-0.61	0.28	-0.21	0.00	0.00	0.56
AREA C	0.20	0.00	1.00	-0.04	-0.25	0.71	0.12	0.32	-0.15	-0.11
AREA D	-0.38	0.00	-0.04	1.00	-0.15	-0.21	0.42	-0.19	-0.20	0.17
AREA E	-0.06	-0.61	-0.25	-0.15	1.00	-0.26	0.24	-0.31	0.13	-0.15
AREA F	0.31	0.28	0.71	-0.21	-0.26	1.00	0.21	0.21	-0.12	0.16
AREA G	-0.26	-0.21	0.12	0.42	0.24	0.21	1.00	-0.13	-0.13	-0.17
AREA H	0.57	0.00	0.32	-0.19	-0.31	0.21	-0.13	1.00	0.33	0.21
AREA I	0.67	0.00	-0.15	-0.20	0.13	-0.12	-0.13	0.33	1.00	0.45
AREA J	0.61	0.56	-0.11	0.17	-0.15	0.16	-0.17	0.21	0.45	1.00

Degrees of freedom: 2

STEP 21 : DETERMINE COPULA FUNCTION

COPULA FUNCTION	0.445	0.251	0.813	0.520	0.701	0.850	0.800	0.613	0.306	0.099

STEP 22 : DETERMINE SCENARIO NET DEFAULT RATES BY AREA

SCENARIO DEFAULT RATE	3.2%	1.9%	2.1%	2.9%	1.7%	6.0%	1.4%	2.8%	1.3%	3.2%

STEP 23 : DETERMINE SCENARIO PORTFOLIO NET DEFAULT RATE

SCENARIO DEFAULT RATE	2.65%

Risk Modeling for Appraising Named Peril Index Insurance Products
http://dx.doi.org/10.1596/978-1-4648-1048-0

15.3.4 Calculation of Value of Index Insurance Decision Metrics (Steps 24–30)

At this point the model has simulated two key scenario parameters (gross and net default rates for the prototype product) for the analysis of the value of index insurance. Based on these parameters, the model now calculates the metrics that help determine the value of the index insurance to the prospective policyholder (table 15.7).

15.3.4.1 Overview

Figure 15.1 provides an overview of how the model generates the cost of the gross default risk, the net default risk, and the value of index insurance.

15.3.4.2 Implementation in Excel (MC_15.3.4_DECISION METRICS)

In Step 24 (case example box 15CB.6), the model generates at least 10,000 scenario gross portfolio default rates and calculates the proportion of these that are greater than the target maximum default rate (Step 1). This figure represents the probability of the policyholder's portfolio having a default rate greater than the target.

In Step 25, the model uses the same 10,000 scenarios to determine the expected gross portfolio default rate. Based on the prediction interval selected in Step 3, the model also calculates the appropriate percentile and tail value at risk (TVaR) values.

Step 26 calculates the required capital and the cost of the gross portfolio default risk.

$$\text{Required capital} = \text{TVaR gross portfolio} - \text{Expected gross portfolio}$$

(gross default rate)   default rate   default rate

                  (Step 25)   (Step 25)

$$\text{Cost of gross portfolio} = (\text{Expected gross portfolio} + \text{Cost of capital} \times \text{Required capital})/$$

default risk   default rate   (1 − Debt recovery expense)

                  (Step 25)   (Step 2)   (Step 2)

The required capital is included in the cost of the default risk because the financial service provider must reserve capital to remain solvent following an extreme event (TVaR). The debt recovery expense is included in the cost of default risk because the financial service provider incurs this cost while trying to recover delinquent loans.

In Step 27 (case example box 15CB.7), the model generates at least 10,000 scenario net portfolio default rates and calculates the probability of the policyholder's portfolio having a default rate greater than the target (Step 1) if the financial service provider has purchased the prototype product.

Table 15.7 Model Computations

Model component	Section	Excel sheet label	Steps	Description
Model computations	15.3.4	MC_15.3.4_DECISION METRICS	Steps 24–30	Calculation of value of index insurance decision metrics

Figure 15.1 Generating the Value of Index Insurance Decision Metrics

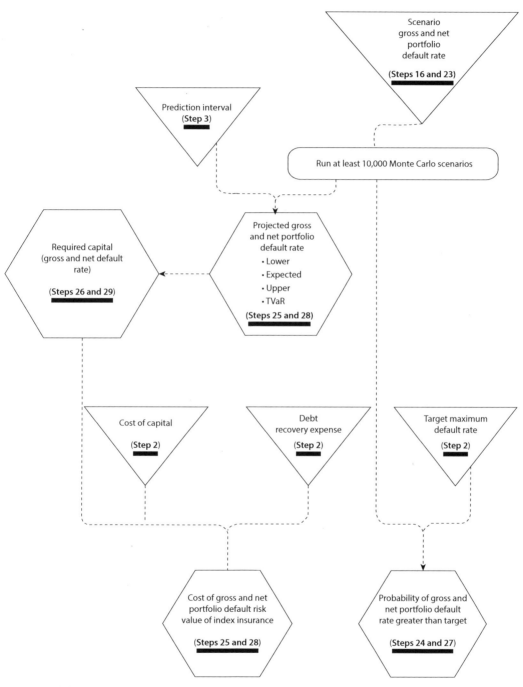

Note: TVaR = tail value at risk.

Case Example Box 15CB.6 Computations—Steps 24–26

STEP 24 : CALCULATE PROBABILITY OF GROSS DEFAULT RATE GREATER THAN TARGET

PROBABILITY	59%

STEP 25 : CALCULATE PROJECTED GROSS DEFAULT RATE

LOWER	2.15%
EXPECTED	4.42%
UPPER	7.03%
TVaR	7.81%

STEP 26 : CALCULATE COST OF GROSS DEFAULT RISK

RISK	5.73%

For the case example, the probability of a default greater than the target maximum (4 percent) in the case in which the large agribusiness does not have index insurance coverage is 59 percent (gross default rate). The expected gross portfolio default rate is 4.42 percent of the total portfolio value. For a 1-in-20 year event, the gross default rate is expected to be 7.81 percent (TVaR).

The required capital for this portfolio is 3.39 percent of the total portfolio value (not shown).

Required capital (gross default rate) = TVaR gross portfolio default rate − Expected gross portfolio default rate

= 7.81 percent − 4.42 percent

= 3.39 percent

The cost to the agribusiness of the gross portfolio default risk is 5.73 percent of the total portfolio value.

Cost of gross portfolio default risk = (Expected gross portfolio default rate + Cost of capital

× Required capital)/(1 − Debt recovery expense)

= (4.42 percent + 5 percent × 3.39 percent)/(1 − 0.2)

= 5.73 percent

Even though the expected portfolio gross default rate is 4.42 percent per year, the actual costs to the agribusiness due to defaults are 5.73 percent because the business incurs expenses for debt recovery and must reserve capital in case of an extreme event (TVaR).

Note: TVaR = tail value at risk.

Case Example Box 15CB.7 Computations—Steps 27–29

STEP 27 : CALCULATE PROBABILITY OF NET DEFAULT RATE GREATER THAN TARGET

PROBABILITY | 0%

STEP 28: CALCULATE PROJECTED NET DEFAULT RATE

LOWER | 1.66%
EXPECTED | 2.41%
UPPER | 3.23%
TVaR | 3.44%

STEP 29 : CALCULATE COST OF NET DEFAULT RISK

COST OF NET DEFAULT RISK | 3.08%

For the case example, the probability of a default greater than the target maximum (4 percent) in the case in which the large agribusiness purchases the Redesigned Prototype 1 is 0 percent, a significant reduction from the situation without index coverage (59 percent). The expected net portfolio default rate is 2.41 percent of the total portfolio value versus 4.42 percent without insurance. The cost to the large agribusiness of the net portfolio default risk is 3.08 percent, down from 5.73 percent. The Redesigned Prototype 1 significantly reduces the default rate and the cost of the default risk for the agribusiness.

The required capital (net default rate) is 1.03 percent (not shown in illustration of steps).

Required capital (net default rate) = TVaR net portfolio default rate − Expected net portfolio default rate

= 3.44 percent − 2.41 percent

= 1.03 percent

The cost of the net portfolio default risk is 3.08 percent.

Cost of net portfolio default risk = (Expected net portfolio default rate + Cost of capital

× Required capital)/(100 percent − Debt recovery expense)

= (2.41 percent + 5 percent × 1.03 percent)/(100 percent − 20 percent)

= 3.08 percent

Note: TVaR = tail value at risk.

In Step 28, the model uses the same 10,000 scenarios to determine the expected net portfolio default rate if the financial service provider is covered by the prototype product. Based on the prediction interval selected in Step 3, the model also calculates the appropriate percentile and TVaR values.

Step 29 calculates the required capital and the cost of the net portfolio default risk.

Risk Modeling for Appraising Named Peril Index Insurance Products
http://dx.doi.org/10.1596/978-1-4648-1048-0

$$\text{Required capital} = \text{TVaR net portfolio} - \text{Expected net portfolio}$$

(net default rate)   default rate   default rate
(Step 28)   (Step 28)

$$\text{Cost of net portfolio} = (\text{Expected net portfolio} + \text{Cost of capital} \times \text{Required capital})/$$

default risk   default rate   (100 percent − Debt recovery expense)
(Step 25)   (Step 2)   (Step 2)

In Step 30 (case example box 15CB.8), the model calculates the value of index insurance.

$$\text{Value of index insurance} = \text{Cost of gross portfolio default risk} - \text{Cost of net portfolio default risk}$$

Case Example Box 15CB.8 Computations—Step 30

STEP 30 : CALCULATE VALUE OF INDEX INSURANCE

RISK	5.73%
COST OF NET DEFAULT RISK	3.08%
INSURANCE	2.65%

In other words, the value of the index insurance is the difference between the cost of default risk without index insurance and the cost of default risk with the index insurance policy in place. Based on the results of this valuation of index insurance, the financial service provider will likely not be willing to pay a premium rate that is much higher than the value of insurance metric calculated by the model. However, to arrive at the final premium for the product, the insurer will need to load the value of insurance metric with expenses and profits (case example box 15CB.9).

See box 15.1 for a summary of the value of insurance metrics.

Case Example Box 15CB.9 Evaluating the Relevance of Insurance to a Specific Financier

In the case example, the value of index insurance for the large agribusiness is 2.65 percent of the total portfolio value. A premium rate of up to about 3 percent should be acceptable to the agribusiness.

Remember that the premium rate for the Redesigned Prototype 1 is 6 percent. At this point, the insurance manager may return to the pricing process completed in chapter 5. If the pricing for the prototype product is close to the value of the insurance, the insurance manager can use the value of insurance metrics to offer the product to the agribusiness. Alternatively, the insurance manager may determine that it is not feasible to offer the product at the required rate and inform the agribusiness of the results from the analysis.

Box 15.1 Overview of Calculations for the Value of Index Insurance Metrics

Derived inputs

- Historical net default rate = Max[0,(Historical gross default rate – Historical payout ratio)]

Scenario metrics (one Monte Carlo scenario)

- Scenario gross portfolio default rate = Scenario gross default rate for Area A × Distribution of loans for Area A + Scenario gross default rate for Area B × Distribution of loans for Area B + …Scenario gross default rate for Area N × Distribution of loans for Area N

Metrics based on at least 10,000 Monte Carlo scenarios

- Probability of the policyholder's portfolio having a default rate greater than the target = Number of scenarios in which default rate > target/Total number of scenarios
- Required capital = TVaR default rate – Expected default rate
- Cost of default risk = (Expected default rate + Cost of capital × Required capital)/(1 Debt recovery expense)
- Value of index insurance = Cost of gross portfolio default risk – Cost of net portfolio default risk

Note: TVaR = tail value at risk.

15.4 Model Outputs (MO_15.4_MODEL OUTPUTS)

The model output sheet (table 15.8 and case example box 15CB.10) summarizes the value of insurance analysis decision metrics for a specific financial institution's lending portfolio. These include the following:

For both gross and net portfolio default rates

- Probability of default rate greater than target
- Expected default rate
- TVaR default rate
- Cost of default risk

For the financial service provider's portfolio

- Value of index insurance

The insurance manager uses these metrics in chapter 8 to answer the key managerial questions about the value of index insurance to a financier.

Table 15.8 Model Outputs

Model component	Section	Excel sheet label	Steps	Description
Model outputs	15.4	MO_15.4_MODEL OUTPUTS	None	Summary of value of index insurance decision metrics

Case Example Box 15CB.10 Outputs

<u>GROSS DEFAULT RATE</u> (NO INSURANCE)

PROBABILITY OF GROSS DEFAULT RATE GREATER THAN TARGET	59%
EXPECTED GROSS DEFAULT RATE	4.42%
PROJECTED GROSS DEFAULT RATE FOR 1 IN 20 YEAR EVENT	7.81%
PROJECTED COST OF GROSS DEFAULT RISK	5.73%

<u>NET DEFAULT RATE</u> (WITH INSURANCE)

PROBABILITY OF NET DEFAULT RATE GREATER THAN TARGET	0%
EXPECTED NET DEFAULT RATE	2.41%
PROJECTED NET DEFAULT RATE FOR 1 IN 20 YEAR EVENT	3.44%
PROJECTED COST OF NET DEFAULT RISK	3.08%

<u>VALUE OF INDEX INSURANCE</u>

VALUE OF INDEX INSURANCE	2.65%

Bibliography

Brehm, P. J. 2007. *Enterprise Risk Analysis for Property & Liability Insurance Companies: A Practical Guide to Standard Models and Emerging Solutions.* New York: Guy Carpenter.

Cherubini, U., E. Luciano, and W. Vecchiato. 2004. *Copula Methods in Finance.* Hoboken, NJ: John Wiley & Sons.

Crouhy, M., D. Galai, and R. Mark. 2006. *The Essentials of Risk Management.* New York: McGraw-Hill.

Embrechts, P., F. Lindskog, and A. McNeil. 2003. "Modelling Dependence with Copulas and Applications to Risk Management." In *Handbook of Heavy Tailed Distributions in Finance*, edited by S. T. Rachev, 329–84. Amsterdam: Elsevier.

Grossi, P., H. Kunreuther, and C. C. Patel. 2005. *Catastrophe Modeling: A New Approach to Managing Risk.* New York: Springer Science Business Media.

Lam, J. 2003. *Enterprise Risk Management: From Incentives to Controls.* Hoboken, NJ: Wiley.

Law, A. M., and W. D. Kelton. 2006. *Simulation Modeling and Analysis.* 4th ed. New York: McGraw-Hill.

Lehman, D. E., H. Groenendaal, and G. Nolder. 2012. *Practical Spreadsheet Risk Modeling for Management.* Boca Raton, FL: Chapman & Hall/CRC.

Ragsdale, C. T. 2001. *Spreadsheet Modeling and Decision Analysis: A Practical Introduction to Management Science*. Cincinnati, OH: Southwestern College.

Tang, A., and E. A. Valdez. 2009. "Economic Capital and the Aggregation of Risks Using Copulas." University of New South Wales, Sydney, Australia.

Yan, J. 2006. "Multivariate Modelling with Copulas and Engineering Applications." In *Springer Handbook of Engineering Statistics*, edited by H. Pham, 973–90. London: Springer-Verlag.

CHAPTER 16

Alternative Probabilistic Modeling Approaches

16.1 Overview of Alternative Approaches

As seen in chapters 11 through 15, the simulation of payout ratios is a key element of many of the model computations related to index insurance in this guide. This fact reflects the modeling solution that we found most appropriate for the set of index insurance problems addressed here. As with any model selection, the approach presented in this guide makes a number of assumptions and has a number of limitations.

Chapter 9 outlines three assumptions and limitations to the models in this guide. It is assumed that the models

- Evaluate the index product in isolation from the insurer's other products.
- Consider only a one-year time horizon.
- Assume no changes in the underlying system over time.[1]

As we have said before and stress again, understanding the assumptions and limitations of any model is important, and that goes for these models as well. This chapter looks in depth at three modeling approaches for simulating payout ratios:

- Simulating the payout amounts directly
- Simulating the index that drives the payouts
- Simulating the weather that drives the index values

The first approach is the one used to simulate payout amounts throughout this guide and the remaining two are alternative approaches.

Figure 16.1 provides an overview of the three approaches. It is important to keep in mind the following three points:

- Approach One is the simplest of the three approaches because it simulates product payouts directly based on historical data.

Figure 16.1 Overview of Three Approaches to Simulating Payout Ratios

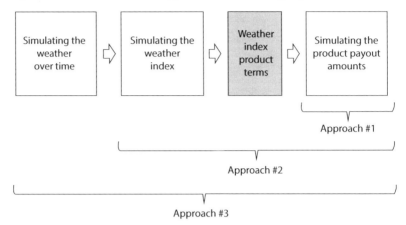

- Approach Three is the most complex because it uses a model to simulate many aspects of the weather. Based on this general weather model, this approach simulates the specific index, then combines it with the product terms, and finally simulates the payouts.
- Approaches Two and Three both explicitly take into account the product terms in the model simulation. Approach One only takes into account the product terms through the historical payout data that are used.

16.2 Approach 1: Simulating the Payouts Directly

Before discussing some of the key assumptions and limitations of this framework, let us summarize the different steps of how total payout amounts are projected for a number of regions.

First, the model uses a Bernoulli distribution to simulate whether there will be a payout greater than 0 percent for each year in each area. This Bernoulli distribution can be seen as a frequency distribution,[2] except that in this case the frequency can only be 0 or 1. This frequency distribution is then combined with a distribution to describe the actual payout as a percentage of the insured amount. The parameter uncertainty for the probability of a payout per region per year is modeled using a beta distribution.

Second, the model simulates the payouts as percentages of the insured amount (payout ratios).[3] The payout amount as a percentage of the insured amount can also be called the severity. In the case example, we used a beta distribution that we fit to all payout ratios greater than 0 percent for the past 30 years of data. The historical data tell us what payouts would have occurred in each of the past 30 years if the index product had been in effect.[4] In summary, we are able to consult the historical data and determine the index values for each year and then use the index values combined with the index product terms to determine the payout ratios for each year. The beta distribution is a sensible choice for the severity distribution because we simulate claim severity as a percentage (ranging from 0 percent to 100 percent).

Third, the model takes into account relationships between the areas by using a copula. It first fits a copula to 30 years of historical payout ratios to estimate the strength of the codependency between areas. In other words, the copula determines whether there is a relationship between payouts occurring in one area and payouts occurring in other areas. We used a t copula, which is suitable in this case because it can accommodate different strengths of relationships between different areas (for example, areas close to each other may be more correlated than areas that are farther apart).[5]

This approach of simulating payouts directly has a number of important characteristics and includes some important assumptions. As explained above, the model is not actually simulating the weather (such as rainfall), nor is it simulating the weather index (for example, drawing from a distribution of index trigger values). Instead the model directly simulates the uncertainty around the actual payout amounts. An important advantage of this approach is its simplicity and the relative ease of explaining and understanding its results. However, this approach has a number of limitations. In addition to those discussed in detail in chapter 9, the limitations of Approach One also include the following:

- The probability of a payout being greater than 0 percent (frequency distribution) is estimated per area (and therefore can vary between areas), but is assumed to be constant over time (that is, not increasing or decreasing over time). For example, if the model estimates the probability of a payout for Area A as 0.06, this value is assumed to have remained the same over time and to stay the same in the future.

- The severity distribution is calculated for each area but is based on the historical payout ratios of all areas because only a small number of historical payouts are available per area (that is, a payout does not occur in each year). In other words, the model assumes that the severity of payouts does not vary between areas. However, the model does not take into account that payout ratios in some areas could tend to be much higher than in others. Because it is based on historical data, the severity distribution also does not take into account changes over time. The model does not take into account that payouts may have been increasing (or decreasing) over time, or that payouts could be expected to increase or decrease in the future.

- With regard to correlation, the model assumes that the occurrence of payouts is correlated among areas. In other words, if one area has a payout, other nearby areas will likely also have payouts. It is important to note that even though the occurrence of payouts is correlated between areas, the payout ratios are not.

- Weather, and therefore the indexes used in a weather-based index insurance product, may go through multiyear cycles of, for example, dry and wet years.

Dry years may be followed by more dry years, and vice versa. Such temporal relationships are not taken into account in the model. The model assumes that any data for the past 30 years are predictive, and more recent data are not more predictive than data from 25 to 30 years ago.

In summary, Approach One takes into account some important risks and the relationships between areas, but also makes a number of assumptions that may or may not be valid, depending on the situation. It is important that the analyst, as well as the managers using the results, be aware of these main assumptions and limitations.

16.3 Approach 2: Simulating the Index

An alternative to simulating the payout amounts directly is for the model to simulate the index or indexes directly, combine them with the product terms, and then simulate the payout amounts.

For example, if the index is the amount of cumulative rainfall over a three-month period, with Approach Two the model first simulates the cumulative rainfall per three-month period. Second, based on the simulated rainfall (for example, 30 millimeters of cumulative rainfall), the model applies the product terms, which indicate that 30 millimeters of rainfall results in a payout of 20 percent of the insured amount.

In reality, index insurance products can be based on multiple triggers, such as rainfall, cumulative hours or days of sunshine, temperature, and so forth. Using Approach Two, these indexes can be modeled individually (taking into account relevant correlations) based on historical weather records.

It is important to note that this approach accounts for relationships between years. The model can take into account that there may be long- or short-term trends in weather patterns. For example, if last year was especially dry, we might be more inclined to predict that next year will be dry. On the other hand, some areas could have been getting wetter or drier or hotter over the past decade, so we might want to account for that in our simulations of possible future events.

Implementation of this approach requires accounting for not only year-to-year correlations in different weather metrics, but also correlations between metrics across different areas. These considerations contribute substantially to the complexity of the final model and the time, effort, and data needed to build it. This complexity can also slow down model run time.

Some advantages of Approach Two include the following:

- Generally, more data are available for modeling the index. When using Approach One to fit the nonzero payout ratio data to distributions, we can only use the years in which payouts would have been made. With Approach Two, we can use all the historical weather data to simulate the index, and then expose it to the index product terms.

- It is easier to take into account that in different areas there are both different frequencies and different severities of payouts. Simulating the actual index for each area can provide a more precise and accurate reflection of the relationships between weather patterns across areas than the copulas used to relate payouts in different areas in Approach One.
- Temporal relationships (that is, index changes over time) can be reflected more precisely by using a time series approach to forecasting next year's indexes. This factor can help reflect both gradually changing weather patterns and multiyear cycles in which weather patterns are related between sequential years.[6]

Although these advantages make Approach Two attractive, keep in mind that with this more comprehensive model comes the need for more data and more assumptions. As the model's complexity increases, the number of assumptions and variables typically do too. Depending on the available data, the experience of the modeling team, the availability of already existing models, the time frame available for building the model, and other issues, the user must evaluate whether the added complexity is likely to result in a better result in the end.

16.4 Approach 3: Simulating the Weather

Approach Three is even more comprehensive and complex than Approach Two. The first step in this approach is to build a more general and comprehensive weather system model of which simulated weather hazard data are the output. Such a model might include multiyear oscillations in weather patterns (for example, El Niño), directional trends in temperature and precipitation, and other large-scale drivers of weather patterns. It would also need to account for correlations among areas and weather metrics. Next, the model uses the simulated weather hazard data to determine the simulated trigger values for each area, which are then combined with the product terms to produce the payout ratios. The key here is that the calculation of trigger values and payout ratios depends on simulated hazard data, not on historical hazard data.

As one can imagine, while such a model may be more flexible and take into account more weather-related factors, it could be a considerable challenge to develop. Weather models of this type do, however, exist, so they might not need to be built from scratch. These models would still require much effort to learn and to adapt their parameters for use in a probabilistic payout model. Approach Three therefore would be more challenging to pursue. We include it here to illustrate the range of different frameworks that might be used for this index insurance problem.

16.5 Which Model to Use?

Every probabilistic (and deterministic) model is by definition a simplification of reality. The key when developing and using probabilistic models for index insurance is to build and use models that incorporate correct and valid inputs and assumptions that can ideally be supported by empirical data. It is also of utmost importance to clearly communicate to all relevant stakeholders the main assumptions and limitations of the model.

In many cases, analysts start off thinking that they need very "realistic" models to capture the behavior of the real world. However, in our experience it is best to start with the simplest model that fulfills all the needed functions and uses valid assumptions. Only then should analysts add more complexity as necessity dictates. Our choice to use Approach One in this guide is in line with our belief that a relatively simple model for which the assumptions and limitations can be clearly understood will be more useful than an extremely complex model that is difficult to understand and explain to decision makers and consumers alike.

Notes

1. By incorporating a time series approach into the modeling, our approach can account for changes over time. This addition can help reflect both gradually changing weather patterns and multiyear cycles in which weather patterns are related between sequential years. However, we have not included this element in the modeling for this guide to reduce complexity and model running time.

2. In modeling losses, a frequency distribution is often used to model the number of loss events.

3. The uncertainty in the actual loss amount (if an event occurs) is also known as secondary uncertainty.

4. The calculations of these historical payout ratios are described in detail in chapter 11.

5. The model fit a t copula to the historical data with the assumption that the correlations between any pair of areas could be unique, as opposed to assuming the same correlation for all pairs of areas. We found this approach more realistic than assuming that all areas were related with the same strength. Goodness-of-fit statistics for the copula actually favored the single correlation approach, but we considered this to be a function of the sparse data for fitting and chose to use the multiple correlation form anyway. This is therefore a case in which our situational understanding and judgment overrode a strictly quantitative method and goodness-of-fit statistic for the copula fitting.

6. With Approach One, some trend parameters can be estimated and included in the model to reflect changes over time. However, given the limited amount of data used in Approach One, such a time series approach will be more challenging.

Bibliography

Banks, E. 2002. *Weather Risk Management: Markets, Products, and Applications.* Basingstoke: Palgrave.

Jewson, S., A. Brix, and C. Ziehmann. 2007. *Weather Derivative Valuation: The Meteorology, Statistics, Financial and Mathematical Foundations.* New York: Cambridge University Press.

CHAPTER 17

Conclusion

This guide covers a lot of ground. Part 1 provides a summary of the insights and decisions required for the insurer to make an informed decision to launch and expand an index insurance business line. Part 2 provides a step-by-step guide to calculating the decision metrics that can be used by the insurance manager. One of our main goals for this guide is to support the improvement of named peril index insurance product offerings through structured and transparent collaboration and communication between insurers, product design teams, and policyholders. With this in mind we would like to leave the reader with two reminders of best practice for using the tools in this guide:

First, remember that because it provides such a high level of coverage, the Base Index is also very expensive and many policyholders will request a lower price—and lower coverage—product. It is extremely important that the insurer always produce a Base Index to explain to the policyholder the difference between complete coverage—that provided by the Base Index—and the coverage provided by other product options. Without this explicit comparison, policyholders often fall into the trap of expecting complete coverage even when they have purchased a lower coverage, less expensive product.

Second, when using the models in this guide, as well as when developing or using any probabilistic model, always be critical of the assumptions that are made in the use of the data, the analysis, and the development of the model. The main, simplifying assumption in a model should be well articulated to all stakeholders so that they are aware of the assumptions and can decide whether the model framework needs refining.

These two strategies, and the additional guidance provided in this guide, are critical for practicing responsible finance. They will help insurers meet consumer protection responsibilities such as providing transparent services and treating policyholders fairly. Failure to implement responsible insurance principles will lead to reputational challenges for the product, the insurer, and the market as a whole. By implementing the tools provided in this guide, insurers can help ensure the healthy, sustainable, and responsible development of index insurance markets.

Glossary

Actuarial analyst The individual (or team) responsible for performing probabilistic modeling and generating decision metrics for consideration by the insurance manager.

Adverse selection A situation in which sellers have information that buyers do not about some aspect of product quality; in insurance, a situation in which the people who have insurance are more likely to make a claim than the average population used by the insurers to set their rates.

Agent An individual or entity that is authorized to represent one or more insurance companies to sell insurance.

Aggregate distribution A distribution that takes into account the frequency of an event happening, and the severity or impact of the event.

Aggregator An entity that accumulates risk exposures of several insured parties within a given geographical area and transfers them to an insurer. Usually acts as the policyholder.

Aleatory uncertainty Inherent randomness associated with a future loss or payout; this uncertainty cannot be reduced by the collection of additional data. Also called randomness, variability, stochastic uncertainty, or irreducible uncertainty.

Base Index An index structure that is designed to exhibit the highest correlation between payouts and inventory losses caused by the insured peril and hence provide the highest level of coverage possible against damage to the insured inventory. As soon as the proxy's behavior starts deviating from its normal level (as defined by subject specialists), the Base Index triggers a payment.

Basis risk The imperfect correlation between the actual losses suffered by an entity or individual and the payments received from a risk transfer instrument designed to cover these losses. In other words, the risk that index measurements of the loss will be different from actual individual losses.

Basis risk ratio Basis risk expressed as a percentage of the sum insured.

Bernoulli distribution A discrete probability distribution of a random variable that takes values of either 1 or 0. The probability of a 1 is often called the probability of success.

Beta distribution A flexible, continuous, and bounded probability distribution described by two shape parameters. It is commonly used when the range of the random variable is known.

Binomial distribution A discrete distribution that is often used to simulate the number of successful outcomes from a certain number of trials in which the probability of success for each of these trials is the same.

Burn analysis contract valuation method An actuarial approach to estimating the premium rate based on the historical performance of the contract.

Capacity Total limit of liability that a company or the insurance and reinsurance industry can assume, according to generally accepted criteria of solvency.

Categorical classification of past damages See *qualitative classification of past damages.*

Claims Payment for losses covered by insurance.

Combined ratio A metric of profitability for an insurer that indicates whether an insurer has made an underwriting loss or gain. It is defined as the proportion of claims paid (or payable) plus administrative and operating expenses (A&O) to premiums earned. A combined loss ratio greater than 1 (or 100 percent) indicates that the premiums collected from the insured are not sufficient to pay the claim (indemnity) and cover A&O expenses. In this case, the insurer faces an underwriting loss.

Conditional value at risk (CVaR) See *tail value at risk.*

Continuous probability distribution A probability distribution that describes a set of uninterrupted values over a range. In contrast to the discrete probability distribution, the continuous distribution assumes there are an infinite number of possible values.

Continuous variable A variable that can take any value within its range.

Contract monitoring Process during the risk period whereby the proxy is continuously evaluated against the contract payout schedule.

Copula A distribution used to describe (or simulate) the dependence between two or more random variables. From a mathematical perspective, a copula is a multivariate probability distribution for which the marginal probability distribution of each variable is a uniform distribution.

Correlation The relationship or interdependence between two or more variables.

Cost of capital Return that shareholders require to keep their capital in a certain investment or line of business. See also required return on capital.

Covariant risks Risks that are likely to affect many individuals or households at the same time, for example, drought that affects adjacent areas during the same growing season.

Cumulative distribution function A function that gives the probability that the random variable X is less than or equal to x, for every value of x. All random variables (discrete and continuous) have a cumulative distribution function.

Cumulative probability The probability that the random variable X is less than or equal to x.

Damage level The amount of damage (expressed as a percentage of the inventory value) for a single insured unit. A 30 percent damage level means that 30 percent of the inventory value was damaged during a particular period (for example, one year).

Data processing Operations on data, often done with the use of a computer, to retrieve or transform information.

Data provider The party responsible for supplying historical and real-time claim settlement data to the parties to an index structure.

Debt recovery expense The cost incurred by the lender in its attempt to recover part or all of the outstanding debt by the defaulting party.

Deductible The proportion (or amount) of an insured loss that the policyholder agrees to pay or bear before any recovery from the insurer.

Default rate The probability per unit of time (often per year) that a borrower will fail to make payments on a loan as required.

Default risk The risk that a borrower will not meet contractual obligations, such as interest payments or principal repayment on a loan, when they are due.

Dekadal rainfall Rainfall accumulated over the period of the 1st to 10th day, 11th to 20th day, or 21st to final day of a calendar month. The third dekad of a month will be 10 days for a month with 30 days, 11 days for a month with 31 days, and either 8 or 9 days for February.

Derived inputs Values used in the model that are arrived at through a structured manipulation of specific input values.

Deterministic model A model in which every set of variable states is uniquely determined by parameters in the model and by sets of previous states of these variables; therefore, a deterministic model always performs the same way for a given set of initial conditions. (In contrast, see probabilistic model.)

Discrete probability distribution A probability distribution that describes distinct values, usually integers, with no intermediate values. In contrast, a continuous distribution assumes there are an infinite number of possible values.

Discrete variable A variable that can take only a distinct value such as 0, 1, 2, 3, 4,... or 0, 1/3, 2/3,....

Distribution fitting The fitting of a probability distribution to data of a random variable. For example, we could fit a continuous distribution to data on annual historical payouts with the goal of forecasting the frequency of occurrence of different magnitudes of payouts.

Economic value added A measure of how much value a company (or business unit) creates. It is calculated by subtracting the cost of capital from the operating profits.

Epistemic uncertainty The lack of knowledge associated with a random variable, for example, future annual payout ratios. Epistemic uncertainty can be reduced by the collection of additional data. Also called statistical uncertainty or parameter uncertainty.

Equitable premium rate The premium rate that each area should be charged to accumulate the total premium suggested for the portfolio should the insurer decide to avoid cross-subsidization and charge fair premiums for each area.

Exceedance probability The chance or probability per certain period of an event (for example, a rainfall or flooding event) occurring that is equal to or larger than a certain threshold.

Exit The threshold amount of the index below or above which the maximum payout will be paid. For example, 50 millimeters of rainfall is the exit for a contract if at 50 millimeters or less of rain the maximum amount of 100 percent pays out.

Expected loss The sum of the probabilities of each insured event multiplied by the estimated amount (in currency) of the loss for each of these events.

Expected value The anticipated value or outcome of a certain event. In probability analysis, the expected value can be calculated by multiplying each possible outcome by its respective probability, then summing those values.

Expense costs Costs of doing business, such as administration costs, commissions, and other overhead costs, that must be included in the premium to allow the insurer to continue providing insurance services.

Expense loading Expense costs expressed as a percentage of gross premium.

Exposed units Units that are likely to be affected by the insured perils during the risk period, when included in the portfolio that defines the index.

Fair coin A coin with an equal probability of landing heads or tails for each throw (that is, 50 percent probability for each side).

Fat-tailed distribution A distribution that belongs to the family of heavy-tailed statistical distributions. Fat-tailed distributions have heavier (fatter) tails than the normal distribution.

Financier A person or entity that controls the use and lending of large amounts of money.

Frequency The number of times a value recurs in a group interval.

Geographical basis risk Basis risk that is caused because of the distance between the insured unit and the measurement location. The measurement location refers to the coordinates where measurements of the proxy are recorded.

Goodness of fit A set of mathematical tests performed to find the best fit between a standard probability distribution and a data set.

Historical hazard data Data on weather parameters (for example, millimeters of rain during a growing season) or recorded classifications or intensities of natural disasters (for example, Category I and II typhoons).

Historical inventory damage data Data on historical damages to inventory suffered by the insured party as a result of the insured peril.

Historical payouts Calculated data on how much an index insurance product would have paid out in the past based on historical index data such as daily rainfall.

Hybrid product (wii + ayii, or wii + indemnity) A product that combines elements from two or more of the following: weather index insurance (wii), area yield index insurance (ayii), and traditional indemnity insurance.

Implied deductible The difference in the amount of risk that is covered by the Base Index and the Redesigned Index. Typically the Redesigned Index has lower costs (and therefore lower coverage of the policyholders' risk); therefore, the implied deductible is the reduction of risk coverage resulting from the lower premium cost.

Indemnity insurance Type of insurance that seeks to compensate the insured party such that the party regains exactly the same financial position as before the occurrence of the loss event. The validity and magnitude of the loss is usually determined by inspection of the damaged inventory by a licensed loss assessor.

Independent risk Risks for which there is no relation between the results of one and those of the other(s). In other words, if one independent risk event occurs, the probability or the impact of the other risk occurring does not change because there is no relationship between the risks.

Insurance intermediary An individual or entity that acts as either an insurance agent or broker in facilitating risk transfer from an insured party to selected insurers.

Insurance manager The staff member of the insurer charged with decision making regarding the insurer's index insurance product line.

Insurance regulator Government agency responsible for approving the issuing of insurance products, monitoring company solvency, and implementing consumer protection rules.

Insured party The individual or entity that transfers away the unwanted residual risk. The insured party can be an individual, a farmer, or small or medium enterprise, or it can be the same organization that is the policyholder.

Insured party basis risk The risk that the Base Index's measurement of the insured party's loss will be lower than actual inventory damage. In other words, a case in which the insured unit suffers a loss that is greater than the payment triggered by the Base Index.

Insured unit An agreed-on measure of the inventory (for example, input cost for an acre of land) that is the subject of the insurance coverage.

Insurer The entity that underwrites the risk; the party legally responsible for the liabilities arising from the insurance policy (up to the limit and minus the deductible).

Insurer basis risk The risk that the Base Index's measurement of the insured party's loss will be higher than actual inventory damage. In other words, the insured unit suffers a smaller loss than the payment triggered by the Base Index.

Inventory damage ratio Damage to inventory as a percentage of the total value of the inventory. For example, an inventory damage ratio of 25 percent for inventory worth $100 indicates that damages to the inventory amounted to $25.

Iteration Within a Monte Carlo simulation model, an iteration (also often called a trial or simulation) is one calculation of the Monte Carlo model that uses a random sample of each of the probability distributions within the model, resulting in one possible outcome of the model. An iteration can also be seen as a possible future scenario. With Monte Carlo simulation models, typically at least 10,000 iterations are used to estimate the range of possible outcomes.

Law of large numbers As the risk pool increases and losses are independent, the actual loss approaches the expected loss.

Liquidity Having sufficient cash or liquid assets to meet day-to-day operating needs.

Loss assessment Determination of the extent of damage resulting from the occurrence of an insured peril and the settlement of the claim.

Mean One of several measures of the location of a distribution. For a data set, the mean is the arithmetic average of all values. For a probability distribution, the mean is the sum of all possible values weighted by their probability. It is also equivalent to the balance point of the distribution.

Modal portfolio The most common portfolio size. For example, if looking at rural banks, the modal portfolio would be the dollar value of outstanding or disbursed loans that is common among those entities.

Monoline insurance A single class of insurance business.

Monte Carlo simulation A computer-based method of analysis developed in the 1940s that uses statistical sampling techniques in obtaining a probabilistic approximation to the solution of a mathematical equation or model. It is a method of calculating the probability of an event using values randomly selected from sets of data, repeating the process many times, and deriving the probability from the distributions of the aggregated data.

Moral hazard A condition that increases the likelihood that a person will intentionally cause or exaggerate a loss. Also, careless behavior caused by the presence of insurance that increases the expected claims filed by policyholders.

Named peril index insurance An index insurance structure that is meant to protect the insured party against the effects of specific perils such as drought, excess rain, or typhoon.

Net fund position The financial status of an insurance fund after paying for claims triggered during the season. The fund is made up of premiums accumulated from previous seasons, current season premiums, and any other funds that management may decide to allocate to the fund.

Net premium income Gross premium less expenses.

Nonperforming loans Loans that are not up to date with scheduled repayments.

Nonproportional reinsurance A type of reinsurance in which an insurer pays a premium to a reinsurer so that the reinsurer will cover all or a proportion of the losses above a certain threshold.

Parameter uncertainty See *epistemic uncertainty*.

Parameterization Selection of the parameters and values of those parameters within a model. Parameterization of a probability distribution means selecting the values that describe the distribution. Probability distributions can often be parameterized different ways, for example, a PERT distribution can be described by a minimum, mostly likely, and maximum, but it can also be described by the 10th percentile, 50th percentile, and 90th percentile.

Pareto distribution A continuous probability distribution with the longest tail of all probability distributions. The Pareto distribution was originally used to model demographics such as income distributions.

Payout level In this guide, the level of payout of an index insurance product, expressed as a percentage of the sum insured. For example, if the payout level over a one-year period was 75 percent and the sum insured was $1,000, then the payout of the policy would be $750.

Percentile Values that divide a sample of data into 100 groups containing (as far as possible) equal numbers of observations. For example, 30 percent of the data values lie below the 30th percentile.

PERT (project evaluation and review techniques) distribution A continuous and bounded distribution that is often used to model expert opinion. The PERT distribution requires the same three parameters as the triangular distribution: the minimum, most likely, and maximum.

Poisson distribution A discrete distribution that models the number of occurrences of an event in a period t with an expected rate of "lambda" events per period t when the time between successive events follows a Poisson process.

Policyholder The party in whose name an insurance policy is issued.

Portfolio-priced product A product with a single premium rate across different areas rather than equitable premium rates for each area. This single premium rate must take into account the risk profiles in each of the individual areas, the correlations in risk between all the areas, and the value insured in each area.

Prediction interval The estimate of the interval within which future observation of a certain metric or outcome will fall, with a certain probability. For example, if the 90 percent prediction interval of the profit margin for next year is −5 percent to +25 percent, it is estimated that there is 90 percent certainty that next year's profit margins will be between −5 percent and +25 percent.

Premium rate The price of the index insurance product, typically expressed as a percentage of the sum insured.

Probabilistic model A system whose output is a distribution of possible values. In contrast to a deterministic model, in a probabilistic (stochastic) model randomness is present, and variable states are not described by unique values, but rather by probability distributions.

Probability density chart A graph that shows a probability density function.

Probability density function A function that describes the relative likelihood that a random variable will take on different values. The probability density function can be integrated to obtain the probability that a continuous random variable takes a value in a given interval.

Probability distribution A list of probabilities or probability densities associated with each of a random variable's possible values, together with those values.

Probability mass function Relates the possible value of a discrete variable to its probability of occurrence.

Probability of fund ruin The annual probability that the net funds position at the end of the year (after paying out all claims) will be negative.

Probability of negative profit The annual probability that the profit margin on the index insurance policy will be negative.

Probability of profit below target profit margin The annual probability that the profit margin on the index insurance policy will be less than a certain profit target.

Probable maximum loss Level representing the largest economic loss likely to occur for a given policy or set of policies (portfolio) when a disaster occurs.

Product design basis risk Basis risk resulting from the failure of the chosen proxies to capture inventory damage caused by the named peril.

Product design team A group of specialists charged with the responsibility for designing index insurance structures.

Projected loss ratio The loss ratio (and its uncertainty range) that may occur during a growing season or year. The loss ratio is the proportion of claims paid (or payable) to premiums earned, usually expressed as the total gross claim divided by the total gross premium. A loss ratio greater than 1 (or 100 percent) indicates that the amount of the claim paid by the insurer exceeds the amount of the premiums collected from the insured.

Projected losses The possible amount of losses (and its uncertainty range) that may occur during the growing season or year.

Projected profit margin The possible profit margins (and its uncertainty range) that may occur during the growing season or year. The profit margin is the amount by which revenue from premiums exceeds expenses and claims.

Proportional (or pro rata) reinsurance A type of reinsurance in which premiums and losses are shared by the insurer (cedant) and the reinsurer on a proportional basis.

Prototype A product or concept in a reduced but fully functional form for the purpose of testing its functionality in the real world. The product or concept is not yet scaled up to full commercial scale or introduced to the broad market.

Proxy A figure that can be used to represent the value of something else, for example, lack of rainfall can represent inventory damage.

Qualitative classification of past damages The classification of historical inventory damage in different qualitative categories such as mild, mild-to-medium, medium, medium-to-severe, and severe.

Random draw See *iteration*.

Reinsurance Purchase of insurance by an insurance (ceding) company from another insurance (reinsurance) company for the purpose of spreading risk and reducing the loss from a catastrophe.

Reinsurer The entity from which an insurance company may buy reinsurance; often described as the insurer of insurer.

Required capital The amount of capital needed to cover payouts of an insurance product with a certain confidence. For example, if the required capital at a 95 percent confidence level is $1 million, we can be 95 percent confident that $1 million will be enough to cover all losses that may be triggered over the season or year.

Required return on capital Return that shareholders require to keep their capital in a certain investment or line of business. See also *cost of capital*.

Residual risk The risk that remains even if all practical and economical risk management measures have been implemented. Typically refers to the amount of risk transferable to the insurer.

Responsible finance or responsible insurance The performance of commercial activities in the financial or insurance sector in accordance with guidelines regarding responsible and positive societal behavior.

Retrospective analysis An analysis aimed at evaluating how a given product would have performed in the past if it had been in force.

Return period The expected time between two occurrences of a specific magnitude of loss event; defined as the inverse of the annual probability of the event occurring. For example, a return period of 100 years corresponds to an annual probability of 1 percent.

Risk-free rate The rate of return on an investment with zero risk. Frequently, the rate of return on U.S. Treasury notes is used as a proxy for the risk-free rate.

Risk management committee A team responsible for implementing the risk management guidelines set by a company's top management. Often, the risk management committee has access to or is part of the board of directors.

Risk mitigation The process of making decisions and implementing measures that will minimize the probability or impacts of adverse effects on an individual or an entity or organization.

Risk modeling The process of designing, building, and using a probabilistic model to gain an understanding of the risks and uncertainties of a certain situation or system.

Risk period The period of time during which an insurable event as defined in the insurance policy is covered.

Risk pooling Aggregation of individual risks for the purpose of managing the consequences of independent risks. Pooling large numbers of homogeneous, independent exposure units can produce an average loss that is close to the expected loss. It provides a statistically accurate prediction of future losses and helps determine premium rates.

Scenario A postulated sequence of development of events. Within a Monte Carlo simulation, an iteration or trial is often referred to as a scenario, or when the model concerns the prediction of certain outcomes, a scenario is often referred to as a possible future scenario.

Secondary uncertainty Both aleatory variability and epistemic uncertainty.

Severity The magnitude of a loss to the inventory.

Sharpe ratio The expected return earned in excess of the risk-free ratio per unit of risk, calculated as the return above the risk-free rate divided by its standard deviation. In other words, the Sharpe ratio shows how much more return (above the risk-free rate) can be expected from an investment per unit of risk. The Sharpe ratio allows the returns on investments with different levels of risk to be compared.

Solvency The ability of an insurer to meet its financial obligations as those obligations become due, including those obligations resulting from insured losses that may be claimed several years in the future, based on existing policies.

Spearman's rank order correlation coefficient A nonparametric statistic for quantifying the correlation relationship between two variables.

Starting fund value The amount of funds available to potentially pay out claims and expenses at the start of offering an index insurance product.

Stochastic Events or systems that are unpredictable because of the influence of a random variable.

Sum insured The monetary value attached to the inventory that is insured, either expressed per insured unit or for an overall region.

Tail The extremes of a probability distribution.

Tail value at risk (TVaR) A risk measure that describes the expected value of a variable, given that an event above a certain probability level has occurred, over a certain period. For example, the TVaR 95 percent is the expected value above the 95th percentile of a probability distribution. Consider a total claims distribution for which the TVaR 95 percent is $10 million. In this case, we expect that 1 in every 20 years (1–195 percent]) the total claims will be $10 million. Also called conditional value at risk (CVaR), mean excess loss, or mean shortfall.

Total funds at risk The total amount available to pay claims triggered during the risk period.

Total sum insured (also called total insured value) Value of all the assets or production covered by the insurance contract.

Trigger An event that causes a payout because an index crosses an agreed-on point. For example, rainfall of less than a certain amount could trigger payout of an index insurance policy to policyholders.

TVaR of projected losses See *tail value at risk* and *projected losses.*

Uncertainty See *epistemic uncertainty.*

Underwriting The process of selecting risks to insure and determining in what amounts and on what terms the insurance company will accept the risk.

Units of exposure Properties or lives at risk from a specific event (for example, floods, earthquake, drought).

Variability See *aleatory uncertainty.*

Environmental Benefits Statement